W9-COS-566

FLORIDA STATE
UNIVERSITY LIBRARIES

MAY 25 1994

TALLAHASSEE, FLORIDA

Uzbekistan

An Agenda for Economic Reform

The World Bank
Washington, D.C.

Copyright © 1993
The International Bank for Reconstruction
and Development/THE WORLD BANK
1818 H Street, N.W.
Washington, D.C. 20433, U.S.A.

All rights reserved
Manufactured in the United States of America
First printing September 1993

*HC
337
49
2922
1993*

World Bank Country Studies are among the many reports originally prepared for internal use as part of the continuing analysis by the Bank of the economic and related conditions of its developing member countries and of its dialogues with the governments. Some of the reports are published in this series with the least possible delay for the use of governments and the academic, business and financial, and development communities. The typescript of this paper therefore has not been prepared in accordance with the procedures appropriate to formal printed texts, and the World Bank accepts no responsibility for errors.

The World Bank does not guarantee the accuracy of the data included in this publication and accepts no responsibility whatsoever for any consequence of their use. Any maps that accompany the text have been prepared solely for the convenience of readers; the designations and presentation of material in them do not imply the expression of any opinion whatsoever on the part of the World Bank, its affiliates, or its Board or member countries concerning the legal status of any country, territory, city, or area or of the authorities thereof or concerning the delimitation of its boundaries or its national affiliation.

The material in this publication is copyrighted. Requests for permission to reproduce portions of it should be sent to the Office of the Publisher at the address shown in the copyright notice above. The World Bank encourages dissemination of its work and will normally give permission promptly and, when the reproduction is for noncommercial purposes, without asking a fee. Permission to copy portions for classroom use is granted through the Copyright Clearance Center, 27 Congress Street, Salem, Massachusetts 01970, U.S.A.

The complete backlist of publications from the World Bank is shown in the annual *Index of Publications*, which contains an alphabetical title list (with full ordering information) and indexes of subjects, authors, and countries and regions. The latest edition is available free of charge from the Distribution Unit, Office of the Publisher, The World Bank, 1818 H Street, N.W., Washington, D.C. 20433, U.S.A., or from Publications, The World Bank, 66, avenue d'Iéna, 75116 Paris, France.

ISSN: 0253-2123
ISBN: 0-8213-2673-2

CURRENCY EQUIVALENTS

CURRENCY UNIT = RUBLE

Exchange Rates[1]

1992

January	121
February	121
March	139
April	139
May	139
June	139
July	159
August	182
September	232
October	339
November	452
December	452

1993

January	600
February	715
March	778
April	878
May	1,156
June	1,141

1/ End of period, selling rates

Source: National Bank of Foreign Activities of Uzbekistan

ABBREVIATIONS

ADB	- Asian Development Bank
BOP	- Balance of payments
CBR	- Central Bank of Russia
CBU	- Central Bank of Uzbekistan
CGSSP	- Committee for Governing State Property and Privatization
CIF	- Cost, insurance and freight
CIS	- Commonwealth of Independent States
CMEA	- Council for Mutual Economic Assistance
CPI	- Consumer Price Index
EAU	- External Assistance Unit
EBRD	- European Bank for Reconstruction and Development
ECAs	- Export credit agencies
EEC	- European Economic Community
EF	- Employment Fund
EIA	- Environmental impact assessment
ES	- Employment Service
FDI	- Foreign Direct Investment
FSU	- Former Soviet Union
G-7	- Group of Seven Industrial Nations
GDP	- Gross Domestic Product
GNP	- Gross National Product
GOU	- Government of Uzbekistan
Goskompriroda	- State Committee for Environmental Protection
Goskomprognostat	- State Committee of Forecasting and Statistics
IBRD	- International Bank for Reconstruction and Development
IFC	- International Finance Corporation
IFIs	- International Financial Institutions
IMF	- International Monetary Fund
MFER	- Ministry of Foreign Economic Relations
MLRWR	- Ministry of Land Reclamation and Water Resources
MMWM	- Ministry of Melioration and Water Management
MOA	- Ministry of Agriculture
MOE	- Ministry of Education
MOF	- Ministry of Finance
MOH	- Ministry of Health
NGOs	- Non-governmental organizations
NMP	- Net Material Product
OECD	- Organization for Economic Cooperation and Development
QRs	- Quantitative restrictions
ROW	- Rest of the world
SANIIRI	- Central Asian Scientific Research Institute of Irrigation
SOEs	- State Owned Enterprises
UNDP	- United Nations Development Program
UNEP	- United Nations Environment Programme
UNICEF	- United Nations Children's Fund
USAID	- United States Agency for International Development
Uzbekzoloto	- Uzbek Gold (gold enterprise)
VAT	- Value-Added Tax
WHO	- World Health Organization
WPI	- Wholesale Price Index

Preface

Uzbekistan became a member of the World Bank on September 21, 1992. This report is based on the findings of two economic missions to Uzbekistan in June and September/October 1992 led by Silvina Vatnick. The report was discussed with the Government in July 1993. These missions would like to express their gratitude to the authorities of Uzbekistan for their hospitality and cooperation and for their involvement in and excellent organization for the discussion of the report.

The report was prepared by a team led by Silvina Vatnick (main author), comprising Suzanne Barnes, Jeremy Berkoff, James Cowie, Jean-Charles Crochet, Asli Demirguc-Kunt, Sunita Gandhi, Jorge Garcia-Garcia, Felix Remy, Ralph Romain, Joseph Saba, Hong Wei, and Charles Cameron, Harold Cole, David Falcon, Sen Gupta, Alistair McAuley (consultants). Valuable contributions to the report were made by Ziad Alahdad, Homayoon Ansari, Michel Cramer, Cevdet Denizer, Hamdy Eisa, Alexander Fleming, Peter Hopcraft, Gordon Hughes, Luciano Janelli, Ruth Klinov, Richard Lacroix, Guy Lemoigne, Walter Ochs, Salem Ouahes, Maurice Schiff, and Elton Thigpen. John Holsen provided very helpful insights for the preparation of the macroeconomic framework. Alan Gelb, and James Hanson (Peer Reviewers), Isabel Guerrero, Parvez Hasan and Costas Michalopoulos provided very useful comments. Tamara Kanterman was responsible for document preparation.

COUNTRY DATA: UZBEKISTAN

GNP per capita in US $ (1992)   860[1]

General

Area (1,000 sq km)	447
Population (1992, million)	21.7
Growth rate (1980-92, percent)	2.6
Density (1991, per sq km)	49

Social indicators

Crude birth rate (percent)	3.5
Crude death rate (percent)	0.6

Health

Infant mortality rate(1991, per 1000 live)	35.5
Population per physician (1990)	297.
Life expectancy at birth	69.5

Gross Domestic Product (billion rubles, at current prices)

	1990	1991	1992
GDP at market prices	32.4	61.5	416.9
Real growth rate (percent)	1.6	-0.5	-9.6
Total Consumption	28.1	48.9	
Private consumption	19.9	37.3	
Government consumption	8.2	11.7	
Gross domestic investment	10.4	15.8	
Resource balance	-6.1	-3.3	

Output by sector (billion rubles)

	1991	1992
Agriculture	22.1	149.5
Industry	17.3	119
Construction	5.4	54.4
Services	16.7	94
Total	61.5	416.9

Government Budget (billion rubles)

	1990	1991	1992
Total revenues	14.6	28	142.7
Union transfers	6.3	12	0
Total expenditures	14.9	31.1	188.4
Overall balance	-0.3	-3.1	-45.7

Prices

	1991	1992
Retail price index (annual percent change)	83	790[2]
Wholesale price index (annual percent change)	147	2700[2]

Source: Goskomprognostat and Bank Staff Calculations

1/ Preliminary estimate subject to revision
2/ From December to December.

)

UZBEKISTAN

AN AGENDA FOR ECONOMIC REFORM

Contents

List of Tables, Figures and Boxes

<u>Tables</u>

Figures

Boxes

EXECUTIVE SUMMARY

THE SETTING

1.   Uzbekistan lies along the famous ancient silk road between Europe and the Far East. Landlocked in the middle of Central Asia, it covers 447,000 square kilometers. Almost three-fifths of its land consists of steppe, desert, and semi-arid terrain and the remainder, fertile valleys that skirt two major rivers--the Amu Darya and Syr Darya. Uzbekistan has the largest population of the four Central Asian republics and is the third most populous republic in the former Soviet Union (FSU). Of its 21 million people, 60 percent live in rural areas and about half the population is under 19 years of age. The majority of the population (about 71 percent) is Uzbek.

2.   The country is a major agricultural producer, and about 39 percent of its net material product (NMP) in 1992 was in agriculture. Cotton is the most important crop, accounting for about 40 percent of the gross value of agricultural production. Uzbekistan is the world's fourth largest producer of cotton and its third largest exporter. Uzbekistan is the largest producer of fruits and vegetables in the FSU. Agricultural production has increased rapidly in recent years--by expanding the irrigated area at the expense of reducing the volume of the Aral Sea and creating serious environmental problems.

3.   Industrial production (33 percent of NMP) centers on the processing of agriculture-based raw materials. Light industry (including cotton) accounted for about 39 percent of industrial production in 1990, agro/food processing 13 percent, heavy industry 41 percent, with the fuel-energy industry taking up the remainder. The machinery sector includes many products that are linked to agriculture as production inputs, such as cotton harvesters and textile machinery, and, within the chemical manufacturing branch, fertilizer.

4.   Uzbekistan is rich in natural resources--primarily gold, oil, natural gas, coal, silver, and copper. It is the world's seventh largest producer of gold, the third largest producer of natural gas in the FSU, and is among the world's ten largest natural gas suppliers. Its annual gold production of about 65 tons is about a third of what the Soviet Union used to produce. In 1992 it produced 42.8 billion cubic meters of natural gas, mostly for domestic consumption, and the export potential is significant. The republic also produced 3.3 million tons of oil in 1992, which is likely to increase substantially in the future as two recently discovered oil fields are developed. Despite this potential, Uzbekistan is one of the poorest countries in the FSU, with a per capita income preliminary estimate of $860 in 1992.

RECENT DEVELOPMENTS

5.   After the breakup of the Soviet Union, Uzbekistan faced difficulties common to republics of the FSU--production inefficiencies, the breakdown of central planning and interrepublican trade and payments mechanisms, highly monopolistic market structures, falling output, repressed inflation, and the loss of significant budgetary transfers from the Union Government. Moreover, world prices were declining for its two major commodities, cotton and gold, and the Government had to manage its economy in an external environment determined largely by Russia. It decided to follow a relatively cautious and partial approach to reform, at least until an articulated approach to reform could be

developed. The Government implemented several new policies in 1992-93, partially liberalized prices, unified the foreign-exchange market, imposed new taxes, and temporarily removed until January 1994 most import tariffs. It has recently removed price controls on foodstuffs with the exception of bread and flour and increased significantly energy prices for industrial use. It also privatized some small shops and residential housing, and enacted banking, property, and foreign investment legislation.

6.   The poor quality and availability of data impose severe limitations on the analyses carried out for this first report on Uzbekistan. Thus, all quantitative estimates of economic indicators should be considered provisional.

7.   Economic performance (as measured by output and investment) in Uzbekistan in 1992 appears to have been better than the average of other FSU republics, but still resulted in a substantial decline in economic activity. Real GDP declined by almost 10 percent, following a decline of 0.5 percent in 1991. Consumption and investment levels were also affected. Real investment fell by an estimated 12 percent in 1992. Inflation in wholesale prices was about 2,700 percent in 1992, and the terms-of-trade deteriorated about 10 percent.   Despite the decline in output, employment was maintained through a significant downward adjustment of real wages. Conventionally measured average real wages declined by 54 percent in 1992. But this figure probably overstates the actual declines because of the extent to which wages had been channelled into "forced savings" before the January 1992 price liberalization.

8.   Uzbekistan had an estimated fiscal deficit (defined as a ruble deficit of the central government) of 11 percent of GDP in 1992, and a current account deficit of 17 percent of GDP, financed by arrears with some FSU republics, by borrowing abroad and by using part of its international reserves. During the first three quarters of 1992, the Government tried, through controls and subsidies, to prevent internal prices from rising as rapidly as they did in Russia and elsewhere in the ruble zone. But in the fourth quarter, a major increase in domestic prices for energy products led to a large increase in the general price level.

9.   According to preliminary estimates, Uzbekistan may have run a trade deficit in its interrepublican trade of about $200 million in 1992, and a trade deficit with the rest of the world of $60 million. Foreign direct investment flows were only beginning in 1992. About $380 million in bilateral loans and export credits were committed in 1992, of which about $125 million were disbursed. In addition, Uzbekistan signed an agreement with Russia on November 2, 1992, whereby Uzbekistan relinquished all responsibility for the share of the old external debt/assets of the former Soviet Union allocated to it under the Debt Allocation Treaty of Succession on Foreign Debt and Assets of the USSR of December 4, 1991. This agreement on the so-called, "zero-variant" with Russia will help Uzbekistan's overall creditworthiness.

THE PROGRAM FOR ECONOMIC REFORM

10.   A comprehensive reform program will be needed to accomplish the Government's objectives of: (1) achieving financial stabilization, (2) reversing the decline in output and improving productivity, (3) promoting sustainable development over the medium term, and (4) protecting vulnerable groups. The program will have to cover macroeconomic management, structural reforms, and sectoral reforms--simultaneously--to make the transition to a market-oriented economy. Early attention should be given to the creation of an enabling institutional and legal environment to support the reform program.

11.   <u>Changing the role of the state and developing markets</u>. In a market economy, resources should move in response to the signals and incentives provided by prices freely determined by markets. The role of the state will need to change from the detailed management of the command economy to combining satisfactory macroeconomic management, establishing and maintaining the legal and regulatory framework for private activity, providing the necessary social services and economic infrastructure, and maintaining an adequate system of social protection.

12.   Phasing out the state order system in all sectors of the economy--along with direct state involvement in both domestic and international trade--is the first step toward increasing resource mobility. This would allow labor, capital, allocation of raw materials, and production and consumption decisions to respond to market prices. The liberalization of the distribution system is essential for the establishment of a market-price-guided incentive system to replace the planned allocation of goods and services. Removing internal trade barriers will allow liberalized prices to work their way through to correct the misallocation of domestic resources and to free up resources for use in the more dynamic activities of the economy.

13.   <u>Establishing property rights.</u> Private sector development requires a legal framework to define and ensure property rights. Property rights must be defined clearly, held largely by private owners, freely used and transferred by such owners without unpredictable or arbitrary governmental intervention, but within a predictable regulatory framework, and enforced by a neutral party based on an effective judicial system and modern civil and commercial laws.

14.   <u>Enterprise governance</u>. Enterprise governance should be strengthened, for public utilities and for the larger state enterprises that will not be privatized in the near future. Budget constraints need to be tightened, and performance monitoring needs to be introduced. An efficient governance structure for enterprises must provide accountability to the owner (the state), an enterprise body responsible for strategic issues and oversight of management performance, substantial operational autonomy and incentives for the enterprise management, and the imposition of financial discipline.

15.   <u>Pro-competition policies</u>. Monopoly power hinders successful reform. The highly concentrated industrial structure in Uzbekistan reduces the competitive pressure for cost minimization and, as a consequence, firms can set higher prices. If productive enterprises are to be forced to behave efficiently, in their resource use and investment policies, they must face competitive pressure in markets with liberalized prices under the discipline of hard budget constraints. International competition, combined with competitive factor markets and competitive markets for nontraded goods, is needed for prices to be effective signals and incentives for economic efficiency. Demonopolization then is an essential element for transforming Uzbekistan into a dynamic market-based economy.

Agenda for Macroeconomic Management

16.   Stabilization can be accomplished after a period of adjustment, which must encompass reform of the economic system and movement toward a market-based economy. The macroeconomic policy measures that would allow the Government to access an IMF Systemic Transformation Facility or a Stand-By arrangement would help the Government establish the fundamental elements of stabilization. As long as Uzbekistan remains in the ruble zone, however, options for macroeconomic policy will be limited. Both monetary and exchange-rate policies will have to follow zone parameters, and success will depend critically on stabilization in Russia. Fiscal discipline is the most critical determinant of stabilization. The challenge to the Government will be to generate revenue efficiently,

while continuing to compress expenditures enough to shrink the deficit in the near future. A stringent fiscal policy will have to be accompanied either by close coordination of monetary policies with other zone members or by Uzbekistan's issuing its own currency, and thereby establishing independent monetary and exchange-rate policies.

17.   Subsidies. Subsidies, at the core of the fiscal deficit and macroeconomic imbalances, have important implications for the efficiency of the economy. To cushion the impact of the economic events of 1992, Uzbekistan maintained most of the direct and indirect subsidies and price controls that are the legacy of the Soviet Union. These subsidies impose a severe burden on fiscal policy. Moreover, relative prices depend heavily on subsidies, creating a severely distorted incentive structure. Input and credit subsidies to agricultural and industrial producers, in addition to their fiscal costs, lead to a tremendous waste of resources. For example, the low domestic price of energy inputs and the absence of water charges for irrigation hamper conservation efforts and induce rationing. Moreover, the systematic underpricing of energy relative to other goods has led to substantially higher consumption of energy per unit of output than in market-based economies.

18.   Social protection expenditures. Priority should be given to restructuring and reallocating social expenditures--particularly to reducing universal subsidies and increasing targeted assistance. Spending on social protection policies (including consumer subsidies) will have to be reduced from today's high level which is higher than in countries with the same per capita income and similar to the level in low-income OECD countries. Funded from both budgetary and off-budgetary sources, spending on social protection (including pensions) represents about 24 percent of GDP, of which almost half is for consumer subsidies. By phasing out all consumer subsidies except those on bread--and adjusting wages and pensions to accommodate higher food prices--the Government could save up to 8 percent of GDP in 1993. As part of the move to a system of direct payments based on need, the Government could also unify the family allowances and switch to a flat-rate allowance per child.

19.   Taxation. The taxation system should be strengthened to enhance revenue, with the tax base widened as much as possible. Special tax exemptions at both the federal and local levels should be reduced. Enterprise profits should be calculated according to revised accounting methods consistent with modern commercial accounting practices and the number of exemptions included in the tax code should be reduced and simplified.

20.   The consolidated public sector budget. Overall budgetary management must be strengthened. All public-sector revenue and expenditures, budgetary and off-budgetary, should be identified to help assess the overall level of Government spending and its financing. As part of the assessment, a consolidated analysis of the entire public sector including public sector enterprises and subsidized credits through the banking system should be undertaken.

21.   Trade policy. Trade policy to open Uzbekistan up fully to the rest of the world and encourage competition in all sectors will accompany both stabilization and structural reform. It will need to have two objectives: achieving efficiency in the economy (in production and consumption) and increasing Government revenue. Quantitative trade restrictions should be eliminated. The medium-term objective should be to work toward treating both FSU and foreign trade equally. A temporary ad valorem export tax could replace differential prices and confiscatory export taxes now in place. The tax on foreign exchange proceeds should be abandoned in favor of a low uniform duty on exports (with a higher rate on minerals and cotton as appropriate).

Agenda for Structural Reform

22.   The Government has indicated that it wants to follow a gradual process of economic transformation. Such a pace is thought to result in fewer social and economic disruptions. However, it is likely to involve the preservation of significant inefficiencies in the allocation of resources which will undermine the Government's capacity to stimulate sustainable long-term growth. Whatever the pace of reform chosen, the success of the reform program will depend on the Government's ability to implement a comprehensive program of structural reform according to a clear timetable. This reform package should cover four priority areas:

- Establishing the legal basis for developing a market-oriented economy and the private sector, especially property rights and contract laws.

- Enterprise reform to restructure and privatize state-owned enterprises in the public sector, improve governance of those remaining as SOEs, and encourage new private sector activities.

- Implementing financial-sector reform so that lending is on a purely commercial basis.

- Providing a social safety net to protect the most vulnerable groups.

23.   <u>Legal and regulatory framework.</u> Uzbekistan would benefit from a thorough reconsideration of legislation necessary for reforming enterprises and developing the private sector. To put in place the minimum requirements for the private sector, new laws (or significant amendments to existing legislation) are required in the following areas: (1) a civil code or new laws governing property (real, personal, and intellectual), contracts (including leases) and secured transactions, (2) company law, (3) accounting standards, with particular attention to standards applicable to SOEs, (4) foreign investment legislation, (5) bankruptcy law, and (6) resolution of commercial disputes. A regulatory framework adequate to encourage and support private-sector development will also require action to rationalize and harmonize existing legislative and legal reform measures and to greatly simplify licenses, permits, and approvals.

24.   <u>Enterprise reform.</u> Enterprise reform lies at the core of the necessary structural reform. At the end of 1991, the SOE sector accounted for 85 percent of GDP and 80 percent of employment in Uzbekistan. Moreover, through its links with the budget and the banking system, the sector controlled most of the country's financial resources. To promote competition, the restructuring accompanying privatization should include both demonopolization and reductions in vertical integration. The change in ownership would thus be accompanied by a consequent change in the size distribution of enterprises.

25.   Despite some legislative initiatives, the Government has not yet developed clear ownership and governance rules for the enterprises that will remain under state ownership in the near future. Nor has it developed a comprehensive privatization program for the SOEs. At present, privatization in Uzbekistan is based on the following principles: privatizing smaller firms and those in trade, catering, services and local industry initially; limiting the dislocation of labor, with employees playing a major role in corporate governance after privatization; leasing or selling firms cheaply to the workforce (often as a collective), rather than auctioning or giving away through a voucher system; placing restrictions on changing lines of business for long periods; and   maintaining the previous control structures and continuing "voluntary" associations into concerns.

26.   The 1991 Privatization Law and the implementing regulations need to be revised in three main ways. (1) The priority given to enterprise staff, particularly collectives, must be de-emphasized. Shares should be given to individuals, not to collectives, and ought to be fully transferable. (2) Competitive sale of enterprises should be the norm, and leases should only be a fall-back solution. Prior to sale, however, all large enterprises should become stock companies, and monopolies should be broken up.   (3) There should be no restrictions imposed on the enterprises' line of business subsequent to privatization.

27.   Financial sector reforms. To sustain enterprise restructuring and privatization and develop the private sector, the banking system must provide a mechanism for mobilizing savings and efficiently allocating resources. Financial institutions in Uzbekistan are not in a position to fulfill this role, or to support the privatization and revitalization of enterprises. Negative real interest rates on deposits are discouraging private bank deposits, so that the financial sector cannot fulfill its primary function of mediating between savers and investors.

28.   The infrastructure of Uzbekistan's financial system must be strengthened as a matter of urgency. This would include the revision of accounting, auditing, and reporting standards, and the adoption of procedures for financial market regulation and supervision. The payment system needs to be replaced by modern clearing and settlement mechanisms, to ensure fast processing of financial transactions. A strong and independent Central Bank, focused on the conduct of monetary policy and on bank regulation and supervision, is the core of any stable, efficient financial system.   Separating the Central Bank's commercial and central banking functions is necessary to avoid conflicts of interest and interference in the conduct of monetary policy. Thus, the Central Bank should no longer funnel 70 percent of deposits in the Savings Bank to the banking system.

29.   As reform progresses, the Government should restructure and possibly privatize some sectoral banks. One option is to create a specialized financial institution that could assist the Government in financing large loss-making SOEs before their privatization, restructuring, or liquidation. Such an institution would lend to SOEs under less stringent criteria than a commercial bank, work closely with the Government and be funded partly (if not wholly) through the budget. Instead of isolating the bad loans in one institution, another option is to adopt strict accounting and regulatory frameworks to ensure that bad loans within each bank will be contained during the transition. To strengthen its commercial banks the Government should enforce prudential regulations (such as limits on loan exposure to owners) and, to reduce risk, it should require diversification of loan portfolios. There is also a need to develop financial institutions and markets to provide term financing and risk capital for the private sector. In the longer term, Uzbekistan also needs to develop other financial institutions, such as a securities market, life insurance companies, and pension funds. Preparing the legal framework and establishing regulatory and supervisory bodies for this purpose could be considered.

30.   Labor mobility. Labor deserves special consideration when discussing reallocation of production factors. Thus far, unemployment in Uzbekistan has remained very low, but this is deceptive, since most enterprises are probably retaining idle workers and many have cut their work week to four days or even three. In the near term, some public enterprises may need to be liquidated and others forced to reduce greatly their employment levels in order to become profitable. As labor in public enterprises is shed, specific measures will be needed to enhance the flexibility of the labor market, such as reducing internal restrictions on mobility and expanding job placement centers. The approval of the Employment Act in 1991, and the beginning of the process of establishing over 100 employment centers around the country, signal some progress in this area. But the perpetuation of residence permit requirements, along

with extensive housing shortages, means that labor mobility in Uzbekistan is still very low.   The rise in unemployment, combined with an expected increase in wage differentials, could lead to a less equitable income distribution, which would reinforce the need for a stronger social safety net.

31.   The social safety net. The social dimensions of stabilization and enterprise restructuring require great attention to the social safety net, which the Government is committed to maintaining.   But the fiscal situation may not support a safety net strong enough to protect against significant unemployment.   Priorities will have to be fixed, and resources will need to be used efficiently.   In this context, the Government should consider (1) offering income support to those who would otherwise fall below the poverty line (such as children in large families and the elderly), (2) extending assistance to those who are affected adversely by the transition, particularly the newly unemployed, and (3) targeting scarce resources to those most in need, rather than providing support indiscriminately.

Agenda for Sectoral Reform

32.   Agriculture. Because yields are relatively low while input use and spoilage rates are high, the productivity gains possible in Uzbekistan agriculture appear to be large. The key to realizing these gains will be to establish the necessary incentives for generating and adopting new technologies in line with Uzbekistan's comparative advantage. The Government has already initiated this process of reform. In the short term, further reforms should focus on providing greater freedom to produce, sell, and trade at prices determined in an increasingly free and competitive market.   This will require Government actions to: (1) liberalize prices and markets, (2) phase out compulsory deliveries at below market prices under the state order system, (3) create a competitive and responsive marketing system, and (4) establish the initial conditions for encouraging more efficient land and water use.   A full-fledged land leasing program could be implemented without major delays.   For the longer term, programs must address two issues: increasing the efficiency of water use in a manner consistent with environmental concerns (for example, through irrigation modernization and water pricing) and supporting sustained growth in land productivity (for example, through land reform, varietal development, and the promotion of improved on-farm practices).

33.   Energy. Provided substantial reforms are undertaken, the medium-term outlook in the energy sector is promising and Uzbekistan could become a significant energy exporter in the longer term. Apart from developing its oil potential, the greatest challenge in the medium to long term is to secure export markets for excess natural gas supplies. The volume of natural gas available for export in the medium term may be much greater than the Government now envisions--domestic consumption could be reduced by raising prices to international levels and promoting greater efficiency in use. If the potential economic benefits from the energy sector are to be fully realized, three policy measures must be implemented in the next 18 months. First, energy pricing and taxation must be reformed. In addition to improving the fiscal situation, this would provide the incentives for resource conservation and more efficient use. Second, an investment framework must be developed to attract outside investment into the petroleum sector and to design petroleum legislation and taxation.   Third, institutional reform in the energy sector is necessary--to restructure energy enterprises and enhance their economic efficiency and development potential.

34.   Mining. The medium-term outlook for the mining sector also appears promising, particularly the gold and copper industries. The sector's success depends on the enactment of a regulatory framework that provides the basis for opening the sector to private investment in exploration --the most critical phase of the mining cycle. Current mining sector policies--state procurement, lack of

access of mineral producers to international markets, exploration reserved to the state--will probably not lead to a strong internationally competitive mining industry. Pricing policies for mineral products distort incentives and resource allocation. Investment decisions are made not on the likely rate of return from a project but on whether a specific commodity is "needed" or whether a geographic region is strategically important. A critical assessment of the competitiveness and productivity of the different subsectors of the mining industry is needed to determine which mines can become competitive in a market-based economy.

35.   In light of the need for modern management expertise and for improved mining technologies, the bulk of the effort to stimulate and maintain growth in the mining sector should come from foreign private investors. To encourage such investment, the Government must adopt a policy and institutional structure that supports stable and transparent regulations to govern the rights and obligations of the investor and the Government, a competitive and well-structured fiscal regime, access to foreign exchange at market rates, and well-organized institutions to monitor and assist the producers effectively.

36.   Transport and telecommunications. The cornerstone of any market-based economy is an efficient system for supplying inputs to producers and distributing the output to customers. Uzbekistan's transport system is well adapted to its geography, but the sector's need for the rehabilitation and replacement of assets is significant. As in the other sectors of the economy, regulatory controls and distorted price and incentive structures create inefficiencies. An improved institutional structure for formulating policy, regulations, and operations effectively is needed.

37.   The main challenge in the telecommunications sector is to take advantage of new technical opportunities to meet the demands of customers for new and improved international, long distance, and local services. Meeting this challenge will require major financing and funding decisions--and a range of planning and operational strategies, appropriate tariff policies, and cost-effective approaches to modernization. The institutional structure of the sector must be reorganized so that the Government can create a framework for encouraging service improvements, privatizing sectoral enterprises, commercializing the sector, and upgrading existing facilities. Only when a strong institutional structure is created will the sector attract investment.

38.   Health. Health status indicators in Uzbekistan are not encouraging. Many rural poor, with large families, suffer from acute infectious diseases, such as enteric illnesses. The interval between births is less than two years for 80 percent of women, maternal and infant mortality are relatively high, and childhood vaccination coverage is dropping in some regions. Poor drinking water, lack of sanitation, and improper clinical management add to the problems. The population now views health care as a right, but fiscal realities are rapidly eroding this belief. Health services face severe problems: (1) the administration of the Ministry of Health, which manages all aspects of the health sector, is weak, (2) there is an unstable financial base, and (3) there are shortages of vaccines, medical supplies, and equipment.

39.   In the short term, consideration should be given to priority setting and development of a sustainable health finance system. A successful prevention program will reduce demand for expensive curative services. Preventive measures such as childhood immunization, diarrhoeal control (clean water and provision of oral rehydration salts), and targeted nutritional supplements for some pregnant women and infants (e.g., dried milk) would save lives, eliminate many expensive in-patient stays, and reduce the need for staff. It should also be possible to eliminate some unnecessary services and increase efficiency in the use of inputs, and there should be a rationalization of drug use and an alignment of service

protocols with international standards. Developing a sustainable health finance system implies the introduction of some charges and fees. There are also needs to empower the Ministry of Health and clarify the roles of other organizations--and to develop a coherent women's health strategy.

40.   Education. The education and training system faces three difficult challenges. First, nationhood has demanded new language policies, focusing learning around circumstances in Uzbekistan and promoting new international links in education. Second, a market-based economy requires changes in the content and purpose of schools and in out-of-school education and training programs. Third, declines in output complicate the reform process by limiting the scope and pace of change and prompting economizing measures that are not necessarily in the best long-term interests of education. The Government should consider (1) reintegrating the management of the sector under one ministry for economy and efficiency; (2) undertaking as early as possible the preparation of a long-term plan (and related short-term programs) for the development of the school system, including both quantitative and qualitative concerns, and the evolution of the management of the system and its staff development needs; (3) assessing the scale of investments needed in the system, establishing priorities and improving coordination; (4) rationalizing the teacher training system; (5) developing selected higher education institutions as centers of excellence in specific disciplines; and (6) undertaking a cost recovery system for higher education.

41.   Environment. The main environmental issues in Uzbekistan derive from the problems of the Aral Sea--land degradation due to high levels of salinity. The expansion of irrigated cotton production has been associated with serious environmental degradation and an erosion of the country's resource base. The most dramatic effect of this has been the shrinking of the Aral Sea--which has led directly to the abandonment of substantial transport, fisheries, and related infrastructure. Since 1960, the Aral Sea has shrunk significantly because of a nearly total cutoff of inflows from the Amu and Syr Rivers for irrigation. The issues relating to the Aral Sea Basin include the reduction of the sea, the destruction of its aquatic ecosystem, the lowering of soil quality in the Aral Sea Basin, the pollution of the surface water and groundwater of the delta draining into the Aral Sea, and the adverse health impact on the population because of lack of potable water and inadequate sanitation. The World Bank is supporting the development of a regional program for promoting sustainable development and use of the basin's land and water resources.

42.   Other environmental issues include: (1) disposal of solid and hazardous waste, particularly where pesticide use is concerned, (2) water contamination from municipal and industrial sources, (3) industrial pollution, particularly in the Fergana Valley, and (4) the impact of mining activities (gold, uranium, lead) on workers' health and safety, on air pollution, and on water quality. Particular consideration should be given to environmental issues while assessing the economic viability of Uzbekistan's industrial sector. Environmental standards in the country seem to be strict but are not observed. Any serious attempt to comply fully with them would be inordinately expensive, so the need is urgent to develop more realistic environmental standards that could be met at a reasonable cost, and then to enforce those standards.

MEDIUM-TERM OUTLOOK

43.   A major reform program will inevitably affect short-term growth, since the agricultural, industrial, and financial sectors have to be substantially restructured. If a reform program along the lines suggested in the report had been initiated in early 1993, GDP may have continued to decline in this year, but at a somewhat lower rate than in 1992--possibly by about 6 percent. The disruption associated with any period of major adjustment and restructuring is also likely to generate a temporary but substantial increase in unemployment. The extent of unemployment will depend on two factors: the pace of enterprise reform in all productive sectors, and the opening of new opportunities in the private sector. A slower pace of enterprise reform and restructuring would imply a lower amount of open unemployment, but continued employment in low productivity activities which would need to be supported by continued subsidies. If the Government were to start implementing a comprehensive reform program in late 1993, benefits would be felt only in 1994.

44.   The reform program in the agricultural sector must proceed at full speed since it is likely to yield the quickest positive growth response to the proposed new incentive structure.   The potential for increasing yields without increasing inputs and for reducing waste, in both the agriculture sector and in the agro-processing industries, could be realized relatively easily. But if reform of the agriculture sector is delayed, the recovery of output and consumption might also be delayed, undermining support for the reform program.

45.   A deepening of structural reform, particularly in the industrial sector, could lead to a further drop in GDP in 1994. However, rapid small-scale privatization, primarily in trade and services, will ensure that at least part of the labor force released by restructuring is absorbed in new activities. Growth of the service sector may also be expected to compensate partially for the decline in economic activity driven by the industrial sector.

46.   In the short term, it is assumed that Uzbekistan will not experience any significant deterioration in its terms of trade. Interrepublican trade now seems to be conducted at exchange ratios quite close to world prices. The relative price of natural gas vis-à-vis Uzbekistan's importable goods was unfavorable in 1992, so some actual improvement in the terms of trade is expected in the near future (along with significant exportable balances of natural gas). Otherwise, no sharp changes are foreseen in the world prices of Uzbekistan's raw material exports and imports.

47.   Trade will certainly play a critical role in the medium-term outlook for Uzbekistan. Trade with countries outside the FSU is likely to gain in significance but trade and current-account deficits may well be substantial in the next few years. In 10 years, however, exports of natural gas, increase of exports of cotton, potential self-sufficiency in oil production, and potential exports of gold could result in a major improvement in the trade balance.

48.   In the absence of comprehensive reform, the few scattered and partial reforms that the Government is implementing would have no major impact. This muddle through scenario would imply that none of the sectors is restructured significantly. This failure to adjust would lead to a supply-led contraction of the level of economic activity, reduction in savings and investment, and unnecessary hardship on the population in the medium term represented by a decline in consumption per capita of not less than 30 percent by 1997.   It is very likely that Uzbekistan will not be able to maintain the level of capital inflows that it experienced in 1992. Thus, not even lower current account deficits are likely to be financeable, affecting even further imports, consumption, and output. The only sources of financing

would be a probably lower amount of technical credits to be made available by Russia, a relatively modest amount of bilateral loans, and use of Uzbekistan's own international reserves.

EXTERNAL FINANCING NEEDS

49.   With good prospects for sustainable development after the transition, Uzbekistan should be able to finance its development without difficulty over the long term.   But, for the next 10 years, it will have significant external financing needs. If the Government implements a comprehensive reform program, it will be well positioned to obtain access to bilateral, multilateral, and trade credits in the short to medium term. Financing from commercial banks and access to international capital markets will probably not develop until later.

50.   Any estimates of Uzbekistan's external financing needs are necessarily preliminary and subject to much uncertainty but they can be useful for assessing the country's prospects under different policy assumptions during the transition. The following analysis should be viewed as scenarios of what may happen under certain policy and other assumptions rather than as projections or forecasts of the future.

51.   Assuming major structural reforms are implemented, exports can be expected to grow at 3.0 percent per year and imports at 1.5 percent in the 1993-97 period. These growth rates are significantly higher in current value terms because of the convergence to world prices and exchange rate valuation adjustment. Imports of capital goods for developing the oil fields and sustaining significant exports of natural gas will be particularly important in terms of balance of payments (BOP) implications in 1994-95.   Uzbekistan could also maintain significant cotton exports through increased productivity, if efforts are made to improve grading capabilities and deliveries. Uzbekistan can also begin exporting up to 65 tons of gold a year. As net oil imports decline to zero, and gold and gas-related export revenues grow, the trade balance could improve significantly. But gross external financing requirements will remain substantial as a result of debt service and profits remittances.

52.   External financing requirements for 1993 could be about $500 million, comprising a non-interest current-account deficit of about $250 million, and interest payments of about $10 million. The balance of about $240 million could be used to build up gross international reserves to back the introduction of a new currency, should the Government decide to withdraw from the ruble zone. For 1994-96, estimated financing needs, to be met by direct foreign investments as well as gross loan disbursements, are $600 to $700 million a year.

53.   In the next few years, mobilizing the desired capital inflow will require a major effort by the Government and the international donor and investor communities. Foreign investors are showing interest in mining, agro-processing, textiles, and commercial vehicle manufacturing. Direct foreign investment flows could reach $200 to $250 million a year by 1997, if the legal and institutional frameworks for such investment are strengthened and there is progress in reform. Despite a significant growth of exports, the import growth needed to sustain expansion in output and investment cannot be financed by commercial sources. Substantial official financing may be needed in the next few years to sustain the reform program. A strong program of economic reform will be needed for these flows to be forthcoming.

54.   Uzbekistan's creditworthiness in the medium and long terms will depend on successful implementation of the reform program, the development of the country's natural gas potential and

recently discovered oil fields, on the timely increase of various commodity exports, as well as on external factors, such as the price of its raw material exports. Weak policies or implementation, and an inability to realize the export potential, could jeopardize creditworthiness. Under these circumstances, Uzbekistan could stagnate. On the other hand, effective reform policies combined with a strong natural resource base may permit Uzbekistan to enter a period of sustained growth with increasing access to international capital markets. Debt service as a share of total exports could reach only 11 percent by 1999, when amortization becomes significant, and could fall to about 8 percent by 2002. These projections depend heavily on Uzbekistan's ability to sustain export performance and to shift a significant portion of its trade to hard currency markets.

55.   Uzbekistan needs technical assistance to design and implement its reform and restructuring activities. Technical assistance requirements are estimated at about $20 million a year for the near term, and are expected to be met to some extent by grant financing. Specific technical assistance needs are discussed throughout the report. At the request of the Government of Uzbekistan, the World Bank has started coordinating technical assistance to Uzbekistan through a Pre-Consultative Group in December 1992 and a Local Consultative Group in Tashkent in May 1993.

CHAPTER 1

THE LEGACY OF THE PAST

1.1   Uzbekistan declared its independence on August 31, 1991. At the time of the breakup, Uzbekistan faced not only the difficulties that were common to the former Soviet Union (FSU)-- production inefficiencies, central planning, highly monopolistic market structures, falling output, and repressed inflation--but also its own problems--declining world prices for its two major commodities (cotton and gold), and the loss of the Union's highest budgetary transfers.

A. THE DISINTEGRATION OF THE UNION[1]

1.2   Hopes for a unified economic reform process in the Soviet Union could not be sustained much beyond mid-1990. The first relatively open elections at the local and republican levels of government in the Soviet Union were held in March 1990, one year after the Union Legislature elections. While communists gained a majority of seats in many institutions, republican legislatures ended up with significantly more reformists than in the Union Supreme Soviet. The growing distress in institutional ideology meant that officials who were more committed to reform began conceiving their policies and programs in a republican, rather than a Union, context. Thus, while the original intent of republic-level legislatures was not to dismantle the Union, the political structure in which they were now operating conflicted with the imperatives of the Union Government to retain its power instruments for the very purpose of undertaking reform. The emergence of dual and subsequently multiple "tracks" of reform was inevitable.

1.3   By September 1990 two competing programs were under active discussion: the Union "Ryzhkov" Plan (named after the then Union Prime Minister, Nikolai Ryzhkov), and the "Shatalin" Plan (after its primary architect, academician Stanislav Shatalin). On the whole, the Shatalin Plan was a challenge by the Russian leadership to the Union authorities' claim to be the arbiters of economic reform. The Ryzhkov Plan, formulated shortly thereafter, was the Union's response to that challenge. The Shatalin Plan called for giving the republics greater decision-making freedom and, in many ways, for undertaking more radical reforms than did the Ryzhkov Plan. The Shatalin Plan envisaged a very specific timetable of reform--particularly privatization and price liberalization. It also assigned primary taxing authority to the republics, and called for funding the Union budget from shares of the republic budgets. The Ryzhkov Plan, by contrast, advocated a slower pace of reform, and did not cede significant powers to the republics.

1.4   The Presidential Guidelines that were issued in the fall of 1990 attempted to capture the fairly narrow field of consensus between these two programs. However, consensus was limited only to some generalized goals, and the guidelines failed to specify a timetable for achieving those goals. In particular, the Guidelines gave the republics considerable freedom to set their own pace for initiating reform and for formulating fiscal policies--without having specified how or whether policy actions by the republics could be limited when those actions threatened the Union reform program. Meanwhile, the economic situation in 1990 had been marked by strikes, interethnic strife, the collapse of the Union-wide market in the face of trade barriers created by the republics, and a breakdown of the system of state

---

[1] This section draws from Chapter 1 of *Russian Economic Reform*, World Bank Country Study, 1992. It provides useful background information on the chronology of events that led to the breakup of the FSU.

orders. As the party apparatus—the core mechanism of informal coordination and management in a planned economy—began to be weaned deliberately from its central role in the economy, the traditional economic structure began to come apart and output declined for the first time in the peacetime history of the Soviet Union.

1.5   By the latter half of 1990, unrest in the republics, including Uzbekistan, had increased considerably. The crackdown in the Baltics confirmed it, fueling separatist tendencies further. In tune with these political and military measures, the economic policies of the Government took a conservative turn; in October 1990 the Government decreed that all Union enterprise ties were to be frozen. Thus, even as some of the objectives outlined in the Presidential Guidelines of 1990 were passed as laws in 1991, general economic, political, and legal disarray precluded their implementation. Although the legislative and fiscal responsibilities of the Union and the republics for 1991 had been agreed upon in April 1990 (and confirmed in January 1991), the republics circumvented implementing the law, by signing treaties and economic cooperation agreements with each other and by withholding tax revenue from the Union budget. Their actions precipitated the so-called War of Laws, in which republic officials began drafting and enacting legislation in areas that were also the bailiwick of Union legislation. In Russia, the same Shatalin Plan that had ultimately been rejected by the Union legislature had been approved by the republican legislature. More significant was the fact that, in defiance of the tax laws of the Union, the Russian republic and most of the republics including Uzbekistan began issuing independent republican tax regulations. For example, the Union tax law imposed a profit tax rate of 45 percent on enterprises, compared with a lower 38 percent rate imposed by the Russian Federation and Uzbekistan. By 1991 it was clear that the blatant disregard of the Union's attempts to achieve macroeconomic stability were grounded in political desires for independence, not necessarily in differences in economic thinking.

1.6   By April 1991 the Union budget had already reached the deficit level that had been projected for the entire year, and was in effect bankrupt. In response, the "Anti-Crisis" program, formulated with the consensus of nine republics (including Uzbekistan), sought "the unconditional fulfillment of obligations as regards budgets and extra-budgetary funds. It also sought to adopt anti-inflationary monetary policy, to liberalize prices further, to take various measures to halt the decline in output, and to secure the social safety net. The program was implemented in recognition that sustaining economic reform was necessary--both politically and economically. Yet agreement among the nine republics could not be sustained.

1.7   Thus, by the spring of 1991, a crisis of governance was superseding the economic reform program in the Soviet Union. The Union no longer had clear authority to implement any program of reform. In May, one of the last Union plans for economic reform that acknowledged the crisis in governance by positing the importance of political restabilization was drawn up (the Allison-Yavlinsky Plan). However, the very process of drafting a new political basis for the Union consolidated the opposition of the conservative forces. Their coup attempt in August 1991 succeeded in destroying the very thing the opposition had set out to preserve--the Union. The following two months were marked by enfeebled Union Treaty negotiations and some puzzling inactivity by the Russian leadership. Uzbekistan declared its independence on August 31, 1991.

1.8   In November 1991, the Russian leadership announced the appointment of a new government, and outlined its commitment to radical economic reform. Most of the elements of reform were not implemented, thus finally exacting Russian Government control over the Union Government by withholding the funds necessary to sustain the legitimacy of the Union. The Soviet Union was declared dissolved on December 8 by the signatories to the Minsk Accord (Belarus, Ukraine, and Russia).[2] The dissolution was finalized upon the resignation of Gorbachev as President of the USSR on December 25, 1991. Uzbekistan joined the CIS on December 21, 1991.

B. UZBEKISTAN IN PERSPECTIVE

1.9   Uzbekistan covers a land area of 447,000 square kilometers, slightly smaller than France. It is landlocked, situated in the middle of Central Asia. Almost three-fifths of its extension consists of steppe, desert, and semi-arid terrain; the remainder consists of fertile valleys that skirt two major rivers, the Amu Darya and Syr Darya. Rainfall is generally low, and the climate is largely desert continental. The country borders Kazakhstan to the north, Kyrgyzstan and Tajikistan to the east, Afghanistan to the south, and Turkmenistan to the southwest. Part of the northern border between Kazakhstan and Uzbekistan includes the inland Aral Sea.

Population and Demographic Characteristics

1.10   Uzbekistan is the largest of the four Central Asian republics of the FSU in terms of population. It is the third most populous republic in the FSU, after Russia and Ukraine, comprising about 7 percent of the total population. It also has a high birth rate (3.5 percent, with about half of the population younger than 19 years of age). In 1991, it had about 20.7 million people, 60 percent of whom were living in rural areas. About 71 percent of the population is Uzbek, and the other major ethnic groups[3] include Russians (9 percent), Tajiks and Kazakhs (about 4 percent each), Tatars and Karakalpaks (about 2 percent each), and Koreans, Persians, and Turks (about 1 percent each).[4] The Fergana valley is one of the most densely populated regions in Central Asia.[5] Uzbekistan's population is largely Sunni Muslim. In terms of administrative structure, Uzbekistan consists of 12 provinces, an independent territory (Karakalpakstan), 123 cities, and 157 agricultural counties.

History and Politics

1.11   Uzbekistan lies along the famous ancient silk road between Europe and the Far East. The region was overrun by the Mongols under Genghis Khan in the 13th century. With the breakup of the Mongol empire in the 14th century, a native empire emerged centered around Samarkand. In the 15th century, feudal Muslim states grew up around the cities of Bukhara, Khiva, and Kokland. Trade with Russia developed in the 16th and 17th centuries, and much of the region was annexed to Turkestan in

---

[2] However, the Union legislature has never voted itself out of existence. The debate about whether the Soviet Union was ever officially dissolved was revisited at the Congress of People's Deputies in spring 1992, when it was argued that references to the USSR in the draft Russian Constitution be retained.

[3] These figures are reported in the 1989 Census.

[4] Russians reside largely in urban areas. The rural population is overwhelmingly Uzbek. However, significant concentrations of other ethnic groups are in villages close to the borders of Tajikistan and Kazakhstan, and a large percentage of Tajiks reside in Samark and Bukhara.

[5] The valley contains more than 300 persons per square kilometer. In the Andhizan oblast, the population density reaches up to 427 persons per square kilometer.

the 19th century. Later, after a brief civil war in 1924, the region was incorporated into the Soviet Union.

1.12   After declaring independence, the former Communist Party was renamed the People's Democratic Party (PDM) in October 1991. Mr. Islam Karimov, former First Secretary of the Party, won the direct presidential elections in December 1991. There are several opposition parties. The largest is the Uzbek Popular Front--Birlik. While the party supports the restoration of the Uzbek national heritage, and a social and educational role for Islam, it opposes the creation of an Islamic state. Rather, the party supports a Western-style democracy, and at its last Congress the party's program called for limiting the powers of the president.

1.13   Two opposition parties were formed by groups that split from Birlik--the Democratic Party--Erk and the Fatherland Progress. Both parties are headed by well-known Uzbek poets. The program of Erk is very similar to that of Birlik, though its orientation is more Western. Its candidate received 12.5 percent of the votes in the recent presidential elections. The Fatherland Progress is a liberal-democratic party advocating parliamentary democracy and a market-based economy. The other remaining party of relevance is the Islamic Renaissance Party, which is the local branch of a party founded originally in the Russian Republic to protect Muslim interests. Thus far, the party has been denied registration given its religious orientation.

1.14   A new Constitution establishing basic principles on civil rights and the division of powers among the executive, legislative, and judiciary branches of the Government was approved by the Parliament on December 8, 1992. Several components of the Constitution are particularly relevant to economic reform because they indicate the enabling institutional structure to support reform in Uzbekistan.[6]

Economic Structure

1.15   In 1990, Uzbekistan generated about 3.3 percent of the gross domestic product (GDP) of the FSU. Although the country's estimated per capita income level for 1991 was US$1,350, it has recently been estimated to be about US$860 in 1992. Uzbekistan is one of the poorest countries in the FSU, with a GNP per capita that is lower than that of all other FSU republics except Armenia, Georgia, Kyrgyzstan, and Tajikistan.[7]

1.16   Nonetheless, Uzbekistan is endowed with substantial natural resources--primarily gold, oil, natural gas, coal, silver, and copper (Table 1.1). Its annual gold production is approximately 70 tons, or one-third of what the entire FSU used to produce. Uzbekistan is the third largest producer of natural gas in the FSU and is among the ten largest natural-gas suppliers in the world. Although most of this production was consumed domestically, and only about 8 percent was exported through a pipeline stretching from Bukhara to the Urals, the export potential of natural gas is significant. A large proportion of local industry uses gas for its energy consumption. In contrast, although oil potential could be significant, current production levels are minor. The republic produced 2.8 million tons of oil in 1991,

---

[6] These are discussed in more detail in Chapter 5, "The Governance of Reform." The structure of the new Constitution is provided in Box 5.1.

[7] These are preliminary estimates subject to revision.

and 3.3 million tons in 1992. This is likely to increase substantially as the newly discovered fields in the Namangan and Fergana regions are developed.

Table 1.1
Uzbekistan: Mineral and Energy Production
(1991)

	Uzbekistan	Central Asian Republics[a] and Kazakhstan	Russia	Uzbekistan/ Russia
Gold Production (metric tons)	70		250[b]	28%[c]
Oil Production (mill. m-tons)	2.8	29.2	516.2	0.5%
Natural Gas	41.9	92.2	640.6	6.5%
Coal (mill. m-tons)	6	131.5	395.4	1.5%

Sources: Uzbekistan Statistical and Forecasting Committee (Goskomprognostat).
World Bank various Country Economic Memorandums.

Notes:
[a] Turkmenistan, Kyrgyzstan, Tajikistan.
[b] Total gold production of the FSU.
[c] Relative to the total production of the FSU.

1.17   Uzbekistan is a major agricultural producer. Approximately 40 percent of the 1992 net material product (NMP) in Uzbekistan was generated in agriculture, 33 percent in industry, 14 percent in construction, and the rest in services. It is the world's fourth largest producer of *cotton* and the third largest exporter. Cotton accounts for about 40 percent of the gross value of agricultural production in the country. Uzbekistan is also the largest producer of *fruit and vegetables* within the CIS. Land used for agriculture comprises over 30 million hectares, two-thirds of which is used for livestock production. The rapid increase in agricultural production in recent years came from an expansion in irrigated areas, which led to reduction in the volume of the Aral Sea and serious environmental problems. At present, the irrigated area is about 4.23 million hectares, about half of which is irrigated by pumping systems.

1.18   Industrial production is based largely on the processing of agriculture-based raw materials. Local processing accounts for 12 percent of raw cotton output, 20 percent of sheepskins, and about 60 percent of silk cocoons. Heavy industry accounted for about 41 percent of the total level of industrial production in 1990, light industry (including cotton) 39 percent, and agro/food processing almost 13 percent, with the fuel-energy industry representing the remainder. The machinery sector includes many products that are linked to agriculture, such as cotton harvesters and textile machinery, and, within the chemical manufacturing branch, fertilizer.

1.19   Production within the state enterprise sector (including agricultural enterprises) is still based primarily on a plan that assigns production quotas to each enterprise. A fixed percentage of the quota is retained by the enterprise, and the rest goes to the Government. However, anything above the quota is the property of the enterprise.

1.20   As in most of the FSU, total trade--but particularly interrepublic trade--represented a substantial proportion of GDP, approximately 67 percent in 1991. In 1991, interrepublic imports accounted for over 83 percent of total imports, almost 29 percent of GDP. Moreover, interrepublic exports amounted to about 89 percent of total exports in 1991. Cotton, machinery, natural gas, and fertilizers are main components in interrepublic exports, amounting to over 70 percent of the total interrepublic exports in 1990. Foreign export represented about 4 percent of GDP in 1991; cotton is the single most significant commodity in foreign export, accounting for about 80 percent in 1992.

1.21   Uzbekistan inherited from the FSU an extensive system of social protection characterized by child allowances, old age pensions, disability benefits, and subsidies on consumer goods and services. In 1989, 44 percent of the population of Uzbekistan were living below the official poverty line, compared with 11.1 for the USSR. The health status of the population started deteriorating in 1990. Moreover, shortages of vaccines, medical supplies, and equipment indicate that Uzbekistan faces uncertain health risks from environmental influences. Uzbekistan also inherited a high literacy rate and a school system which has suffered prolonged underinvestment in the physical plant, and is isolated from the mainstream of current actual practices in countries outside the FSU. However, it does have a large number of mature and well-educated staff at all levels who have coped well with some of the deficiencies of the system.

1.22   Uzbekistan has a relatively well developed transport system that is adapted to its geography (42,000 km of main roads, 90,000 km of local roads, and 3,500 km of rail lines). However, the economy is unusually transport-intensive, and the needs for rehabilitation and the replacement of assets are significant. Uzbekistan inherited a telecommunications network organized centrally with international routing via Moscow with obsolete equipment and poor-quality service, which is deteriorating further.

Economic Performance until the Breakup

1.23   Since 1988, real output growth rates have declined rapidly, and became negative in 1991 (Table 1.2). The substantial decline in output in 1991 preceded any attempt to undertake substantial reform toward a market-based economy and was a response to the breakup of the FSU and a corresponding decline in both the overall terms of trade and the volume of interrepublic trade.

1.24   The share of agriculture in production has been growing steadily to 36 percent in 1991 (see Table 1.3). At the same time, the share of industry declined to 21 percent in 1990 and has recovered thereafter. The shares of construction and services in total GDP dropped sharply in 1991, to 9 percent and 27 percent, respectively.

1.25   The share of agricultural employment has remained constant at approximately 40 percent since 1985,[8] while industry's share has grown slightly, representing about 15 percent in 1990. Employment remains heavily skewed toward the state enterprise sector, which accounted for almost 65

---

[8] However, agricultural employment varies within the year owing to temporary seasonal labor.

Table 1.2
Uzbekistan: Main Macroeconomic Indicators for 1988-1991

	1988	1989	1990	1991
Output (Real Growth Rates)				
Gross Domestic Product	10.2	3.7	1.6	-0.5
Net Material Product	9.6	3.1	4.5	-0.91
Trade Balance (as % of GDP)	-6.3	-13	-16.4	-3.0
Interrepublic	-5.7	-11.4	-11.4	-0.7
Foreign	-0.6	-1.6	-5.0	-2.3
Prices and Wages[a] (percentage change)				
NMP implicit deflator	-2.2	0.8	4.0	98.2
Retail price	0	0.9	3.8	83.1
Wholesale price	NA	2.1	7.2	147.3
Average nominal wage	7.3	6.5	11.2	51.2
Real wage index[b] (1991=100)	107	113	121	100
Real minimum wage index (1991=100)	-	-	183.6	100

Source: State Statistical and Forecasting Committee (Goskomprognostat) and Bank staff estimates.

[a]   Period averages.
[b]   Deflated by retail prices.

percent of total employment in 1991. Employment in cooperatives represented about 18 percent in 1991. The fastest-growing employment sector was self-employment in trade and services, which absorbed part of the drop in the state enterprise share, increasing from 10 percent in 1985 to 17 percent in 1991, although it still represents a comparatively small portion of overall employment (see Table 1.3).

1.26   Since Uzbekistan's per capita income was quite low relative to the average for the Soviet Union as a whole, it led to sizable net budget transfers to the republic, which stopped by the end of 1991. Modest fiscal deficits were recorded in the Government's finances during 1987-90, ranging from 0.3 percent to 1.4 percent of GDP. However, net transfers from the Union rose significantly from about 7 to 9 percent of GDP during 1987-89 to 19 percent of GDP in 1990. The Government deficit rose to about 5 percent of GDP in 1991 in spite of a further increase (up to 19.5 percent of GDP) of Union transfers to Uzbekistan.[9] The underlying deterioration in Government finances reflected an increase in expenditures mainly associated with efforts to maintain the living standards of the population through subsidies.

[9] Source: Ministry of Finance and IMF estimates. Union transfers may be overestimated because gold transfers from Uzbekistan to the center are not considered. It is estimated that in 1991 they represented about 2 percent of GDP.

1.27   Aggregate expenditures increased rapidly during the 1987-90 period. The shares of household and government consumption and investment in GDP all rose. Household consumption increased from 58 percent of GDP to 61 percent. During this period, Government consumption also increased from 21 percent of GDP to 26 percent (see Table 1.4). Investment grew from 28 percent of GDP in 1987 to 32 percent in 1990.

1.28   The increase in total expenditures during this period led to more than a doubling of the republic's resource imbalance with the rest of the FSU, from −8 percent of GDP in 1987 to −19 percent of GDP in

Table 1.3
Structure of Employment
(in percent)

	1985	1990	1991
Percentage of Population			
Employed	37	39	40
Retired	11	12	12
Employment by Sector			
Industry	15	15	14
Construction	8	9	8
Agriculture	38	39	42
Forestry	4	3	3
Transportation and communication	4	3	3
Trade and related sectors	7	6	6
Other	28	28	27
Employment by Enterprise Type			
State sector	72	66	65
Cooperatives	18	20	18
Self-employed	10	15	17

Source: State Statistical and Forecasting Committee of Uzbekistan (Goskomprognostat).

1990. Although the data for 1991 suggest that the resource balance improved sharply, to −5 percent of GDP, the magnitude of this improvement may not be accurate. It is very likely that the interrepublic trade deficit was underestimated.[10]   The share of total consumption declined in 1991, driven by a reduction in the consumption of state enterprises, which fell by 5 percent, to 15 percent of GDP.

1.29   Inflation had been repressed within the FSU until quite recently. For example, retail prices rose at an annual rate of 1 percent between 1988 and 1990. The NMP deflator, retail prices, and wholesale prices all accelerated gradually in 1990, and jumped abruptly upwards in 1991 (shown earlier in Table 1.2).

1.30   The constraint to nominal household consumption, due to the repressed inflation, led to involuntary savings. Between 1988 and 1990, real wages rose by approximately 13 percent relative to retail prices and 8 percent relative to wholesale prices. Household income grew by around 21 percent in real terms in the same period. Although wages declined in real terms in 1991, household income continued increasing throughout the year. Most of this increase in real income was held in the form of liquid assets (monetary overhang). Rapid increases in nominal wages and household incomes without an increase in the supply of goods for consumption and repressed prices led to excessive accumulation of household savings. Household financial savings increased significantly throughout the period and,

---

[10] This apparent inconsistency of the data will be resolved when more detailed data become available.

while in 1988, about 58 percent of those savings were deposited in the Savings Bank, by 1991 that share reached 65 percent.

1.31   Investment was substantially more volatile than either output or consumption; its rate of decline in 1991 was more than twice that of either output or consumption. A net transfer of resources from enterprises to households seems to have taken place. The composition of investment changed over time. The share devoted to housing and social benefits expanded at the expense of agriculture and industry.

Table 1.4
Uzbekistan: Structure of Production and Expenditures
(as % of GDP)

	1987	1988	1989	1990	1991
Sector Shares					
Industry	29	26	22	21	28
Agriculture	26	28	31	33	36
Construction	11	11	11	11	9
Services	35	36	36	36	27
Expenditure Shares					
Household consumption	58	58	59	61	61
Government consumption	21	20	23	26	19
Investment	29	27	32	32	26
Resource balance[1]	-8	-6	-13	-19	-5[2]

Source: State Statistical and Forecasting Committee of Uzbekistan.

[1]   Resource balance differs from trade balance reported in Table 1.2 because of non-factor services.

[2]   The 1991 reported figure should be considered with caution. These data are inconsistent with the amount of total transfers from the Union reported in the budget.

CHAPTER 2

THE NEED FOR REFORM

2.1   By the end of 1991, when the Government of Uzbekistan began to manage its own economy, the external environment was largely determined by Russia. At the start of 1992, following the dissolution of the Union, Russia initiated ambitious reforms. The centerpiece of the reform was significant price liberalization. Similarly, in Uzbekistan's neighboring republics--particularly Kazakhstan and Kyrgyzstan--reform measures were under way.

2.2   At that time, the Government of Uzbekistan adopted a cautious and partial approach to reform, until an articulated program could be developed. Prices were partially liberalized, foreign-exchange markets unified, new taxes imposed, import tariffs removed, small shops and residential housing privatized, and new laws on banking, property, and foreign investment enacted.

2.3   By June 1993, Uzbekistan had, however, still not designed a comprehensive reform program for its transition to a market-based economy. The problem is that a slow, partial approach runs the risk of sending confused signals to economic agents from a hybrid system--neither the old command system nor a viable alternative. Uzbekistan needs to stabilize the economy and reverse long-term declines in productivity. Without reforms to do that, the negative effects of recent shocks to the economy will be increasingly felt, and economic deterioration is likely to continue. This could in the medium-term lead to a significant fall in per capita consumption and economic stagnation. A decline in economic activity in the short-term probably cannot be avoided but far-reaching reforms will now establish the necessary basis for sustainable and significant economic growth over the medium and long terms.

A. THE SETTING FOR REFORM

2.4   In 1992, Uzbekistan experienced a large decline in real output (10 percent), high inflation (about 2,700 percent in wholesale prices between December 1991 and December 1992), and a substantial terms-of-trade shock (10 percent). To cushion consumers and the enterprise sector, the Government tried to prevent internal prices from adjusting to FSU levels, which simply exacerbated inherent distortions in production. The result: an even more distorted incentive structure, in which relative prices depend primarily on relative subsidies. Productivity has continued to decline owing partly to the requirement for SOEs and farms to maintain employment when output is falling. Given the present macroeconomic instability and distortions in the economy, Uzbekistan will not be able to generate the necessary supply response to promote the Government's developmental objectives. Comprehensive reforms are needed if the Government is to:

- Stabilize the economy,

- Reverse output decline while improving productivity,

- Achieve sustainable development in the medium term, and

- Be able to protect vulnerable groups of the population effectively.

2.5   While detailed estimates of economic aggregates are still preliminary, there is little doubt that Uzbekistan has significant macroeconomic imbalances. In 1992, it had a fiscal deficit -- central government deficit in rubles -- of 11 percent of GDP and a current account deficit of 17 percent of GDP. These deficits were financed through arrears with some FSU republics, foreign domestic and foreign borrowing, and gold reserves. Such high financing requirements are not sustainable.

2.6   As long as Uzbekistan remains in *the ruble zone*, monetary and exchange-rate policies (both crucial to successful macroeconomic management) will have to follow zone parameters, and stabilization will depend, to a significant extent, on what happens in Russia. Meanwhile, financing the fiscal deficit with Russian rubles is being paid for, in part, by an effective inflation tax on the people of Uzbekistan. Despite growing consumer subsidies, high inflation is hurting the most vulnerable groups of the population.

2.7   Subsidies lie at the heart of the fiscal problem in Uzbekistan. Through subsidies (direct and indirect) and price controls, the Government has tried to cushion the population from the impact of recent economic events. However, *consumer goods subsidies* have not been targeted at the most vulnerable and have encouraged the overconsumption of subsidized goods and services. Moreover, in 1992 many of Uzbekistan's highly subsidized products were apparently bought by citizens of neighboring republics, effectively spreading Uzbekistan's social safety net abroad. In July 1993, the Government reduced the number of products of the consumer basket subject to direct consumer subsidies. In principle, only bread and flour remain subject to controlled prices. Subsidies must be reduced to avoid further pressures on the budget. Moreover, the economic cost of subsidies is greater than the allocation in the ruble budget; foreign exchange is allocated for consumer goods imports (mainly, wheat and sugar) at a fraction of the market exchange rate.

2.8   *Input and credit subsidies to agriculture, industry producers and enterprises* are also costly for the Government and the economy of Uzbekistan. For example, low domestic prices for energy inputs and the absence of water charges inevitably lead to rationing and hamper conservation. Moreover, systematic underpricing of energy relative to other goods has led to massive overconsumption per unit of output relative to market-based economies. Reducing energy consumption and increasing energy efficiency will both reduce imports and free up energy supplies for export. Increasing energy prices to fully reflect costs of supply will be the primary catalyst for lowering energy intensity.

2.9   There is another damaging (implicit) subsidy--very negative real interest rates. Despite the abolition of central planning, financial resources in Uzbekistan are still allocated to state enterprises through non-market mechanisms. State enterprises are borrowing for working capital without undertaking fixed investment, while their output is declining.

2.10   Apart from the "inflation tax,"[1] these economic subsidies are financed by large net taxes on agriculture and foreign borrowing. Transfers out of agriculture result from the Government's pricing policy on inputs and output and, in particular, from the *state order system* which requires that much of the output of state and collective farms be sold to the state at significantly lower than market prices. Such a system does not convey market-price signals to producers to allow for market-based production

---

[1] Inflation is a tax on the holdings of real monetary balances. Anyone who holds money loses part of the value of the money owing to inflation (can buy fewer goods and services with the same quantity of money).

decisions and it fails to create incentives for production investment and innovation. In agriculture and agro-processing, for example, yields are low relative to inputs and spoilage is very high; moreover, incentives for efficient distribution (storage and transportation) do not exist.

2.11   While *output declines* can be seen as part of adjustment (that would lead eventually to a production structure more in line with Uzbekistan's resource base), there are strong signs that this is not so. The decline so far does not reflect adjustment, nor the reallocation of labor and capital towards more productive uses. Rather, it reflects disruption and low capacity utilization. Hence, allowing output to decline further without changing how state-owned enterprises are run will not improve the economic situation. SOEs must be restructured to face new relative prices of inputs and output, and use capital and labor efficiently. Output per worker has been falling at not less than 10 percent a year, since there has been no reduction in SOE employment. Estimates of value added in some parts of industry are negative.[2]

Table 2.1
Output Decline in FSU Economies
(percentage change in GDP)

	1991	1992
Armenia	-12	-53
Azerbaijan	-2	-26
Belarus	-2	-10
Estonia	-11	-25
Georgia	-28	-45
Kazakhstan	-7	-14
Kyrgyzstan	-4	-26
Latvia	-8	-44
Lithuania	-15	-39
Moldova	-18	-21
Russia	-8	-19
Tajikistan	-9	-25
Turkmenistan	-1	- 9
Ukraine	-11	-20
Uzbekistan	**-0.5**	**-10**

Source: World Bank CEMs Goskomprognostat and Bank staff calculations.

2.12   If stabilization is not achieved and if the minimum structural change is not in place, long-term investment in areas such as energy, mining, and agro-processing will continue to suffer, which will have detrimental economic consequences. Uzbekistan's export potential is considerable but without a clear and articulated reform strategy and (at least the beginning of) removal of incentive distortions, capital inflows will remain well below optimal levels.

B. RECENT ECONOMIC DEVELOPMENTS

2.13   This section presents recent economic trends in several areas in 1992-93 that set the stage for the macroeconomic framework and agenda for reform presented in chapter 3. The poor quality and availability of data impose severe limitations on the analyses carried out below. Thus, all quantitative estimates of 1992 economic indicators should be considered provisional.

OUTPUT AND EMPLOYMENT

2.14   Given the strength of agriculture and the export of raw materials to both the FSU and the rest of the world, the economy of Uzbekistan was affected somewhat less by the trade disruptions accompanying the breakup of the FSU than were most of the other republics (see Table 2.1). However, the rate at which real output is declining accelerated in 1992, owing to a significant terms-of-trade shock

---

[2] Chapters 9 to 14 of this report discuss specific problems with the current system in the context of the different sectors of the economy of Uzbekistan.

and a decline in trade volumes and investment. Real GDP declined by 0.5 percent in 1991, and a further decline of about 10 percent has been estimated for 1992. The sharpest decline in output occurred in the construction subsector (see Table 2.2). The decline in the industry subsector was not nearly as severe. The chemical and agro-industrial subsectors suffered the largest declines in output. Agriculture showed a decline over the year, despite a good harvest in 1992. Real investment in 1992 is estimated to have fallen significantly. Official estimates indicate a fall in investment of about 12 percent relative to 1991.[3] While output decline in Uzbekistan was the lowest in the FSU, both consumption and investment levels have been severely affected.

2.15   Employment levels are being maintained through a significant downward adjustment of wages, resulting in underemployment. Real wages showed a significant decline in 1992-93. The average real wage declined by 54 percent and the minimum real wage by 74 percent in 1992 (see Table 2.2). Wage differentials have also contracted throughout 1992. It is estimated that the real aggregate monetary income of households (measured as wages, pensions, and other allowances) fell by slightly over 50 percent in real terms in 1992.[4]

Table 2.2
Uzbekistan - 1992-93 Macroeconomic Indicators

	1992	1993
Output (Real growth rates)		
GDP	-9.6	-4.5[b]
NMP	-12.9	
Agriculture	-7.3	
Industry	-12.3	
Construction	-42.3	
Transport and telecom	-7.3	
Other	-5.1	
Trade Balance (as % of GDP)	-12.2	
Interrepublic	-9.4	
Foreign	-2.8	
Prices and wages (percentage change)		
Retail prices	790[c/d]	300[a]
Wholesale prices	2700[c]	245[a]
Average nominal wage	612	300[a]
Real wage[e]	-54	
Real minimum wage[e\f]	-74	

Source: Goskomprognostat, IMF, and Bank staff calculations.
[a]   Between December 1992 and June 1993.
[b]   The first quarter of 1993 with respect to the first quarter of 1992.
[c]   Calculated point to point--percentage change over same period one year earlier.
[d]   Evidence indicates that this index has been underestimated.
[e]   Deflated by wholesale prices.
[f]   From Jan. 1993 to Jan. 1992.

---

[3] This figure is not consistent with the estimated fall in the construction sector NMP of 39 percent.

[4] The figures on real wages and real household incomes almost certainly overstate the actual declines because of "forced savings" (the growth of the monetary overhang) prior to the scale price liberalization in January 1992.

PRICES

2.16   Although most domestic prices were initially liberalized in January 1992, overall prices in Uzbekistan remained below the levels of the other FSU republics until October 1992.   According to a comparison of the prices of 12 basic food commodities (such as flour, bread, beef, butter, and vegetable oil), 7 of which are controlled, the price gap between Uzbekistan and Russia had widened in 8 of the 12 categories. On October 16, 1992, the Government significantly increased domestic prices for energy products. This increase in energy prices had a significant impact on other prices of goods and services and inflation rates accelerated in the last quarter of 1992 (Table 2.3.). Direct energy subsidies remain only for residential consumption and transport. Energy price ceilings have been established, which are generally above energy prices in other FSU countries. By the end of December 1992, the seven controlled prices of basic food and urban transport remained below neighboring republics' prices. However, in July 1993 further price liberalization took place. Only bread, flour, and urban transport remain heavily controlled.

Table 2.3
Price Behavior in 1992[a], Monthly

Year	Month	Wholesale Prices		Retail Prices (Goods and Services)	
		Index	Inflation Rates	Index	Inflation Rates
1991	12	100	7	100	5
1992	1	475	375	241	141
	2	511	8	293	22
	3	563	10	328	12
	4	602	7	278	-15
	5	698	16	320	15
	6	757	9	357	11
	7	799	6	409	15
	8	865	8	503	23
	9	978	13	537	7
	10	1595	63	605	13
	11	2378	49	739	22
	12	2788	17	887	20
1993	1	4077	46	1551	76
	2	4546	12	1754	13
	3	5376	18	2004	14
	4	5572	4	2498	25
	5	7458	34	2908	16
	6	9608	29	3490	20

Sources: Goskomprognostat and Bank staff calculations.

[a]   Inflation rates were calculated based on point to point indices--relative to the same month of previous year.

2.17   It is very difficult to determine Uzbekistan's "true" rates of inflation for 1992 because of statistical biases embedded in the methodologies presently used by the Statistical and Forecasting Committee. The rates of inflation for wholesale and retail prices from December 1991 to December 1992 measured point to point were about 2,700 percent and 790 percent, respectively. Rates of inflation measured by monthly indices were about 8,900 percent and 900 percent, respectively.[5]

---

[5] However, since these calculations are based on indices that reflect unweighted averages of commodity baskets, the high volatility of price increases in 1992 caused the aggregate indexes to be overestimated. Inflation rates in Russia measured in the same way during the same period were about 6,040 percent in wholesale prices and 2,430 percent in retail prices. Wholesale prices in Russia measured point to point increased by about 3,270 percent and urban retail prices by about 2300 percent. Therefore, price data should be considered with a lot of caution.

STATE ORDERS

2.18   While the Government has started reducing the proportion of production that must be channeled into the state order system, there is still significant room for improving the incentive mechanisms in the production sectors of the economy. For example, cotton production is currently subject to a state order quota of 80 percent, fruits and vegetables 50 percent, and industrial products between 20 percent and 80 percent.

FISCAL DEFICIT

2.19   Despite the upheaval caused by the breakup of the Soviet Union, and the consequent loss in transfers from the Union and the decline in real output, Uzbekistan has managed to keep the Government's real expenditures under control. Although the Government has restricted itself largely to spending from current revenue receipts in order to contain expenditures, estimates of the executed federal budget for 1992 indicate that total expenditures represented 45 percent of GDP and preliminary estimates for the first quarter of 1993 indicate that they represented 56 percent of GDP. A significant proportion of these expenditures constitutes expenditures on social programs. Total revenue dropped substantially, to about 34 percent of GDP, with the cessation of the Union transfers.   Therefore, according to the narrow definition, the ruble fiscal deficit in 1992 reached approximately 11 percent of GDP.[6] Although Table 2.4 indicates a surplus for the first quarter of 1993, this preliminary result should be taken with caution.

2.20   Until September 1992, actual revenue and expenditures were roughly at the planned levels. However, the sharp increase in energy prices in October 1992

Table 2.4
Federal Revenue and Expenditures
(as shares of GDP)

	1991	1992	1993[d]
Total Revenue	45.5	34.2	60.9
of which			
VAT	-	9.2	18.6
Excise	-	8.4	12.2
Export tax[a]	-	1.9	4.2
Enterprise income tax	5.7	5.9	10.7
Personal income tax	2.6	2.6	3.5
Others	8.3	6.1	11.7
Union grants (net)	19.5	-	-
Turnover tax	9.4	-	-
Total Expenditures[b]	50.6	45.2	56.5
of which:			
National economy	18.0	3.7	3.4
Social and cultural programs	17.9	16.7	17.5
Others	6.1	10.1	18.4
Subsidies	8.6	11.8[c]	12.3
Expenditures for financing centralized state capital investment	na	2.9	4.7
Deficit	5.0	11.0	-4.4

Source: Ministry of Finance.

[a]   Export taxes refer to raw material taxes on inter-republic trade only. The revenue from trade with the ROW is not large and is included in the category "others."

[b]   Expenditures financed by the Pension Fund and the Social Insurance Fund do not appear in the budget. These include such items as pensions, child allowances, and maternity benefits.

[c]   Budgetary compensation on consumer goods and on children's goods.

[d]   As share of first quarter GDP.

---

[6] The Government still keeps two budgets: one in rubles, the other in hard currency. Estimates on the latter were not made available to the Bank or the IMF.

affected the budget by, among other things, increasing the amount of direct subsidies. Subsidies still remain, primarily for residential energy consumption and public transportation. The fiscal impact of the cessation of transfers from Moscow, which represented about 19.5 percent of GDP in 1991, was significant (Table 2.4). Moreover, the impact of the negative terms-of-trade shock on the reduction in national income was not negligible.[7]

2.21   The Government financed the ruble deficit in 1992 (1) by issuing domestic bonds and placing them through auctions throughout the country (an estimated 6 billion rubles or 1.5 percent of GDP); (2) by Central Bank credits; and (3) by interrepublican food credits.

Revenue

2.22   The Government tried to compensate for the loss in revenue by imposing a new tax structure. However, due to the high inflation rate, the tax base for most of the taxes has been eroded throughout 1992, and ineffective collection methods have also affected revenue. Four types of taxes are collected in Uzbekistan: (1) commodity taxes, (2) an enterprise profits tax, (3) a personal income tax, and (4) a wage tax. The major *commodity tax* is the value added tax (VAT), whose single rate of 25 percent is high by international standards. It was introduced in January 1992. The VAT covers commodities through the manufacturing stage and does include wholesale and retail margins. The VAT is not applied on exports but on the value added of imports. The second major type of commodity taxes is excise taxes imposed on a small list of commodities, including alcoholic drinks, cigarettes, rugs, gold jewelry, and gasoline. The third major category of commodity taxes is those on external trade. External trade is treated differently according to whether it is interrepublic trade or foreign trade. On foreign trade, 70 product categories have export duties ranging from 2 to 40 percent. The combined effect of both taxes on foreign exports is a total tax rate that ranges between 36 and 75 percent. Foreign imports (38 product categories) have import duties ranging from 2 to 40 percent. A 1 to 3 percent fee is also charged for handling and processing on all foreign trade. These taxes do not collect much revenue, since ROW trade encompasses a large barter component that enables exporters to avoid both export taxes and, reportedly to some degree, the enterprise profits tax. On the other hand, exports to the FSU are taxed at a much lower rate. All goods exported to FSU countries under an intergovernmental contract or agreement are subject to a 10 percent export tax. There are differentiated rates for a few goods such as cotton fibre and natural gas. There are no import duties on FSU imports.

2.23   An unusual feature of the enterprise *profits tax* is that the tax base is the sum of wages and profits. The tax was originally introduced as a way to discourage excessive wage increases in SOEs. This so-called profits tax has a basic rate of 18 percent, but can vary from 12 percent to 30 percent depending on the sectoral rate set by the Council of Ministers. A wide variety of specific exemptions apply to this tax. For example, newly established enterprises are taxed on 25 percent of their income in their first year and 50 percent in the second, but foreign direct investment through joint ventures (with 30 percent of foreign participation) is exempt.[8]

---

[7] For an analysis of the terms-of-trade shock, see the section on Trade Policy in this chapter.

[8] Foreign direct investment through joint ventures in the Government's priority sectors is exempt from the enterprise income tax for five years.

2.24   For the majority of taxpayers, the *personal income tax* is collected from the enterprises directly when they make wage payments. In 1992, seven income brackets imposed tax rates ranging from 12 to 60 percent. The tax had a basic exemption of 1,000 rubles per month. At present, the tax exemption is the minimum wage. Almost all taxpayers recently are in the first bracket, because the income distribution is so tight and the lower bracket is so wide. The income tax allows a 50 percent income deduction for those with three or more dependents. The personal income tax also grants several additional exemptions, such as student stipends, pension income, charitable donations, and income used to purchase shares in state enterprises. Interest income on bank deposits and government securities is not taxed.

2.25   A new 35 percent tax on hard currency proceeds was introduced in May 1993. The tax base includes all hard currency earned by activities conducted in Uzbekistan, minus a few selected items that can be deducted from the tax base (transport cost, freight, insurance, interest, etc.). Under this tax, all barter transactions with non-ruble countries are to be taxed from July 16, 1993 based on the cost of the contract. Twenty-five percentage points of the tax go to the central Government of which 20 percent is deposited in the new Republican Monetary Fund and 5 percent has to be surrendered to the Central Bank at the market exchange rate. The remaining 10 percent goes to the hard currency funds of the City of Tashkent, the 12 oblasts, and the Republic of Karakalpakstan. Enterprises must deposit the remaining foreign exchange income in the authorized banks from which they can draw according to the foreign exchange regulations for hard currency use.

2.26   In addition to the personal income tax, a *wage tax* has been imposed since 1991. Employers pay 37 percent of the wage bill, and employees pay 1 percent of their wages. These taxes feed two extrabudgetary funds for social protection. In 1991, the Pension Fund was established by the Government to replace the old Union Pension Fund, and it receives 82.5 percent of the taxes collected by the wage tax. In addition to pensions, this fund provides child allowances. The remainder of these tax receipts goes to the Social Insurance Fund, which provides a range of benefits at the enterprise level under the discretion of the local trade union. A third fund was established in 1992--the Employment Fund, which is financed by an additional 3 percent tax on the wage bill of enterprises and apparently by direct transfers from the budget. This fund is to provide unemployment benefits, retraining, and job placement services.

Expenditures

2.27   After the breakup of the USSR, most of the social programs continued under the direction of the Republic, financed through a variety of significant budgetary and off-budgetary funds. Total social expenditures represented approximately 29.1 percent of GDP in 1991, 22.3 percent of which were subsidies and family allowances, and 6.8 percent were pensions.[9] In 1992, social expenditures reached about 23 percent of GDP, 12 percent of which (representing consumer subsidies) was financed through the federal budget. The present policy is not sustainable.

---

[9] Chapter 8 of this report, "The Framework for Social Protection," provides a detailed explanation of the structure of the social safety net in Uzbekistan.

2.28   Because energy prices are subsidized indirectly by price regulation,[10] these indirect subsidies largely do not appear in the narrowly defined fiscal budget, and the direct impact will thus be smaller. However, the impact on the consolidated budget will be much larger, since here the pass-through of the higher oil prices cannot be disguised, but must appear on the profit and loss statements of the affected enterprises. Since these enterprises are the property of the state, this loss is actually a loss to the consolidated state budget. This fiscal structure highlights the need for a consolidated budget accounting system.[11]

FINANCIAL SYSTEM

2.29   While the financial structure in Uzbekistan has changed since independence, many of the old features have been retained. Initially, four banks operated in the Soviet Union, differing according to their function: the commercial bank, or *Gosbank;* the Savings Bank, or *Sberbank;* the foreign trade bank, or *Vneshekonombank;* and the construction bank, or *Stroibank*. The role of the Gosbank has been assumed by the Central Bank; the role of the foreign trade bank has been assumed to a certain extent by the National Bank. Although the local branches of the Sberbank have been regrouped into the Savings Bank of Uzbekistan, they continue to operate under the direction of the Central Bank, without much change. At the same time, Uzbekistan has two major sectoral banks--one for agriculture and one for industry--as well as several small commercial banks that serve largely as intermediaries between enterprises and the rest of the banking system.

2.30   Real interest rates remain extremely negative under the current financial structure of Uzbekistan. By June 1993, the average nominal interest rate for deposits reached only 25 percent, the Central Bank's rediscount rate reached a maximum of 40 percent, and the highest lending rate of the National Bank reached 100 percent.

PAYMENTS SYSTEM

2.31   The clearing process has slowed down with the gradual replacement of the old clearing system with a new multi-bank system. Now, at each stage, successive payments are held up because payments are not made by other participants. Since an end-of-production cycle adjustment no longer exists, this sequential system of payment can quickly lead to financial gridlock if the enterprises do not maintain positive balances in their accounts. As the delays accumulate, so do arrears.[12] Because commercial and sectoral banks do not maintain correspondent accounts with each other, the payments system clears only through the Central Bank of Uzbekistan. This arrangement slows the clearing process even further, as a large mass of payments must flow through a single institution. At the same time, the general perception that the Central Bank will in effect bail out loss-making enterprises has not diminished. This perception erodes the incentive that an enterprise might normally have to care about the likelihood of repayment before deciding to extend credit, by allowing another enterprise to accumulate accounts receivables with it. However, the resulting delays in payment are very costly to creditor enterprises.

---

[10] Energy prices in 1992 had both an implicit subsidy (i.e., prices were below world prices) and an explicit subsidy (i.e., prices were below cost).

[11] No reliable figures are currently available on extrabudgetary funds.

[12] Arrears are defined as any debt overdue for more than two months.

2.32   The end result of these factors, combined with a decline in real working capital due to a policy of tight credit, has been an extremely rapid buildup of interenterprise arrears within Uzbekistan. Interenterprise arrears grew in real terms by a significant amount in 1992. The ratio of arrears to GDP rose from 4 percent in 1991 to about 20 percent of GDP by September 1992.

MONETARY DEVELOPMENTS

2.33   Because Uzbekistan remains in the ruble zone, the money supply is determined by the magnitude of cash ruble shipments from the Central Bank of Russia, by credit from the Central Bank of Uzbekistan, and by the change in net claims on other FSU republics. In the second half of 1992, Russia fulfilled almost entirely the requests for rubles from the

Table 2.5
Monetary Indicators[1]
(1992-3)
(million rubles)

	Mar 1992	Jun 1992	Dec 1992	Mar 1993
1. Cash held by population	14450	26080	96784	207637
2. Personal deposits	18775	20412	23882	45425
3. Total deposits of enterprises & organizations	21856	30277	141003	183388
Total (1+2+3)	55081	76769	261669	436450
Retail price index (Mar92=100)	100	135	648.9	941.5

(as percent of GDP[2])

1. Cash held by population	6.0	7.0	6.2	9.2
2. Personal deposits	7.8	5.5	1.5	2.0
3. Total deposits of enterprises	9.1	8.1	9.1	8.1
Total (1+2+3)	23.0	20.5	16.8	19.3

Source: Central Bank of Uzbekistan, Goskomprognostat and Bank staff calculations.
[1]   End of period.
[2]   Ratios of money components to GDP are calculated by $(M_i/P_j)/(GDP/P_{avg})$, where M_i is money component i; and P_j is retail price at time j; and P_{avg} is an average retail price.

Central Bank of Uzbekistan. Real monetary balances declined throughout 1992, owing primarily to high inflation levels and the decline in the level of economic activity (see Table 2.5).

2.34   Velocity of circulation of money appears to have increased substantially in the second half of the year. Personal deposits in the financial system dropped drastically, most likely because of the very high negative real interest rates. The ratio between currency in the hands of the public and currency deposits almost doubled in the second half of 1992, indicating a serious possibility of a financial crisis in the near future. Until now the potential crisis has been kept under control owing to several administrative measures that do not support the emergence of an efficient financial system. The Central Bank has established cash offices at commercial banks and is strictly controlling the flow of cash. In addition, individuals are not having easy access to their cash holdings and are required to use cash certificates (similar to checks) for their purchases. In this way, the Government is attempting to control the flow of cash in the economy. Enterprise deposits in the financial system also dropped significantly owing to a tight credit policy and their need for working capital.

2.35   The Central Bank of Uzbekistan can affect the nominal demand for money directly only by controlling the domestic credit to the Government and enterprises, but indirectly by setting interest-rate and rediscounting policy. The spread over the Central Bank's cost of borrowing has been set at 4 percent by a Government decree. Because the interest rates on loans were negative in real terms (in fact, nominal rates were lower than in Russia), interest-rate and rediscounting policies are not effective policy instruments. Domestic credit to the banking system behaved erratically in 1992, reaching in October 1992 the same value in real terms as in January 1992 after a continuous decline between February and September.

2.36   The distinction between cash and credit rubles evolved in 1992 as a way to separate the financing of interenterprise trade and final-goods trade. Because these two types of rubles are not freely convertible, they are in effect parallel currencies. The public has access only to cash rubles, since all wage and pension payments are made in this form. Box 2.1 on cash versus credit rubles analyzes the implication of both types of currency on interenterprise trade and all monetary aggregates. Credit to enterprises is made in the form of credit rubles. It declined 15 percent in real terms between December 1991 and December 1992 owing to a conscious effort by the Central Bank to keep domestic credit policy under control.

Box 2.1: Uzbekistan: Cash versus Credit Rubles

Cash rubles are created solely by the mints in the Russian Federation, and allocated to the Central Banks of the different republics at the discretion of the Central Bank of Russia. Conversely, credit rubles are created through the banking system of each of the different republics and are differentiated by country of origin. This distinction in the source of credit ruble is pertinent to all those transactions that had formerly been but are no longer domestic. These inter-republic noncash transactions are now cleared through bilateral correspondent accounts at the Central Banks of the respective republics.

Since clearing is made on a bilateral basis, the trade balance—particularly the ruble credit balance between the two republics in question—combined with the degree of political cohesion between the two republics and the efficiency of each republic's Central Bank, determines the speed at which these transactions will clear. Since the magnitude of interrepublic inter-enterprise trade was very large, the financial flows that were effected were also quite large. Thus, substantially greater delays have been associated with inter-republic than with intra-republic trade, since transactions that had taken several days can now take as long as several months. Uzbekistan is a net creditor with respect to almost all its significant FSU trading partners.

Interenterprise trade is conducted with credit rubles. Credit and cash rubles are allocated to enterprises through the banking system, largely by the Central Bank. In fact, enterprises are allocated only cash sufficient to pay for their wages, to procure farm products, and to conduct business trips. All cash earnings by enterprises must be returned to the Central Bank via the banking system in exchange for credit rubles. Enterprises face much softer budget constraints with their credit rubles.

Although in monetary aggregates cash and credit rubles are lumped together, they are not generally convertible, and they do not trade at par. The monetary aggregates thus provide a misleading description of the present situation. This is particularly true if the relative value of these two currencies is changing over time.

TRADE

Interrepublican Trade

2.37   Both interrepublican and foreign trade[13] declined in 1992 with the breakup of the FSU.   The structure of interrepublican trade differs sharply from the structure of foreign trade. In interrepublic trade, the Government has entered into a system of bilateral trade agreements with FSU countries to ensure that key commodities are available at prices that those countries feel they can afford.   The agreements cover petroleum and petroleum products, rare metals, cotton, and some chemical and metallurgical products.   The two key export commodities covered under these bilateral agreements are cotton fibre, which it exchanges for Russian oil, and petroleum products.   Other important export goods include

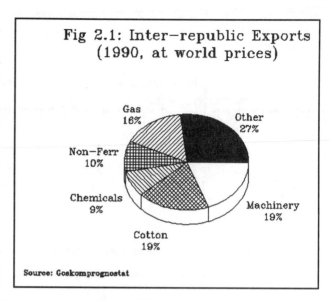

Fig 2.1: Inter-republic Exports (1990, at world prices)

Gas 16%
Other 27%
Non-Ferr 10%
Chemicals 9%
Machinery 19%
Cotton 19%

Source: Goskomprognostat

machinery, vegetables, fruits, and nonferrous metal.   Major imports include oil and certain agricultural products, textiles, fertilizers, and machinery (see Figures 2.1 and 2.2).

2.38   In the 1992 bilateral agreements, the quantities to be supplied by each republic had been determined so that the value of the commodities being exchanged--calculated at world-market prices at the time of the agreement-- were balanced.   However, the agreements did not specify prices.   Rather, the governmental agencies responsible for overseeing interrepublic trade-- which for Uzbekistan is Uzcontractorg--granted domestic enterprises the right to purchase a certain amount of the commodity in question from an enterprise suggested by the other government, at a price to be negotiated between the two enterprises.   For commodities that Uzbekistan had pledged to the other republics, particularly cotton, Uzcontractorg acted as the sales agent for Government stocks of these commodities, which

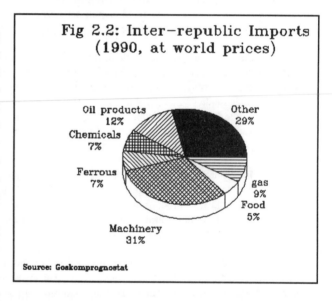

Fig 2.2: Inter-republic Imports (1990, at world prices)

Oil products 12%
Chemicals 7%
Other 29%
Ferrous 7%
gas 9%
Food 5%
Machinery 31%

Source: Goskomprognostat

were acquired through a state order system that specified the share of total output that had to be sold to the Government (up to some ceiling) at the price set by the Government (which naturally is substantially below the market price).   While Uzbekistan continues to exert substantial state control over the economy, and is thus more able to keep up its end of these bilateral agreements, the increasing decentralization of control in other republics--particularly Russia--is making implementation of these types of agreements more difficult.

---

[13] Foreign trade defines trade with the rest of the world--outside the FSU.

Foreign Trade

2.39   Two major developments have affected foreign trade. First, as has already been mentioned, the world price of cotton deteriorated substantially, creating a negative terms-of-trade shock. In addition, the discount on world-market prices for Uzbek cotton reflects recent problems with quality and reliability. Cotton represents about 80 percent of Uzbekistan's foreign exports (see Table 2.6). This deterioration in the price of cotton implies a loss to the net trade balance that may be as high as $250 million.

2.40   The second major development in foreign trade was the shift from a commercial rate to a unified exchange rate. On August 15, 1992, Uzbekistan moved to a unified exchange-rate system. Moreover, the 60 percent surrender requirement on foreign currency earnings was going to be substantially reduced. Until May 1993, the surrender requirement was redeemed at the market exchange-rate. The unified exchange rate follows the rate in Russia with a time lag. Although the exchange-rate premium between Russia and Uzbekistan was approximately 15 to 20 percent in the second half of 1992 no significant arbitrage took place owing to various

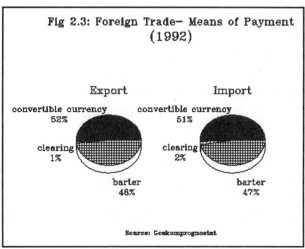

exchange controls. Export earnings from the rest of the world are subject to export taxes, as well as to an 18 percent income tax. In light of the high total tax rate on exports, a substantial portion of foreign trade is made in the form of barters to avoid the surrender requirement and the income and export taxes. Barter trade comprised 48 percent of total foreign trade in 1992 (Figure 2.3).[14]

2.41   The nominal ruble/dollar exchange rate, as measured by the Moscow auction market, has been depreciating rapidly since January 1992, but not as rapidly as the rate at which domestic prices have increased. Thus, the real exchange rate has appreciated substantially, in particular in the first half of 1992.

Trade Policy

2.42   Foreign trade is restricted more heavily and is subject to harsher tax treatment than is interrepublican trade. In order to export to the rest of the world, an enterprise must acquire a license for most commodities, and then conduct its trade through the Ministry of Foreign Economic Relations,

---

[14] The shift to barter trade has substantially reduced export tax revenue. Partially in response, the Government is considering whether to further weaken the incentive to engage in barter trade. The proposal would require that 10 to 15 percent of foreign exchange revenue be given up, while 10 percent be purchased at the market rate. The key, however, is that the 10 to 15 percent amount surrendered would count towards the 18 percent income tax on revenue on the remaining 90 to 85 percent of value. This would lower the effective income tax on revenue from 18 to 16 percent in the 10 percent surrender requirement. In the proposal, the 10 percent surrender requirement would apply to ready-made goods, while the 15 percent surrender requirement would apply to raw materials.

which also determines the price to be charged. For goods not covered by licensing requirements, few direct restrictions are imposed, though several key consumer goods are rationed.

2.43   The Government has taken several actions to increase interrepublican and foreign trade flows. For example, it has reduced the number of commodities that are subject to export restrictions in the form of licensing requirements--from 176 to 76--though most important commodities in the trade flows are still subject to them. It has also removed tariffs on most imports from the rest of the world until January 1, 1994, in order to increase the supply of consumer goods. In addition, it has signed several bilateral agreements with other FSU republics (for example, Russia and Ukraine) in order to reduce the restrictions on interrepublic trade.

2.44   A new bilateral agreement signed with Russia in January 1993 specifies that trade between the two countries, focusing primarily on cotton-for-oil trade, should be based only on international prices. The agreement amounts to $1.4 billion in 1993, 50 percent of which is on a barter basis (no cash ruble or credit ruble payments will be involved). The agreement was ratified in March 1993. Russia had recently withdrawn from a 1992 free trade agreement with Uzbekistan, and introduced custom duties as of February 1, 1993. However, trade under the new bilateral agreement will not be subject to duties. Bilateral trade agreements with Kazakhstan, Kyrgyzstan, Turkmenistan, and Belarus have also been finalized.

Table 2.6
Composition of Foreign Trade
1992

	Unit	Quantity	Value (mln $)
Total Exports:			**869**
Cotton-fibre	1000 tons	601	673
Nonferrous metal	1000 tons	22	40
Fertilizers	1000 tons	317	39
Ferrous metals	1000 tons	77	18
Electric-energy	mill. kwh	131	13
Petroleum products	1000 tons	137	8
Silk cocoons	1000 tons	5	7
Cotton-waste	1000 tons	27	6
Cotton wool	1000 tons	7	4
Cotton fabric	na	na	2
Textile & clothes	na	na	2
Vegetable oil	1000 tons	4	4
Others na	na	54	
Total Imports:			**929**
Grain	1000 tons	4,005	573
Meat, food, and poultry	1000 tons	30	45
Textile & clothes	na	na	32
Footwares	1000 tons	889	14
Butter, other milk fats	na	6	9
Fresh potatoes	1000 tons	41	5
Tea	1000 tons	6	10
Sugar	1000 tons	145	44
Cigarettes	1000 tons	43,732	1
Fertilizers	1000 tons	0.3	3
Silk fabric	na	na	1
Cotton fabric	na	na	3
Sedan cars	1 unit	63	1
TV & radio sets	1 unit	16	2
Others na	na	189	

Source: State Statistical and Forecasting Committee of Uzbekistan.

2.45   Attempts to reduce trade barriers are constrained by the present structure of subsidies and the highly distorted internal pricing system. A substantial reduction in foreign trade barriers is forcing Uzbekistan to be consistent with those in the rest of the FSU, and is exerting pressure to eliminate the implicit subsidy system. This pressure will affect the implementation of the current social protection policy. This apparent contradiction between trade policy (reduce tariffs and QRs) and social sector policy (maintain subsidies for many products) indicates the need for a coherent policy framework.[15]

2.46   Uzbekistan's *terms of trade* are estimated to have fallen by about 10 percent from their level in 1990.[16] The interrepublic terms of trade, particularly driven by the cotton for oil trade, appear to have deteriorated more than the international terms of trade. This negative shock combined with the fall in output caused a decline in domestic absorption, which was under way in 1991, and continued in 1992.

Table 2.7
Uzbekistan - Balance of Payments 1992

	in rubles (billion)	in convertible currency (million U.S. dollars)	Total
Current account	-39	-170	-369
Non-interest current account		-160	-359
Trade balance			-259
Interrepublic balance	-39		-199[1]
Exports[2]	123		
Imports[2]	162		
Foreign trade balance		-60	-60
Exports		869	869
Imports		929	929
Factor Services (net)		-110	-110
Interest component		-10	-10
Capital account		165	165
Foreign direct investment		40	40
Net increase in foreign credits		125	125
Errors and omissions	19	-	97
Overall balance	-20	-5	-107
Financing			
Interrepublic arrears	-40		-204
Correspondent accounts	60		306
Increase reserves (-)			5

[1] Converted from the ruble deficit using the average market exchange rate.
[2] Estimates.
[3] Average nominal exchange rate in 1992 Rbs/$=196.

---

[15] See chapter 3.

[16] The methodology used to estimate the overall terms of trade shock is based on available information on the cotton for oil trade. It represents a pure change in relative prices weighted by the respective shares in both interrepublic and foreign trade. It also assumes that all other traded goods except for oil and cotton had compensating relative price changes. Two types of changes have been estimated: (1) an intertemporal change that occurred between 1990 and December 1992, and (2) a discrete change due to convergence toward world market prices in December 1992. Both changes are estimated separately for interrepublic and foreign trade. The two changes are then aggregated using appropriate trade shares.

BALANCE OF PAYMENTS

2.47   Despite this reduction in expenditures, according to preliminary estimates Uzbekistan may have run an interrepublic trade deficit of about $200 million in 1992 and a foreign-trade deficit of approximately $60 million. The current account deficit may have reached about $370 million (see Table 2.7). Foreign direct investment flows were only incipient in 1992. Approximately $380 million in bilateral loans and export credits were committed in 1992, of which about $125 million were disbursed. Uzbekistan also had access to the equivalent of approximately US$300 million in technical credits from Russia. In addition, Uzbekistan signed an agreement with Russia on November 2, 1992, whereby Uzbekistan relinquished claims on USSR assets in return for Russia's accepting responsibility for Uzbekistan's share of the USSR's external debt.

CHAPTER 3

MACROECONOMIC POLICY FRAMEWORK AND THE REFORM PROGRAM

3.1 Although Uzbekistan is pursuing a gradual approach to economic reform to avoid social unrest, any reform program must be comprehensive, simultaneously covering macroeconomic stabilization, structural reform, and sectoral reform. Partial reforms could worsen the situation in the short run and not accomplish much in the medium term.

3.2 In the medium term Uzbekistan will benefit from accelerating a broad systemic transformation, rather than postponing it (chapter 2). The recent decline in economic welfare occurred in the absence of any substantial reform. Unless there are reforms to improve incentives and facilitate goods and factors mobility, to reverse the decline in economic activity and productivity levels, economic deterioration is likely to persist, leading to economic stagnation in the medium term. Comprehensive reform is unlikely to halt the decline of economic activity in the near term, but it will establish the basis for sustainable and significant economic growth in the medium and long terms.

3.3 One major question is that of how to sequence reforms. Experience in other transforming economies suggests that, although country-specific factors will influence the pattern of reforms, some components of reforms are prerequisites for success. Moreover, a broad set of reforms from the outset will enhance the chances of success over the medium term. The key for Uzbekistan is to design and implement a sensible program that can attain the transformation and development objectives in a reasonable time, while preserving a minimum social safety net.

A. THE KEY ELEMENTS OF A SUCCESSFUL REFORM PROGRAM

3.4 A successful macroeconomic stabilization program is a necessary condition for the successful transition of Uzbekistan to a market-based economy. Without it, there could be a fiscal or financial crisis, without a corresponding decline in inflation. Liberalizing domestic prices, reducing subsidies, and moving toward positive real interest rates over a reasonable time horizon are critical policy measures for achieving stabilization. Without fiscal discipline, the Government's increasing inability to maintain its program of social protection would be hurt further by declining output levels and a deepening of the negative trade shocks already faced, thus prompting a genuine fiscal crisis.

STABILIZATION

3.5 Successful stabilization depends not only on effective economic management, but also on factors outside the Government's control, such as developments in the ruble zone. Because the monetary policy of the ruble zone is determined largely by Russia, the Government cannot substantially affect the price of goods without wide restrictions on trade. Thus, recent trade shocks have been driven primarily by movements towards world-market relative prices on goods traded among FSU republics. Negative terms of trade shocks are not expected in the near future. However, a significant adjustment in domestic relative prices will take place, if the Government implements a comprehensive reform program.

3.6   Full stabilization will be accomplished only after a period of adjustment, which must encompass real reform of the economic system and movement towards a market-based economy. Several elements are key to ensuring macroeconomic stabilization in Uzbekistan, and the basic policy measures and targets of a Stand-By arrangement or a Systemic Transformation Facility with the IMF could help the Government establish these.

Fiscal Issues

3.7   Fiscal discipline is the most critical determinant of stabilization. The challenge to the Government will be to generate revenue in the most efficient manner, while continuing to compress spending sufficiently to shrink the budget deficit as part of the overall fiscal adjustment. It must move further from central planning, where enterprise surpluses are transferred to the center and then allocated to governmental spending and enterprise investments. While the Government has attempted to shift to a tax system based on objective rules, the traditional planning approach prevails to a large extent.

3.8   Priority should be given to restructuring and reallocating social expenditures and, in particular, reducing universal subsidies provided through price controls and increasing targeted assistance, while reducing the overall share of GDP that goes to social protection. The share in Uzbekistan is higher than that in countries with the same per capita output and is similar to that in low-income OECD countries. Social protection (including pensions) that is presently funded from both budget and off-budgetary sources represents about 26 percent of GDP, of which almost 12 percent is consumer subsidies. The Government should phase out all consumer subsidies, except those on bread, which could save up to 8 percent of GDP in 1993. In parallel, new concrete programs involving direct payments based upon need should be put in place (chapter 8).

3.9   On the revenue side, taxation should be improved and strengthened. Discretionary taxes (both federal and local) should be reduced. The tax base should be widened as much as possible and collection improved. A new methodology, consistent with Western accounting practices, would have to be introduced to calculate enterprise profits. Moreover, exemptions in the tax code should be simplified. Structural measures to strengthen the tax system have been identified by the IMF, including broadening the base of value-added tax (VAT) to cover wholesale and retail margins and most services; all excise taxes should be *ad valorem*.

3.10   A temporary ad valorem export tax could replace differential prices and confiscatory export taxes. It would be simpler than the present system, would tax excess profits generated by the undervaluation of the currency and would apply only to a small number of commodities whose domestic prices would approach the international price level over the next one to two years. For taxes on trade, the treatment of interrepublic and foreign exports should be unified, especially if Uzbekistan issues a national currency. The differential tax treatment on foreign exports, according to whether or not the trade is part of a barter arrangement, should be eschewed. Taxing export earnings at world market value, regardless of any barter agreements, could improve revenue during transition by simultaneously increasing incentives to export. To protect fiscal revenues in the short run, the Government may wish to consider a temporary excise tax on cotton.

3.11   The Government should use profits only as the tax base for enterprises, and set an appropriate tax rate.[1] Tax breaks for new enterprises seem excessive and are likely to encourage fraud. Instead, the Government might consider some type of loss carry-over provision for the first few years in which a new enterprise operates.

3.12   Overall budgetary management must be strengthened. All public-sector revenue and expenditures, budgetary and off-budgetary, should be identified to support assessing the true overall level of Government expenditures and their financing. As part of the assessment, a consolidated analysis of the entire public sector should be undertaken. State enterprises can be taken into account by including their retained earnings (or losses) plus depreciation allowances as current receipts, and including SOE investment expenditures and their financing in the capital account. At the same time, the Government should switch to narrowly targeted consumer subsidies rather than producer subsidies wherever possible in order to reduce the misallocation of resources induced by distorted prices and interest rates. It should also consolidate and allocate expenditure categories on a more rational basis. In this regard, it should unify the system of family allowances, and switch to a flat-rate allowance per child.

Monetary Issues

3.13   Monetary policy should be consistent with fiscal and exchange-rate policies. If Uzbekistan remains in the ruble zone, macroeconomic management will be heavily dependent upon coordination with Russia and other zone members in monetary, interest rate, and exchange rate policies. Such coordination has hardly been evident in the recent past. To achieve it in the future would require much improvement in institutional and implementation capabilities. Successful stabilization in Russia (a necessary condition for stabilization in Uzbekistan) will depend on implementing a restrictive monetary policy, which will probably include some tightening of technical credits to Uzbekistan.

3.14   If Uzbekistan were to leave the ruble zone, it could pursue independent monetary and exchange rate policies and concentrate fully on serious fiscal reform. Uzbekistan would have to finance its own fiscal deficits; domestic inflation would depend on domestic fiscal and monetary policies. Leaving the zone might result in forgoing some benefits from temporarily subsidized prices in interrepublican trade. But there are already indications that at least some recent bilateral agreements are being formalized at international prices. When the Government decides that the net benefits of leaving the zone seem to outweigh its costs, the Government will face three major decisions: (1) which currency system to adopt, (2) how to undertake the transition, and (3) when it will issue the new currency. Before issuing a new currency, it is very important to undertake the proper strengthening of the Central Bank and other institutions. Assistance in developing the appropriate system and policies in this area should be sought from the IMF.

Trade Policy

3.15   Trade policy reforms should accompany both stabilization and structural reform, allowing Uzbekistan to open up fully to the rest of the world and encourage competition in all sectors. Trade policy can work toward two objectives: to achieve efficiency in the economy (in production and consumption), and to increase Government revenue. Quantitative trade restrictions should be eliminated. The medium-term objective would be to work toward treating both FSU and foreign trade equally.

---

[1] The IMF has recommended a tax rate of 40 percent.

3.16   Domestic relative prices would also be expected to adjust over time with the implementation of trade policy. But only after consumer and input subsidies are removed, and the state order system is abolished will relative prices be corrected fully.

STRUCTURAL REFORM

3.17   Successful macroeconomic stabilization will not by itself establish the basis for reviving growth, generating sources of employment as the economy is restructured, and encouraging development. The success of the reform program will ultimately depend on the Government's ability to implement a comprehensive program of structural reform and a clear timetable for implementing it. The economic objective of structural reform is to improve the incentive system for efficiency, innovation, and growth. The major elements of this program should seek to increase resource mobility in an effort to allow the factors of production and production and consumption decisions to respond to market prices.

3.18   Phasing out the state order system in all sectors of the economy (procurement by the state at below market prices fixed by the Government), along with direct state involvement in both domestic and international retail and wholesale private trade, is the first step toward ensuring resource mobility. In addition, a reform package should simultaneously cover four key areas:

- Establishing the legal basis for developing the private sector, especially property rights and contract laws;

- Restructuring and privatizing state owned enterprises (SOEs);

- Implementing financial-sector reform so that lending takes place on a purely commercial basis and public and private enterprises have access to credit; and

- Providing a social safety net to protect the most vulnerable groups.

Changing the Role of the State

3.19   In a competitive market-based economy the state is responsible for macroeconomic management, provision of some social services and economic infrastructure, and establishment and enforcement of the legal and regulatory framework for competitive markets. If Uzbekistan wants to move towards a market-based system, the Government must progressively change the role of the state in the economy, liberalize the distribution system, and create a market-price-guided incentive system to replace the planned allocation of goods and services. Ideally, the only role for the state in trade would be to collect taxes, regulate sales practices and standards, promote effective free entry, and implement anti-trust and trade policies that support the development of competitive markets. The current internal marketing system is highly constrained, with product marketing operating through one or another large ministry.[2] Individual enterprises have very little scope for marketing their products directly either to other enterprises or to the public. This problem is compounded by the lack of an adequate independent internal distribution system, and by barriers that inhibit enterprises from obtaining retail market space directly to sell goods or services. Removing internal trade barriers is as important as liberalizing prices for the

---

[2] For particular examples of the Government's activities in different sectors, see chapters 6 to 12 of this report; chapter 5 discusses the overall institutional structure of the Government and how it can respond to the reform program.

misallocation of domestic resources and for freeing up resources so that they can be used by the more dynamic elements of the economy.

3.20   The continuation of bilateral trade agreements with other republics to ensure an adequate supply of key commodities forces the Government to be involved actively in internal trade (since trade provides many important inputs for the production process), while also forcing the Government to maintain some system for acquiring the commodities that it has committed to the other republics. However, the current system under which the Government allocates the right to buy the key inputs virtually ensures that small and/or private enterprises will be the last to be supplied. This restraint limits the ability of enterprises, particularly private or leased enterprises, to develop or adapt to new circumstances. The Government can mitigate the negative impact of its bilateral trade agreements on enterprise development by implementing market-type incentives. It can do so most effectively by auctioning those commodities that it acquires directly through bilateral agreements, or, when it merely authorizes its enterprises to acquire a certain number of units of a particular key commodity from a supplier in another FSU republic, by auctioning these purchase rights. In either case, the enterprise with the highest valuation of the commodity would eventually acquire it, which is a desirable outcome.

3.21   Similarly, it may be time for the Government to reassess its policy of entering into bilateral trade agreements. Only if those agreements lead to a net subsidy relative to world market prices does it makes sense that the Government continue them. However, even in this case, the growing fragmentation of economic control in the other republics, particularly Russia, makes implementing such agreements at subsidized prices increasingly problematic and thus expensive. If there are no net subsidies involved, the Government should not engage in these trade agreements and should allow trade to be undertaken simply on the basis of correspondence accounts in dollars at the various Central Banks, with any net trade deficit or surplus being covered in foreign exchange.

Providing a Legal Basis

3.22   The Government must also construct a legal framework for developing the private sector, especially property rights and contract laws. Regulation of natural monopolies, and antitrust and regulatory legislation also deserve particular attention. The fundamentals for a sound market economy are clear property rights and the commercial accountability of enterprise governance. Private sector development, including privatization, will be unsuccessful unless Uzbekistan creates a system in which property rights are (1) defined clearly, (2) held largely by private owners, (3) used and transferred freely by such owners without unpredictable or arbitrary governmental intervention, but within a predictable regulatory framework, and (4) enforced by a neutral party based on an effective judicial system and modern civil and commercial laws. This system is the foundation of a private sector. Without it, the reform measures that seek to establish a market-based economy would not be built on a firm basis. Yet this system does not exist in Uzbekistan.

Reforming the SOEs

3.23   Enterprise reform lies at the core of structural reform.[3] The structural transformation of Uzbekistan's economy is ultimately related to the organization and ownership of its productive sectors, which are dominated heavily by state-owned enterprises (SOEs). As of the end of 1991, the SOE sector

---

[3] For this reason, it is discussed at length in chapter 6. The discussion here summarizes the main issues to be considered in designing a structural reform program.

in Uzbekistan accounted for 85 percent of GDP and about 80 percent of employment, and, through its links with the budget and the banking system, it controlled most of the country's financial resources. Thus, the destatization of the economy through enterprise reform is a key requirement for establishing a market-based system and a necessary condition for achieving both macroeconomic stability and the sustainability of economic reform.

3.24   The Government must reform SOEs by privatizing some and rationalizing the structure and improving the performance of those that will remain in the public sector. Change in ownership should be accompanied by a consequent change in the size distribution of enterprises, and enterprises must be demonopolized.

3.25   Monopoly power is a constraint on the reform process. The highly concentrated industrial structure in Uzbekistan reduces the competitive pressure to minimize costs, and the consequent market power allows firms to set prices at distorted levels. The key elements of reform are to remove excess demand, harden the budget constraint, and move to a less concentrated and more competitive industrial and distribution structure facing a set of clear price signals and relative prices that reflect the scarcity values of inputs and outputs.   In addition, the sequencing of demonopolization, domestic price liberalization, and trade liberalization are critical policy concerns, which are discussed further in chapter 6.

3.26   Another requirement for a sustainable market-based economy is that enterprise governance adhere to commercial principles and bear legal and financial liability for failure.   The Government must reform the yardstick by which the performance of state enterprises is measured. These revised measures will enable the Government to ascertain the true efficiency of a public-sector enterprise more effectively, and thus reward the management and workers more appropriately, either by offering bonuses or tying salary increases to performance. This performance-based system would improve the incentive of both workers and management to cooperate in an effort to operate the enterprise more efficiently.

Reforming the Financial Sector

3.27   Successful financial sector reform is very closely linked to enterprise reform. Financial institutions in Uzbekistan are not currently in a position to allocate resources efficiently or to support the privatization and revitalization of existing enterprises.   The extremely negative real interest rates on deposits are discouraging private deposits in the banking system; consequently the sector does not fulfill its major function of intermediating between savers and investors.

3.28   Today, the financial system is making loans to enterprises that might not be viable in the long run. Uncertainty, the absence of information, political pressures, and the ownership structure of financial institutions are at the root of the problem. Much of bank lending goes to enterprises and corporations that own the banks. Thus far, the high rates of inflation have continuously eroded the real value of bank assets and liabilities, thereby reducing the real magnitude of potential portfolio problems and the potential budgetary costs of financial restructuring. Finally, the financial infrastructure is inadequate. Legal codes and enforcement mechanisms, and the payments, accounting, auditing, and bank supervision and regulation systems are not developed enough to support a market economy. Although steps can be taken to improve the financial infrastructure, to strengthen bank supervision and regulation, and to change the ownership structure of banks, the problems of the financial sector ultimately reflect those in the other sectors of the economy.

3.29   To sustain enterprise restructuring and privatization, and to support the developing private sector, Government must create a true banking system. The so-called commercial banks that have been established are inadequate. The primary reason is that the major equity holders of these banks are in fact the SOEs and the Ministries, and weak restrictions apply to the proportion of a commercial bank's loans that can be made to its stockholders. Thus, these banks act largely as intermediaries between the SOEs that established them and the state banks, particularly the Central Bank and the Savings Bank. Only by establishing a private market for credit can market incentives and market prices allocate credit in the most efficient manner. It is unlikely that public-sector banks will show much initiative in seeking out private-sector enterprises to lend to; they would instead continue to lend to the SOEs. Thus the ownership structure of the banks should be modified to ensure that they follow truly commercial banking principles and begin to allocate the flow of credit into the public and private enterprise sectors more equitably. Just as with privatized enterprises, it is critical that the Government not retain residual liability for private banks.

Social Protection

3.30   As part of restructuring production factors, labor deserves special consideration. Surplus labor in public-sector enterprises can be reduced while measures are taken to enhance the flexibility of the labor market, such as reducing internal restrictions on mobility and expanding job placement centers. The approval of the Employment Act in 1991 and the beginning of the process of establishing over 100 employment centers around the country are signals of some progress in this area. However, the perpetuation of residence permit requirements, along with extensive housing shortages, implies that labor mobility within Uzbekistan is still very low. Employment agencies do not seem to deal effectively with a substantial number of job seekers. This factor is an important consideration, since unemployment is an inevitable part of the transitional period towards a market-based economy, as labor gradually shifts to a more efficient configuration.[4]

3.31   Thus far, unemployment in Uzbekistan has remained very low, yet the low rate is deceptive, since most enterprises are probably retaining idle workers, and many have cut their work week to three or four days. Some public-sector enterprises may be forced to reduce their employment levels by as much as 50 percent. Non-viable enterprises would have to be closed down and their workers would need to seek alternative employment. The combined effects of the rise in unemployment and the increased wage differentials would be a less equitable income distribution, which in turn would reinforce the need for a stronger social safety net system.

3.32   The social dimensions of stabilization and enterprise restructuring require greater focus on the social safety net. The challenge is to reconcile these demands for macroeconomic and structural change with ways to channel public resources most efficiently to social protection. The Government is committed to maintaining a social safety net. However, the fiscal situation cannot support a social safety net strong enough to protect against significant increases in unemployment accompanying a substantial restructuring, in particular of the industrial sector. In the present context, the Government should consider the following. First, income support must be offered to those who would otherwise fall below the poverty line--such as children in large families and the elderly. Second, assistance should be extended to those who are affected adversely by the transition, particularly the newly unemployed. Third, scarce

---

[4] In fact, it is unemployment, or the anticipation of it, that is one of the major motivations for workers to seek alternative employment.

resources must be targeted at those in need, not at those who are not. The foremost task for the Government is to prioritize social expenditures according to the degree to which they benefit the poor.

B. MEDIUM-TERM OUTLOOK UNDER TWO SCENARIOS

RECOMMENDED REFORM PROGRAM

3.33   The depth and scope of the policy changes and their sequencing will determine the final impact of economic reform in Uzbekistan. How the economy actually responds to each policy change and the speed at which the factors of production adjust are quite uncertain. Thus, the analysis provided here reflects a preliminary benchmark assessment of a likely adjustment path for the economy of Uzbekistan in the 1993-97 period, if the Government decides to implement a comprehensive reform program immediately. The analysis assumes that a package of measures aimed at stabilization and structural and sectoral reform is implemented in 1993.

3.34   The reform program that is discussed is gradual in the following sense: it assumes that stabilization and a minimum set of structural measures are implemented at the beginning of the program (Phase 1). At the end of this period, the economy would not as yet have completed the transition to a market-based economy, since goods and factor markets would not be completely liberalized by then, competition and decentralized decision-making would be in their preliminary stages, property rights would still be in the process of being redefined, and many of the necessary large-scale privatizations would not yet have been made. Thus, the program would seek to deepen structural and sectoral reforms over time (Phase 2). Table 3.1 presents the policy measures sequenced in two phases.

3.35   The measures to be implemented in Phases I and II represent the core of what is considered absolutely necessary to achieve a successful and sustainable transition to a market-based economy. This gradual but comprehensive approach is consistent with the Government's desire to reform the economy of Uzbekistan gradually.

3.36   It is very difficult to anticipate the future turn of events. However, it is reasonable to expect that if a new currency is successfully introduced and conservative fiscal and monetary policies are adopted, the credibility of the reform program will grow over time. It is reasonable to expect that this would cause a medium-term appreciation of the real exchange rate relative to the initial situation.

3.37   The implementation of structural reforms, combined with stabilization, could help stabilize relative prices between Uzbekistan and the rest of the world, thus promoting an increase in foreign trade. It is likely that over time trade would shift away from heavy dependence on the FSU. This might hasten the adjustment process in both agriculture and industry, given the greater degree of openness with the rest of the world and the greater certainty associated with domestic prices.

3.38   It is assumed that significant stabilization efforts are undertaken quickly and the rate of inflation reduced substantially over the next several months. In addition, the following assumptions were made. First, the Government manages to avoid a fiscal crisis. Second, the Government pursues financial reform and infrastructure rebuilding--particularly for Central Bank supervision.

3.39   Agriculture in Uzbekistan is a leading candidate for economic reform. To enable farmers to use natural resources more effectively and induce them to increase output, Uzbekistan must reform its pricing and marketing policy. In particular, input and output markets for agricultural products must be

Table 3.1
Sequencing of Key Structural and Sectoral Reforms

Phase I	Phase II
• Achieve macroeconomic stabilization	

• Implement price reform:
    Full pass-through for oil energy products
    Border pricing for natural gas	

• Implement trade reform: remove QRs, and impose transitional export tax and an excise tax on cotton	• Adjust tariffs to moderate levels
• End the direct decision-making role of Associations and Ministry of Trade in trading. Reorient the role of ministry towards facilitating trade and developing wholesale markets.	
• Remove consumer subsidies (except on bread)	• Eliminate remaining state order purchases
• Phase out indirect subsidies on electricity and inputs to agriculture and industry	• Continue implementing institutional reform
• Implement land-leasing program	
• End state order system in agriculture	
• Implement institutional reform--redefinition of the basic accounting framework, budgeting techniques, and Government structure	• Continue demonopolization and implement medium and large-scale privatization
• Implement small-scale privatization fully	• Implement industrial restructuring
• Privatize and demonopolize wholesale trade, related storage and transport	• Implement mining sector restructuring
• Introduce corporate governance in large PSEs and begin demonopolization	

• Implement legal reform:
    Reformulate: banking and foreign investment
    Prepare: commercial code, mining code, petroleum legislation
	• Restructure the financial system

• Begin developing financial system infrastructure
    Adopt consistent system of accounting, auditing, financial disclosure
    Implement clearing and settlement mechanisms
    Implement Prudential regulation and Supervision	

• Labor market: deregulate hiring, eliminate residence permits	• Deepen social sector reforms in terms of pensions, social security, unemployment insurance, and the delivery of social services
• Social safety net: Replace consumer subsidies for direct cash payments to the needy Determine a poverty line in absolute terms based on a minimum consumption basket.	

created, trade barriers should be removed, and a large-scale land-leasing program implemented. Raising input prices will hurt agriculture, but comprehensive agricultural price reform should boost profitability of farmers, because the sector transferred roughly $600 million to the rest of the economy in 1991. Because these transfers represent revenue to the Government, reform of agricultural price policy must be linked to the ability of the Government to create and benefit from alternative sources of revenue. Today, farmers are the only ones who can deliver productivity gains and increased savings, but they can do so only if the large amount of resources they transfer to the rest of the economy goes back to them. Under a generalized program of land leasing, the Government would receive around $500 million a year in revenue. Moreover removing input subsidies could save perhaps $1 billion. At the same time, eliminating the state order system would cost about $1.5 billion in forgone income. Thus, the proposed reforms for agriculture would be revenue neutral.[5]

3.40   Energy sector reform should focus on pricing policy changes to promote energy efficiency, thus reducing domestic energy consumption and increasing the surplus for export, while expanding petroleum production and implementing broad institutional reforms.

3.41   Industrial reforms should first work towards a set of policy measures aimed at achieving competitiveness, enhancing the value of viable enterprises, and creating the enabling environment for developing the private sector. In a second phase of reform, a strong link between privatization and industrial restructuring will be present as the enterprise prepares itself for sale. For large-scale SOEs, privatization could be the most decisive way to improve management.

3.42   Mining reform should address the low productivity of state-owned mining enterprises. A possible combination of policy options would involve commercialization of these enterprises -- setting commercial goals, introducing a hard budget constraint and increasing accountability for managers, and opening up exploration to private investment.

Supply Response

3.43   A major reform program will have a significant impact on the economy of Uzbekistan. This impact is inevitable, since the agricultural, industrial, and financial sectors would have to be substantially restructured. In the short run, the disruption associated with any period of major adjustment is likely to generate a substantial decline in the level of output and an increase in the level of unemployment, while also making the distribution of income more uneven. In 1993 the real decline in output may well decelerate to about 6 percent (Table 3.2). This decline is consistent with the experience of other reforming socialist economies that have undergone adjustment in the recent past.

3.44   In this respect, it is also critical that the reform program in the agricultural sector proceed at full speed, since it is likely to yield the quickest positive growth response to the incentives created by the reform program. The tremendous potential both for increasing yields substantially without increasing inputs and for reducing waste in the agricultural sector itself and in the agro-processing industry could be realized relatively easy. But if the Government delays the process of reforming the agriculture sector, then a serious possibility exists that output might not rebound as quickly as forecasted, thus undermining support for the reform program.

---

[5] A detailed analysis of these issues is presented in chapter 9.

Table 3.2
Uzbekistan - Key Macroeconomic Projections
(in percentage)
Reform Scenario

	1993	1994	1995	1996	1997
Real GDP Growth	-6	-2	1	3	4
Agriculture	3	7	7	8	4
Industry	-10	-15	-5	-1	4
Other	-12	-4	-2	-1	3
Total Consumption	-5	-1	-1	2	2
Investment	-8	-7	1	7	12
Current Account (deficit)					
(in million $)	260	425	445	485	470
As % of GDP	13	13	14	14	13

Source: Bank staff estimates.

3.45   A deepening of the structural reform, particularly in the industrial sector, could lead to a further drop in GDP in 1994. However, rapid small-scale privatization primarily in trade and services will ensure that at least part of the excess supply of labor generated by restructuring in the economy is absorbed in new activities. Growth of the service sector may also be expected to compensate partially for the decline in economic activity driven by the industrial sector. Positive growth could be achieved by 1995 and sustained thereafter.

3.46   Adjusting interest rates would have both fiscal and financial implications. The foremost is that a consequent increase in the interest rate on loans would substantially reduce the profitability of the enterprise sector, which would then try to seek Government assistance. However, the Government would have to resist that pressure and implement a harder budget constraint. The cost of borrowing for the Government will be higher. Besides, many of the loans on the books of the banks would become nonperforming. In addition, liberalizing interest rates on deposits would tend to increase the level of savings deposits and thus the level of credit that could be extended by the banking sector and, through this, the level of the money supply.

3.47   No further major terms-of-trade shocks are expected for Uzbekistan. The primary justification for that assumption is that interrepublic trade seems to be conducted currently at exchange ratios that are quite close to world-market relative prices. In addition, the relative price of natural gas vis-à-vis Uzbekistan's importable goods was unfavorable in 1992. Thus, a gain in terms of trade could be expected in the near future, leading to significant exportable balances of natural gas. Furthermore, no sharp changes in the world market prices of Uzbekistan's raw material exports or imports are foreseen.[6]

---

[6] This projection is consistent with the Bank's forecasts of future oil and cotton prices.

3.48   Trade will certainly play a critical role in the medium-term outlook of Uzbekistan. Trade with countries outside the FSU will gain significance. On the other hand, the share of interrepublican trade will decline over time. Trade deficits are expected to be incurred during the transition to a market-based economy. However, in the medium term, the potentially significant exports of natural gas, an increase in the exports of cotton, potential self-sufficiency in oil production and exports of gold will turn around the external balance.

3.49   In terms of the social dimension of the reform program, the unemployment rate under the reform scenario could rise gradually up to 12 percent by the end of the third year of the reform program, driven by an active industrial restructuring and large-scale privatizations. These hypothetical unemployment estimates under this scenario are consistent with the experiences of the Eastern European countries that have progressed much further in the transition toward a market-based economies. It is estimated that the corresponding level of unemployment compensation as a share of GDP could reach about 1.5 to 2 percent of GDP in 1993-95.[7]

Aggregate Demand

3.50   Domestic demand is expected to decline by about 11 percent in 1993, as a consequence of declines in both Government and private consumption and investment. Fiscal deficits are assumed to decline over the 1993-95 period to reach about 5 percent of GDP as a result of a reduction in the subsidy level, redesign of tax policy, and improvement of tax administration and budgetary management. In the medium term, consumption may be expected to grow on average at about 2 percent per year. Although substantial domestic savings could be generated in the rural sector after the initial period of reform--that is, after 1995-- foreign savings will be critical at the beginning. Domestic savings could be channeled into small investments in the industrial sector.

3.51   Investment rates have fallen substantially in response to the recent decline in output, and are likely to continue to be low in the future. Gross fixed investment is not likely to start growing before 1995. Foreign direct investment is likely to be quite modest and probably restricted to a few sectors, such as oil, gas, and mining and possibly manufacturing in the medium term.

Sectoral Adjustment

3.52   Changes in pricing and marketing policies, combined with a land-leasing program, can be expected to generate an increase in agricultural output (of 3 percent) in the first year of the reform, of which a large part would be due to reductions in spoilage. The output increase could even reach 7 to 8 percent in later years, owing to the new incentives and land-leasing arrangements. Judging from the Chinese experience, agricultural growth could be high by the second year of reform before moderating. The potential upside of the agricultural sector would translate into a significant increase in rural consumption and savings, which might also generate an increase in small-scale rural industry, especially for processing agricultural products.

---

[7] Unemployment and declining output result as the unemployment compensation scheme becomes increasingly less generous as the duration of unemployment continues.

3.53   Industrial output is expected to fall by about 10 percent in 1993 and by about 15 percent in 1994-95, when medium-size and large enterprises are privatized, the remainder are demonopolized, and active restructuring is implemented. Initially, the major impact on industrial output will come from the higher input prices and a harder budget constraint. In the second phase of reform, privatized small and medium enterprises would show gains in efficiency and improvements in performance. Light industry, agro-industry, and building materials, which depend less on the FSU for inputs and output and are labor-intensive, could lead the supply response of the sector. Tourism is one area where big benefits from private-sector development can be realized. For a relatively modest amount of foreign direct investment and know-how, a supply response in the services sector could be expected in the medium term.

3.54   The medium-term outlook for energy is promising. Natural gas exports should increase significantly in the medium term, owing primarily to a reduction in domestic consumption in the next three to four years. This assumes that prices are at world market levels within the first two years of reform and that a viable export market is developed. On the marketing side, the priority in the near term is to negotiate export contracts and to reach agreements with Russia and Turkmenistan on the accessibility and tariff structure of gas transmission. The outlook in mining, too, could be favorable. Increases in production of gold and other minerals could materialize with only modest investment, if significant reforms are implemented in the sector.

MUDDLE-THROUGH SCENARIO

3.55   It would appear that in the absence of comprehensive reform, an alternative scenario is for the Government to continue along its present course, without implementing any major reform initiatives, and the few scattered and partial reforms that are implemented have no major impact. This muddle-through scenario assumes that fiscal and financial crises are avoided. In this case, it is also assumed that the organization of economic activity is expected to continue to deteriorate, but without a major collapse in economic activity.

3.56   Under these circumstances, prices would be forced to accommodate primarily to the change in FSU--particularly Russian--price levels and the nominal exchange rate, and thus the real exchange rate will be determined largely by factors outside the control of Uzbekistan. It is assumed that inflation rates remain well below those associated with hyperinflation. This is consistent both with the Government's current fiscal condition and with the assumption that the Government maintains the current level of trade barriers, and does not seek to raise them substantially, reversing some of their recent progress.

3.57   For trade, the country is assumed to continue to depend highly on interrepublic trade, and foreign trade will develop only slowly. Trade and payments arrangements among FSU republics are likely to continue to present serious problems. However, the direct impact on trade of staying in the ruble zone on interrepublic trade is likely to be quite small.

3.58   The muddle-through scenario assumes that none of the sectors is restructured significantly. This failure to adjust is likely to lead to a supply-led contraction of the level of economic activity, reduction in savings and investment, and unnecessary hardship on the population in the medium term represented by a decline in consumption per capita of not less than 30 percent by 1997. In addition, it is very likely that Uzbekistan will not be able to maintain the level of capital inflows that it experienced in 1992. While the scenario shows a lower current account deficit than the reform scenario, even that

Table 3.3
Uzbekistan - Key Macroeconomic Projections
(in percentage)
Muddle-Through Scenario

	1993	1994	1995	1996	1997
Real GDP growth (in percent)	-9	-7	-5	-3	-1
Agriculture	-2	0	1	1	1
Industry	-10	-10	-10	-6	-6
Other	-15	-12	-8	-6	0
Total Consumption	-8	-10	-4	-3	-2
Investment	-12	-10	-3	-1	0
Current Account (deficit)					
(in million $)	175	210	135	135	140
As % of GDP	9	7	5	5	5

Source: Bank staff estimates.

deficit is not likely to be financeable because Uzbekistan is not likely to be viewed as creditworthy (see Chapter 4). Thus, the only sources of financing would be a probably lower amount of technical credits to be made available by Russia, a relatively modest amount of bilateral loans, and use of Uzbekistan's own international reserves.

3.59   There is no reason to expect a major improvement in the performance level of the agricultural sector unless it undergoes major reform. Dependence on cotton might actually increase given that it is the major agricultural export crop to the rest of the world, especially if any further disruptions in interrepublic trade occur in the future. Agricultural output will stagnate.

3.60   In the industrial sector, it is expected that a continued decline in the level of activity would probably slow down the outer years. Deterioration is projected to arise owing to a worsening of the incentive structure of the enterprise system as a whole, the aftermath of the breakup of the Union, and a gradual erosion of the capital stock.

3.61   In the mining sector, progressive declines in production are expected because of the falling head grades caused by the depletion of the richest sections of the mineral deposits used to amortize recent investments.

RISKS ASSOCIATED WITH THE COMPREHENSIVE REFORM PROGRAM

3.62   Should the Government commit itself firmly to both the substance and phasing of the stabilization and structural reform program outlined herein, then the prospects for Uzbekistan to be supported fully by the international financial community are considerable. Such support would enable Uzbekistan to start moving along a path of sustainable development on a relatively firm footing with a significant level of direct foreign investment and financing flows.

3.63   Should a comprehensive reform program be implemented, five main risks to the overall success of the program should be considered:

- Policy slippage on the stabilization and structural reform program;

- Inability to sustain implementation because of a lack of popular support owing to declines in output and employment;

- Limited policy implementation capacity;

- Adverse changes in the external economic environment;

- Restricted access to external financing in the short-term.

Policy Slippage

3.64   Failing to broaden, deepen, and hasten the reform process poses a significant risk to the overall success of Uzbekistan's transition. The Government must become fully committed to a comprehensive program to move toward economic recovery. In particular, slippage on macroeconomic stabilization and an indecisive stance regarding the ruble zone would postpone developing a stable environment. Such an environment would allow producers to begin following clearer price signals, trading at a more stable real exchange rate, and undertaking new investments with some certainty. However, relative price adjustment to world prices, and closer alignment of the real exchange rate to purchasing power parity for tradeables, will certainly take time. Similarly, significant progress on the structural front is necessary to provide enterprises and individuals with the appropriate institutional and market incentive structures. Major slippage on structural reform would slow the supply response in the economy and reduce potential increases in productivity and output in the agricultural sector, and would impede developing energy resources further in an effort to facilitate the adjustment process.

3.65   Slippage on the fiscal side will also pose a major risk to the economy. The fiscal deficit may be much worse than projected if anticipated revenue does not materialize and/or expenditures increase. Should Uzbekistan decide to move away from the ruble zone and concentrate on its own stabilization and structural and sector reform, then it would be imperative for the Government to keep the fiscal situation under tight control. A tight fiscal stance would ensure the credibility and sustainability of the program. A loss of fiscal control would inevitably lead to economic decline, as shown by the experience of many developing and industrialized economies. Only long-run fiscal adjustment and a firm commitment to enterprise reform can create the conditions for stabilization and the recovery of growth.

3.66   Assuming a decision is made to adopt a national currency, poor implementation of new currency issuance may also prove to be very disruptive, to undermine the credibility of the reform effort, and to trigger a financial crisis and macroeconomic instability. In that case, instability would be generated by Uzbekistan, as opposed to being imported from Russia.

Sustainability of the Reform Program

3.67   Popular discontent with the stabilization measures, and growing unemployment, may generate political instability and thus slow down the reform process. The Government may face strong pressures from the enterprise sector and the population at large to abandon the program after a few months of implementation. This risk is closely linked to the policy slippage risk discussed earlier. Failure to broaden the scope of the program enough could certainly lead to the abandonment of it and to future macroeconomic instability.

Implementation Capacity

3.68   Given the complexity of and linkages among the policy decisions underlying a comprehensive reform program, and thus the necessity of implementing appropriate institutional arrangements to support them, the proposed reform timetable in two phases is feasible. However, some delays are conceivable. In particular, given Uzbekistan's limited experience with a market-based economy and its inadequate knowledge of the key macroeconomic linkages that would be determinants of the success of the program, many of the reforms may take substantially longer to implement than is currently anticipated. Furthermore, the pace of change may be constrained by the ability of the Government structure to implement the policy measures. In such circumstances, the timing of the supply response built into the projections may be somewhat optimistic.

3.69   Moreover, should it take a long time for economic agents to adjust to the new environment, the output decline may be deeper and more sustained than has been suggested in the discussed scenarios. Should misguided investment decisions be made in the context of a delayed implementation of the program, the country's indebtedness and consequently its creditworthiness may be adversely affected.

External Environment

3.70   Uzbekistan is exposed to developments in its key trading partners and, more generally, to developments in the global economy. Given its close economic integration with the rest of the FSU, and despite the fact that Uzbekistan has had high bargaining power with Russia, Uzbekistan is vulnerable to adverse developments in the FSU, until a substantial diversification of trade towards foreign trade takes place. Macroeconomic instability in Russia would hinder Uzbekistan's efforts at stabilizing its own economy, notwithstanding the issuance of new currency. As was noted earlier, as long as Uzbekistan remains within the ruble zone it will be exposed to even greater negative macroeconomic effects of possibly large Russian fiscal deficits and relaxed monetary and credit policies. Moreover, since many enterprises remain closely integrated with suppliers and end-users in other parts of the FSU, the development of some sectors of the economy will be closely linked to the pace of economic recovery throughout the FSU. To reduce this risk, the Government should encourage domestic agricultural producers and enterprises to seek alternative suppliers and markets outside the FSU. Doing so will imply significant efforts to improve the quality of the produce to international standards, distribution channels, and reliability. Ongoing discussions among the Government and its neighboring countries about gaining relatively easier access to the sea may prove to be a critical factor in hastening trade diversification beyond interrepublic markets.

3.71   The conflict in the neighboring republic of Tajikistan may also impose some delay in the adjustment process in Uzbekistan. Deterioration of the regional conflict may divert the Government's attention from the reform efforts.

External Financing Constraint

3.72   Should Uzbekistan be unable to mobilize sufficient external financing in the short term, then the economy will be exposed to a binding foreign-exchange constraint on trade, and the Government would be forced to rely more heavily on its gold production to generate foreign exchange. Although Uzbekistan has a significant level of gold production, it would probably lower imports in the short-term and reduce the future growth potential of the economy. This policy would impose a harsher adjustment on the economy, lower the income of the population, and reduce consumption more than is suggested under the reform scenario. A reduction in imports will also constrain the ability of Uzbekistan to import capital goods, thus slowing the rate of investment and technological transfer. Finally, if Uzbekistan decides to move away from the ruble zone, it may need access to a significant amount of foreign exchange to ensure the viability of the new currency. (The external financing issue is discussed more extensively in the next chapter.)

CHAPTER 4

EXTERNAL FINANCING

4.1   For the next five to seven years, Uzbekistan will have significant external financing needs. Provided that the Government implements reforms, however, Uzbekistan is well placed to obtain mostly bilateral, multilateral, and trade credits in the short to medium term. Financing from commercial banks and access to international capital markets will probably develop only in the medium term. A partial approach to reform would, however, inhibit the availability of foreign resources.

4.2   In 1992, Uzbekistan may have run a trade deficit in its interrepublic trade of roughly $200 million,[1] and a deficit with the rest of the world of roughly $60 million. Foreign direct investment flows were only beginning in 1992. Approximately $380 million in bilateral loans and export credits were committed, of which roughly $125 million were disbursed. Uzbekistan signed an agreement with Russia (on November 2, 1992) whereby it relinquishes claims on USSR assets in return for Russia's accepting responsibility for Uzbekistan's share of the USSR's external debt. This will have a positive impact on Uzbekistan's creditworthiness.[2]

Table 4.1
Composition of Resource Balance[a]
(in million U.S. dollars)

	1993	1994	1996	1999	2002
Resource Balance (deficit)	225	340	250	-95	-385
Exports[b]	2,940	3,670	4,280	5,620	7,000
Gold	740	790	840	930	1,020
Cotton	1,350	1,600	1,940	2,250	2,530
Gas	300	500	600	840	1,160
Other[c]	550	780	900	1,600	2,290
Imports	3,000	3,780	4,280	5,200	6,220
Oil	600	680	360	160	30
Current Account (deficit)	260	425	485	350	240

[a]   It reflects the mid-point of the range presented in the external financing requirements.

[b]   The real annual average growth rates of exports for 1993-2002 were assumed to be: cotton (0.6 percent); gas (6.5 percent); gold (0 percent); and other (2.8 percent). The growth rates in current value terms are significantly higher because of the convergence to world prices and exchange rate valuation adjustment.

[c]   Other exports include non-ferrous metals, silk, textiles, agro-industrial machinery, chemicals, etc.

A. ESTIMATED EXTERNAL FINANCING REQUIREMENTS

4.3   Any estimates of Uzbekistan's external financing needs are necessarily preliminary and subject to much uncertainty, but they can be useful for assessing the country's prospects under different

---

[1] Note that the interrepublic trade balance in 1992 was estimated by converting the ruble's deficit to dollars based on market-exchange rates. This figure is biased downwards, since the exchange rate is undervalued.

[2] It is worth mentioning that, until Russia formalizes arrangements with foreign creditors that it will assume the FSU's external liabilities, the "zero debt option" is not legally in effect. This may affect the disbursement of specific bilateral loans that have already been approved.

policy assumptions during the transition. The following analysis should be viewed as scenarios of what may happen under certain policy and other assumptions rather than projections or forecasts of the future. Uzbekistan's external financing requirements for 1993 could reach about $500 million, comprising a noninterest current-account deficit of about $250 million, interest payments of about $10 million, and buildup of gross reserves. Estimated financing needs for 1994-96 average $600 to $700 million, which assumes that the Government implements comprehensive reforms that stabilize the economy (including currency reform), as well as structural measures (see chapter 3).[3]

4.4   Imports of capital goods for developing oil fields and sustaining natural gas exports will be

Table 4.2
Medium-Term Projections: External Financing Requirements
Under the Reform Scenario[a]
(in million U.S. dollars)

	1993	
	Lower Bound	Upper Bound
Total Financing Needs	**455**	**555**
Non-Interest Current Account (deficit)	230	280
Debt Service		
Amortization	0	0
Net interest	9	11
Change in Reserves[b]	225	275
Total Financing Sources	**455**	**555**
Direct Foreign Investment (net)	90	110
Multilateral	20	25
Bilaterals	250	300
Export Credits	47	68
Short Term	18	22
Grants	30	30

Source: Bank staff estimates.

[a] The ranges indicated above reflect uncertainties around the midpoint of each of the components rather than alternative policy scenarios. Thus, neither the lower nor upper bounds can be added up to represent an independent balance of payments scenario.

[b] These figures reflect resources needed to build up reserves equivalent to three months of imports. The stock of reserves as of end of 1992 was

particularly important in terms of balance of payments (BOP) implications in 1994-95. Uzbekistan could also maintain significant cotton exports from increased productivity, provided an effort is made to improve grading capabilities and deliveries. Uzbekistan could also begin exporting gold--up to 65 tons, its annual production. As net oil imports decline to zero and gas-related export revenues begin to rise significantly, the resource balance could improve substantially (see Table 4.1). However, external financing requirements will continue to increase because of debt service. Tentative estimates of Uzbekistan's BOP and corresponding external financing requirements for the period 1993-2002 under the reform scenario described in chapter 3 are presented in Tables 4.2 and 4.3.

---

[3] It is assumed that (1) the Government undertakes agricultural and energy pricing reform; (2) the real exchange rate appreciates significantly in 1993-94 and remains stable thereafter; (3) cotton and oil trade takes place at world prices throughout the period; (4) natural-gas trade moves to world prices in 1994; and (5) gold trade takes place at world prices.

4.5   Let us now look at somewhat more optimistic assumptions[4]-- availability of domestic or foreign investment to finance the development of two new discovered oil fields, convergence of natural-gas prices to world-market levels, adjustment of domestic prices, vigorous energy conservation, and the corresponding steady and significant decline in domestic consumption of gas. All this could generate up to $190 million in extra net gas exports in 1993, up to $600 million in 1995, and possibly up to $700 million in 1997. For oil, Uzbekistan could become self-sufficient by 1995 and a net exporter by 1997. Should these assumptions materialize the current account would turn into surplus by the year 2000.

Table 4.3
Medium-Term Projections: External Financing Requirements
Under Reform Scenario[a]
(in million U.S. dollars)

	1994		1996		1999		2002	
	Lower Bound	Upper Bound	Lower Bound	Upper Bound	Lower Bound	Upper Bound	Lower Bound	Upper Bound
Total Financing Needs	**540**	**665**	**685**	**835**	**745**	**910**	**565**	**695**
Non-Interest Current Account (deficit)	355	430	340	410	160	190	30	40
Debt Service								
Amortization	10	15	170	210	380	470	310	380
Net interest	25	35	100	120	160	195	185	225
Change in Reserves[b]	150	185	75	95	45	55	40	50
Total Financing Sources	**540**	**665**	**685**	**835**	**745**	**910**	**565**	**695**
Direct Foreign Investment	135	165	160	200	225	275	225	275
Multilateral Financing	100	120	185	230	235	285	260	320
Bilateral Loans	210	260	195	240	200	245	40	45
Export Credits	50	65	85	95	85	105	40	55
Short Term	25	35	45	55	0	0	0	0
Grants	20	20	15	15	0	0	0	0

Source: Bank staff estimates.

[a]   The ranges indicated above reflect uncertainties around the midpoint of each of the components rather than alternative policy scenarios. Thus, neither the lower nor upper bounds can be added up to represent an independent balance of payments scenario.
[b]   These figures reflect resources needed to build up reserves equivalent to: (1) three months of imports for 1993-97; (2) less than a month of imports for 1998-2002.

4.6   Uzbekistan's exposure to commodity price risks (for example, in cotton, gold, oil, and natural gas) could become a significant issue in the medium term, because Uzbekistan's exports will remain highly concentrated in primary commodities, for which price movements are strongly correlated. This exposure will affect Uzbekistan's economy--directly through its impact on export revenue (and thus government tax revenue) and on enterprise net income, production, and consumption decisions, and indirectly through its impact on macroeconomic policy management and potentially on the equilibrium exchange rate.

[4] These were discussed in chapter 10 on the Energy Sector but are not reflected in the reform scenario presented in this chapter.

4.7   Foreign savings will play a critical role in the short and medium terms. Assuming that: (1) the fiscal deficit declines in 1993-94 and stabilizes at 5 percent of GDP; and (2) domestic savings could only become significant in the longer term, foreign savings generated through a declining current account deficit would be necessary. This would allow Uzbekistan to finance public and private investment during the transition to a market-based economy and a smooth recovery of private consumption levels (see Figure 4.1).[5] Initially, most of the external financing will be channeled to the Government and to SOEs. However, as the structural reforms deepen foreign savings are expected to increase financing to the new private sector.

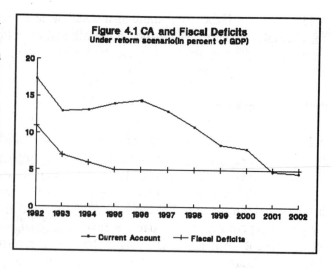

Figure 4.1 CA and Fiscal Deficits
Under reform scenario(in percent of GDP)

POTENTIAL FINANCING SOURCES

4.8   While FDI can be a significant financing source in the medium to long term, a large proportion of Uzbekistan's short- and medium-term financing requirements may need to be met by official borrowing in the form of bilateral loans, export credits, loans from multilateral institutions such as IBRD, IMF, EBRD, and possibly ADB, and EC and grants for technical assistance and humanitarian reasons. Under the assumption that a new currency is introduced in 1993, a significant amount of international reserves will be necessary to support its convertibility. It is estimated that Uzbekistan has a significant stock of international reserves in the form of gold, and that the country produces about 65 tons of gold annually (amounting to about $760 million at April 1993 world-market prices). However, in order to build up a minimum of international reserves that would ensure access to imports, Uzbekistan would need to borrow externally.

Private Financing

4.9   *Foreign direct investment (FDI)*--equity investment and joint ventures could represent significant resources for Uzbekistan in the medium term. Potential foreign investors will require attractive returns, a regulatory framework and a stable environment to invest in Uzbekistan. Since this will take time to put in place, significant flows are not expected in the short run. In 1992, an $80 million to $100 million commitment for 1993-94 was made by a well-known U.S. mining company to invest in gold extraction from existing deposits. However, should Uzbekistan decide to open up the mining sector for exploration, it could attract several foreign companies. The oil and natural-gas sectors could also attract FDI. It is expected that FDI in Uzbekistan could increase from $100 million in 1993 to $180 million in 1995, to up to $250 million in 1997.

4.10   *Trade credits* from commercial private sources represent an alternative source of financing for Uzbekistan in the medium term. They could become a significant source of short-term financing as the economy is stabilized and a consistent trade policy is implemented.

---

[5] Note that the current account to GDP ratio is overestimated. It reflects the undervaluation of the ruble at the market exchange rate given the 1992 initial conditions.

4.11   Uzbekistan could also obtain access to *commodity-linked financing* as an alternative to, for example, finance investments in the mineral or cotton subsectors. The potential amount that can be attained through the issuance of bonds linked to gold, for example, is limited in the medium term but could prove significant in the longer term.[6]

Official Financing

4.12   Both multilateral and bilateral financing could play a significant role during the transition to a market-based economy in Uzbekistan. *Multilateral institutions* can be expected to be instrumental in supporting Uzbekistan as it implements a comprehensive reform program. An agreement with the IMF on a Systemic Transition Facility or a Stand-By Arrangement would provide the framework for substantial bilateral and multilateral assistance. The Bank could also be a catalyst in mobilizing additional resources by providing cofinancing or parallel financing arrangements. It is premature to anticipate the timing of an agreement with the IMF. The Bank is currently preparing an Institutional Building/Technical Assistance Loan. Beyond 1993, depending on the progress of the reform program, the Bank will continue to develop a pipeline of projects in agriculture, irrigation, human resources, privatization, and energy. Multilateral financing, in terms of commitments, could amount up to an average of $60 million in 1993 and to an average of $400 million in 1994-96. Provided there is a continued progress on reforms, a steady flow of lending from multilateral sources could be expected for the remainder of the decade.

4.13   *Bilateral financing* of about $280 million in direct government loans has partially been committed for 1993. Should Uzbekistan undertake a comprehensive economic reform program, further assistance could become available. A loan of approximately $130 million from the EC tied to food and pharmaceutical imports had been approved in 1992 but is still undisbursed due to the legal obstacles associated with the "zero option" agreement.

4.14   *Export credit agencies* can also play a significant role as Uzbekistan develops stronger commercial ties with the rest of the world. Several foreign government ECAs have already established credit lines for Uzbekistan, usually combining bilateral loans with export credits--Turkey, Spain, Indonesia, Switzerland, India, and China. Uzbekistan could obtain access to at least $100 million annually through this type of financing.

4.15   A significant amount of *technical assistance* is expected to be provided to Uzbekistan in the short and medium term. From the Pre-Consultative Group meeting that took place in Paris in December 1992, chaired by the World Bank, Uzbekistan received commitments for a significant portion of the technical assistance needs that it proposed to official donors. Thus, Uzbekistan can obtain about $30 million in the form of technical assistance grants in 1993, and about $20 million per year over the medium term. This scenario assumes that Uzbekistan will benefit from a broad program of assistance in different areas and sectors. A description of technical assistance needs is presented throughout the report. In sum, Uzbekistan would benefit from a variety of technical assistance programs in economic management, public-sector management, privatization, private-sector development, the social safety net, the financial sector, agriculture, energy, mining, transport, and industry. These programs are critical to a successful reform program in Uzbekistan.

---

[6] Note that a precondition for Uzbekistan to access commodity linked financing or any financing that involves pledging of assets would require a negative pledge waiver from the country's creditors.

4.16   Uzbekistan has been receiving humanitarian grant assistance from both private and official agencies since the breakup of the FSU. During the transition period, possibly to assist in health and environment related problems, Uzbekistan is likely to benefit from more grants in kind--such as pharmaceutical products--and some other tied financial assistance.

UNDER THE MUDDLE-THROUGH SCENARIO

4.17   While the reform scenario foresees the relatively heavy involvement of official creditors in financing Uzbekistan's needs in the medium term, the muddle-through scenario does not envisage significant external financing or foreign direct investment flowing into the country. Thus, Uzbekistan would have to rely primarily on its own reserves and a modest amount of foreign loans to finance its external imbalances.   Bilateral loans--mainly from Russia and Turkey--would probably represent a significant share of total foreign loans. Estimated financing under this scenario would increase from about $300 million in 1993 and 1994, to about $350 million in 1997. At that point, higher requirements in the absence of loans from official and commercial sources would be very difficult to finance, thus adversely affecting consumption per capita levels and the growth prospects of the country (see Table 4.4).

4.18   These projections assume that the Government follows a partial approach to reforms without implementing any major reform initiatives. Heavy dependence on interrepublic trade also imposes a constraint on the total volume of trade and therefore on the level of economic activity.[7]

Table 4.4
Medium-Term Projections: External Financing Requirements
Under Muddle-Through Scenario
(in million U.S. dollars)

	1993	1994	1996	1999	2002
Total Financing Needs	315	280	295	390	310
Non-Interest Current Account	165	190	80	110	5
Debt Services					
Amortization	-	8	130	170	180
Net interest	10	22	55	75	105
Change in Net Reserves	140	60	30	35	20
Total Financing Sources	315	280	295	390	310
Direct Foreign Investment (net)	50	60	80	90	90
Multilateral Financing	25	30	35	40	40
Bilateral Loans	185	150	145	200	130
Export Credits	30	25	25	50	40
Short Term	5	10	10	10	10
Grants	20	5	0	0	0

Source: Bank staff estimates.

[7] It is assumed that (1) the real exchange rate appreciates in line with developments in the ruble zone in 1993-95 and remains constant thereafter; (2) cotton and oil trade moves to world prices by the end of 1993; (3) a very modest trade of natural gas moves to world prices in 1994; and (4) gold trade takes place at world prices.

B. CREDITWORTHINESS

4.19   Uzbekistan's creditworthiness in the medium and long terms will depend on successful implementation of the reform program and on export performance. Because of existing uncertainties, various simulations (with blends of market and concessional lending terms) were analyzed to derive an idea of the sensitivity of Uzbekistan's creditworthiness to borrowing conditions.   Under the reform scenario, Uzbekistan could enter a period of sustained growth with increasing access to international capital markets (Table 4.5). A rapid buildup of external debt during the transition is reflected in total debt outstanding as a share of exports of about 44 percent by 1997. Thereafter, rising amortization payments should stabilize external debt at less than $3.0 billion, with increasing exports. Debt service as a share of exports could reach only 11 percent by 1999, when amortization becomes significant, but the debt service ratio would fall to about 8 percent by 2002. These projections depend heavily on Uzbekistan's ability to sustain export performance and to shift a significant portion of its trade to hard currency markets.

Table 4.5
Creditworthiness[a]

	1993	1997	1999	2002
		(in percent)		
Full Market Terms (100% market financing)				
DOD[b]/Total Exports	16	44	43	38
Debt Service[c]/Total Exports	0.2	9	11	8

External debt is assumed to be at market terms
[a] External debt is assumed to be at market terms.
[b] DOD: total external debt outstanding.
[c] Debt service: amortization plus interest payments.

4.20   The country has the potential for considerable exports of natural gas, becoming self-sufficient in oil in the future and maintaining a significant amount of cotton and gold exports. However, its creditworthiness could be jeopardized by policy slippages, delays owing to implementation capacity, difficulties in realizing its export potential, and the lack of foreign direct investment to develop pipeline capacity.

C. INSTITUTIONAL ARRANGEMENTS

4.21   Any of the alternative financing sources described earlier have institutional preconditions. For example, (1) the domestic legal system must provide effective enforcement of contractual terms, and should have transparent regulations; (2) domestic financial institutions should have the capacity to intermediate the foreign funds; (3) technical expertise to manage the foreign flows effectively should be well developed; and (4) institutional arrangements should be in place, such as an external assistance unit, a procurement unit, and an external debt management unit.

EXTERNAL ASSISTANCE MANAGEMENT UNIT

4.22   The restructuring of Uzbekistan's economy into a market-based system requires substantial technical and financial assistance. However, the Government has no direct experience with external assistance and is thus unfamiliar with the terms and conditions of this assistance, and with the different procedures of the various donors. The mobilization and effective utilization of aid would thus depend on the Government's ability to manage and coordinate the needs for different types of aid in the economy, matching them with domestic resources, and using available aid resources effectively in line with the financial and procurement requirements of various aid agencies. Hence, the recent establishment of the External Assistance Unit in the Cabinet of Ministers to manage and coordinate external assistance is a step in the right direction.

4.23   The Unit will serve as a facilitator of contacts between donors and ministries and will be the single focal point in the Government for coordinating relations with donors. It will disseminate to other Government agencies any information on sources of funds, donor procedures, and probable flows of financial and technical assistance, thus helping to match needs with potentially available resources. It will not have authority to set economic priorities, nor to evaluate the economic validity of projects, but will verify that project financing is realistic and prepared according to generally accepted standards. It is critical that the Unit be well staffed. While the Bank is providing an IDF grant for establishing the Unit, its full cost and technical assistance needs are estimated to be higher than the grant.

4.24   Beyond managing and coordinating external assistance from all sources, the Unit would help the Government determine the sources of the country's external assistance needs in the medium term.

External Asset and Debt Management

4.25   Although the Government is cognizant of the importance of effective external debt management, it still lacks a proper institutional and legal framework for this purpose. Currently, the Ministry of Finance (MOF) is responsible for authorizing, recording, monitoring, and reporting all external debt transactions. The Central Bank is excluded from managing the country's foreign exchange reserves and has no say in the external borrowing strategy. In market-based economies, external borrowing is managed jointly by the Ministry of Finance and the Central Bank. Uzbekistan should adopt this approach. The MOF should maintain all records on Central Government borrowing, and the Central Bank should monitor and report the external debt of commercial banks and enterprises, whether publicly or privately owned. In addition, the Central Bank should be responsible for managing the country's international reserves on behalf of the Government.

4.26   In order to develop an effective institutional structure, the Government should create debt offices within the MOF and the Central Bank. The Government should define the role of each institution--that the MOF is the policymaking body, while the Central Bank is its executing agency. The relationship and communications and the exchange of information between the MOF and the Central Bank should be clear. Since Uzbekistan has no experience in debt management the two proposed debt offices will need substantial technical and financial assistance. In order to improve external debt management, the Government must always have access to detailed, accurate, and up-to-date data on its external debt, on both a loan-by-loan and an aggregate basis. It could do so by creating a computerized debt management system. Staffing issues, including their structure, size, and training needs, will also require technical assistance. It is estimated that the technical assistance requirements of these two units would be about $350,000.

CHAPTER 5

THE GOVERNANCE OF REFORM

5.1   As Uzbekistan makes its transition from a command economy dependent on other FSU republics to an independent nation pursuing a market-based economy, it must pursue several tasks simultaneously: create a system of government based on a democratically elected executive and legislature, and liberalize financial and legal regimes to support creating a private sector; decide which public organizations and services would be privatized, and how it will provide social services independent of commercial enterprises; and create a new pattern of external relationships with FSU countries and others throughout the world.

5.2   These tasks must be coordinated by the Government of Uzbekistan. To do so successfully requires skills, knowledge, attitudes, and organizational arrangements that are quite different from those used in the former regime. Thus, the institutions of governance must go through a transition no less significant than that which the state itself is experiencing. Building this capacity--and thus sustaining the reform process--requires clarity in the distribution of powers among elements of the governing system,[1] analytical capability to drive the policy formulation process, and management and administrative systems able to sustain the implementation process.

A. GOVERNANCE

5.3   Governance generally encompasses three broad aspects: (1) the form of the political regime; (2) the processes by which authority is exercised in managing a country's economic and social resources; and (3) the capacity to design, formulate, and implement policies, and, in general, to discharge governmental functions. The first aspect is outside the mandate of the Bank, and thus the discussion herein focuses on the other two aspects.

5.4   The functions of the modern state provide scope for much debate, with governments examining, and re-examining, the extent to which they should intervene in the management of economic affairs and the provision of social services. Yet it is clear that certain functions can be undertaken only by the state, however committed its government is to a market-based economy:

- Protection of the state, citizens, and property

- Relations with other governments and multinational agencies

- Macroeconomic policy design and management

- Enabling conditions for private-sector development

---

[1] Box 5.1 highlights several key components of the new Constitution approved by Congress on December 8, 1992, as they pertain to the structure of governmental authority.

- Financial regimes

- Legal structure

- Infrastructure (energy, transport, and communications)

- A trained and healthy workforce

● Minimum social-service provision (education, health, housing, and social security)

● Cultural and scientific development.

5.5   Executing these functions efficiently and effectively is critical if the economy is to flourish and the citizens of the state are to be secure, healthy, educated, and well housed. Thus, the Government must be able not only to formulate and design appropriate policies but also to secure their effective implementation. Developing the capacity of the government system and the administrative machinery that supports it is a matter of primary importance to a country passing through the transition from a command economy to a market-based economy.

B. THE SETTING FOR REFORM

5.6   The breakup of the Soviet Union and the transition to a market-based economy are the two major determinants of the change in the system of Uzbekistan government and public-sector management. Uzbekistan must articulate the values that will underlie its development, and exercise its independence within an economically and politically uncertain regional and international environment. A population deprived for many years of opportunities for active political involvement will develop political literacy; contrasts between the rural and urban traditions and conditions in Uzbekistan must be recognized in fostering participation in the process of governing the nation's activities.

5.7   The system of administration has traditionally been based on central control and direction, with limited delegation of authority. The emphasis on control extended to relations between bureaucrats and the public; bureaucrats had to implement controls and constraints rather than focus on providing services to members of the public as individual citizens. This administrative environment has limited the range of attitudes and skills possessed by public servants.

5.8   External audits of Government expenditures have been absent, and scrutiny of executive power and actions has been limited. The media were not free in the past to report and comment openly on Government actions. The exercise of power without public scrutiny and accountability creates opportunities for industries to abuse their authority, leading to unfair treatment. Again, this has a lasting impact on the attitudes and skills of public servants.

5.9   Two major structural changes have occurred thus far in the Government: the creation of new ministries after the breakup of the Soviet Union (for example, the Ministry of Foreign Affairs and the Ministry of Defense) and the redesignation of ministries into concerns, associations, or companies.[2]

---

[2] The organizational structure of the Government of Uzbekistan is presented in Annex 1 of this volume.

While it was inevitable that initial changes would reflect immediate priorities, a greater emphasis might now be placed on developing an overall strategy for institutional reform and development.

PRIORITIES FOR THE FUTURE: STRENGTHENING THE STRUCTURE OF GOVERNMENT

5.10 Developing a coherent strategy for public-sector reform requires public debate to articulate national values and to develop Uzbekistan's philosophy on the role of Government in a market-based economy. Without this background, a framework for the civil service, an appropriate management structure, and efficient operational procedures cannot be developed.

5.11 The organizational structure of Government should be derived from its functions. The central teams supporting the President, the Prime Minister, and Cabinet of Ministers play a critical role in the policy-making function, and their work must reflect the priority functions of Government.

Box 5.1. Uzbekistan's Constitution–Distribution of Powers

- A single-chamber representative parliament (the Oliy Majlis) wields legislative power (Article 76)

- The legislature has the power to (Article 78):

    - Adopt and amend the Constitution
    - Pass laws
    - Determine legislative, executive, and judicial powers
    - Admit new state units
    - Regulate customs, currency, and credit activities
    - Oversee the operation of state banks
    - Determine internal and exernal frontier issues
    - Adopt the national budget and control its execution
    - Determine the dates of national and local elections
    - Elect its Chairperson and Deputy-Chairpersons
    - Elect the Constitutional Court
    - Elect the Supreme Court
    - Elect the High Economic Court
    - Elect the Chairperson of the State Committee on Environmental Protection
    - Confirm the President's appointments of the Prime Minister, Deputy Prime Ministers, and other members of the Cabinet of Ministers
    - Confirm the President's appointment of the Procurator General
    - Confirm the President's nomination of the Chairman of the Board of the Central Bank
    - Confirm the decrees of the President on establishing ministries, state committees, and other governmental bodies
    - Confirm the decrees of the President on conscription and emergency situations
    - Ratify and annul international treaties
    - Institute state titles and awards
    - Determine local government arrangements

- The right of legislative initiative rests with the President, the autonomous Republic of Karakalpakstan, the deputies of the Oliy Majlis, the Cabinet of Ministers, the Constitutional, Supreme, and High Economic Courts, and the Procurator General (Article 82)

- An elected President is head of state and chief executive (Articles 89 and 90)

- The President has the power and duties to (Article 93):

    - Guarantee the rights and freedoms of citizens, the Constitution, and the laws
    - Safeguard the sovereignty, security, and integrity of the state

---

5.12 The basic structure of seven major clusters within the Cabinet of Ministers, coordinating the work of uni-functional ministries and central services and cross-bracing state committees, is sound. However, the areas of responsibility covered by the seven major clusters can be reviewed to ensure that the division of responsibility reflects the major priorities of the future. Following this review, organizational entities must be rationalized and procedures simplified. The number of Ministries should be reviewed and reduced to minimize overlap. For example, separate Ministries of Public Education and Secondary and Higher Education may not be very effective, and the activities of the Ministries of Health, Labor, and Social Security can be redefined.

5.13   Both the efficiency and effectiveness of the operational procedures followed by the Government should be scrutinized. The practice of having separate forecasting teams to project school enrollments, the supply of teachers, and school building requirements is one example of unnecessary duplication. To give a second example, the scrutiny of draft legislation appears to be a duplicative activity, while the need for developing legislative drafting expertise within the Ministry of Justice deserves critique. If this scrutiny process is to be of lasting value, it should be an internal exercise, operating according to centrally determined guidelines and subject to continued evaluation by the Office of the Prime Minister.

Box 5.1 (cont.)

- Negotiate and sign treaties
- Appoint diplomatic and other representatives in foreign states
- Present annual reports on internal and international situations to the Oliy Majlis
- Form and supervise the Government and its executive administration, subject to the requirement to present decrees to the Oliy Majlis for confirmation
- Appoint the Prime Minister, Deputy Prime Ministers, members of the Cabinet of Ministers, and Procurator General, subject to confirmation by the Oliy Majlis
- Nominate candidates for membership of the Constitutional, Supreme, and High Economic Courts, the Chairperson of the Board of the Central Bank, and the Chairperson of the State Committee on Environmental Protection subject to consideration by the Oliy Majlis
- Appoint and dismiss judges of the regional, district, town, and economic courts
- Appoint and dismiss the *khokim* of the regions and City of Tashkent subject to confirmation by the respective Soviet of People's Deputies
- Repeal the acts of ministries and khokims
- Sign the laws
- Return a law to the Oliy Majlis for further consideration
- Declare a state of emergency, subject to confirmation by the Oliy Majlis within three days
- Act as Commander in Chief of the Armed Forces
- Declare a state of war, subject to confirmation by the Oliy Majlis within three days
- Resolve questions of citizenship
- Dissolve the Oliy Majlis (Article 95)

- A Cabinet of Ministers (Article 98)

- A system of local administration with elected Soviets of People's Deputies and appointed khokims with significant personal authority and responsibility (Articles 98 and 101)

- Independently exercised judicial power through the Constitutional Court, the Supreme Court, the High Economic Court, the Supreme Court of the Republic of Karakalpakstan, and regional, district, town, and economic courts

- A Procurator's Office, responsible for supervising the observance of the law

Source: Constitution of the Republic of Uzbekistan

5.14   The Government of Uzbekistan faces a major task in developing the individuals and institutions that are critical to its economic reform program. While an overall strategy is necessary to ensure coherence, certain institutions are of such importance that it would be appropriate to focus attention on them. They include:

- The Offices of the President and Prime Minister, including coordinating activities for the Cabinet of Ministers

- The Central Bank

- The State Committee on Privatization

- Central financial and personnel management functions

- Management development and training for senior civil servants.

The Civil Service

5.15   As Uzbekistan develops as an independent state, a clearer delineation between career civil servants and those holding political office will be necessary, even if senior positions in the bureaucracy are held by individuals with political affiliations. Thus, a civil service model is required, defining its role in relation to the Government.

5.16   A major change in strategy should be made at all levels of the civil service. In the past, the emphasis has been on control and direction. If the civil service is to adopt a managerial approach, concerned primarily with service quality, then a completely different emphasis is needed.

The civil service should have the following capabilities:

- Policy analysis and advice to the President and Cabinet of Ministers

- Financial planning and expenditure control

- Execution of Government and legislative decisions and routine management of government business based on clear target-setting for devolved management units

- Evaluation of executive activities based on explicit performance measures

- A review of targets based on the evaluation.

5.17   The structure of the civil service would follow the structure of the Government. Clusters within the Cabinet of Ministers, liaising with the Office of the President, should have the major responsibility for policy development and evaluation. State committees can provide the main analytical support for policy-making, with advice on the implications for implementation being provided by the ministries. Ministries can then focus predominantly on executing policy decisions and could be structured into executive units that would each operate within clear policy, resources, and evaluation frameworks.

5.18   The role of public servants as servants of the public must be highlighted, and the quality of the service provided by the Government to citizens should be assessed.

5.19   In order to develop a merit-based civil service in which the highest standards of integrity can flourish, the Government must create a transparent personnel management strategy, covering recruitment, selection, promotion, appraisal, training, counseling, dismissal, remuneration and other benefits (including pensions), and retirement. By creating a coherent personnel policy, discrimination among different ethnic groups and the barriers that inhibit career development among women can be removed. The Prime Minister's Office must provide the central focus for developing and monitoring this strategy. The present arrangement whereby the Ministry of Labor and Ministry of Finance share these responsibilities is inappropriate for the future civil service. Personnel policies should be implemented only by individual ministries and other organizational units.

5.20   The training function deserves attention also; a program of institutional strengthening should be implemented to provide focused training programs for all levels of staff in the civil service. Responsibility for ensuring that these training programs are implemented should rest with line managers, not with the central personnel policy unit or the providers of training. A training market should be developed with institutions of higher education, as well as with state training institutions.

5.21   An integrated financial information system must be developed to support all elements of financial management--budgeting, expenditure control, cash management, accounting, and auditing. The existing arrangements in which ministries operate incompatible computer systems is a waste of resources. The financial system should be developed as an essential component of the overall management system, so that financial control and financial targeting are part of performance evaluation arrangements.

The Legislature and Scrutiny

5.22   The Constitution confirms the separation of powers between the executive and the legislature. An important element in the work of any legislature is its scrutiny role. The Committee structure of the Supreme Council provides the basis for scrutinizing draft legislation and the conduct of Government business, but it is important that members of the legislature have access to sufficient information, requiring an appropriately staffed support function. Access to information is particularly important in relation to the Government's use of public funds. The absence of an independent external audit function is a major deficiency, depriving the legislature of independent advice on Government expenditures and their impact.

Local Government

5.23   As set forth in the Constitution, the arrangements for local governments subject them to central control and direction and limit the powers of the locally elected bodies. This is understandable at the early stage of national development. There is also much merit in treating local government staff as part of the civil service, permitting transfers among all levels of Government.

The Constitution gives the following authority to local government:

- Law enforcement, social order, and the security of citizens
- Economic, social, and cultural development
- Local taxation and the use of such revenue

- Environmental protection
- Registration of the acts of the civic state
- Normative acts and other powers within the Constitution and law.

5.24   Evolution into a politically mature state is made difficult if local democratic organs have limited autonomy.   Thus, in the longer term, increasing the autonomy of locally elected bodies must be considered.

Public-Sector Management

5.25   The specific steps recommended to the Government of Uzbekistan to clarify its role and purpose in a market-based economy so as to strengthen its public-sector management are as follows:

- The structure of Government should be reviewed, with clusters, ministries, and state committees organized to reflect the major priorities of Government. Explicit statements of purpose should be formulated for each entity within the structure.

- The structure of the team of special advisors to the President could be reviewed to reflect the priorities of Government and their relationship to policy development in the Cabinet of Ministers.

- Transitional arrangements should be reviewed to ensure their long-term suitability--for example, responsibility for external debt management, balance of payments preparation, etc.

- Consideration should be given to creating an external audit service, accountable to the legislature.

- A major review of the organization of the state administration should be undertaken with a view toward developing a coherent and transparent management structure for the civil service.   This review should be coordinated by a project unit based in the Prime Minister's Office, with the work of the review devolved into organizational units as the organizational structure evolves.

- A major review of operational procedures used throughout the state administration should be organized in conjunction with the organizational review.

- A program of workshops, seminars, and training courses should be designed to develop new attitudes, skills, and knowledge at all levels in the civil service, including the staff who work in local government. Emphasis should be placed on legislative drafting.

- A central personnel management policy unit should be created within the Prime Minister's Office to develop and monitor the implementation of personnel management policy.

- An integrated financial management system should be developed.

Technical Assistance

5.26   The capacity of the Government must be strengthened in several areas related to public-sector management to enable it to carry out structural and sectoral reforms,[3] by:

- Creating local capacity to coordinate and manage external assistance, including financial aid and technical assistance.

- Strengthening the capacity of the Government to design and implement macroeconomic policy. Furnishing Government officials with up-to-date analytical information on macroeconomics and facilitating both the transition to the market-based economy and the working requirements of the new environment.

- Improving external debt management and strengthening the country's capacity to develop a suitable strategy consistent with sound macroeconomic policies. Installing a computerized debt management system and training relevant Government officials in its use.

- Providing long-term support to civil service reform program.

- Clarifying the role, purpose, and structure of the emerging civil service.

5.27   This list is not comprehensive, but it illustrates the range of issues that came to the attention of the World Bank Mission in September 1992. An overall review of the work of Government is necessary to identify all areas in which individual and institutional capacity development is required.

---

[3] Technical assistance needs related specifically to structural and sectoral issues are presented in chapters 6-14 of this report.

CHAPTER 6

REFORMING STATE-OWNED ENTERPRISES AND DEVELOPING THE PRIVATE SECTOR

6.1   The economic objective of structural reform is to improve incentives for efficiency, innovation, and growth. In the case of Uzbekistan, it is ultimately related to the organization and ownership of its productive sectors, which are dominated by state-owned enterprises (SOEs). At the end of 1992, SOEs accounted for roughly 85 percent of GDP and about 80 percent of employment. Moreover, through its links with the budget and the banking system, the sector absorbs most of the country's financial resources. Therefore, reforming enterprises is a key requirement for establishing a market-based system and effecting both macroeconomic stability and the sustainability of economic reform. Structural transformation should include changes in the size of enterprises, the introduction of competition, and the prevention of new monopoly formation. The challenge for the Government now is to design and implement policies to break down the systems of market segmentation and vertical integration and remove the structural impediments to competition.

6.2   Despite some important reforms in other sectors, the Government has not yet made significant *structural* changes in SOEs to improve efficiency. To effect the necessary changes, policies and action programs are needed in four interdependent areas: enterprise governance, financial discipline, privatization, and competition. First, SOEs are not currently subject to effective governance. Through tax, trade restrictions, profile requirements and the continued exercise of ownership rights by Government regulators, the state interferes with SOEs' operational autonomy. Yet, as owner, the state does not exercise its ownership rights through the imposition of clear rules of financial accountability. The Government continues to use the banking system and the budget as tools for financing expenditures of most SOEs, largely eliminating incentives to restructure. This, in turn, has led to the expansion of credit, exacerbated the fiscal situation, and seriously undermined other macroeconomic reforms and stabilization. While a strong privatization law is in place, actual programs to date have focused primarily on small retail shops and public services. Major sectors of the economy are unaffected. Restructuring (both corporatization and privatization) of medium and large enterprises has been left to the initiative of existing workers and management who lack both the incentives and means to impose the needed ownership and financial discipline required to restructure many of the enterprises. Finally, serious impediments to competition remain and, unless removed, will undermine enterprise ownership and financial reforms. Market entry, exit, and operation are severely restricted by overly discretionary regulation. Market information is very limited. SOE control of critical services and distribution networks continues the rigid market segmentation of the command economy. Unfortunately, there is no formula or model for the steps to be taken or for guaranteeing success in all cases. However, continuation of the currently slow ownership reforms and neglect of the competition, governance, and financial issues is almost certain to bring further economic declines.

A. SETTING FOR ENTERPRISE REFORM

COMPOSITION AND STRUCTURE OF THE SOE SECTOR

6.3   SOEs operate in almost all sectors. Uzbekistan's enterprise sector consists of approximately 76,502 enterprises. The industrial sector comprises approximately 2,000 enterprises employing over 900,000 workers (see Table 6.1). Agricultural enterprises, collectives and state farms employ about 1.9 million. Construction and building supply enterprises number about 1,163, employing over 400,000. The trade sector employs about 253,000 with 10,969 enterprises. Transport employs 220,000, with about 740 enterprises. Many enterprises are combined in vertically structured groups that emerged from former branch ministries. Most markets are dominated by such groups or individual SOEs, including particularly distribution and transport at the local level.

Table 6.1
Uzbekistan's Industrial Structure in 1991

	Number of Enterprises	Employees		Output	
		(Thou.)	(Percent)	(billion rubles)	(Percent)
All Industry	2,006	915	100	61	100
Heavy Industry	897	482	53	24	39
Fuel and Power	53	47	5	4	7
Metallurgy					
Ferrous metallurgy	6	9	0	1	1
Nonferrous metallurgy	16	50	5	6	10
Metal Processing					
and Machine Building	289	208	23	6	10
Forestry Woodworking,					
Pulp and Paper	96	26	3	1	2
Building Materials	231	69	8	2	3
Chemical and Petrochemical	49	44	5	3	4
Light Industry	708	335	37	26	43
Agro Industry	405	99	11	11	18
Other Industry	153	31	3	1	2

Source: Goskomprognostat.

Industrial Concentration and Entry

6.4   The structure and organization of the enterprises (including most of those privatized to date) continues to inhibit competition, undermining the efficient distribution of goods and impending the transition to a market-based system. The industrial sector is currently organized into large associations (also called amalgamations, consortiums, and so forth), each of which generally embraces all the activities of individual subsectors that were under ministries of the FSU. Such associations control various umbrella enterprises, each of which, in turn, controls others. Under the old system, the branch ministries allocated production targets to enterprises and offered incentives to the enterprise managers to meet the targets. The flow of information and the incentives were unrelated to the true production capacity of the enterprises and the requirements of the consumers. Moreover, the incentives discouraged competition. Larger enterprises were rewarded for producing larger targets by receiving orders for yet larger production targets.

6.5   Two features of the old system continue in the present environment. First, small firms were not encouraged. As a result, smaller firms do not exist in significant numbers and are unable to play the critical roles that they could play in market economies--innovation and the fostering of entrepreneurial, managerial skills. In addition, enterprises were isolated, divided along branch ministerial and geographic lines. Central planning resulted in a highly segmented industrial structure in which enterprises had no communication outside their small sphere of activity. The isolation separated individual enterprises from knowledge about the identity of their customers and suppliers. Gosplan and Gossnab controlled both.

6.6   Although the Gosplan and Gossnab central planning system has collapsed, no new reorganization has been permitted yet to take hold. The old problems persist. Most distribution in Uzbekistan continues to be organized by enterprises or associations that are replicas of the planning system. They continue to distribute for the supply organizations and industrial ministries to which they has previously belonged. While many have been "destatized," they have not been privatized nor do they act differently. Changing behavior requires changing the incentive system and more active systemic reform. The enterprise managers remain captive to a vertical chain that they cannot escape from and which is reinforced by implicit subsidies. Until new forms of accountability to owners, distribution and competition emerge, the past inefficiencies will continue.

6.7   Reform and rationalization could be accomplished by (1) desegregating, reorganizing, and privatizing most of the enterprises; (2) establishing clear lines of accountability from managers to owners (including the state), separating the state's ownership, regulatory and management functions; (3) providing the appropriate legal and regulatory environment for fostering private property rights; and (4) creating competitive markets through the removal of barriers to free trade and entry, and improvements in public infrastructure, especially communications. No one of these steps, without the others, will ensure success.

PRODUCTIVITY OF THE SOE SECTOR

6.8   Real GDP declined by 1 percent in 1991, and by almost 10 percent in 1992 (chapter 2). In 1991, the sharpest fall in output was in construction; the decline in industry output was not as severe. In the first half of 1992, chemical and agro-industrial subsectors suffered the largest declines. These output declines, however, are not necessarily part of an inevitable adjustment process that will lead to the emergence of a new production structure more in line with Uzbekistan's resource base. Allowing output to decline further without altering the operational structure and practices of SOEs will not improve the production outlook in either the sector or the economy. Thus, SOEs must be restructured so that industrial assets, both capital and labor, can be used efficiently. Since there has been no reduction in SOE employment, output per worker has been declining at about 10 percent a year.

6.9   The Government has partially liberalized prices and trade, altering the relative profitability of sectors and companies by shifting relative prices in favor of tradeable goods. Under normal conditions, this shift (driven by changes in the structure of prices and by changes in demand) should encourage the reallocation of resources towards newly profitable sectors. More specifically, firms would be expected to respond by lowering wages and laying off surplus labor to cut costs, allowing labor resources to be reallocated across sectors to match the relative prices. In addition, some firms should go bankrupt, freeing capital assets for reallocation, while others should be selling off some plant, equipment, and underutilized space, also encouraging the reallocation of capital. Yet continued access to soft credit, continuance of state orders and the lack of an efficient governance structure owing to unclear ownership rights have prevented the free movement of production-related factors--a key condition for allocative efficiency--which in effect blocks the necessary adjustments in the SOE sector.

FINANCING ARRANGEMENTS FOR SOEs

6.10   Loss-making state-owned enterprises can be financed in one of three ways -- bank credit, inter-enterprise arrears, and direct budgetary outlays. Unless the Government finances losses directly, they are "hidden" in bank or inter-enterprise arrears. Allowing either the banks or other firms to make loans that cannot be repaid merely defers a government obligation. Ideally, the Government itself should explicitly finance loss-making SOEs that it has chosen to keep afloat, and not force banks or other enterprises to do so.

6.11   The relationship between the SOEs and banks complicates the problem. The SOEs are major shareholders in banks and most bank lending goes directly to SOEs. The Government even allows SOEs to take equity stakes in newly established banks. This is damaging to the incentive structure and makes banks hostage to SOEs. Banks are unlikely to assess loan requests on commercial criteria; even if they did, they would not have the power to deny loans for unworthy projects.   This organizational/ownership deficiency, coupled with the Government's unwillingness to control the flow of credit to SOEs, not only complicates monetary management but also contributes to the growth of low-quality (nonperforming) loans in bank portfolios. Many loans to enterprises finance their current expenditures and losses, not investment. Hence, the ability of enterprises to repay debts is in question. This situation will (or is likely to) increase the accumulation of poor-quality loans and further reduce the viability of the banking system, creating future problems for the Government.[1]

MACROECONOMIC ADJUSTMENT AND SOEs

6.12   Macroeconomic adjustment and enterprise reform are interrelated. To reach sustained macroeconomic improvement, the Government must take measures that invite innovation and investment. But innovation and investment depend on the existence of a stable economic environment and a productive enterprise sector. Macroeconomic stabilization and adjustment thus becomes a necessary condition for achieving microeconomic (efficiency) gains. However, without microeconomic reform to create the necessary price responsiveness, stabilization is likely to be unsuccessful.

6.13   The absence of adjustment by SOEs and the Government's inability to deal with the situation negatively affects these two interrelated factors. The Government should try to eliminate the causes of macroeconomic disequilibrium by corporatizing enterprises, imposing on them financial discipline, containing budget deficits, and controlling monetary aggregates.

6.14   SOEs are still operating because they continue to have access to credit without having to adjust to new economic conditions. This is seriously undermining the necessary fiscal and monetary adjustment and is the root cause of current macroeconomic disequilibrium. Although the budget deficit (narrowly defined) was about 11 percent of GDP in 1992, the consolidated public-sector deficit, which includes the borrowing requirements of the SOEs, is estimated to be substantially higher.

6.15   Another SOE-related factor that is likely to complicate fiscal policy is the collapse of enterprise profitability. The 1992 budget included 6 percent of revenue derived from the tax on enterprise profits, and the 1993 estimated budget includes a higher share. Given that their output is declining, it may not be realistic to expect such sources of funds from the enterprises in the short term.

---

[1]   See Chapter 7 on the "Financial Sector."

In 1991, before the breakup of the Soviet Union, their contribution to revenues was 5.3 percent of the total. This supports the recommendation that the Government should intensify its tax reform efforts to broaden the tax base and find alternative revenue sources.

PRICING POLICY AND DEMONOPOLIZATION

6.16   Monopoly power and market segmentation constrain reform. If productive enterprises are to be forced to behave efficiently in both resource use and investment policies, then they must face competitive pressure in markets with rational prices and hard-budget constraints. Demonopolization requires restructuring enterprises, breaking up segmented markets, and removing the numerous regulatory and trade barriers to new market entrants. International competition, combined with competitive factor markets, competitive markets for nontraded goods, and market clearing would create an efficient set of market prices in the absence of market failures. The highly concentrated industrial and market structure in Uzbekistan sustains vertical dependence which in turn inhibits the competitive pressure for cost minimization. The segmented market power of one or more firms so organized permits them to set prices at distorted levels.

6.17   What is the desirable sequencing of demonopolization, domestic price liberalization, and trade liberalization? Key to restructuring is removal of excess demand, hardening the budget constraint, and moving to a less concentrated and more competitive industrial structure facing a set of rational prices.

6.18   On one hand, the danger of liberalizing domestic prices but not imports, and delaying demonopolization, is that it would do little to force managers to reduce costs and improve efficiency through restructuring, and it would provide little incentive to banks to assess the creditworthiness of borrowing firms. On the other hand, several problems are associated with trade liberalization without demonopolization.   First, trade liberalization will do little to impose competitive pressure on the nontradeable sector. Aside from public utilities, the main nontradeables are transport, distribution, construction, and services. None of these except railways is a natural monopoly. Thus, these enterprises are clear candidates for privatization, and, where possible, it would be desirable that they be demonopolized before they are privatized.[2] Moreover, transport and many services are inputs into the production of tradeables. If they are not forced to become more efficient by demonopolization and exposure to competition by new entrants, the tradeable goods sector in Uzbekistan will remain at a competitive disadvantage.   Second, given the present structure of vertical integration and market segmentation, it may be hard to determine which lines of activities are profitable if they remain integrated. The signals for restructuring will be muted as internal cross-subsidization allows inviable units to survive. And third, concentrated industries are better placed to be the focus of interest groups that would attempt to lobby for protective tariffs or quotas and an undervalued exchange rate in order to protect inefficient production.

---

[2]   Evidence from transport liberalization in the United States and the Great Britain suggests that significant efficiency gains can be realized from increased competition. If foreign imports remain in the hands of monopoly distribution networks, trade liberalization will be seriously compromised.

B. THE ENABLING ENVIRONMENT FOR DEVELOPING THE PRIVATE SECTOR

PROPERTY RIGHTS AND ENTERPRISE GOVERNANCE

6.19   Uzbekistan has not established the foundation for a market-based economy yet: clear property and ownership rights, a supportive business environment, the application of commercial principles to productive enterprises whether or not state owned,[3] and accountability. Private-sector development, including privatization, will not succeed unless Uzbekistan designs and implements a policy aimed at the creation and maintenance of a system in which property rights are:

- Clearly defined

- Held, largely by private owners

- Used and transferred freely by such owners without unpredictable or arbitrary governmental intervention, but within a predictable regulatory framework

- Enforced by a neutral party, based on an effective judicial system and modern civil and commercial laws

- Determined and allocated by a policymaking authority that itself neither exercises nor enforces them.

6.20   This system is the foundation of a private sector. It does not exist in Uzbekistan and its emergence is constrained by vestiges of the old system and the absence of decisive steps leading to the creation of mechanisms to put such a system in place.

6.21   The second requirement for developing the private sector is the creation of a supportive business environment. Such an environment is shaped by a complex interaction of formal policies and laws, informal practices, institutions and infrastructure. A supportive business environment requires as a minimum stable rules, ease of business entry and exit, access to facilities and information, and a government policy aimed not at controlling private entrepreneurship but promoting it as an engine of growth. A supportive business environment also requires contestable markets.

6.22   The third requirement for a strong market economy is the application of commercial principles to enterprise governance. This requires providing managers with the right market incentives

---

[3]   An anomaly is the Uzbek reputation for enterprise and initiative as contrasted with the incipient reform program. In the bazaars of the former Soviet Union, Uzbek nationals were known for their trading and marketing skills. They are generally perceived to be good negotiators, possessed of an instinct for individual enterprise. These talents, said to have survived within the command economy, would now be expected to provide great impetus to the transformation of Uzbekistan. Yet, there is still not enough evidence in the country of such activity. Privately, many frustrated entrepreneurs argue that what is needed is massive deregulation and a cessation of arbitrary bureaucratic interference with private economic activity. If coupled with an orderly property rights regime, the skills of the traders and entrepreneurs could increase efficiency and productivity. While a latent talent is difficult to assess, additional work must be undertaken to explore how to encourage growth in the trades and services. These sectors could be the source of a considerable number of new jobs to compensate for losses in inefficient industry.

for success while also causing them to bear legal and financial liability for failure. Market rules and institutions for corporate finance, governance and capital markets are needed. Enterprise governance in Uzbekistan has changed somewhat since the breakup of the Union, but the reforms have not led to improved performance because changes were sometimes misconceived. A heavy structure of subsidies continues, managers bear little responsibility for enterprise debts, and hard budget constraints are rare.

THE LEGAL CONSTRAINTS

6.23   While the Government has enacted many laws and regulations that seek to develop a market-based economy, these measures do not provide the clarity, detail, or harmony required to support a clear property rights system--a fundamental requirement for a market economy. In many ways, the new legal measures actually prevent the emergence of market-based economic structures. There are several key weaknesses in the existing legal regime. A stable and known set of rules governing central issues such as asset transferability, investment, taxation and land is only beginning to emerge.

6.24   The Law on Property (31 October 1990), the Law on Enterprises (15 February 1991), and the Law on Entrepreneurship (15 February 1991) should be repealed and replaced by either a single piece of legislation or by new provisions in a Civil Code reformed to accommodate a market-based economy. Although these laws were amended in 1993, the amendments do not address or remedy the most serious problems which are:

* *Limitations on Property Rights*. All three laws subordinate private property rights to a list of undefined, general rights and interests of citizens, institutions, legal entities, and the state, which can and have been determined administratively by bureaucratic agencies (e.g., the numerous restrictions on transfer of housing). Since there are still many laws that are biased toward state interests, there is serious doubt on the boundaries of ownership rights, and some profiles and restrictions are continually imposed on private property rights by local authorities. The Civil Code should be substantially revised.

* *The Laws Do Not Recognize the Inviolability of Private Property or the Free Exercise of Property Rights by Private Owners*. The three laws reflect a fundamentally socialist view that all property rights belong primarily to the state, to be handed out as, when, and how the state so chooses. Many provisions are unclear or inappropriate. While stating who may own what and how, the laws are notable for what is not provided. Property rights essential to a free market economy are not fully developed, e.g., there is no clear right of a person or firm to acquire and alienate property, nor protection of contract rights; land ownership is unclear.

6.25   In addition to the confusion over property rights, there are gaps in the legal system. There is an absence of procedural rules, and transparency in resolution of disputes and recourse for arbitrary administerial acts. Subordinate legislative and related regulatory bodies in Uzbekistan often take away the property rights granted by the reform legislation. Regulatory bodies interpret the new legislation in ways that deprive new owners of the rights to use property in their best economic interest. Further restrictions exist because the laws give the workers' collectives extensive management rights and preferred rights to profits. Complex licensing, registration, and application procedures and increased fees contradict the policy underlying the reform towards a market-economy legislation.

Economic Legality

6.26   Laws and official documents are enacted frequently by different levels of government, but are not always coordinated and are rarely published in a systematic, official manner. It is often difficult to determine which laws are in force and which have been abrogated. Uniformity and consistency are nonexistent. Numerous enterprise managers, small businesses, and commodity-exchange brokers believe that they cannot keep pace with ever-changing economic legislation. In any event, they have little confidence that economic laws will be enforced uniformly and impartially where the enforcer is the single largest economic player.

Enforcement

6.27   Institutions for resolving civil disputes remain basically unchanged, although a new Arbitration Law is a welcome step. However, the institutional capacity for enforcing property rights of market participants is limited, and resources have not been allocated for the additional judicial personnel, facilities, and training necessary to support the new laws. Independent commercial arbitration has not yet been developed, and the Arbitration Law does not contain a provision for recognizing either arbitration agreements or their enforcement. Yet without an expeditious, fair, and neutral way to resolve disputes, there is unlikely to be the sort of trust necessary for the economically meaningful exercise of property rights in Uzbekistan.

REGULATORY BARRIERS TO ENTRY: ESTABLISHMENT OF NEW ENTERPRISES

6.28   Despite the Government's intentions to promote the development of the private sector over the past two years, the persistence of obstacles and constraints inhibits it. The most serious constraints are:

- Entry and exit rules

- Lack of access to commercial space

- Tax burden

- Financial constraints

- An absence of competition and state control over trade flows

- Lack of competition

- Limited access to business information and services and skills.

Entry and Exit

6.29   Despite recent legislation clarifying the basis for the creation of companies and partnerships, the actual registration of a new enterprise remains difficult. Extensive documentation is necessary, and finalization ultimately depends on the decisions of a local administrative committee (soviet) about whether (1) the intended business supports the social and economic goals of the community, and (2) the owners are fit to conduct the business. The economic actor is not free to choose in his own best economic interest. Rather, decisions are often based on informal incentives. Transparency is non-existent.

6.30   Most business activities require licenses (for example, wholesale trade, services, importing, and exporting). The staff of ministries and state trading organizations that grant licenses say that they must avoid overcapacity or "excessive" and "wasteful" competition. Thus, they routinely reject or delay licenses. The laws that require permits and licenses are straightforward and not always complex. However, these laws are at odds with legal procedures for obtaining them. These conflicts are typically resolved by a local Executive Committee's President who is also a deputy of the local soviet and, reportedly, they favor existing SOEs over new enterprises. The entire process reflects the perpetuation of a centrally planned system, in which individual initiatives, risk taking, and competition with SOEs are not permitted. Bureaucratic decisions preempt market mechanisms. The result is that Tashkent and other cities have no significant, legally legitimate private sector, and no examples of how private property rights can create efficiency and prosperity. Moreover, the license permit system also discourages competition, an essential requirement for a successful transition.

Office Space

6.31   Uzbekistan has no functional commercial real estate market. Desirable, available properties are typically controlled by local authorities and state enterprises. Even when leases are obtained, tenants have no assurance that they will be honored because most oblasts have no clear method of registration of title and thus an aggrieved tenant often has little basis for demanding continued occupancy. Further, most leases contain numerous restrictions, and are typically short term (one to three years). Subleasing is discouraged by high taxes on payments. Property rights in such leases are negligible and invariably non-transferable. At the same time, entrepreneurs and enterprise managers alike report significant underutilized space in the state enterprises. This space constitutes unused wealth, yet the enterprises have little incentive to divest.

6.32   The formulation of a real estate policy and program is necessary, to be undertaken in conjunction with the privatization program. Such a program would carefully consider the incentives/disincentives to segmentation of unutilized space (to take place at corporatization or privatization) for auction to the highest bidder (examples exist in Poland and the Czech and Slovak Republics). Ownership of space and land and means of transfer should be established at the same time. Transfer should be free and clear of all profile restrictions except generally applicable zoning and environmental regulations. Subleasing should be unrestricted.

6.33   Further actions that could be taken would be the acquisition of land and fixed assets by a state agency for the development of basic infrastructure and sale or long term lease (on commercial terms) to new private entrepreneurs. Other measures could include tax and/or other incentives for enterprises to sell, utilize, repair, or sublease existing unutilized space.

Tax Burden

6.34   The effective tax burden has become a significant constraint to the development of private businesses. The level and complexity of the present system of taxation make it very difficult for prospective new businesses to be established. Tax burden on enterprises in Uzbekistan is comparably high. For example, enterprises have to pay a social security tax amounting to 37 percent of the wage bill. The profit tax rates are between 15 and 35 percent. Furthermore, a 30 percent tax on amortization and a 6 percent resource tax for industrial enterprises on the use of electricity, fuel, etc., were introduced in January 1993. A 35 percent tax on hard currency proceeds was introduced in July 1993. In addition, registration fees for private enterprises were introduced in July 1992.

Financial Constraints

6.35   **Access to Credit.** New small and medium enterprises, not linked directly to large associations, have little access to credit. Credit in Uzbekistan has been allocated primarily through low-cost refinance credit from the Central Bank and the granting of credits by commercial banks to SOEs or to the banks' shareholders, which are primarily SOEs. The practical result is that small and medium private enterprises do not have access to credit unless it comes from an SOE. Unfortunately, the allocation of credit appears to be based on nonmarket factors--mainly on an enterprise's part ownership of a bank and personal contacts.

6.36   Term-credit facilities are essential for private development, since private capital remains limited. The Government could seek external assistance for studying and funding the development of at least one strong financial institution for catering to the needs of the private sector. This institution should then be well isolated from the liquidity needs of the public sector, and should focus on long-term investments and development (see Chapter 7).

6.37   **Financial Assistance.** The Fund of the Support of Entrepreneurship was established in 1991 under the auspices of the Union of Entrepreneurs. The Government has contributed 2 million rubles to it. According to the Union, the Fund is ineffective, since it has insufficient resources to support new enterprises.

6.38   **Collateral.** There is no mortgage market, nor any legal basis for secured lending. Consequently, new and newly privatized enterprises are at a distinct disadvantage in daily transactions. Although rural housing and a small share of rural land is private, an owner has no mechanisms for leveraging his assets, and a lender has no mechanisms for enforcing a mortgage. Moreover, since land is not being fully privatized (its use may be inherited and leased, but not sold), the value of a mortgage on an apartment, villa, or official space will always be volatile and, thus, risky. The problem is acute for small- to medium-size new enterprises.

State Control over Trade Flows

6.39   Private entrepreneurs and privatized enterprises invariably quote supply as one of their main problems. In part, this stems from the trade disruptions across the FSU. However, it is due also largely to the state's continued control over both domestic and external trade flows, which leaves little room for the private firms to compete and grow. Most output of national agricultural and manufacturing producers is reserved by "state order" to the state-controlled sector and its centralized procurement and distribution system. These state order shares still stand at 50 percent for fruit and vegetables, 75 percent for silk cocoons, and 80 percent for cotton and most other agricultural products (poultry, milk, leather hides, and so forth), despite a few reductions over the year (for vegetables, cotton, and silk). Much of the remaining output is used by the producers to procure equipment and additional inputs, primarily from state enterprises and concerns, thus reducing the availability of free tradeables further. Imports are also subject to large state orders, and private operators have limited direct access to the remaining external trade, except through Government-licensed barter trade with FSU countries.

6.40   Access to inputs is a serious problem because the state gives priority to its own enterprises. Private operators cannot secure reliable supplies, and pay prices at least twice as high outside the "state order." Newly privatized enterprises have more limited access to state supplies, even when they had access initially. Some state enterprises resist privatization because they would lose their supply or remain dependent on a monopoly supplier. Privatization will stall, or privatized firms may well be crowded off the market, under such conditions. To support private-sector growth and successful privatization, the Government should gradually relax and eventually eliminate the state order and procurement system, starting at the producers' level. At the same time, wholesale monopolies, such as Uzbeksavdo, should be fragmented to preserve fair prices and availability through competition.

6.41   Overall, the flow of supplies not controlled at some point by state entities is estimated at only 10-20 percent. Many of these private supplies were usefully channeled through the commodity exchanges in the major cities (see Box 6.1). Owing to new trade licensing requirements and taxes, however, exchange business has reportedly fallen sharply, and shifted primarily to barter in 1992.

Lack of Competition

6.42   Sourcing, trade, distribution, and related support services remain highly concentrated. The state's continued control over both domestic and external trade flows leaves little room for the private firms to compete and grow. For many prospective domestic and international investors, dealing with vertical integration and market segmentation and its inefficiencies and shortages is a strong deterrent to investment. A particular problem is undeveloped wholesale trade and trade services in Uzbekistan, particularly in food processing and common consumer goods. Without a dynamic competitive network of distributors, wholesalers, agents, and other middlemen, a market is unlikely to emerge. These actors provide the basis for the market to take over from the state order.

6.43   The so-called "black market" provides growing supplies of consumer goods. However, the continued ambiguity of the legal status of these activities has generated an emerging network of *ex* legal operations, which in turn discredit the private sector while depriving the Government of necessary tax revenue.

6.44   The new Enterprise Law of December 1992 contains a provision which is an incentive to continued vertical integration, market segmentation, and monopoly control. It provides that the shareholders or participants in a society

Box 6.1. Commodity Exchanges

Commodity exchanges in Uzbekistan could serve as important institutions in the transition to a market-based economy. While most exchanges are owned by SOEs, they engage in transactions outside the state order, providing a useful mechanism for private growth. They are essentially spot markets and some are attempting to establish their own insurance companies, banks, and dispute resolution mechanisms to facilitate transactions. Unfortunately, business has fallen by 80 percent since May 1992, when the Branch Ministries and State Trade Organizations imposed licensing requirements for buying and selling items--even items not subject to state orders. The exchanges now suffer from the recent Government practice of granting the local authorities and monopolistic trade organizations the right to license most transactions. Coupled with the currency-surrender requirements and increased taxes, the measures have led to a general decline in trade and the virtual elimination of trade for money on the exchange.

The Tashkent Commodity Exchange (reportedly the largest) is a closed joint stock company with 598 shareholders, approximately 80 percent of which are state-owned structures (that is, corporations that are at least partly privately owned), and 20 percent are individual brokers. The first trade was in June 1991. Trades previously were three times a week but are now down significantly. Most trades are barter arrangements. The Central Asian Association of Exchanges, headquartered in Tashkent, provides a database and clearing facilities for interrepublic trades. It has little experience in trading outside the FSU.

or partnership "will enjoy a right of priority to obtain products (services) manufactured (rendered) by the society and the partnership" (Part I, Chapter 2, paragraph 2). The provision also detracts from the independent identity of a company (vis-à-vis its shareholders), confuses creditor and shareholder rights, and encourages anti-competitive tying arrangements.

Business Information and Skills

6.45   The lack of information, accounting standards, and general business skills is a major barrier to the formation and success of private enterprise. Little printed material is available on market business practice. Educational institutions are rapidly changing their curricula, but lack of experienced teachers and social experience with market-based mechanisms will continue to impede private-sector development. The problem is manifest in the difficulties associated with the collection and transmission of information, the virtual absence of a corporate culture as understood even in the former socialist states of Central Europe, and a continuing mistrust of market mechanisms. Business information should be regarded as a critical element of the market infrastructure needed to encourage private sector development.

C. PRIVATIZATION

6.46   Privatization began later in Uzbekistan than in most other FSU countries (see Box 6.2). Since late 1991, the Supreme Soviet and the highest Government executives have shown determination, and broad plans for privatization have proceeded rapidly. However, an initial reliance on conservative policies, lack of institutional capacity, and the absence of a framework to promote private-sector development will curtail any economic benefits. The current program does not address the current problems of SOE governance. Based on its own and other countries' experience, Uzbekistan appears willing now to strengthen the design and implementation capacities of the program. With the experience of the past two years, a second generation of design issues has emerged for Uzbekistan to confront the importance of: transparency, dealing with the potential social costs of privatization, initiating programs for effective commercially based SOE governance and accountability, and establishing a post-privatization environment that stimulates competition, promotes equity, and inhibits concentration of ownership and economic power.

6.47   Privatization in Uzbekistan currently follows certain principles:

- For 1992-93, privatization efforts concentrate on small firms in trade, catering, services and local industry, with emphasis on those serving consumers;

- The program seeks to limit the dislocation of labor;

- Initiative of individual privatization action is left to collectives and managers;

- The state, through Uzgosfund, is to retain a significant equity percentage in medium and large enterprises;

- "Profile" requirements and restrictions on changing lines of business for long periods are imposed;

Box 6.2. Current Status of Privatization

Institutional Framework. A permanent committee was set up by Presidential Decree in February 1992 (and organized by resolution of the Cabinet of Ministers in August 1992) to participate in policy formulation, set procedures, prepare and implement privatization programs, and manage enterprises to be privatized. The Committee for Governing State Property and Privatization (CGSPP) reports directly to the Supreme Soviet and Cabinet of Ministers. In principle, associations and ministries must accept its privatization policies, but its authority outside of agreed-upon programs remains vague. CGSPP has territorial branches and a staff of 500. The local branches of the CGSPP work with the executive committees of local soviets, which can initiate privatization of communal property. For assets with a book value of less than 5 million rubles, applications can be approved locally; for larger transactions, the local branches act as agents for headquarters. However, according to the Privatization Law, provincial and municipal authorities are to approve the privatization of enterprises allocated to them, and they have already tended to control privatization, particularly by extending leases to smaller enterprises.

CGSPP put together a commission to evaluate proposals and see whether they conform to the Law, to assess the business plan for the enterprise, and to value property and payout conditions of sale. Terms of up to five years are possible, but with high inflation, the Commission tries to limit terms to less. The commission also checks on the source of finance and on the willingness of banks to continue lending to the privatized enterprise. In many cases, the state retains a shareholding, sometimes a controlling one. The commission presents its plan to the CGSPP for approval. The final price cannot be lower than the initial valuation of the commission.

INFORMATION ON PRIVATIZATION OF ENTERPRISES AND ORGANIZATIONS IN UZBEKISTAN IN 1992-1993

(by number of enterprises)

Total	Planned to be privatized	Number of applications for Privatization				Number of enterprises privatized			
		total	joint stock/ collective	private/ family	leasing	Total	joint stock/ collective	private/ family	leasing
76502	22285	12714	1681	10356	157	9645	1286	8298	53

Source: The Committee for Governing State Property and Privatization (July 1, 1993).

- SOEs are leased or sold (cheaply) to the workforce (often as a collective), rather than divested through an auction; or a voucher system[4];

- There are no provisions for widespread public ownership.

---

[4] Some of the very small service establishments are to be given away to their proprietors, who, it is argued, have long made personal investments in their businesses.

THE CURRENT PROGRAM

6.48   Uzbekistan's program for destatization and privatization contemplates a gradual, case by case, approach to transformation with significant state equity to remain in most medium and large enterprises.[5] All property has been divided into republic property and local (or communal) property. Some of the local enterprises apparently are large (defined as having net assets in excess of 5 million rubles (as of 1991); no classification by number of employees exists, though most are small. All Republic and local property is included in the program. The republic CGSPP has the authority to transform all SOEs whose assets exceed 5 million rubles, while its local offices handle the smaller properties.

6.49   SOEs have been classified into five groups by Cabinet of Minister Resolutions. These are:

(1)   Trade

(2)   Construction and Transport

(3)   Material Supply, Food and local Industry

(4)   Public Facilities

(5)   Others.

The programs and their status for 1992-93, as of July 1, 1993 are set forth in Table 6.2.

6.50   The Government has stated that enterprises in sectors that have important forward linkages with the rest of the economy (such as mining, metallurgy, air and rail transport, pharmaceuticals, and other technology-intensive industries) would not be privatized. This means that a large portion of SOEs will remain in public hands for years to come. Unfortunately, no comprehensive program of reform exist for these critical enterprises.

Methods of Privatization

6.51   The Law permits virtually any party to initiate a privatization, but subject always to the assent of the existing collectives and guaranteed social protection (basically job security). To date, virtually all privatization and destatization has been initiated by collectives or, in the case of very small enterprises, individuals or families which were already engaged in the business. Most of the activity has centered on the small enterprises which have less than 5 million rubles net worth. This activity has been conducted by the local CGSPPs with a considerable role for the local governmets. For example, of the total 9,645 enterprises privatized as of July 1, 1993, 8,298 were transferred by local CGSPPs to

---

[5]   The present program is authorized by the Law on Destabilization and Privatization of November 1991 as amended in May 1993, and implemented by several Resolutions of the Cabinet of Ministries and the CGSPP. Article of the Law confuses destabilization (defined as transformation of SOEs into collective, leased, associations, and companies which are not the state property) and privatization (defined as the acquisition of State property by physical persons and non-state entities). As in the Property Law, the difference between the character of the owner (state, mixed or private) and the organization of ownership (corporate, collective) is confused. This definitional confusion undermines the process.

individuals and families. Of the remainder, only 53 privatizations were completed by the republic, central CGSPP which during the period received only 380 applications (i.e., from 380 enterprises with net worth over 5 million rubles as of 1991 (see Box 6.2 and Table 6.2).

Table 6.2. Privatization in Uzbekistan
(as of July 1993)

	Total	Planned	No. of Applications for Privatization				No. of Enterprises Privatized			
			Total	Joint Stock/ Collective	Private/ Family	Leasing	Total	Joint Stock/ Collective	Private/ Family	Leasing
Trade	10,969	4,466	2,242	1,054	1,176	12	1,246	674	556	16
Construction, Transport	740	187	54	54			3	3		
Material Supply, Food and Local Industry	48,716	6,592	5,740	272	5,426	42	5,623	618	4,983	22
Public Facilities	15,598	1,070	4,408	544	3,782	82	2,654	231	2,412	11
Other	479	334	270	122	140	8	119	35	84	
Total	76,502	22,285	12,714				9,645			

Source: CGSPP and Bank staff calculations.

6.52   The steps to privatization are numerous, complex and time-consuming with repetitive approvals by often large interministerial committes. The steps are as follows:

(a)   Workers' Collective of SOE calls meeting and by 2/3 initiates (or approves a third party's suggestions for) transformation and submits application to local CGSPP.

(b)   Local CGSPP determines whether application is proper (i.e., SOE not on list of companies or sectors not to be privatized) and whether it should be referred to CGSPP in Tashkent for process. (Most applications are handed locally.) CGSPP forms a Privatization Committee, which if the SOE is large, can be up to 12 members drawn from different ministries and agencies.

(c)   Collective prepares data for CGSPP and CGSPP then prepares privatization plan with proposed concessions and shareholding split (usually 60 percent collective and up to 40 percent retained by state) or leasing terms.

(d)   Two-thirds of Privatization Committee must approve the CGSPP plan.

(e)   If plan approved, privatization documentation prepared by CGSPP and submitted for approval to Committee and experts selected by the Committee and CGSPP. Agreements and certificates are then issued.

(F)   The SOE forms the new entity and transfers property on shares. New entity concludes new collective agreement.

6.53   For privatizations to date in the form of joint stock companies, a majority of the shares have been registered to individuals. The state shares are formally registered to Uzgosfund (see discussion below) which does not exercise substantive management influence. The state's interest continues to be exercised through means other than share ownership, such as allocation of credit and control of trade and distribution. The joint stock companies have been closed form. In such cases, there is no transferability of shares outside the pool of existing shareholders. Formally, the general assembly of workers has the authority to elect the management (previously appointed directly by the relevant ministries). But in practice, state organizations, through the continued domination of distribution of goods and services, continue to play a role in management selection. Thus, the transformation structure closely resembles (one manager said he saw no difference) the old forms.

6.54   The mandate to hold the state's shares in the privatization program (and responsibility for stock exchange development) was transferred to Uzgosfond, part of the Ministry of Finance, in November 1992. Uzgosfond is represented on the board of 10 enterprises, but this number will increase dramatically as privatization speeds up. Uzgosfond will have to manage many companies, deal with corporate restructuring issues, and prepare some companies for privatization. Uzgosfond, however, needs substantial assistance to fulfill its responsibilities efficiently. It lacks the capacity to monitor and manage the companies it partially owns.

Deficiencies in the Methods

6.55   The method of privatization to date has not addressed the most serious problems posed by the organization of the SOEs. It does not subject them to the discipline of owners motivated by market incentives and does not provide the governance needed for a successful transition. The current methods do not result in meaningful management reform. Also, by denying workers and managers a fundamental ownership right--the right of asset transferability--the method denies the owners the right of private ownership of equity capital. Hence, without such full rights, there is not discipline of capital. Finally, the structures of the old branch ministries are repeated in the new Associations.

6.56   Under central planning, managers had little opportunity to build up experience in managing their supply, marketing, finances, or even independent accounting. Current staff alone can seldom meet all future management, capital, technical, and market needs. Without outside help, they will not be able to cope in a market-based economy, and staff may (ironically) suffer greater job losses. Even enterprises with dynamic management will not be able to benefit from privatization (through, for example, technology and supply sources) and to broaden financial support to invest and grow. Moreover, the interests of current managers and staff will conflict at times with the enterprise's longer-term survival and growth. For instance, staff tend to focus on higher salaries, not reinvesting surpluses, and managers may unduly favor a form of privatization that offer the best chances to keep their jobs. Priority to staff may also appear unfair: the rest of the population may resent the privileges given to staff. Privatization should shift from transfers to staff to competitive sales, both to improve enterprise support bases and to ensure equitable returns to the public purse.   Staff could propose, but not decide on, forms of privatization, with a share price discount of up to 30 percent to staff.

6.57   The dependencies of the privatized firms on the old vertical systems of control and market segmentation have resulted in these enterprises' continuing linkage in the new Associations. These Associations very much resemble the old branch ministries and perpetuate their non-competitive feature, keeping enterprise managers dependent on a small number of customers and suppliers and soft credit, all orchestrated from the top and usually by actions not motivated by economic efficiency.

6.58   The current enterprise reform program is notable for its lack of a corporatization program for SOEs remaining in state ownership.   Corporatization is an essential first step to delineate property rights and liabilities, clarify the enterprises' legal status, determine the rights and responsibilities of the managers and those who exercise state's ownership rights, and install accountability for the enterprises' finances and performance.

6.59   The small-scale privatization program, while picking up momentum, has not achieved the visible changes that such programs caused in Poland, Hungary, and China.   The key problems have been the imposition of "profiles" on the enterprises (discussed below) and the highly confused structure of private rights in the small enterprise sector.   The large Trading Association controls the distribution of goods; the municipalities control the land and other real estate; transferability is prohibited or severely limited; and change of use or product is also prevented.   These restrictions give small-scale private investors little cause for confidence.   Purchasers of small shops and service businesses find themselves tied down for years with little prospect for innovation or profit.

Obligations of Privatized Enterprises

6.60   The existing law encourages agreements to preserve enterprise profiles, for example, output, delivery to certain clients, jobs, social protection, and facilities.   However, the rationale for privatization is that enterprises become more efficient without interference, within market competition and conducive sectoral policies.   Imposing restrictive obligations will reduce benefits, diminish the property rights of the new owners, and make the enterprise difficult to monitor equitably.

Box 6.3 Leasing or Transfer to Collectives - a Weak Form of Privatization

Many privatizations so far have been leases, generally in favor of the staff collective. In other countries, however, such an approach has been disappointing. Leaseholders (particularly as collectives) are far less motivated than individual or corporate buyers to invest in and maintain the plant. They pursue independent interests, while remaining dependent on the state and may, for instance, try to delay the competitive sale of the enterprise. Leases should thus be a fall-back solution, only if competitive sale is impossible at an acceptable price.

INSTITUTIONAL CONSTRAINTS

Administrative Capacity

6.61   Despite recruitment efforts, CGSPP's staff is still relatively small and lacks experience with privatization and private enterprises.   It remains a passive processor of applications rather than an active designer and implementor of action policy. It is staffed and organized along enterprises' sectors. It has yet to affirm its authority in investigating and settling high-level issues, such as the privatization of national wholesale trade.

Lack of Domestic Private Capital

6.62   The accumulation of private capital is limited, though perhaps underestimated. This shortage of capital in the private sector will curtail competition, and thus the pace or equity of privatization. If enterprises are priced close to their real long-term market value, privatization could stall. With large discounts it may be viewed as selling off public wealth and being overgenerous to foreign investors. These (and other) constraints on privatization could be overcome, however, through a voucher scheme (see Box 6.4).

Box 6.4. Early Experience in Voucher Schemes

Vouchers distributed to the people for buying state property have been planned or initiated in some Eastern European countries. In the Czech and Slovak Republics, Poland, and Russia, only shares in the large State enterprises may be acquired with vouchers. In Lithuania and Mongolia, vouchers can also be used to buy real estate or small enterprises. In Hungary, they are limited to meeting restitution claims.

These schemes seek primarily to increase the speed and equity of privatization, by supplementing the lack of domestic private capital and the underdevelopment of stock markets. Early results are encouraging. In Lithuania, for instance, voucher subscription was virtually universal, and some 600 large and medium enterprises and 1,300 small firms had been privatized after about one year. Even so, difficulties in designing and implementing these schemes had generally been underestimated. In the Czech and Slovak Republics for example, there are 600 intermediate funds for investing in enterprises. Set up with little initial regulation, they have mobilized about 70% of the vouchers, sometimes by promising high returns. There is now real concern that many will fold.

Privatization through vouchers does little to improve efficiency of large enterprises in the short term. A lead shareholder able to meet the enterprise needs (for example, investment, technology, exports, and so forth) is often warranted. In the Czech and Slovak Republics, vouchers have been combined with foreign direct investment in large enterprises, and on average 62% of the shares of enterprises in the first batch were put up for sale through vouchers. The Russian program contains provisions for seeking strategic investors and for selling up to 35% of an enterprise's shares against vouchers.

Contrary to some fears, issuing vouchers might not reduce the state cash returns from sales. Without vouchers, prices of shares would be lower, since they would reflect the shortfall of private capital available. As long as the amount of vouchers issued does not exceed this shortfall, cash payments from domestic buyers may be maintained, while the additional demand in the form of vouchers should increase the share prices paid by foreign investors. Issuing vouchers may, however, worsen inflation. The trading of vouchers as liquidities could be expected to develop during the lag between their distribution and the sale of enterprise shares. Even if this lag is shortened, many recipients are likely to sell them for cash to fulfill more immediate consumption needs. Even if voucher trading is restricted, the sudden increase

---

D. RECOMMENDATIONS

LEGISLATION

6.63   To put into place the minimum requirements for a private sector, new laws or major amendments to existing legislation are required in the following areas:

- A revision of the Civil Code and/or new laws governing property (real, personal, and intellectual) contracts (including leases), and secured transactions (pledges)

- Company law (the new Enterprise law could be amended)

- Accounting standards, with particular attention to standards applicable to SOEs

- Intellectual property

- Foreign Investment Law

- Securities

- Bankruptcy

- Commercial dispute resolution mechanisms.

THE REGULATORY REGIME

6.64   A regulatory framework to encourage and support private-sector development requires efforts in:

- Rationalizing and harmonizing existing legislative and legal reform measures

- Deregulating licenses, permits, and approvals

- Formulating and enacting legislative and regulating guidelines for contracts, the recording of individual, business, and creditor property rights, including personal and intellectual property, bankruptcy and secured transactions, negotiable instruments, real estate

- Disseminating information on the reform measures, including the establishment of a legal database and regular publication of business-related legal information

- Training legislative and regulatory staff members to draft and harmonize laws

- Establishing mechanisms for enforcement

- Training a core of lawyers and judges for the new commercial arbitration and bankruptcy courts

- Identifying training needs of governmental agencies in business law

- Providing support to existing training centers and academic institutions in teaching business law.

REVISING THE PRIVATIZATION LAW

Fuller Privatization

6.65   Prudent initial policies must now be upgraded to reap the full economic benefits of privatization. This calls first for revising the 1991 Privatization Law and the implementing resolutions as follows:

- The scope of the program should be broadened to include the large enterprises, transport, telecommunications, agriculture, and all other productive enterprises.

- The priority given to enterprise staff, particularly collectives, must be de-emphasized. Decisions about the form of privatization belong not to the staff, but to the state. Preemptive acquisition rights of staff should be limited to 30 percent of enterprise value and voting shares; staff discounts should also be limited to about 30 percent. Shares should be to individuals, not to collectives, and ought to be fully transferable.

- The full, competitive sale through various techniques of enterprises should be the norm. Leases should only be a fall-back solution. Prior to sale, however, all large enterprises should become stock companies, and monopolies should be broken up.

- Conditions imposed subsequent to transformation should be removed or strictly limited.

- A comprehensive program for strengthening enterprise governance and accountability is needed.

IMPROVING INSTITUTIONAL AND FINANCING CAPABILITIES

CGSPP

6.66   In order to privatize enterprises effectively, the Government must reassert CGSPP's central privatization responsibility. The privatization of all large enterprises should be conducted by CGSPP, with the operating support of local authorities (for example, enterprise valuing).   Small enterprises could be privatized locally, according to common guidelines issued by CGSPP, and subject to selective, primary ex-post control by CGSPP. Generally, CGSPP should be clearly responsible for making decisions on the forms of privatization on the state's behalf, and for coordinating all privatization issues. CGSPP should also complement its staffing, and concentrate on strengthening its functional capabilities and procedures for selecting forms of privatization and searching for partners.

6.67   To achieve rapid and equitable privatization, CGSPP could also prepare a simple mass voucher scheme for supplementing the shortage of domestic private capital. The proportion of shares of large enterprises to be sold against vouchers should leave room for attracting qualified partners as leading shareholders. Preferably only eligible funds would be allowed to purchase shares with vouchers on behalf of the recipients.

Uzgosfund

6.68   To exercise the state's ownership rights and bring enterprises to commercial accountability, Uzgosfund must begin programs of active participation in enterprise management with a view to further marketing the segmentation and the creation of capable accountable enterprise management. It should turn its attention to the constraints imposed on transformed firms, removing profiles and restrictions on asset transferability.

E. TECHNICAL ASSISTANCE NEEDS

TO SUPPORT PRIVATIZATION

6.69   Substantial technical assistance is needed to realize the full benefits of privatization, and continuous field expertise and know-how will be necessary for adapting privatization policy to national conditions. Technical assistance could thus cover:

- Long-term residential advisors in privatization policies, including forms of privatization and voucher schemes, for the CGSPP and a pilot local authority (such as the Tashkent municipality) along with study tours and round-tables for relevant international exchanges

- Long-term residential advisors to the CGSPP for privatization operations (partner search and enterprise valuation), with supporting short-term consulting services (foreign partner search, technical negotiations, and model contracts and bidding procedures), and microcomputer systems (enterprise database).

TO SUPPORT PRIVATE-SECTOR DEVELOPMENT

6.70   There is need for broad technical assistance, covering new legal and economic policies and structures. Such assistance should supply high-level experience in economic transition policies, and should combine:

- Long-term residential legal advisor(s) for law drafting and on-the-job training, and short-term experts for training trainers and legal staff

- Long-term residential foreign investment advisor(s) for policy formulation, promotion, and on-the-job training, and investment forums in relevant countries

- Long-term residential economic policy advisor(s) for formulating market reforms and providing on-the-job training, and short-term experts to help set up a representative, independent Chamber of Commerce and for broader, regular training events.

F. FOREIGN DIRECT INVESTMENT

6.71   The Government of Uzbekistan wants to promote foreign direct investment (FDI), which, so far, has been insignificant. Most has come through new joint ventures; roughly 400 such ventures were registered as of December 1992. The challenge for Government is how to balance its open policy toward FDI with overall economic reform. At the moment, both approaches seem to be inconsistent.

FOREIGN INVESTMENT LAW

6.72   Though containing many desirable liberal provisions, the new law remains vague or silent on several matters (for example, access to foreign exchange, redemption rates, the modality for profit remittances, expatriate taxation, price controls and quotas, and so forth). It provides for discretionary tax rebates, which are likely to be called upon given the high tax rates. Disputes must be settled in local courts, which have no experience in FDI. (Uzbekistan has not yet adhered to the usual international arbitration conventions.) It does not specify the critical foreign investment promotion, registration, and licensing modalities necessary.

6.73   Serious foreign investors will be sensitive to the overall regulatory framework, and will be deterred by customs procedures, local travel restrictions, and numerous other administrative (sometimes irrelevant) controls.

6.74   Removal of existing references to corporate formation would avoid any confusion about the formation, governance, and legislation of Uzbek juridical entities with foreign participation relative to those that are wholly Uzbek. It would also prevent the formation of companies with foreign participation whose sole purpose is to obtain more favorable legal treatment but not to engage in true economic activity.

6.75   Other issues merit re-examination. First, what incentives are necessary to attract foreign investment, and how should they be implemented (primarily tax issues)? Second, the foreign investment law should address and permit widespread foreign participation in privatization, limiting involvement narrowly or perhaps only to "strategic" sectors such as defense. Third, the foreign investment law should provide the "modern traditional" assurances for expropriated property, which would ensure "prompt, adequate, and effective" compensation.

6.76   The Government would benefit from technical assistance in FDI policy and strategy for implementing a review of (1) the strengths and constraints of the existing legal and institutional framework and (2) linkages and consistency with the privatization program.

CHAPTER 7

THE FINANCIAL SECTOR

7.1   In a market economy, the financial system provides a mechanism for mobilizing domestic savings and allocating credit to its most efficient uses. Uzbekistan must establish an efficient financial system to support the emergence and growth of a vibrant private sector. However, given the radical nature of the adjustments required, the challenges that confront the Government in converting from a command to a market-based financial system are daunting. Uzbekistan currently has few of the financial institutions, markets, and instruments that characterize a market-based financial system. Moreover, as in other FSU republics, reform in the financial sector must proceed in a difficult and uncertain macroeconomic environment. Since nominal interest rates have not been adjusted to reflect inflation, holding financial assets is becoming less and less attractive. Inflation is rapidly eroding the size of the financial system, with holdings of ruble balances as a percentage of GDP down from 23 percent in March 1992 to 19 percent at the end of March 1993. As financial institutions would seek to adopt rational profitability criteria in lending to their clients, they will confront an enterprise sector that is moving slowly through a difficult period of restructuring. Pressure from the Government to continue to lend to nonviable enterprises to support their operations during the transitional period is strong. The risks of undermining the solvency of the banks, and precipitating a collapse of the financial system, are high.

A. THE SETTING FOR SECTORAL REFORM

THE FINANCIAL SYSTEM OF THE FORMER CENTRALLY PLANNED ECONOMY

7.2   The extent of reform and transition required in the financial sector of Uzbekistan can be gauged from its condition before independence. Under the centrally planned system that existed prior to 1988, financial strategy was made in Moscow, and resources were mobilized and allocated according to the central plan. Uzbekistan's financial sector comprised the regional branches of the Soviet banks situated in Moscow--Gosbank (Central Bank), the Savings Bank (Sberbank), the Construction Bank (Promstroibank), the Agricultural Bank (Agroprombank), and the Foreign Trade Bank (Vneshtorgbank).

7.3   Tax revenue and financial resources were channelled from Uzbekistan to Moscow, which then amalgamated these resources with those generated by the other republics. A share of these financial resources was channelled back to Uzbekistan primarily through the Uzbekistan branch of Gosbank. The fiscal resources that flowed from the central budget to the Uzbekistan budget then went directly to state enterprises throughout the republic.

7.4   The regional branch of Gosbank in Uzbekistan used resources from its headquarters in Moscow (as well as some enterprise deposits) to grant credits to enterprises. While major investments were financed primarily from the central and Uzbekistan budgets, credits from Gosbank were granted to enterprises that required short-term working capital. The Uzbekistan Foreign Trade Bank and the sectoral banks also granted credits to enterprises to support investment (long-term credits) and trade.

Box 7.1. Uzbekistan: Present Financial System

Institutional Structure

A move to a two-tier banking system began in 1988. The Central Bank (called the State Bank until September 1992) was placed at the hub of a financial system comprising large joint-stock sectoral banks, the Savings Bank, and other commercial banks. This new structure was confirmed in the Banking Law passed in February 1991. Since then, several new nonbank intermediaries have emerged--primarily insurance companies--and an embryonic commodity and stock exchange has been established. The present structure of the banking system can be seen from the following table:

Structure of the Banking System[a]
in millions of rubles

Type of Bank	No. of Banks	No. of Branches	Total Assets	Total Loans	Total Deposits	Capital
Central Bank	1	13	179,080	3,936	2,117	2,692
Sectoral Banks	4					
Agro-Industrial Bank	1	181	71,329	55,632	15,110	1,476
Industrial-Building Bank	1	58	80,606	54,813	20,525	2,045
Savings Bank	1	1,814	1,052	-	21,127	150
National Bank	1	8	1,540	25	2,107	110
Commercial Banks	20	n.a.	5,881	2,405	6,178	470

Source: The Central Bank of Uzbekistan

[a] As of October 1, 1992.

The Central Bank. In March 1992, the statute of the Central Bank was approved. This institution is responsible for formulating monetary policy, providing prudential control of the banking system, issuing currency, and operating the payments system. The Central Bank continues to serve as a domestic financial intermediary, siphoning off 70% of the deposits of the Savings Bank and resources from the other banks by way of reserve requirements--20% on demand deposits, 17% on term deposits of less than one-year maturity, and 15% on term deposits of maturity longer than one year. The Central Bank then channels these resources back to commercial banks for up to one year (currently at a rediscount rate of 15%, but which can be as high as 40%). In principle, the Central Bank can influence monetary conditions through its rediscount operations and reserve requirement policy. However, because Uzbekistan is a member of the ruble zone, the current ruble money supply is determined by the magnitude of cash received from the Russian Central Bank and the cash trade surplus with members of the FSU. In addition, inflation is determined by the direct pricing decisions of the Government and by the rate of inflation in the rest of the FSU. Given that the National Bank for Economic Activity holds the Government's international reserves, the Central Bank cannot use them to manage exchange rate and monetary policy. Thus, the scope for monetary policy is quite narrow, and will remain so as long as Uzbekistan remains in the ruble zone.

Box 7.1 (cont.)

The Agro-Industrial Bank (Uzagroprombank). As with the Industrial-Building Bank, the Agro-Industrial Bank was made a joint-stock commercial bank in 1991. It has a capital of 1.5 billion rubles and almost 4,000 staff employed in an extensive branch network--176 branches--throughout Uzbekistan. However, it is now owned by Government ministries and other state-owned entities. The bank still retains a link with the Russian Agro-Industrial Bank through cross-ownership of stock. Under the former system, it had been a specialized bank. And, despite changing its status, it still concentrates its lending in the agricultural sector and related agroindustry. About 60% of the bank's resources are obtained from the Central Bank at the discount rate, and the rest from the population at 12 to 13% interest rate. Due to its extensive branch network, the Agro-Industrial Bank is starting to compete with the Savings Bank in mobilizing household deposits. The bank lends a small fraction (up to one-fifth) of these deposits in the interbank market to the Russian Agro-Industrial Bank and to Uzbeki commercial banks, at 20%. On the assets side, 80% of its portfolio consists of loans to state enterprises at very low rates. The rest of the loans are made to associations and small businesses. According to Central Bank regulations, the bank must charge an average margin (between borrowing and lending rates) of 3 to 4% on its loans. However, on individual loans, it can charge margins as high as 30%, based on the riskiness of the loan. Although, in theory, the bank is free to make its own lending decisions, in practice there seems to be substantial amount of Government interference. But, given the influence of the Government, the bank also expects to be bailed out in case of difficulty.

The Industrial-Building Bank (Uzpromstroybank). This bank, with over 2 billion rubles in capital, concentrates its lending in industrial and construction-related activities throughout the country and has 57 branches to support its activities. It is also involved in export/import financing. It became a joint-stock commercial bank in April 1991 but is still owned by various state entities. Together with the Agro-Industrial Bank, the two banks account for well over 90% of credit channelled to the enterprise sector. The bank receives almost all of its funding from the Central Bank and the Savings Bank, and lends almost exclusively to state enterprises. Its deposit and lending rate structure is similar to that of the Agro-Industrial Bank. While the bank is said to be operating according to market principles, it continues to lend also at the urging of ministries. Accordingly, the bank also expects Government backing if it runs into financial difficulties.

The Savings Bank (Uzsberbank). This bank has an extensive branch network throughout Uzbekistan (1,574 branches). Ownership of the bank has been retained by the state. It is the country's main mobilizer of household deposits (guaranteed by the state), a role that has not changed since its independence from the Soviet Savings Bank in early 1991. The bank pays 3% on demand deposits and up to 12% on term deposits. Reportedly, withdrawing large sums of deposits is not easy and may involve long delays. As already noted, the Savings Bank is required to pass on 70% of its deposits to the Central Bank. It on-lends the remainder of its resources to other banks and enterprises, as well as to the household sector, primarily in the form of housing construction loans. An amount of 7.8 billion rubles of the assets of the Savings Bank, formerly transferred to the Soviet Savings Bank in Moscow, has not been repatriated to Uzbekistan. This issue was discussed during the recent international debt agreement with Russia, and a decision was reached to defreeze a large portion of these assets.

National Bank for Foreign Economic Affairs. This bank was established in October 1991 as a joint-stock commercial bank. Its function is to undertake international financial business on behalf of the Government (export/import financing, foreign currency trading, and so forth), and it currently holds the foreign currency reserves of the public sector. It has recently been expanding both its branch network and its staff, and was converted into a state bank. This bank is the primary point of contact for foreign financial institutions that wish to provide external financing for the country. It conducts business (borrowing and lending) in both dollars and rubles. Dollar deposits pay dollar interest of LIBOR plus a few percentage points. Its lending (both dollar and ruble) is directed primarily at state enterprises. It does not mobilize deposits from households except for dollar deposits. Although staff are well trained, lending decisions appear to be made according to pre-set priorities that are not necessarily consistent with market criteria.

Box 7.1 (cont.)

Other Commercial and Cooperative Banks. Uzbekistan has 34 other joint-stock commercial banks. All of them have been registered since 1990. Most are owned by ministries, unions, and state enterprises, although some foreign capital has begun to flow into the banking sector in the form of joint ventures. These banks have begun to take deposits from both households and enterprises in competition with the larger sectoral banks. The bulk of their lending goes to state enterprises--in many instances to those entities that own them--at substantially lower rates than those of other borrowers. One wholly privately owned bank has recently been registered, capitalized by an Uzbeki entrepreneur and his family. He intends to create a large bank with multiple branches. It would lend predominantly to the emerging private sector. The main constraint against its establishment has been the availability of property for the main branch.

Other Institutions and Markets. A commodity exchange and a stock exchange have recently been established by the same company, capitalized by a mix of state enterprises and private entrepreneurs. The commodity exchange has now been trading for several months and is increasing its trading activity. The stock exchange has just begun to trade on the basis of the stocks of about 40 listed companies. There are 370 licensed commodity brokers and 120 stock brokers. Total stock-market capitalization and turnover are 800 million rubles and 0.125%, respectively. Trading currently takes place only every other Tuesday, and prices have reportedly fluctuated significantly. The commodity market is more active, with trading taking place every week. Insurance business is dominated by a state insurance company, which offers property, life, animal, and agricultural insurance. There are also 40 small private insurance companies (20 domestic and 20 foreign-based) but they have an insignificant share of the market, since they do not deal with agriculture or individuals. The state insurance company is required to invest its reserves (a not significant 300 million rubles in 1991) with the Agro-Industrial or Industrial-Building Banks as deposit or equity. There are no private pension funds.

7.5   Fundamentally, banks played a passive role in the intermediation process. For instance, they did not perform a credit analysis of their customers, as their counterparts would in a market economy. Rather, the central planning process dictated the volume and pattern of lending regardless of the solvency or viability of the borrowing enterprise. Furthermore, whereas monetary and prudential authorities in a market economy typically use market-based instruments (open-market operations and interest-rate mechanisms) and a well-defined regulatory and supervisory framework to influence the lending behavior of banks--in terms of both loan volume and its allocation--the central planning process implied a direct intervention in the credit decision.

THE TRANSITION TO THE CURRENT SYSTEM: MOBILIZING AND ALLOCATING RESOURCES

7.6   With inflation repressed and interest rates controlled by a centralized structure, Uzbekistan's former financial system could not mobilize and allocate resources efficiently. By March 1992, the ratio of personal and enterprise deposits with respect to GDP was almost 17 percent (see Table 7.1); this ratio declined abruptly over the year, reaching 10 percent as of end of March 1993 owing to high inflation rates, low real rates, and decline in the level of economic activity. (Box 7.1 provides an account of the changes in the institutional structure of the sector.)

7.7   Despite the partial elimination of central planning and the existence of other reform measures, the effects of the old command structure continue to be felt. An important institutional constraint against mobilizing resources in Uzbekistan is the role of the Savings Bank as the main depositor for household savings, without enough competition from other banks (see table in Box 7.1). Moreover, highly negative interest rates in real terms have not stimulated the mobilization process. As is shown in

Table 7.1, the cash/deposit ratio has been increasing steadily in 1992. This trend is not likely to reverse itself in the near future unless positive real rates are established.

7.8   Financial resources in Uzbekistan continue to be *allocated* through nonmarket mechanisms to state enterprises at highly negative real interest rates. Furthermore, state enterprises are borrowing for working capital. They are not making fixed investments and their output is declining.   Enterprises are financing current expenditures and hence possibly losses. Given that current expenditures do not generate future income, the ability of enterprises to repay their debts is questionable.   However, inflation is continuously eroding the real value of bank assets and liabilities, thereby reducing the real size of potential portfolio problems and the potential budgetary costs of financial restructuring.

Table 7.1
Monetary Indicators[1]
(1992-3)
(million rubles)

	Mar 1992	Jun 1992	Dec 1992	Mar 1993
1. Cash held by population	14450	26080	96784	207637
2. Personal deposits	18775	20412	23882	45425
3. Total deposits of enterprises & organizations	21856	30277	141003	183388
Total (1+2+3)	55081	76769	261669	436450
Retail price index (Mar92=100)	100	135	649	941

(as percent of GDP[2])

	Mar 1992	Jun 1992	Dec 1992	Mar 1993
1. Cash held by population	6.0	7.0	6.2	9.2
2. Personal deposits	7.8	5.5	1.5	2.0
3. Total deposits of enterprises	9.1	8.1	9.1	8.1
Total (1+2+3)	23.0	20.5	16.8	19.3

Source: Central Bank of Uzbekistan, Goskomprognostat and Bank staff calculations.
[1]   End of period.
[2]   Ratios of money components to GDP are calculated by $(M_i/P_j)/(GDP/P_{avg})$, where M_i is money component i; and P_j is retail price at time j; and P_{avg} is an average retail price.

B. SECTORAL REFORM: BACKGROUND ISSUES

7.9   Financial institutions in Uzbekistan are not currently in a position to allocate resources or to support the privatization and revitalization of existing enterprises efficiently. Today, the financial system is making loans to enterprises that may not be viable in the long run. It is doing so in the absence of sound financial information, but in the face of political pressures and an ownership structure in which much of the bank lending goes to enterprises and corporations that own the banks. Moreover, the financial infrastructure is inadequate. *The legal codes, enforcement mechanisms, and the payment, accounting, auditing, and bank supervision and regulation systems are not developed enough to support a market-based economy.*

7.10   Although steps can be taken to change the ownership structure of banks and to improve the financial infrastructure by strengthening bank supervision and regulation, the problems of the financial sector ultimately reflect those in the other sectors of the economy. In other words, successful reform in the financial sector is very closely linked to reform in the enterprise sector. The remainder of this section discusses these linkages as background to the financial reform program delineated in the next section.

LINKAGES BETWEEN FINANCIAL AND ENTERPRISE REFORM

7.11   Uzbekistan contains many large state-owned enterprises (SOEs) that will not be viable in the long run. At present, their problems are masked behind the substantial interest subsidies they receive, and by their different accounting practices. Eventually, these enterprises will be closed. However, enterprise reform will not occur overnight; throughout the transitional period, some loss-making enterprises will be subsidized.

7.12   Loss-making SOEs can be financed in three ways: direct budgetary outlays, bank credits, and inter-enterprise arrears. Unless the government finances losses directly, they are "hidden" in bank or inter-enterprise arrears. Allowing either the banks or firms to make loans that cannot be repaid merely defers a Government obligation. To avoid this process, the Government should explicitly finance loss-making SOEs that it has chosen to keep afloat, and not force banks or other enterprises to finance the losses. The banking system can channel Central Bank credit or household savings to loss-making enterprises (rather than to profitable enterprises), but doing so involves inflationary financing or the taxation of household savings. Thus, the more the financial system is used to finance loss-making firms, the fewer opportunities will be available to establish a sound, market-oriented financial system.

7.13   Since both loss-making enterprises and financially viable enterprises will co-exist during the transition, the challenge is to develop a financial system that will finance both types of enterprises. However, this stage must be a truly transitional stage, during which an increasing number of loss-making enterprises will be liquidated, requiring that less and less credit be extended on a noncommercial basis. At the same time, the resources allocated to the viable enterprises will increase, and the number and size of private banks that serve these institutions will grow. The transitional period will be over when the loss-making enterprises and the institutions that finance them shrink out of existence. The transition should not last more than four to five years, and the subsidization of loss-making enterprises should decline each year throughout.

7.14   The following section discusses how Uzbekistan's present financial system can be restructured to best meet the challenges it faces. However, here it must be stressed that a prerequisite for financial sector reform is adopting significant price and trade liberalization policies so that reasonable price signals for resource allocation exist. In the absence of price and trade liberalization, a liberalized and competitive banking system would channel resources to the enterprises that, although they may be most profitable because they receive the largest subsidies, are not necessarily the ones that will be viable in the long run. Thus, to the extent that prices differ greatly from world prices, financial sector reform may intensify the financing of sectors not viable in the long run.

C. SECTORAL REFORM: AREAS AND RECOMMENDATIONS

7.15   As a key sector in the transformation from a command to a market-based economy, Uzbekistan's financial system should (1) strengthen its infrastructure; (2) change its pattern of intermediation and strengthen its Central Bank; (3) restructure and privatize its sectoral banks; (4) strengthen its commercial banks; and (5) develop institutions/markets to provide term financing for the private sector during the transitional period and in the long run. Strengthening the financial infrastructure is the most immediate concern, while all the reforms will continue into the medium term. A timetable for reform is provided in Section D, in which technical assistance needs are also identified and prioritized.

FINANCIAL INFRASTRUCTURE AND OTHER INSTITUTIONAL ISSUES

Financial Infrastructure

7.16   As a first priority, the Government should adopt a consistent and transparent system of accounting, auditing, and financial disclosure at both the enterprise and bank levels, so that the solvency of the banking system and its borrowers can easily be assessed. The inefficient payments system must be replaced by modern clearing and settlement mechanisms to ensure that financial transactions are processed promptly.

7.17   The legal structure is equally important. Although the July 1992 session of the Supreme Soviet attempted to establish a more comprehensive legal framework for the private sector and foreign investment, a framework still does not exist. The Property Law still reflects a fundamentally socialist view that all property rights belong primarily to the state, to be handed out by the state as it so chooses. The Contract Law specifies the legislation that governs relationships among state enterprises, but not more complex market operations. Bankruptcy and liquidation laws must be enacted. Finally, institutions for resolving civil disputes are not capable of enforcing the laws, owing to staffing constraints and a lack of facilities and training.

7.18   Some legislative progress has recently been made to strengthen financial institutions; both a banking and a stock exchange law have been enacted by Uzbekistan. The Law on Banks and Banking Republic Uzbekistan assigns an independent role to the Central Bank to maintain the stability of the currency and to regulate and supervise the banking system. It also gives the Central Bank the main responsibility for foreign-exchange operations. However, the Central Bank is also assigned responsibility for allocating the resources mobilized by the Savings Bank, which is merely the perpetuation of the central planning function, conflicting with the role of a central bank in a market-based economy. The law also establishes conditions under which commercial banks operate in Uzbekistan. The commercial banking model that has been adopted is the universal bank, empowered to take equity positions and to engage in a wide range of retail and wholesale financial activities. Yet, given the absence of risk-management skills and supervisory capabilities, such broad powers may be destabilizing for the financial system in the short run. The Law of the Republic of Uzbekistan on Stock Exchange and Stock Exchange Activity describes the commodities and stock-exchange activity. The law contains tight licensing requirements that restrict activity; state regulation activity consists of this licensing function only. No separate regulatory or supervisory body has been established for exchange operations.

Interest Rate Controls

7.19   Real interest rates in Uzbekistan are severely negative. A 4 percent cap has also been placed on the average spread between deposit and lending rates, as determined by the Central Bank. Although rapid price liberalization in most markets is desirable, the price of credit (interest rate) is one price that must be dealt with carefully. The main problem is that, in the absence of controls, undercapitalized banks may bid up deposit rates and fund the riskiest investments, which would in turn destabilize the rest of the banking system. In general, the complete liberalization of interest rates should be considered only when macroeconomic conditions have been stabilized, and banks are well capitalized. However, during the transition to full interest liberalization, authorities should gradually eliminate large interest subsidies and strive for positive real rates. Short-term interest rates should be raised when overall deposits cease to grow commensurately with inflation. Similarly, the cap on spread is a transitional measure that should be eliminated in time. However, as it stands, 4 percent is too low to support financing projects with a high rate of return in a risky environment.

Prudential Regulations and Supervision

7.20   Procedures for regulating and supervising financial markets should be strengthened. The Central Bank has recently issued new prudential regulations for the commercial banks, covering capital adequacy, liquidity, asset classification, and provisioning. Yet, despite this positive step, much room for improvement remains. Capital requirement is low (at 4 percent of assets), overexposure is allowed (banks are allowed to lend up to 50 percent of their capital to individuals, and up to three times their capital to a group of five individuals), and interest is not suspended on nonperforming assets (actually, interest keeps accruing at a higher penalty rate, until the bank decides to take the borrower to court, a move that may take a couple of years).

7.21   Prudential regulations will remain ineffective until they are enforced. However, the supervisory function of the Central Bank is severely limited, and can be strengthened only with increased staffing, better technology, and more effective training. Off-site supervision should concentrate on compliance with prudential ratios and determine whether on-site supervision priorities are being met, rather than on monitoring whether Central Bank credit has been channelled to the correct final users. On-site supervision does not exist. To establish this, the Government should merge the existing Independent Auditors (owned by the banks themselves) with the off-site regulators of the Central Bank, forming a supervisory department.

7.22   Improving the regulatory and supervisory capabilities of the Central Bank is crucial in the transition from a centrally planned economy to a market-based system. The pace of liberalization will depend on the speed with which prudential regulations and supervision can be strengthened. This process will require a substantial amount of technical assistance.

Barriers To Entry and Exit

7.23   Regulatory barriers to entry include restrictions on the licensing of domestic banks, restrictions on branching, and restrictions on foreign bank entry. The most common exit barrier is implicit or explicit deposit insurance.

- *Licensing of New Banks*. Given the weakness in the supervisory capabilities of the Uzbekistan Central Bank, the Government is apparently reluctant to license new domestic banks. The minimum capital requirement for establishing a commercial bank was recently raised to 50 million rubles. However, despite the weak supervisory capability of the Central Bank, it is still important that entry not be restricted completely. Applications for new charters should be evaluated according to objective criteria, and the process should be completed as quickly as possible.

- *Branching Restrictions*. The opening of branches is subject to Central Bank approval, a process that is perceived to be subjective and to favor sectoral banks. Branching is important in banking because it allows banks to diversify their sources of funds and to expand into retail banking. Although the costs of building large branch networks are high and few new banks will ever want to establish nationwide networks, selective branch openings by private banks are likely to strengthen the level of competition and enhance efficiency. Banks with strong capital and that are in sound financial condition should be allowed to establish bank branches freely.

- *Foreign Bank Entry*. Foreign banks in Uzbekistan are allowed representative offices or branches. They can also have a noncontrolling share in joint venture banks. However, a joint venture bank must have a minimum capital of 500 million rubles, of which a maximum of 49 percent can be from the foreign participant. This capital requirement is too high relative to the requirement for domestic entry, and restricts the inflow of foreign capital unnecessarily, which is a critical necessity in privatizing sectoral banks. Regional restrictions and portfolio limitations also discourage the entry of foreign banks. These inequalities should be rectified. Furthermore, as the Central Bank improves its staffing and technological capacity in an effort to strengthen its supervisory capability, foreign banks should be allowed to establish fully owned subsidiaries and operate on an equal footing with the domestic banks.

- *Exit Mechanisms and Deposit Insurance*. Competition and efficiency also require that effective exit mechanisms be established. Financially weak banks, which are allowed to operate with the implicit or explicit backing of the authorities, can have serious detrimental effects on the soundness of the banking system. The Uzbekistan Government currently guarantees only the deposits of the Savings Bank. Other banks that are trying to compete with the Savings Bank in mobilizing household savings--the Agro-Industrial Bank and the Industrial-Building Bank--have opted to set up their own insurance reserves. At this point, the Uzbeki authorities would do well to consider the pros and cons of deposit insurance regulation. One common mistake is to establish deposit insurance schemes for a financial system that is experiencing widespread insolvencies, since doing so may destabilize the financial system by distorting risk-taking incentives and undermining market discipline. Clearly, these cases require that the entire financial system be restructured. Insolvent banks are expected to establish a deposit insurance fund, and to bail each other out. A deposit insurance system established under these unstable conditions is a "hidden" bailout of insolvencies. A deposit insurance scheme should be considered only after banks are solvent, as a way to retain public confidence in the system, to put all institutions on an equal footing, and to protect the small, unsophisticated depositors. However, it is very important that institutions that are not managed prudently be denied insurance or have their insurance discontinued. The fund should have very well-defined powers; its purpose should be to protect small, unsophisticated investors rather than mismanaged institutions.

Staff Training

7.24   Finally, the lack of skilled human resources in the financial sector constrains its development. The Government could strengthen the skills and capabilities of financial sector personnel by supporting the development of a banking school, training courses by international experts (in Uzbekistan), and study tours, seminars, and secondments abroad. Universities should include business, economics, and financing courses, and invite exchange professors to accelerate the training of future financial-sector personnel.

Changing the Pattern of Intermediation and Strengthening the Central Bank

7.25   One of the major reform issues to be addressed in the financial system is how the central banking and domestic intermediation activities of the Central Bank of Uzbekistan can be separated and responsibilities reallocated. A strong and independent Central Bank, engaged primarily in formulating and implementing monetary policy and in regulating and supervising banks, is the core of any stable, efficient financial system. The Central Bank should no longer be responsible for funnelling 70 percent of the deposits mobilized by the savings bank to the banking system. The Central Bank's commercial and central banking functions must be realigned to avoid conflicts of interest and interference in the conduct of monetary policy, thus enhancing the credibility of the Central Bank both domestically and internationally. Furthermore, the reallocation of responsibilities will enable the management and staff of the Central Bank of Uzbekistan to concentrate their efforts on establishing the institutional framework necessary to implement monetary policy efficiently; moreover, the process will improve the regulatory and supervisory capabilities of the Central Bank, which, as was already discussed, is especially critical in the transitional period and is a primary determinant of the pace of reform in the financial sector.

RESTRUCTURING AND PRIVATIZING THE SECTORAL BANKS

7.26   The Government has different options to accomplish this task. One option is the creation of a special financial institution to help the Government finance large loss-making state enterprises prior to their privatization, restructuring, or liquidation. This institution would lend to state enterprises according to less stringent criteria than those used by a commercial bank, would work closely with Government, and would be funded partly through the budget and partly through deposits. A specialized institution would contain the bad loans within one part of the financial sector so that healthy institutions that are operated on the basis of commercial criteria can emerge and develop. Another option is, instead of isolating the bad loans in one institution, adapting strict accounting and regulatory frameworks to ensure that the bad loans within each bank will be contained during the transition. Implementation of this alternative may turn out to be very difficult because of the need to assess and monitor the quality of the banks' portfolio.

7.27   The other state or joint-stock institutions in the banking sector should also be restructured and privatized. To the extent that restructuring will create new commercial banks, *the following discussion assumes that the financial infrastructure has improved, that enterprise restructuring is proceeding, and that a strong regulatory and supervisory framework for banks is in place. Since these are preconditions for a stable and sound banking and financial system, progress in these areas will determine the pace of financial system reform. A complete reform can only be expected in the medium term.*

The Savings Bank

7.28   With over 1,500 branches and 95 percent of household deposits (18 billion rubles), the Savings Bank is the largest retail bank in Uzbekistan. Its deposits are guaranteed by the Government. On the asset side, however, 7.8 billion of its loans are with the former Soviet Savings Bank in Moscow. Although a decision was made in the recent external debt agreement between Russia and Uzbekistan to defreeze a large portion of these assets, it is not clear when these assets will be repatriated. In its present form, it is likely that the bank is insolvent. One possibility is to convert the Savings Bank into the special financial institution mentioned above (see para 7.26). However, it should be significantly downsized before such a move is made. Bad loans made by the bank can be carved out and kept. The "good" part of the bank and the majority of its branches can be sold to private banks, or groups of branches can be reconfigured into private banks. If the bad loans comprise a large part of the bank's portfolio, they can be replaced by government bonds before the bank is privatized. A specialized institution can lend directly to the enterprises whose subsidization the Government considers essential during the transition. As enterprise reform proceeds and loss-making enterprises are liquidated, the bank will become increasingly less important or necessary. Eventually, at the end of the transitional period, the institution would have to be restructured and capitalized or go out of business, given that so much of its portfolio would comprise nonperforming loans. The transparency resulting from isolating the financing of loss-making firms in a special institution, as opposed to allowing the various institutions and their activities to remain indistinguishable, may help limit the financing of loss-making enterprises and help accelerate enterprise reform as the magnitude of the problem becomes clear to all relevant entities.

7.29   Another possibility is to gear the Savings Bank to raise household deposits and to allow it to lend only to households and interbank markets in a limited way. The rest of the deposits would be used to purchase Government bonds. Under this option the Savings Bank would provide households throughout Uzbekistan with a safe window to deposit their savings, access to the payments system and a source for credit.

Agro-Industrial and Industrial-Building Banks

7.30   Together, these two banks account for well over 90 percent of credit channeled to the state-enterprise sector. Assessing the actual quality of this loan portfolio is difficult, given that, on paper, most enterprises appear to be profitable, owing to the accounting technique they use and the subsidized credits they receive. However, as the amount of interest subsidies decreases, and as generally accepted accounting rules are adopted, the profitability of the enterprises, and thus the quality of the banks' assets, is expected to deteriorate; also, the two banks obtain most of their funding from the Savings Bank. Yet, with over 200 branches, the Agro-Industrial Bank and the Industrial-Building Bank should be able to mobilize deposits on their own. If responsibility for funding the state enterprises rests with the new specialized institution, the Government can undertake a comprehensive audit of the banks in order to determine whether they should be restructured and/or consolidated in an effort to reduce inefficiencies and trim costs. The restructured bank should be operated according to purely commercial criteria, and should focus on lending to viable private enterprises. The ultimate objective should be to privatize this reconfigured financial institution.

National Bank for Foreign Economic Affairs

7.31   This bank is responsible for acting on behalf of the Government to address issues associated with international financial relations; it holds all public-sector foreign exchange reserves, and recently converted its charter from a joint-stock commercial bank into a state bank. With only 200 staff, this is the smallest national bank (although it has recently been opening new branches and increasing its staff). Given that all central banking activities should be concentrated under one authority to support efficient monetary policy and the credibility of the Central Bank as discussed, the central banking activities of the National Bank should be transferred to the Central Bank. What remains of the National Bank can become a commercial bank, which could ultimately be privatized.

STRENGTHENING THE COMMERCIAL BANKS

7.32   The ownership structure of existing commercial banks is unsound. Many of these banks exist primarily to borrow from the Savings Bank and the interbank market in order to finance the very enterprises that own the banks. Consequently, far from funding the most efficient enterprises, this regressive lending practice strains the fragility of the financial sector.

7.33   As one solution to this problem, state enterprise loans could be written off against their share capital and bank deposits, even though doing so may still leave the state-owned enterprises in a dominant position. As loss-making enterprises are liquidated, many of their ownership structures will also be disentangled. In the meantime, the Government must enforce certain prudential regulations (such as limits on loan exposure to owners) and reduce risk by requiring that loan portfolios for sectors and firms be diversified.

7.34   The new private banks, chartered as a result of restructuring and privatization, should be operated prudently according to commercial criteria. These banks should mobilize resources from the enterprise and public sectors and apply them toward the most efficient investments. To support the privatization of both the commercial banks and enterprises, the Government should encourage the entry of foreign capital. Foreign banks, in addition to bringing in much needed capital, would increase the efficiency of the market and enhance bank staff training by contributing modern financial technology.

DEVELOPING NEW INSTITUTIONS/MARKETS TO PROVIDE TERM FINANCING FOR THE PRIVATE SECTOR

7.35   In addition to the banks, the financial sector of Uzbekistan should include other financial institutions, both complementing and competing with banks. For example, a well-functioning securities market may support the process of privatization. And Uzbekistan already has an embryonic stock market, whose legal framework and regulatory and supervisory bodies have not yet been established. In time, the market should also help support the privatization process, and reap the benefits of the process itself. In addition, efforts should be made to develop contractual savings institutions, particularly life insurance and pension funds. Over time, these institutions could become the main avenue for mobilizing term financing for the private sector. The insurance market in Uzbekistan is currently dominated by a state insurance company. Although foreign/domestic private companies also exist, their business is limited. Owing to existing regulations, the state insurance company can invest in the Agro-Industrial Bank and Industrial-Building Banks only in the form of deposits or equity.

7.36   Developing a competitive banking market, stock market, and contractual savings institutions will take time. Nevertheless, during the transition, private enterprises will still have long-term financing needs that may be too risky to be supported by newly privatized commercial banks. In this interim period, a donor-funded and donor-controlled development bank should be established, to be operated solely on the basis of purely commercial criteria, so as not to become a mechanism for funding loss-making institutions. Thus, profit would be its most important objective, and it would provide term financing to private enterprises during the transitional phase. At the end of the transition, the donors would leave and the institution would be privatized.

D. TECHNICAL ASSISTANCE NEEDS IN THE FINANCIAL SECTOR

7.37   To support the reform of various institutions in the financial sector, the Government must mobilize and coordinate the technical assistance efforts of international agencies, focusing on four priority areas: (1) strengthening the financial infrastructure; (2) improving the functions and clarifying the responsibilities of the Central Bank; (3) restructuring and privatizing the banks; and (4) developing other institutions and markets. These areas constitute the core of financial reform as discussed in Section C. The following technical assistance programs are proposed to address them; each program is prioritized, and a preliminary costing and time frame for its implementation are provided.

THE FINANCIAL INFRASTRUCTURE

7.38   Strengthening the financial infrastructure requires technical assistance to develop legal, accounting, and auditing systems, to improve the payments system, to computerize banking operations, and to train financial-sector personnel both at the Central Bank and at commercial banks.

7.39   This program is the most immediate priority; a strong financial infrastructure is a pre-condition for establishing a modern financial sector. With prompt and adequate support and commitment, the financial infrastructure can be improved significantly within one year. The cost would be around US$10 million.

THE CENTRAL BANK

7.40   The Central Bank requires technical assistance to strengthen both its knowledge of central banking functions and its supervisory and regulatory activities.

7.41   *Central Banking*. Technical assistance is required to improve the bank's ability to manage and eventually to formulate monetary policy (direct to indirect monetary control), and to develop a computerized database that contains economic and financial information (to improve forecasting tools).

7.42   *Supervisory and Regulatory Activities*. Technical assistance is required to strengthen on-site supervision (upgrade the skills of examiners, and align examination practices with international standards), and off-site supervision (develop a computerized database of operational and organizational information to support the synthesis and analysis of immediate problems, and to prioritize on-site monitoring efforts).

7.43   Improving the operation of the Central Bank, particularly its regulatory and supervisory role, will also help improve the financial infrastructure, and is thus an essential ingredient of bank restructuring throughout the sector. Therefore, progress in this area must be made immediately, since it will determine the pace of reform of the rest of the financial sector. With proper training and institution building, the regulation and supervision capabilities of the Central Bank can be improved significantly within one year.

BANK RESTRUCTURING

7.44   To restructure and privatize Uzbekistan's banks, the Government requires three areas of technical assistance: diagnostic efforts (in depth audits to identify the extent of losses and analysis of accounts); expertise in the restructuring options available to the financial institutions (international consultants and so forth, or perhaps the creation of a restructuring agency); and the privatization of commercial banks.

7.45   Although this technical assistance program is important, it is also very complicated; in particular, diagnostic efforts and restructuring expertise must be advanced significantly before the restructuring process can be completed. Thus, even though diagnostic efforts can be initiated as soon as an accounting system is in place, the bulk of the restructuring/privatization process must wait for the financial infrastructure to improve, for enterprise restructuring to proceed, and for a strong regulatory and supervisory framework to be put in place. Thus, the technical assistance program can start approximately in a year. However, bank restructuring is a time-consuming process. It may be three years before the major part of the effort is in fruition.

OTHER INSTITUTIONS AND MARKETS

7.46   The Government also requires technical assistance to develop contractual savings institutions and stock markets (expertise to support building the legal framework and establishing the regulatory and supervisory bodies), and to establish a donor-funded and donor-controlled development bank for the transitional period.

7.47   The availability of long-term capital is essential for supporting development in the private sector.   Since a competitive banking market will evolve only over time, other financial institutions/markets should be cultivated in the interim--particularly a development bank to provide funding during the transitional period. Although a full-fledged stock market will also evolve only over time, the technical assistance can begin to lay the groundwork for establishing the necessary legal and regulatory framework. Work can start immediately and be completed in six months (but may go on up to one year).

CHAPTER 8

THE FRAMEWORK FOR SOCIAL PROTECTION

8.1   Uzbekistan is one of the poorest countries in the FSU. Owing to the decline in economic activity and the discontinuation of the transfers from the center, the level of real economic resources available for social protection declined in 1992 and is expected to continue to decline in the near future. Furthermore, the drastic price increases in 1992-93 affected the poor disproportionately, and, moreover, if the Government decides to shift to a market-based economy, some groups are expected to experience a greater level of poverty in the transitional period. Under those circumstances, despite the reduced overall resources, a social protection policy has to be designed to prevent families from sliding below a specified minimum living standard--that is, a poverty line. Three measures will have an impact on living standards: price liberalization, output decline, and unemployment. Liberalization of controlled consumption goods prices, particularly food, is expected to reduce the real income of consumers, but at the same time to increase the income of agricultural producers; consequently, relative urban income is expected to decline. Then, the structure of production and employment is expected to change, leading to frictional unemployment as new skill levels are required and displacement occurs; moreover, when a market-based economy is introduced, the population will be exposed to new risks that will necessitate modifying existing social insurance and social security programs.

8.2   The Government recognizes that it must provide a social safety net that responds to these challenges. Yet it also faces several serious problems that will complicate the transition to a market-based economy. Uzbekistan inherited an extensive system of social protection from the FSU, but this system used resources inefficiently, and was expensive to operate. It was also not well suited to the types of risks that would be imposed by a market-based economy. The authorities have made certain changes to the system of social protection since independence, but the changes have not always worked toward improving the potential efficiency of the system. Moreover, recent economic developments have reduced the availability of resources and, thus, the average standard of living. Further significant changes--and hard decisions--are necessary if the Government is to provide a social safety net at a price that the new state can afford.

A. STRUCTURAL POVERTY

8.3   The analysis of poverty in Uzbekistan at the end of the Soviet period calls for an assessment of whether the all-Union poverty line (or the consumption basket on which it was based) provides an appropriate benchmark for Uzbekistan--that is, how the line was related (and now relates) to the minimum consumption basket necessary. Then, at whatever level the poverty line is drawn, a substantial number of poor children and others (for example, pensioners) is likely. Anti-poverty policy should focus on how their plight can be addressed.

DEMOGRAPHIC PRESSURES

8.4   Uzbekistan's demographic characteristics have implications for social protection policies both in the present and the future. A significant relationship exists between per capita income and family size--or, more properly, the number of children in the family. High dependency ratios in Uzbekistan mean that a substantial number of children live in poverty, thus providing a focus for anti-poverty policy. Rapid population growth means that the labor force is also growing rapidly. In 1991, 8.3 million people were in the labor force. In the absence of substantial job creation, it is likely that unemployment--and particularly youth unemployment--will increase substantially, thus providing a focus for labor-market policy. The scarcity of land and water in many rural areas means that a substantial part of these new jobs will not be in the agricultural sector, but will instead require that the manufacturing and service sectors be expanded. Along with this expansion will come an increase in rural-to-urban migration, which will in turn require a substantial investment in the urban infrastructure, and in new houses, shops, and schools.

8.5   The annual birth rate in Uzbekistan is high, at about 3.5 percent, and the annual rate of population growth is about 2.8 percent--implying that the population will double in approximately 25 years. Infant mortality is also high--37.7 children per 1,000 live births died in 1989 within the first year of life. The high birth rate implies that the average size of families is large-- 5.12 persons; in urban areas 4.56, and in rural areas 6.1. The average family contained only 2.2 to 2.4 working members; the remainder were pensioners, children, or adult dependents. According to the most recent census, about 51 percent of the population were under 19 years of age. Another 6 percent were older than age 60--the retirement age for men. Only 43 percent of the population were between 20 and 59.

Table 8.1
Income Distribution
1989-1992
(percent)

	Poor Families	Middle-Income Families	Affluent Families	All Families
Share of Population, 1989	44	23	33	100
Share of Income, 1989	29	22	49	100
Share of Wages, 1989	27	22	50	100
Income in 1992 (billion rubles)	54	40	90	184

Sources: Row 1, Narodnoe khoziaistvo SSSR v 1989 godu Finansy i Statistika, Moscow, 1990, p. 91; row 2, derived from expenditure shares N.F. Belova and I.I. Dmitrichev Semeinyy biudzhet Finansy i Statistika, Moscow, 1990, p. 68; row 3, pertains to state employee households; data from Sostav sem'i, dokhody i zhilishchnye uslovia semei rabochikh, sluzhashchikh i kolkhoznikov Goskomstat: informatsionno-izdatel'skii tsentr, Moscow, 1990, p. 206; row 4, estimated from expenditure in the first six months of 1992 and for the month of August; data from Goskomprognostat Uzbekistan.

Note: Poor families are those whose per capita income is below 75 rubles a month; middle-income families are those whose per capita income is between 75 rubles and 100 rubles a month; the affluent are the remainder.

8.6   According to a 1989 sample survey, average per capita gross income in Uzbekistan was 91 rubles a month.   For state employees, it was 99 rubles a month, but for collective farmers (*kolkhozniki*) it was only 73 rubles.[1] In 1988, it was estimated that the average USSR family needed a per-capita income of 78 rubles a month to attain a minimum material standard of living; thus, 75 rubles a month came to be accepted as the semi-official poverty line. According to the 1989 survey, some 44

---

[1] Only Tajikistan had lower incomes. By contrast, average per capita income in Russia was 179 rubles a month; for the USSR as a whole, it was 159 rubles.

percent of the population of Uzbekistan had a per capita income of 75 rubles a month or less; of these, 16 percent were living on 50 rubles or less a month (see Table 8.1). Tajikistan was the only republic in the FSU with a greater incidence of poverty.

B. RECENT DEVELOPMENTS

LABOR MARKETS AND EMPLOYMENT

8.7   A labor market has begun to emerge in Uzbekistan, as have the institutions required to support an effectively functioning labor market. Still, the structure of employment reflects the Soviet legacy of a high share of state employees (about 80 percent in 1990); high participation rates, especially for women; a relatively underdeveloped service sector; and the propiska system of residence that constrains labor mobility (Figure 8.1). The economy is largely rural--about 40 percent of all employment in 1990 was in agriculture. In 1990 about 15 percent of the labor force was engaged on private agricultural plots, and 5 percent in producer and consumer cooperatives (Figures 8.2 and 8.3). It is expected that private sector employment, both individual and enterprise, will grow rapidly but from a small base. Early indications of such activity have already emerged in recent months; many small businesses are operating as cooperatives and making consumer goods such as clothing.

The Prospects of Unemployment

8.8   Despite significant falls in output since 1991, there has been little adjustment to employment. Any adjustment has tended to be on the price side of the labor market, since real wages have fallen by about 70 percent since 1990. Hence, as in the other former Soviet republics at this stage, open unemployment remains low-- probably well under 2 percent--but is likely to rise substantially when stabilization and structural reforms take place. In December 1992, about 10,000 people were receiving unemployment benefits (0.1 percent of the labor force) and in July 1993 about 16,000 people.

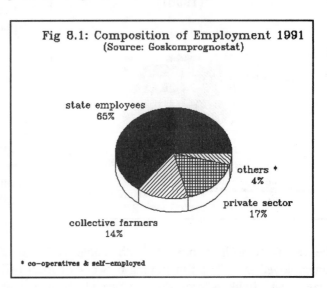

Fig 8.1: Composition of Employment 1991
(Source: Goskomprognostat)

state employees
65%

others *
4%

private sector
17%

collective farmers
14%

* co-operatives & self-employed

8.9   The current structure of the labor market in Uzbekistan has certain implications for the evolution of employment and unemployment in the new market-based economy (see Box 8.1). First, a sharp increase in unemployment is expected. Although much of the search for jobs in the private sector before 1992 occurred on the job, this pattern is not likely to continue. Enterprise restructuring and privatization will change the size distribution of firms, thus reducing the number of private employment positions. Such frictional unemployment will become more widespread as manufacturing contracts and the service sector expand. Furthermore, endemic underemployment is believed to exist in rural areas.[2]

---

[2] Some Soviet economists have claimed that structural unemployment was pervasive in Central Asia (Razvitie). The planned economy failed to create jobs fast enough to match the growth in the working-age population. This structural unemployment was partly or largely hidden by how labor-force statistics were recorded. But it affected a substantial

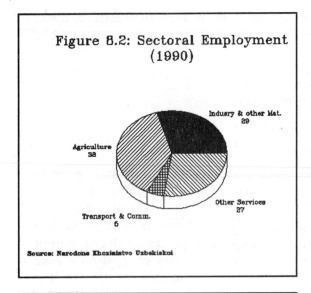

Figure 8.2: Sectoral Employment (1990)

Indusry & other Mat.
29

Agriculture
38

Transport & Comm.
5

Other Services
27

Source: Narodona Khoziaistvo Uzbekiskoi

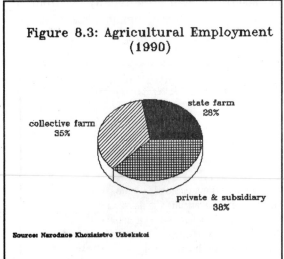

Figure 8.3: Agricultural Employment (1990)

state farm
28%

collective farm
35%

private & subsidiary
38%

Source: Narodnoe Khoziaistvo Uzbekskoi

Unless it can be eliminated, it will deepen the sense of alienation often found in the countryside.

8.10   Labor-force participation among women is high by international standards. Some women may voluntarily retreat into the domestic sphere; others may opt for part-time employment. This will ease the problem of job creation.

8.11   Much of the Government's efforts in social policy have been devoted to coping with the consequences of high inflation and the fall in output. The Government has also recently enacted a law on employment to introduce an unemployment benefit scheme (Box 8.2 provides an overview of social protection policy in Uzbekistan). The collapse of the Soviet Union, the declaration of independence, and the decision to maintain a certain level of social protection called for substantial change in the labor market of Uzbekistan. These changes were embodied formally in the Law on Employment of the Population, passed by the Supreme Soviet and signed by the President on January 13, 1992. The law responded to three issues that are relevant to the framework for social protection and the transition to a market-based economy: first, it ended the commitment to full employment; second, it created the Employment Service (ES) and delineated its responsibilities; and, third, it established the Employment Fund (EF) to finance unemployment benefits and proactive programs.

8.12   The Employment Services appears to be relatively well resourced, with ample staff for current needs (the ratio of staff to registered unemployed is 1:5), a functioning network of local offices, and a first wave of computerization under way. The Bank is proposing to provide technical assistance to familiarize staff with the work of employment services in industrial market economies, to promote the application of such experience in Uzbekistan, and to provide staff training, the purchase of essential office equipment, and further progress on automation.

8.13   As mentioned earlier, there is large potential for small business development in Uzbekistan. These enterprises are currently eligible for loans from the Employment Fund, through the regional offices of the Employment Service. It is projected that such activities will represent up to 30 percent of EF expenditures next year. If this is to be effective, there is an urgent need to review loan procedures and support to small entrepreneurs.

---

number of persons--particularly the young.

Box 8.1: Statistics on Employment and Unemployment

Available statistics on employment and unemployment in Uzbekistan have certain problems, primarily because the concepts used under socialism do not correspond to those used in the West. In particular, Soviet statistics did not capture the concept of the labor force; they referred only to the population of working age and the employed population.

Table 1: Employment and Unemployment, 1991-1993
(in thousands)

	1991	1992	1993
Population of Working Age	10,155	10,393	10,631
Labor Force	10,215	10,464	10,706
Employed	7,268	7,357	7,569
Unemployed	*	9[a]	110
Not in Labor Force	977	1,014	1,031
of which:			
Full-time education	959	993	1,005
Domestic activities	17	21	26

Sources: Ministry of Labor.
a/ This figure corresponds to the second half of 1992.
b/. Concept was not used by Soviet sources. Since the concept of unemployment did not traditionally exist in the sense that individuals were both available and actively looking for work, the unemployed have been confounded with the nonemployed.

Note:
1. A registration scheme started in operation in January 1992.

2. Projected by the Ministry of Labor, this figure seems low in view of the persistent claims that extensive underemployment exists in rural areas and in light of the likely impact of the privatization and stabilization programs on total employment. Judging from the experience of other socialist economies in transition, this may be realistic in the short run. But the projections in chapter 3 of this report (which suggest an average unemployment rate of 5.6 percent in 1993) provide a more plausible scenario of the medium term.

8.14   The law made labor-force participation voluntary. Further, it defined what was meant by unemployment and specified who would be entitled to unemployment compensation.[3] The law envisages four main categories of unemployed persons: those who have been declared "redundant" at their previous place of employment; those who have been discharged from the armed forces or the security services; those who seek to return to the labor force after a long interruption; and, finally, those who are new entrants into the labor force. Individuals in each of these categories who are actively seeking work are entitled to unemployment compensation. The value of the compensation differs: for those declared redundant, it is set at half their previous earnings (but not less than the minimum wage); for new entrants it is set at 75 percent of the minimum wage, and so on. Persons are entitled to receive benefits for up to 26 weeks in any 12-month period.[4]

[3] Briefly, the unemployed are defined as those who register with the Employment Service, who are actively looking for work, are available for work, and are willing to undergo training, if necessary. These individuals would be entitled to unemployment compensation.

[4] New entrants are entitled to 13 weeks of benefits.

Box 8.2: Social Protection Policy

Uzbekistan social protection policy consists of three primary components:

(1)   Anti-poverty policy, which is designed to raise the real income of those who work

(2)   Income maintenance policy, which is intended to support those no longer able to work

(3)   Employment policy, intended to help those who lose their jobs to find work

In Uzbekistan, three ministries and three quasi-autonomous funds are responsible for administering these policies: The Ministries of Labor, Social Security, and Finance, and the Pension Fund, the Social Insurance Fund, and the Employment Fund. However, the ministries, funds, and policies are not coordinated. This incoherence is part of the Soviet legacy.

The system of social protection that Uzbekistan inherited from the FSU was deficient in two major respects. First, it did not provide for the unemployed. This deficiency may not have been important while Uzbekistan formed part of a planned economy that could ensure full employment. But it will clearly be an important shortcoming when the Government commits itself fully to a market-based economy. Second, it contained only the most meager provision for public assistance to those who did not qualify for particular benefits. The only such "safety net" was the social pension, which was available only to those of pensionable age and to orphans. Again, this lacuna may not have been important in a highly regulated society where a permanent excess demand for labor exists (which may not in fact have been the case in Soviet Central Asia). But it is a weakness for the more open society that is expected to emerge from the process of economic transition. Here, a general means-tested benefit should be introduced to respond to unforeseen contingencies. The Government has recognized the first of these shortcomings and has introduced an unemployment compensation program. Yet, it has done little about the second.

Table 1: Persons Receiving a Pension, 1980-1991
(in thousands)

	1980	1985	1990	1991
Pensioners--All	1844.0	2018.0	2377.0	2499.0
of whom:				
Working	199.0	261.0	319.0	328.0
By Category of Pension				
Old age	1132.0	1267.0	1538.0	n.a.
Disability	235.0	234.0	259.0	n.a.
Survivor	392.0	402.0	422.0	n.a.
Other[a]	85.0	115.0	158.0	n.a.
Persons of Pensionable age	1300.0	1443.0	1592.0	1602.0

Sources: Rows 1, and 3-5, Narodnoe Khoziaistvo Uzbekskoi SSR v 1990 g Uzbekistan, Tashkent, 1991, p.42. Rows 2 and 6, unpublished estimates of the Ministry of Labor, Uzbekistan.

a/ Includes personal pensions paid from the republic budget; it may also include military pensions payable to residents of Uzbekistan; finally, it may include those who receive a so-called social pension.

Box 8.2 (cont.)

The Soviet pension scheme was recodified in 1990. This law still governs the payment of pensions in Uzbekistan. (A draft law has been prepared by the Government, but as of September 1992 it had not yet been adopted by Parliament.)

The origins of anti-poverty policy in Uzbekistan are found in the policies adopted by all-Union ministries in Moscow. For much of the Soviet period, there was no such policy, since the authorities refused to acknowledge that families could be living in poverty under socialism. In the 1960s, however, that attitude began to change under pressure from academics--and officials in such organizations as the State Committee on Labor and Wages. In 1974, the Soviet government introduced a benefit payable to families with children younger than age 7 whose per capita income was below the "poverty line." This was the first explicit attempt to alleviate poverty in the USSR. In April 1991, Prime Minister Pavlov merged this allowance with the system of child allowances (payable to all mothers with three or more children), and the structure was upgraded to compensate families for the significant increase in retail prices introduced at the same time. This revised system of allowances for mothers and children forms the first component of Uzbekistan's anti-poverty policy.

The Soviet government also operated a system of price controls and subsidies for so-called necessities, which was also conceived as a component of the state's anti-poverty policy. In April 1991, the Soviet Prime Minister sanctioned a significant increase in retail prices in an attempt to reduce the budgetary cost of these subsidies. After the failed coup of August 1991, the Government, acting independently, extended the system of retail price controls and subsidies in the face of accelerating inflation. These controls were accompanied by a system of rationing in order to restrict the sale of most goods in Uzbek stores to citizens of the republic or to bona fide visitors.

8.15   The ES is responsible for providing job-placement sources. It is required to create a data bank that contains all vacancies in the economy; firms risk fines if they do not notify the service about vacancies. The ES also organizes the retraining of redundant employees, and coordinates public works programs. Finally, it is required to maintain a register of the unemployed and to certify that the registered unemployed are actively seeking work.

8.16   The Employment Fund is a quasi-autonomous organization similar to the Pension and Social Insurance Funds. The Employment Fund is financed by a payroll tax (currently set at 3 percent of the wage bill). It is responsible for unemployment compensation payments, for public works, and for part of the cost of retraining redundant workers.

EVOLUTION OF WAGES AND CONSUMPTION

8.17   Rapid inflation has adversely affected real wages and the standard of living (see Table 8.2). Between 1990 and January 1992, the retail price index increased fourfold. Real average wages fell by an estimated 47 percent between June 1991 and 1993.[5] Wage differentials have also contracted throughout 1992. In 1990, average earnings were about three times the minimum wage. In July 1992, they were only twice the minimum wage.

---

[5] It is possible that these figures overstate the decline in welfare, since there are doubts about whether the prices used in the index in 1990 were market-clearing. But it is certain that they reflect a marked decline in the standard of living.

8.18   This collapse in real wages has been accompanied by changes in the composition of household income; it has also led to changes in the composition of household expenditures (see Table 8.3). The relative importance of income from work has increased, which is reflected in the increased share of income accruing in the form of wages and salaries; it is also reflected in the growth of income from private subsidiary economic activity. In contrast, the share of income derived from the state's income maintenance programs has fallen by a third--from 27 percent to 18 percent of the total, owing primarily to inflation.

8.19   Equally dramatic changes in the composition of household expenditures have occurred. In 1991, the average family spent 43 percent of its money income on food; in the first half of 1992, this expenditure had increased to 49 percent. To make room for this increase in expenditures on food, families have cut back on their purchases of non-food goods and other expenditures. Further, it can be argued that the average levels of consumption in Uzbekistan in the second quarter of 1992 were similar to those of the poorest 10 percent of households in the FSU (see Table 8.4).[6]

EVOLUTION OF SOCIAL PROTECTION

8.20   The Government's current response to the erosion of the wages and social security payments of families seems to be ad hoc: it has focused on increasing the minimum wage and the minimum pension, and it has committed resources to support the system of price subsidies. Other elements of its anti-poverty policy have been ignored.

8.21   In January 1992, the minimum wage was raised from 70 rubles a month to 350 rubles. Given the nature of the wage-determination system, inherited from the FSU, the effect of this policy was that the majority of the wages were paid by state enterprises. In this way, the Government ensured that a majority of families were able to maintain their entitlement to minimum quantities of foodstuffs. In the ensuing 18 months, the President decreed eight further increases in the minimum wage, merely to ensure a minimum level of consumption for a large number of state employees and their families.

Table 8.2
The Evolution of Wages, Monthly

	Nominal Average Wage (rubles)	Nominal Minimum Wage (rubles)	Real Average Wages[a] (Dec 91 rubles)
December	460	70	460
1992			
January	614	350	129
February	659		129
March	927		165
April	1,158		192
May	1,300	550	186
June	1,595		211
July	1,908	1,000	239
August	2,098		243
September	2,660	1,350	272
October	3,798	2,000	238
November	4,716		182
December	5,919		212
1993			
January	5,919[b]	2,500	145
February	6,196	3,000	136
March	7,357		137
April	8,386		150
May	9,386		126
June	23,456	7,500	244
July	na	11,250	

Source: Ministry of Labor, Bank staff calculations.

a/ Deflated by wholesale prices.
b/ It is assumed to be equal to December 1992 nominal wage for lack of consistent data.

---

[6] Uzbeks consumed more bread than poor Russians, but fewer potatoes; they purchased more fruit and vegetables but less sugar; their consumption of meat, fish, milk and eggs was similar. The consumption of the least well off families in Uzbekistan was clearly inferior to that of the poorest Russians.

8.22   As was pointed out earlier, the 1990 All-Union Pension Law did not contain a provision for the indexation of pensions. Nor did its predecessor. Rather, from time to time the authorities had arbitrarily decreed an increase in the minimum pension to take into account inflation and increases in average incomes. If a person's designated pension was below the new minimum, he or she received the new minimum pension instead. Thus, there was a concentration of pensioners-- particularly the elderly--at the minimum. Uzbekistan has followed the same approach since January 1992. It has raised the minimum pension at the same time that it has raised the minimum wage. (The minimum pension was set slightly higher than the minimum wage in July 1993.)

8.23   The Government controlled prices for a range of basic foodstuffs, including flour, meat,

Table 8.3
The Structure of Income and Expenditure,
1991-1992

	1991	1992 1st Quarter	1992 1st Half
Money Income[a]	100.0	100.0	100.0
Wages and salaries	48.0	54.1	56.2
Earnings from kolkhoz	8.9	11.3	8.1
Pensions and allowances	26.9	17.2	17.6
Other receipts	16.3	17.3	18.1
Money Expenditures[b]	100.0	100.0	100.0
Food	42.7	46.9	49.0
Non-food goods	34.3	32.0	30.6
Alcoholic beverages	2.8	3.6	3.3
Services	6.8	5.3	5.6
Taxes	4.3	4.4	4.6
Other	9.1	7.8	6.9

Source: Goskomprognostat.

a/ The figures are derived from the ongoing family-budget survey; the concept of income thus differs from that used in Tables 8.1 and 8.2.

b/ This includes income from the sale of produce grown on private plots and from other private subsidiary economic enterprises.

milk, and sugar until July 1993. However, consumers were entitled to purchase only a limited quantity at these prices; additional supplies could be purchased at higher market prices. In a significant move towards reducing direct subsidies, the Government now only controls the price of bread and flour. There appears to be no formal limit on the amount of bread that can be purchased at this price, but supplies are not always available. Private bakers also sell higher-quality bread at higher market prices-- and seem to find sufficient customers to make it worthwhile to remain in business.

8.24   In addition to these price controls and subsidies on bread and flour, the Government operates a range of other subsidy programs. Subsidies are available for such items as children's clothing and detergents; coal for household heating; waste heat from power stations used for district heating in some towns; and urban mass transport systems. The rents charged for publicly owned housing are controlled; they are so low that they do not cover the costs of construction and maintenance.[7] Subsidies are also available to consumers for various medical services and pharmaceuticals, as well as for higher education costs. In 1991, the Government spent 4.4 billion rubles on these subsidy schemes; in the first half of 1992, the cost rose to more than 14.2 billion rubles. For 1992, the planned budgetary expenditures on subsidies were about 30.7 billion rubles (see Table 8.5).

---

[7] This was the main incentive for the Government to accelerate privatizing residential housing in 1992. In Tashkent, almost 99 percent of the total stock of residential housing was privatized, having been sold to the tenants at a very low nominal value.

Table 8.4
Changes in the Consumption of Foodstuffs, 1990-1992
(Kg. per capita)

	1990	1991	1992	RSFSR 1992 poorest 10 percent	Uzbekistan in 1991 families with <75R per-capita
Bread	41	39	35	26	37
Potatoes	9	9	8	26	6
Vegetables	26	25	41	12	18
Fruit	9	8	14	2	
Sugar	4	3	2	4	2
Meat	8	6	6	5	2
Fish	0	0	0	1	0
Milk	52	47	41	39	29
Eggs	25	20	20	21	13
Margarine	3	3	4	1	2

Source: Ministry of Labor; col. 6 from Rossiiskie Vesti 29, 1992.

8.25   The second component of the Government's anti-poverty policy consists of the various child allowances that have been introduced since 1974. The structure of these payments is complex. The levels at which most of these allowances are paid were increased 3.5 times from the April 1991 level. Thus, at their present levels, the allowances make very little contribution to alleviating poverty.

THE COST OF SOCIAL PROTECTION

8.26   In sum, Table 8.6 presents the estimated total cost of Uzbekistan's social protection. The table includes both programs that are financed directly from the budget and those that are paid for from various extra-budgetary funds. The table shows that the costs of social protection increased inexorably through the 1980s and that they have exploded in the past two years. In 1980, the cost of social protection was equal to about 7.4 percent of GDP; by 1990, it had risen to about 12 percent of GDP. In 1991, it reached almost 29 percent of GDP, and in 1992 it is estimated to have fallen back to about 24 percent. Present policies are clearly unsustainable from a fiscal point of view.

8.27   Table 8.6 also provides estimates of the value of transfers received from Moscow until the breakup. In 1985 and 1990, transfers covered roughly the cost of the social safety net. In this sense, the system of social protection under socialism was free in Uzbekistan. This is no longer the case. Uzbekistan must now assume full fiscal responsibility for whatever social safety net is introduced.

8.28   Total expenditures on social protection must be reduced. As a guide to what might be appropriate, the experience of various countries is enlightening (see Table 8.7).[8] Expenditures on pensions in Uzbekistan are of the same order of magnitude as those in the other comparison states; expenditures on health and on education are substantially higher, except for education in Kazakhstan.

---

[8] It is more appropriate to compare Uzbekistan with the low-income states than with the so-called welfare states. (However, per capita GDP in Uzbekistan is less than in these OECD countries.)

Differences in the composition of the population and overinvestment in tertiary education in Uzbekistan may explain some of those differences. Expenditures on unemployment in Uzbekistan in 1991 were rather low; however, they are expected to increase in 1993-94 if the Government begins to implement a serious reform effort. The major difference is to be found in the category "other social expenditure." This category includes both price subsidies and allowances. Allowances have been eroded significantly in 1992. However, consumer subsidies have almost doubled in 1992. It is here that savings must be made. Owing to fiscal considerations (discussed in chapters 2 and 3) and in an effort to minimize the negative effects on the incentives structure, the Government must reduce subsidies and price controls.

Table 8.5
Budgetary Cost of Selected Subsidies, 1991-92
(billion rubles)

	1991	1991 (% of GDP)	1992*
Foodstuffs			
Bread, Flour	2.1	3.4	4.6
Meat & Meat Products	.9	1.5	1.6
Milk & Milk Products	.5	0.8	1.0
Sugar	.0	.0	1.7
Tea	.1	.1	.6
Eggs	.0		.2
Non-Food Goods			
Soap & Detergent	.0	.0	.1
Children's Clothing	.0	.0	3.0
Pharmaceutical	.6	1.0	.1
Coal--for House Heating	.1	.2	.4
Utilities			
District Heating	.1	.2	.5
City Transport	.0	.0	.6
Total	4.4	7.2	14.2

Source: Ministry of Finance.
* Subsidies for 1992 reflect only the period from January to June of 1992.

STRATEGIES FOR THE FUTURE

8.29   The evident unsustainability of the current set of social protection policies means that the Government must choose its priorities; available resources must be committed in the first place to these objectives. The measures chosen to attain the Government's social policy goals must ensure that available resources are used efficiently. Existing programs are reviewed here with those considerations in mind. But the system must also respond to the new demands being placed on it. Of these, perhaps the most important is unemployment. The recently introduced unemployment benefit scheme is also analyzed herein.

C. RECONSTRUCTING THE SAFETY NET

Anti-Poverty Policy

8.30   The Government must reconsider its approach to anti-poverty policy. The procedures used to determine both the composition of vulnerable groups and the programs that are implemented to alleviate poverty must be reformed.

8.31   T h e Government continues to measure poverty according to the methodology developed under the Soviet regime. The Uzbek statistical service, G o s k o m p r o g n o s t a t , determines the so-called subsistence minimum by defining how much it costs to purchase a basket of goods. On August 1, 1992, this was 1,371 rubles a month per capita.[9] Procedures used in this calculation have two shortcomings. First, the consumption basket used in the calculation is still based on expert assessment, rather than on the expenditure patterns of the poor; furthermore, it depends on opinions about what was appropriate for the FSU as a whole, not for Uzbekistan alone. Second, in determining costs, Goskomprognostat still relies substantially on official or list prices; its researchers do not sample actual prices paid.

8.32   This approach must be changed. First, the consumption basket must be based more clearly on behavioral patterns and economic conditions in Uzbekistan. Second, the cost of this basket-- the so-called poverty line--must reflect more closely the prices actually paid in stores and on the kolkhoz market. Since the prices and expenditure patterns in urban and rural

Table 8.6
Expenditures on Social Protection, 1980-1992
(in billion rubles)

	1980	1985	1990	1991	1992[a]
Total Budgetary Expenditures				9.8	49.1
as Percent of GDP				16.0	11.8
Family allowances	0.3	0.5	0.7	5.4[c]	
Subsidies[b]				4.4[c]	49.2
Total Extrabudgetary Expenditures				8.1	49.5
as Percent of GDP				13.1	11.9
Pension Fund	1.1	1.5	2.1	4.2	42.4
Old age	0.9	1.2	1.8		31.8
Disability	0.2	0.2	0.3		..
Other					10.6[d]
Unemployment Fund					1.1
Benefits					
Retraining					
Social Insurance Fund	0.3	0.6	0.7	1.0	6.0[d]
Sick pay[e]	0.2	0.2	0.3	0.6	
Maternity[e]	0.1	0.3	0.3	0.5	
Child Allowances	0.1	0.3	0.4	2.9	
Total Expenditures on Social Protection	1.8	2.8	3.9	17.9	98.6
As percent of GDP	7.4	10.1	11.9	29.1	23.7
As percent of NMP		10.4	14.0	38.6	26.3
Transfers from Moscow					
As percent of NMP[f]	5.1	14.0	23.2	26.0	..
As percent of GDP			19.4	19.5	..

Sources: columns (1) to (3), Bank staff calculations based on Ministry of Labor; columns (4) to (5), Pension Fund, Social Insurance Fund, Ministry of Finance, and IMF.

a/   Actual values unless indicated.

b/   Subsidies were provided on food prices in earlier years, but there is no evidence about their amounts; they were transferred from the all-Union budget.

c/   The Government budget in 1991 reports only 5.3 billion rubles for expenditures on these two items combined; it is believed that the budget underreports by 4.4 billion rubles.

d/   In 1992, includes child allowances which are financed partially through the Pension Fund and partially through the Social Insurance Fund.

e/   Columns (1) to (3), Narodnoe khoziaistvo Uzbekskoi SSR v 1990 Uzbekistan, 1991; columns (4) to (5) Social Insurance Fund.

f/   Before 1991, figures were calculated as the difference between NMP utilized and NMP produced.

[9] It also determines the cost of a lower standard, which in August 1992 was set at 971 rubles a month per person.

Table 8.7
Levels of Social Expenditure: Uzbekistan and OECD Countries
(as Percent of GDP)

	Uzbekistan		OECD Lower-Income States, 1986[a]	Romania	Kazakhstan	Russia
	1991	1992		1990	1992	1991
Pensions	6.8	10.2	7.8	9.2	4.7	7
Unemployment		0.3	2.5		0.5	.0
Other Social[d]	22.2	13.2	2.9	.0	5	3
Total Social Protection	29.1	23.7	12.5	9.2	10.2	10
Education	6.0	10.8	3.7	3.4	7.7[b]	4.7[c]
Health	5.9	5.1	4.8	3.4	3.7[b]	2.6[c]
Total	41	39.6	21.0	16.0	21.6	27.3

Notes & Sources: Ministry of Finance and World Bank reports: Reform of Social Policy and Expenditures, Washington, D.C., 1992.
a/ Greece, Ireland, Portugal, Spain, and Turkey.
b/ For 1991.
c/ Refers to the FSU in 1989.
d/ Including child allowances, and consumer and child goods subsidies.

areas differ substantially, the authorities might consider calculating the poverty line separately for each. Third, since the objective of anti-poverty policy is to alleviate the suffering of the most needy, the poverty line must be set at a realistic level, whereby a reasonable prospect exists for providing assistance to those whose incomes fall below it. Finally, when these concepts have been established, their cost should be monitored regularly--on a monthly or quarterly basis. All anti-poverty and income maintenance payments should be formally linked to it rather than to the minimum wage.

Price Subsidies

8.33   The second component of the Government's anti-poverty policy must also be reformed. Much of the price-subsidy program should be abolished. The objective of anti-poverty policy is to target expenditures at the poor; without means-testing, which is not currently feasible in Uzbekistan, the Government cannot do so. The next-best approach would be to concentrate expenditures on goods and services that the poor use disproportionately. In Uzbekistan, subsidies could thus be provided for bread. In view of the cost and the tightness of the budget constraint, subsidies for other foodstuffs should be phased out. The subsidies for non-food goods should also be phased out; many of them would be used more by the affluent than by the needy--contradictory with the objectives of anti-poverty policy. The savings from reducing the scale of consumer price subsidies could be used to increase direct cash support for the poor, or they could be used to reduce the burden of social protection on the economy as a whole.

8.34   In this context, it would be desirable if the complex structure of child allowances were superseded. It could be replaced either by a single child-allowance or by a child allowance plus means-tested benefit for those whose income falls below the cost of a lower standard. In principle, the second scheme is more efficient, since fewer resources are diverted to the non-poor. But it suffers from one major drawback: means-testing is politically unpopular, and it requires substantial administrative capacity.[10]

Income Maintenance

8.35   The pension scheme is the major income maintenance program operated by the Government. At present, its demands on resources are not excessive in relation to those of low-income OECD countries. But the scheme may still benefit from reform. The Ministry of Social Security is currently engaged in an extensive program to introduce a degree of differentiation into the structure of pensions. This program is expensive, in terms of both the administrative effort involved and the resources it will require. It is estimated that expenditures on pensions will increase by 56 to 87 percent, plunging the pension fund into deficit (and probably increasing the payroll tax). Further, since individual files are not maintained, and hence there is no explicit record of contributions, the exercise is based on a dubious concept of equity.

8.36   The current pension scheme is based on pay-as-you-go principles: today's employees provide the resources used to pay the pensions of the elderly, with the implicit promise that, in turn, their pensions will be paid for by the succeeding generation. Since the Government is operating under tight financial constraints, it can be argued that the most equitable arrangement is for all current pensioners to receive the same pension. In practice, more than 90 percent of pensioners receive the same pension-- an arrangement that should be formalized. The authorities should consider introducing a flat-rate pension scheme linked to the poverty level and indexed formally to the cost of living. It might also be augmented where the recipient was responsible for dependents.

8.37   At a later date, the Government might consider introducing a partially funded pension scheme that would allow the better off to make appropriate provision for their retirement. This scheme would complement the array of private schemes expected in a market-based economy. But a funded pension scheme should not be introduced in the presence of rapid inflation. The Government might also reduce the number of circumstances in which workers can retire early. But it makes little sense to make any of these changes when the unemployment rate is expected to increase significantly.

Social Insurance

8.38   The present sickness benefit system contains elements of moral hazard that probably lead to overuse. In particular, if employers and employees were to be responsible for some of the costs of sickness, they might reduce the demands on the system. Second, the maternity benefit and leave program contains hidden incentives toward increasing the number of births; this is not what is required in present circumstances. Although such incentives have been eroded by inflation, they impose costs on employers. In particular, the requirement that enterprises keep a woman's job open for her for up to three years after the birth of her child is an excessive burden that should be reviewed. Finally, although this has little bearing on costs, the trade unions should discontinue administering the state's social insurance program.

---

[10] In particular, it is worth pointing out that both conceptual and practical difficulties are associated with determining the incomes of households engaged in subsistence agriculture, as is the case with many rural Uzbek families. Since per capita income falls as the number of children in a family rises and because a majority of children were classified as poor according to the old poverty line, the first scheme would certainly concentrate resources on the major source of poverty. Furthermore, since it is easy to establish the number of children in a family, it would be relatively cheap and nonintrusive to administer.

THE PROBLEM OF UNEMPLOYMENT

8.39   It is widely acknowledged that economic reform will lead to unemployment, and that it will impose an additional burden on the social protection system. Experience is available from other transforming economies to indicate that unemployment rates could reach at least 10 percent during the initial phase of a program. To assess the burden imposed by unemployment on the social safety net, analysts must rely on elementary models.[11]

8.40   An alternative approach for modeling the growth of unemployment assumes that a given (but varying) proportion of existing jobs are eliminated each month, owing perhaps to a decline in demand or, possibly, to improved productivity. At the same time, new jobs are created--at a rate which depends on the stock of unemployed labor. In this model, a ceiling is placed on the level of unemployment. But as the calculations show, the unemployment rate could rise as high as 12 percent, according to the assumptions made.

8.41   As was pointed out earlier, recent legislation provides for unemployment compensation at 50 percent of average earnings (but not less than the minimum wage) for 26 weeks in any 12-month period. If one ignores the fact that average earnings are currently less than twice the minimum wage, the law provides for a replacement ratio of one quarter; that is, on average, four individuals unemployed for a year will receive the same monetary compensation as an average worker. The EF, which pays unemployment compensation, is financed by a 1 percent payroll tax. If the unemployment rate exceeds 4 percent, then the EF will go into deficit. Given the level of unemployment projected, it is clear that the EF--or the unemployment benefit scheme--must be reformed radically. On the one hand, either the payroll tax rate must be raised or the deficit financed from general revenue. On the other, the ratio of benefits to previous earnings may have to be reduced. Furthermore, it is not possible to abandon workers who "exhaust their benefit." Some arrangements must be made to provide limited support for those who have been without work for six months or longer. This arrangement will add to the cost of the social safety net.

E. SUMMARY OF RECOMMENDATIONS

8.42   While macroeconomic stabilization requires adopting tight fiscal and monetary policies, the social dimensions of stabilization and enterprise restructuring require increased attention to the social

---

[11] Suppose that the relationship between the output of and input for labor and capital in Uzbekistan can be described by a Cobb-Douglas production function. Suppose further that the capital stock does not change over the relevant period. One can then derive the following relationship between the proportionate change in output and the proportionate change in labor utilized:

$$dQ/Q = \alpha dL/L,$$

where α is the share of labor in total income. To an order of magnitude, α in Latin America or in a new industrialized country such as India is 0.6 to 0.7. Hence a 1% fall in output should lead to a 1.4-1.6 percent reduction in the amount of labor utilized. If this decline in utilization is translated directly and immediately into unemployment, the implications of the reform scenario suggested in chapter 3 are significant: real output would fall by 40 percent between 1991 and 1994-95, which would mean a decline in employment of 60 percent. Yet the relationship between unemployment and reductions in the utilization of labor on private plots or collective farms is unclear. If one assumes that no one from these sectors registers as unemployed, the unemployment rate could still rise to 30-40 percent. Unemployment at this level would impose an intolerable strain on the social safety net, besides leading to political unrest.

safety net. The challenge, therefore, is to reconcile these demands and to find ways to channel public resources most efficiently to social protection.

8.43   The Government is committed to maintaining a social safety net. In the present context, this has three dimensions. First, income support must be provided to those who would otherwise fall below the poverty line--such as children in large families and the elderly. Second, assistance should be extended to people who are affected adversely by the transition--in particular, the newly unemployed. Third, scarce resources must be targeted at those in need, and exclude those who are not, in order to remain within fiscal constraints.

8.44   Existing programs go only part way toward meeting these objectives. Significant amounts are being spent in ways which do not benefit the poor; yet at the same time, many of the poor do not receive adequate support. The foremost task for the Government is to prioritize social expenditures according to the degree to which they benefit the poor. The following recommendations focus on measures that the Government could use to reallocate and reduce social expenditures, while, to the extent possible, also preserving a minimum level of support for Uzbek people in need.

Consumer Subsidies

8.45   Subsidies are conceived to be a component of anti-poverty policies. Rapid inflation and changes in relative prices have dramatically driven up the cost of various subsidies financed by the Government budget. As a proportion of GDP, the cost increased from 7.8 percent in 1991 to 11.8 percent in 1992. This trend is clearly unsustainable. Moreover, many of the subsidies may not in fact benefit the poor.

8.46   *The Government should phase out all subsidies, except those on bread*. This would have saved an estimated 7.8 percent of GDP in 1992, reducing the budget deficit to 4 percent of GDP. *The poor will receive cash compensation for the price rises, if their benefits are indexed as recommended below.*

Establishing a Minimum Subsistence Income

8.47   Government attempts to alleviate poverty should be guided by the concept of a "minimum consumption basket," based on expenditure patterns of the poor and regional prices. This would represent a poverty line set in absolute rather than relative terms. This level, rather than the minimum wage as at present, would be the anchor of the system of benefits.

Targeting the Poor

8.48   A means-tested approach would be useful to target assistance, so that only those who fall below the minimum subsistence income would be eligible. But this is very difficult to implement in the short term, particularly because rural household income is hard to measure. Work should begin on developing a program of social assistance based on an income test. This could be a useful area for technical assistance.

8.49   In the interim period, especially given the increasing social strains imposed by the transition, a workable alternative to selecting recipients of social assistance is required. The best approach is to continue to rely on family and child allowances. The presence of children is empirically correlated with poverty in Uzbekistan. Two-thirds of the poor in 1991 were in fact children. At the same time the existing system should be simplified, possibly by replacing the array of existing benefits with a single child allowance. Further analytical work could help determine how the existing system should be improved--for example, by making the amount of child allowance a positive function of the number of children.

8.50   *In the short term, the foundation of anti-poverty policy should be family allowances. A single benefit should replace the present complicated system, and its level should be maintained in real terms.*

Preserving an Adequate Level of Assistance

8.51   In the midst of high inflation, the real value of benefits is rapidly eroded. Yet automatic indexation of all benefits can have adverse fiscal and inflationary implications. One approach, which tries to reconcile these competing goals, is to set minimum benefits at least as high as the poverty line, and defend the minimum benefit fully against inflation. All benefits would receive uniform price adjustments, so that higher benefits increase proportionately less, and the benefits structure is effectively compressed. It will lead to sizable cost savings (in Russia, for example, 2 percent of GDP for pensions only). This is an appropriate short-term measure. It targets resources at those in need, and helps ensure that no Uzbek falls below the poverty line. It could be reversed when fiscal circumstances allow, and the Government could then adopt its plan to introduce a differentiated structure of earnings-related benefits.

Further Cost Savings

8.52   At a time of fiscal crisis, it is essential to identify and implement cost savings wherever possible. In addition to the measures outlined above, there are further areas where the Uzbek government could reduce current spending.

8.53   **Pensions**. Public pension schemes in the former Soviet republics differ from those elsewhere in the world, in that the elderly are permitted to work without any dimunition of pensions benefits, and pensionable age is relatively young. In Uzbekistan, about 13 percent of pensioners also receive income from work. It is advisable to at least limit this provision--so that people who are earning substantial sums from work cannot concurrently receive a full pension. *The Government should consider introducing a work test for pensions, or at least a partial "clawback" system where earnings exceed a certain level.*

8.54   *The age at which Uzbeks become eligible for a pension could be gradually increased. Beginning January 1996, the pension age would increase by six months each year until it reaches age 65 for both men (2005) and women (2015).*

8.55   **Maternity Benefits**. Current provisions, which allow three years leave, and the payment of maternity benefits for half of that period, appear to be relatively generous. It might be appropriate to curtail these benefits, given fiscal constraints and the objective of encouraging family planning.

8.56   **Sick Pay**. Consideration should be given to shifting from payroll-tax-financed public provision, with full replacement, to a system whereby employers are mandated by the Government to provide sick pay, with or without a waiting period of, say, one or two days. The advantage would be that employers who bear the cost of sick pay will have the incentive to scrutinize absenteeism more closely. The disadvantage is that potential employees who are perceived to have a higher incidence of illness (for example, women of childbearing age) will be discriminated against in hiring decisions.

Employment Policies

8.57   The Government could take several steps to develop effectively functioning labor market in Uzbekistan. It could:

- Abolish administrative constraints on labor mobility--for example the propiska system of residence permits should be eliminated

- Encourage the widest possible range of channels for job placement

- Review the operation of small business loans granted through the Employment Service--in particular, the conditions and eligibility criteria, and the provision of practical short courses in bookkeeping and marketing to borrowers.

CHAPTER 9

AGRICULTURE

A. THE SETTING FOR REFORM

9.1   Uzbekistan has limited natural resources and a large and rapidly growing population, concentrated in densely settled oases and recently developed irrigation tracts. Its vast deserts are of little productive use. Only 10 percent of its land area is cultivated, 95 percent of which is irrigated. Yet, the country's economic livelihood comes from agriculture. Though there are areas suitable for development, water resources are fully utilized and the agriculture sector will almost certainly have to release water to other sectors. Agricultural strategy must, therefore, focus on increasing productivity from already developed land and water.

9.2   Despite Uzbekistan's meager resources, agriculture has played a dominant role in development, owing primary to massive (Moscow financed) irrigation to increase cotton production (see Box 9.1). Between 1960 and the early 1980s, the irrigated area rose from about 2.3 million to 4.5 million hectares, more than 50 percent of the Central Asian total. By the mid-1980s, however, it became clear that water resources were being over-exploited, and that water transfers from the Siberian rivers and other sources were unsustainable. Rising environmental concerns coincided with a deteriorating fiscal situation in the USSR, and irrigation expansion slowed markedly. Since independence, budgetary transfers have ceased completely and--irrespective of water constraints--limited domestic savings rule out major land reclamation for the foreseeable future. In contrast to area expansion, agricultural technology appears to have changed little, and crop yields have stayed fairly constant. Trends in agricultural value-added have reflected the growth in cultivated area, and, since the mid-1980s, value-added has stagnated.

9.3   Productivity gains in Uzbekistan agriculture are potentially large, since yields are relatively low, and both input use and spoilage rates are high. Realizing these gains will depend on establishing incentives for generating and adopting new technologies in line with Uzbekistan's underlying comparative advantage. Important policy and institutional changes will be required, both in the transition from a planned to a market-based economy and over the longer term, to sustain technical progress and efficient resource use.

9.4   Reform has already begun. In the short term, it should emphasize greater freedom to produce, sell, and trade at prices that the market can bear. Measures include: liberalizing prices and markets; phasing out the state order system; creating a flexible and responsive marketing system; and establishing the initial conditions for encouraging more efficient land and water use. For the longer term, reforms should induce policies that increase efficient water use and are consistent with environmental concerns (for example, through irrigation modernization and water pricing), at the same time supporting sustained growth in land productivity (for example, through land reform, varietal development, and better on-farm practices). In agriculture (or any other sector), self-sufficiency is incompatible with high growth, and reform in both the short and long term must adjust agricultural production in line with the country's comparative advantage.

Box 9.1: The Agriculture Sector

Uzbekistan's climate is typical desert continental, with high-temperature summers and low-temperature winters. Average rainfall ranged from 176 to 302 mm from 1986 to 1992 (Figure 1), and was not enough to support agriculture, which is wholly dependent on irrigation. About 80 to 89 percent of available water resources are used for agriculture. Because frost occurs frequently from late September until April, only one crop can be grown a year, with double cropping limited to vegetables.

Total cultivated area was 4.22 million hectares in 1991, of which 41 percent was under cotton, 32 percent grain crops, 11 percent fruits, 4 percent vegetables, and 12 percent was used for other cultivation. Between 1987 and 1991, the share of cotton in the cultivated area declined by 16 percent, the share of grain increased by 3 percent, and the shares of fruits and vegetables increased by 2 percent and 1 percent, respectively (Figure 2). The total cultivated area fell by 155,000 hectares (about 4 percent).

Although grain production increased by 38 percent in 1986-91, yields fell by 3 percent. Vegetables followed a similar pattern. Cotton production, however, declined by 7 percent, but yields increased by 11 percent (Figures 3 and 4). Yields in Uzbekistan are lower than those in other developing and industrialized countries with similar climatic conditions. Therefore, the potential for productivity improvements is extensive.

In the former Soviet Union (FSU) the states' involvement in agriculture was comprehensive, and the main features of that system still exist. Thus, the Government of Uzbekistan (1) owns and exploits the land, and sets production targets and the share of it accruing to the Government (100 percent until 1990); (2) determines the requirements of chemical inputs for collective and state (CS) farms; (3) sets farm, input, and consumer-goods prices, and monopolizes the processing and distribution of agricultural goods and inputs; (4) monopolizes the import and export of agricultural products and inputs; and (5) restricts the movement of labor within the rural sector and between the rural and urban sectors.

Pricing Policies. The Ministry of Finance (MOF) has primary responsibility for pricing policy. Producer prices are established separately from quotas, often after planting, and have played little part in determining production levels. However, farm managers have known that the Government will compensate them for any difference between production costs and farm receipts, either through budgetary transfers (the state farms) or through input subsidies (the collective farms). Moreover, only those farms that have agreed on a production plan with the Government are assured of inputs at subsidized prices. In the past year, some input prices have been increased, thus squeezing farm profits. Even so, prices for tradeable goods remain well below international prices, while water, a key input, is free.

Consumer prices are established without consideration of international prices. Any difference between the full cost of delivering products to consumers and the consumer price is covered by subventions to government enterprises and state shops.

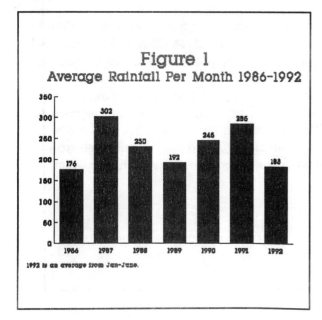

Figure 1
Average Rainfall Per Month 1986-1992

1992 is an average from Jan-June.

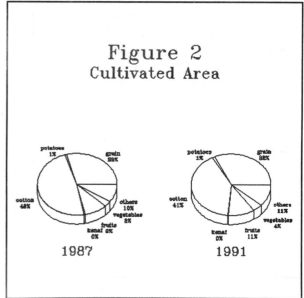

Figure 2
Cultivated Area

1987   1991

Box 9.1 (cont.)

Subsidized food products include bread, macaroni, flour, rice, oil, tea, sugar, meat, eggs, and yogurt. For 1991, it is estimated that food subsidies represent 7 percent of GDP.

Production Decisions and Rights to Farm Output. Planned (quota) output has traditionally been treated as belonging to the state rather than the farm. The composition and size of quota obligations are determined by the Forecasting and Statistics Committee (FSC, the former GOSPLAN), the Ministry of Agriculture (MOA), and the Ministry of Land Reclamation and Water Resources (MLRWR). The FSC estimates the country's overall requirements for food and foreign exchange and, in agreement with MOA and MLRWR, establishes the level of production quotas. Inputs, including water and farm finance, are allocated accordingly. Quotas and input allocations are then passed on to the regions, to be distributed at the district level.

Since 1990--as an incentive to increase agricultural (especially food) production,--the CS farm can retain a share of the planned production, provided that it meets its quota. This farm-refined proportion has been increasing and varies among crops, currently varying from 20 percent for cotton to 50 percent for fruits and vegetables. The farmer, however, must sell its nonquota output through the CS farm that sells it on the emerging private markets (mainly the urban bazaar). Proceeds are distributed among CS farm members. Differential prices for quota and "free" market output are an implicit heavy tax on agricultural production.

Distribution. Apart from the important "farmers' markets," internal distribution is monopolized by state enterprises. In addition, state enterprises or official "contractors" are responsible for all international trading--import and export--of agricultural products (see below).

Families in the rural sector could always retain 100 kg. of the grain they produced. The purchase of selected commodities (rice, milk, meat, soap, tea, and sugar) at official prices is subject to rationing. Purchases over the ration can be bought in the free market. Subsidized bread is an exception. Its price is controlled, but it is freely available. However, private bakeries are rationed flour from state enterprises, and restaurants must buy bread or rice at market prices.

International Trade. External trade is controlled by the Minister of Foreign Economic Relations (MFER)-- through of import and export licenses and through the direct trading of commodities by state enterprises. In the past, these enterprises were fully controlled by the MFER. However, in mid-1991, the Ministry of Agriculture also created a unit to intermediate agricultural commodities abroad.

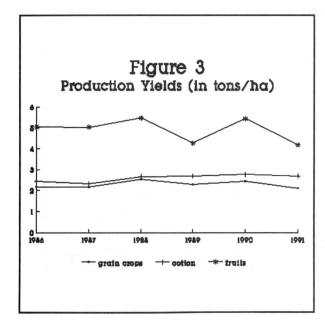

Figure 3
Production Yields (in tons/ha)

grain crops — cotton — fruits

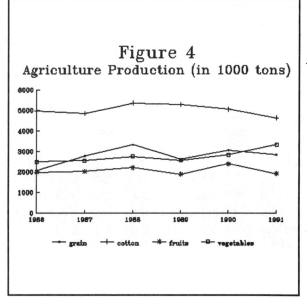

Figure 4
Agriculture Production (in 1000 tons)

grain — cotton — fruits — vegetables

B. SHORT-TERM ISSUES AND RECOMMENDATIONS:
STRUCTURAL REFORM TO PROMOTE THE IMMEDIATE EXPANSION OF OUTPUT

INSTITUTIONAL STRUCTURE

9.5   Uzbekistan's agriculture is controlled by the Government, which dictates what farmers produce and the inputs they use (see Box 9.1). The state owns the land and the water, and production is predominantly by collective and state (CS) farms; state processors of agricultural products buy from farmers at predetermined prices, and then sell to Government stores, whose prices are also Government-determined. CS farms receive their inputs from Government-owned concerns and Government agencies, and the quantity and composition of those inputs are allocated according to the production plan agreed by the CS farm and Government. The result is that the farmer, **a primary decisionmaker in a market-based economy**, has little freedom to decide what goods to produce, where to sell them, and which inputs to use and where to buy them. In short, wholesale and retail markets and markets for factors of production (for example, labor, capital, land, and water) barely exist.

9.6   Thus, the country is wasting a valuable asset: the knowledge and expertise of farmers, and their entrepreneurial abilities. The absence of well-developed markets inhibits the generation and dissemination of information and the allocation of resources to the most productive activities. This means that actual output is lower than potential output, perhaps by a substantial margin.

9.7   In the short term, Uzbekistan must pursue a comprehensive strategy for improving the agricultural productivity and profitability. To increase productivity, it must allow for more attractive incentives, including:

- Elimination of the state order system in agriculture

- Removal of trade restrictions on inputs and output

- Creation of markets and elimination of entry barriers for marketing and distribution.

To increase profitability, Government must implement a more efficient pricing policy for output and inputs, including:

- Movement towards international prices

- Reassessment of tax/policy on consumption subsidy and on production.

INCREASING PRODUCTIVITY: IMPROVING THE INCENTIVE STRUCTURE

The State Order System

9.8   The state order system regulates economic relations between collective and state farms and the Government. The Government determines the output (*planned* output) of farms and the proportion of output (*quota* output) that they must sell to Government enterprises. Both forms of output are sold at procurement prices fixed by the Government and, until 1990, quota and planned output were one and the same. In 1991, the Government allowed farms to keep a small percentage of their output and authorized that nonquota and overquota output could be sold in bazaars (open markets) at market-determined prices. In 1992, the farmers' retained share of output was increased. The Government plans to reduce further the share of quota output that farmers must sell to the state, and to abolish it completely for such output as fruits and vegetables within three years.

9.9   Whether this has helped increase production is hard to say, given the dearth of information on agricultural production. Collectives certainly have more freedom, but this may not extend to individual farmers. They must sell output through the collective, which determines how the fruits of the extra effort are distributed. Although the allocation rule applied by the collective links additional production and reward, the rule does not apply specifically to rewards for individual farmers. That must change; any output that exceeds the state order must be the (owned) property of the farmer, who should be free to sell where and how he wishes. Moreover, planned output is linked to past performance. Thus, if, say, last year's output was higher than planned output, this year's planned output is increased. Farmers do not have any incentive to disclose the true amount produced.

9.10   In China, "rural reforms also contributed significantly to output growth during 1978-1984," and "among the various components of reform, the shift from the production-team system to the household responsibility system (HRS) is clearly the most important one. This institutional reform alone produced 48 percent of the output growth, as much as the combined effects of input increases."[1] In 1978-84, agriculture in China grew at 7.7 percent a year, and total output by 56 percent. Thus, approximately 28 percent of the increase in output was obtained *without the help of additional productive inputs*.[2]

9.11   Giving such farmers institutional freedom is a significant change that should encourage and enable them to use resources more effectively and to specialize. Uzbekistan must also allow farmers to market and distribute output through channels other than the collective and state farm; also, they must be allowed to establish and run activities such as trucking, distribution, and retailing.

9.12   Uzbekistan's agriculture and its agroindustry do not have a marketing system for most production (or, for that matter, inputs) and there are huge impediments to a well-functioning and competitive system. Private shops account for less than 3 percent of all shops -- insufficient for any meaningful competition for public outlets or to increase efficiency. With the new direction in economic policy, alternative market intermediaries are only just beginning to emerge but are still dwarfed by government parastatals, which dominate processing and distribution of products and inputs, and thus enjoy considerable monopolistic powers. Private parties and state enterprises do not have the right to export and import agricultural commodities and inputs directly.

9.13   The present system does not convey the correct market-price signals to producer and processor to allow for market-based production decisions, and it fails to create incentives for investment in agriculture, in processing, and, in particular, in support services such as storage and transportation. Furthermore, the absence of open-entry into--and competition within--distribution means that facilities for processing, transporting, and storing output are inadequate, and the quality of finished products is

---

[1] Justin Yifu Lin, "Rural Reforms and Agricultural Growth in China," American Economic Review, March 1992, p.46.

[2] D. Gale Johnson, The People's Republic of China: 1978-1990, San Francisco: International Center for Economic Growth, 1990.

often far below international standards. It is estimated that post-harvest losses in fruits and vegetables are 20 to 25 percent of farm output.

9.14   Under the present system, production enterprises bring goods to the consumer on the basis of pre-ordained plans and using a mechanistic distribution system. Prices are based on rigid cost formulas and are merely intercompany transfer values. Independent decisionmaking by the management of individual enterprises is limited to daily operational issues. Since the distribution system has many imperfections, a shadow market of goods and services developed a long time ago, and (in the absence of market-based banking) much of that was barter. This primitive system of exchange repaired some of the supply problems, but did not nothing to bridge the gap between the producer and the consumer, nor to help direct investments and make distribution more efficient.

9.15   In the initial stages of transition from central planning to market-based production, the Government has relaxed compulsory supplies through the quota system. However, the infrastructural constraints remain. Nevertheless, a real market is developing, based partly on the nonquota component of production. Most, if not all, enterprises are circumventing closed-accounts payment by opening retail shops, but these are often an extension of the old shadow economy: obtaining retail space, owned primarily by municipalities, requires favors.

9.16   Institutional constraints on developing a market site are formidable, given the absence of an enabling environment. The usual trade-facilitating services, laws and regulations, and physical and institutional infrastructure taken for granted in market economies are missing. There is no established way to obtain retail. Wholesale markets for farmers, traders and agroindustries do not exist. Neither, do national or even regional price information systems to create market transparency. Even if such markets existed, agroindustries would be hard pressed to procure because of the unavailability of cash. Furthermore, the image that internal trading was not a valid and useful economic activity lingers on and is an added impediment to market development.

9.17   Although apparently flourishing, farmers' retail markets in urban centers are no substitute for a wholesale network. Rather, they should be supplied by wholesale markets. The production of individual farmers is now limited to what can be sold in a small market, providing no room for expansion. The same possibility for expansion through supply arrangements with processing enterprises and other bulk buyers, such as supermarket chains, is made difficult by the absence of laws governing contractual relations and entities to enforce the obligations of parties to a contract.

9.18   The absence of a true marketing system creates problems, including the following:

- Production enterprises cannot adapt activities and prices to the wishes of the consumer or other parties because there is no feedback from the consumer.

- Production monopolies have become bloated cost structures, passing high costs to the consumer.

- Incentives for establishing efficient distribution facilitating services, such as adequate storage and transportation, do not exist.

- Product losses tend to be high, since production is based on quantitative targets. Plan fulfillment is paramount. Anything over a norm has limited value. Quality is usually not an important consideration.

9.19   Government intervention in trade goes beyond the direct taxation of exports; it also includes the actual importing and exporting of commodities. International trade can be effected only through government organizations, and exporters require a license to trade, and, moreover, must go through many intermediaries to market their output.

9.20   Barter is the primary mechanism for effective international trade, since high export taxes deter hard-currency transactions. Exports other than cotton incur a uniform 40 percent tax when bought in hard currency. Moreover, exporters are subject to surrender requirements. In contrast, when commodities are exported on barter terms, not only is the 40 percent export tax avoided, but exporters specify the commodities they want without having to request an import license.

9.21   The tax treatment of cotton is complex. The price for free cotton is fixed according to prices prevailing on the Commodity Exchange of Tashkent. Because a license is required to export cotton, the domestic price is invariably below the international price (represented by the Liverpool index). Thus, exporters are taxed directly through a lower export price. Export taxes also discriminate between quota output and "free output." In 1992, the tax on "free" output comprised a 40 percent export levy on the 20 percent of quota production retained by farmers and a 20 percent tax on the excess over quota.[3] The tax on quota output was 60 percent, discounted directly by the MOF. Barter trade on quota production is handled by the MFER, and exports of barter cotton are exempted from any export tax.

9.22   Moreover, cotton producers must pay other fees to export. Export intermediaries get 5 percent of the exported value, while the state organization is relieved of paying the fees for processing the license. In 1992, producers also had to pay a fixed 10,000 rubles to collective and state farms (or 20,000 rubles to a Government agency) if they made the export arrangement.

INCREASING PROFITABILITY: PRICING POLICY AND SECTORAL TRANSFERS

9.23   The Government fixes prices for agricultural products and inputs, and, enforces them through state quotas orders, and the control of distribution, imports, and exports. In Uzbekistan, prices serve as an accounting device, and as a mechanism for effecting income transfers among social groups. Ancillary activities such as transportation and storage are also Government controlled. Thus, the main role of prices--to provide general information on the status of markets and to serve as a signaling mechanism--has been suppressed. For this reason, the prices for inputs and farm products in Uzbekistan bear little relation to their scarcity in the domestic market or to international prices.

9.24   Official prices for farm products are far below both domestic free-market (bazaar) prices and international prices, and adjustments in official prices follow price changes in free-market prices. Similarly, official input prices are way below international prices and have not necessarily been adjusted

---

[3] The procedure is slightly more complex than as described in the text. If exports correspond to the production over quota, 80 percent of the foreign exchange proceeds goes to exporters in hard currency, and the remaining 20 percent must be sold to the Central Bank at the market exchange rate. To import commodities with the retained 80 percent of foreign currency, the importer must pay a 25 percent import tax at the market exchange rate.

to the change in the general price level. It is likely that these interventions have led to a significant misallocation of resources, to distorted consumption patterns, and to a substantial transfer of resources from agriculture to the rest of the economy.

9.25   The large differences between bazaar prices and official prices indicate the distortions that exist (see Table 9.1). As early as September 1992, bazaar prices were twice or three time as high as controlled prices. Between December 1991 and September 1992, however, the ratio of bazaar to official prices for most commodities declined, as partial liberalization of markets has reduced distortions. Further liberalization is needed not only to provide appropriate production incentives but to compensate farmers for the profit squeeze as the costs of imported inputs (agrochemical and fuel) are shifted to farmers to avoid further deterioration in the Government's fiscal situation.

Table 9.1
Uzbekistan: Ratio of Market to State Prices, 1989-1992

	12/30/89	12/30/90	12/30/91	9/2/92
Milk	1.8	2.0	1.8	1.5
Meat	1.6	2.8	1.3	1.3
Butter	1.1	2.3	2.2	2.5
Edible Oil	n.a	n.a	2.3	2.0
Sugar	n.a	n.a	1.7	4.0
Rice	3.8	4.0	3.0	2.7
Potato	3.1	6.1	2.0	1.3
Tomato	2.5	2.0	3.0	2.5
Grapes	3.0	2.5	2.5	2.1
Tea	2.0	2.0	1.6	1.5
Coffee	1.3	1.5	1.6	n.a
Melon	2.0	2.0	2.0	1.4
Apple	1.5	2.3	2.5	2.0
Vodka	2.0	1.3	1.5	2.3

Source: Bank staff estimates based on information from Ministry of Agriculture.

THE PROFITS SQUEEZE: OUTPUT-INPUT PRICES

9.26   Between December 1989 and September 1992, state-price increases varied from 90 times for potatoes and 7 times for fruits (melons and apples); bazaar-price increases were as much as 90 times for butter and 5 times for melons. The price of inputs also increased, ranging from an increase of 5 times for electricity up to 60 times for urea and 150 times for pesticides.

9.27   The decline in the profitability of agriculture is significant because the increase in the price of some products has been larger than the price rise of its required inputs, while the reverse has been true of others. It is hard to estimate the full impact on the profitability. Yet, between the end of 1991 and September 1992, the Government increased the price of inputs substantially, and the profitability of agriculture (measured as the ratio of either state-to-input prices or bazaar-to-input prices) has declined. Output prices have fallen dramatically relative to the price of inputs, sometimes by 80 to 100 percent (Table 9.2). Profitability has declined even according to the ratio of output to electricity input prices (for which official prices were not adjusted too far upwards); the exceptions are seedcotton, maize, and tomatoes.

9.28   This profit squeeze has been exacerbated by an inadequate supply of fuel and spare parts. This is due to the lack of foreign exchange, and to the disruption in the production of machinery and inputs in the FSU. Thus, the prices for output, input, and spare parts do not reflect their true opportunity costs to farmers, and the absence of a well-functioning marketing and distribution system prevents quick delivery of these products. So, liberalizing these prices alone will not correct the problems. To do so, entry barriers in the distribution of outputs and inputs must be lifted, and competition must be introduced.

Table 9.2
Uzbekistan: The Decline in Profitability of Selected Agricultural Products:
Change in the Output-Input Price Ratio Between
December 1991 and September 1992

Milk Output/Input			Maize Output/Input	
Electricity	-31		Electricity	100
Nitrogenous fertilizer	-81		Nitrogenous Fertilizer	-44
Meat Output/Input			Seedcotton Output/Input	
Electricity	-47		Electricity	136
Nitrogenous fertilizer	-85		Nitrogenous fertilizer	-33
Rice Output/Input			Wheat Output/Input	
Electricity	-20		Electricity	50
Nitrogenous fertilizer	-77		Nitrogenous fertilizer	-58
Potato Output/Input			Oats Output/Input	
Electricity	33		Electricity	-50
Nitrogenous fertilizer	-62		Nitrogenous fertilizer	-58
Tomato Output/Input			Alfalfa Output/Input	
Electricity	100		Electricity	-14
Nitrogenous fertilizer	-44		Nitrogenous fertilizer	-76
Grapes Output/Input			Barley Output/Input	
Electricity	-7		Electricity	38
Nitrogenous fertilizer	-74		Nitrogenous fertilizer	-61
Apple Output/Input				
Electricity	-40			
Nitrogenous fertilizer	-83			

Source: Bank staff estimates based on information from Ministry of Agriculture.

Note: Output prices are bazaar prices, except for cotton which is the state price.

TRANSFERS INTO AGRICULTURE: INPUT SUBSIDIES

9.29   Again, direct Government intervention in pricing agricultural products and inputs has led to substantial differences between domestic and international prices. Crude comparisons indicate that between 1989 and 1992 the domestic prices of agricultural products were falling well below international prices (see Table 9.3). In 1992, the falling ratio of domestic to international prices reversed, but domestic prices are still below international prices.

9.30   The Government subsidizes the prices of farm inputs to compensate farmers for the low returns on their output. Yet, subsidies do not offset them fully. The bulk of the subsidies to farmers are the free distribution of *water*, the free use of *land*, and cut-price *electricity*, *agrochemical inputs*, and *fuels*. Although estimates of subsidies is constrained by lack of data, an effort was made to estimate the amount of subsidies based on a subset of subsided inputs (Table 9.4). Even so, this method underestimates the subsidies.

9.31   Given the absence of information, comparisons of domestic and international prices of inputs and outputs exclude transport costs, except for cotton. Transport is highly subsidized. The cost of moving cotton by rail from Tashkent to the Baltics is roughly $9 a ton. That compares to $165 a ton from Mexico to Georgia and the Carolinas in the United States. Using that cost would reduce the overestimate of transfer out of agriculture. Because the relevant price to farmers for imported commodities is the f.o.b. price plus internal transport costs from the shipping port to the domestic market, excluding transport costs from the price comparisons would underestimate the size of the transfers out of agriculture. This would be the case for wheat, milk, and butter.

Table 9.3
Uzbekistan: Ratio of Domestic to International Prices
(In percent)

	12/30/89	12/30/90	12/30/91	9/2/92
Procurement				
Rice	28	30	9	17
Coffee	310	621	367	-
Tea	56	32	14	23
Sugar	32	13	18	33
Edible Oil	18	10	4	10
Cotton Fiber	15	6	3	16
Bazaar				
Wheat	28	27	9	21
Maize	25	40	11	41

Source: Bank staff estimates based on information from Ministry of Agriculture.

TRANSFERS OUT OF AGRICULTURE

9.32   The net result of Government input and output pricing policy is that (1) imports and the domestic consumption of commodities not produced by the country (for example, tea and sugar) are subsidized; (2) imports and the domestic consumption of commodities that the country does not produce (for example, grains) are subsidized but their production is taxed; and (3) the production of commodities exported by the country (for example, cotton) is taxed but their consumption is subsidized.

9.33   Gross transfers out of agriculture, resulting from the Government price policy on inputs and output, are US$1.5 billion, of which US$1.2 billion relates to cotton. Grains is the second most taxed commodity, at US$200 million, followed by rice (US$81 million), and maize (US$27 million) (Table 9.5). With total transfers into agriculture from input subsidies of US$916 million (Table 9.4), the net result is a transfer out of US$0.6 billion dollars, equivalent to roughly 8 percent of the sector's GDP.

9.34   Who benefits and who loses? The net loser is the farm sector, because it is a net seller of agricultural products. Urban consumers are obvious gainers, because in monopolizing cotton exports, the Government can buy cotton from farmers and sell it to Russia for oil. Thus, the Government can sell electricity and fuel to consumers at low prices. The difference between the price paid and the export price of cotton permits the Government to sell the imported grain to urban and rural consumers at subsidized prices.

9.35   While low consumer prices benefit urban consumers, they may hurt or help the rural population depending on whether they are net sellers or buyers of agricultural products. Moreover, as the sector becomes market-oriented, low consumer prices are likely to create artificial shortages as producers shift resources into more profitable activities. Agricultural pricing policy is a critical determinant of the allocation of budgetary resources, yet consumer protection is also an important policy concern during adjustment and transition. The two objectives should now be treated separately in the budget allocation and the policy process.

Table 9.4
Uzbekistan: Input Use in Agriculture and Subsidies Received

	Unit	Consumption (1990)	Subsidy (in US$ million)
1. Electricity (Alt. B)	Million kwh	14883	790
a. Irrigation	"	7121	380
b. Agriculture Production	"	4574	243
c. Homes/Rural Areas	"	3188	167
2. Diesel Fuel	1000 tons	1416	48
3. Motor Gasoline	1000 tons	144	2
4. Urea	1000 tons	690	76
TOTAL			916

Source: Bank staff estimates.

Note: All prices are as of October 1992. Because the irrigation system is a heavy user of energy (50 percent of the electricity used in agriculture), the value of its subsidy is obtained by comparing the price of energy used in irrigation with the export price of energy; this yields a lower (underestimated) bound for the value. In addition, the subsidy for the rest of the input consumption of energy is obtained in a similar way. The subsidy on fuel consumption is calculated as the difference between its domestic price and its ex-refinery price in world markets. And the subsidy for the consumption of agrochemicals is calculated for urea only. Pesticides and other fertilizers are left outside of this calculation given the limitations of available information.

RECOMMENDATIONS

9.36   To enable farmers to use natural resources more effectively and induce them to increase agricultural output, Uzbekistan needs to reform its pricing and market policy. Farm prices should be liberalized by (1) eliminating the farmers' obligation to sell some output to the Government; (2) lifting restrictions on the export and import of agricultural products and inputs; (3) dismantling the entry barriers to distribution of farm output and inputs; and (4) pricing some of the Government-supplied inputs at international prices.

9.37   A full liberalization of prices should generate a permanent increase in the general price. Raising input prices will hurt agriculture, but a comprehensive package of agricultural price reform should give a boost to the sector, because the sector transferred around $0.6 billion to the rest of the economy in 1991.

9.38   By controlling prices and trade, the Government can also purchase cheap products abroad (through barter) and pass these low prices to consumers. Thus, because the Government is the direct recipient of some transfers, the reform of agricultural price policy must be linked to its ability to create and benefit from alternative sources of revenue. Pricing policy reform is necessary and urgent, because only then will agriculture be able to increase its output and generate gains in productivity. While output growth in the past was made possible by the expansion of area through massive land reclamation schemes, these alternatives are not now feasible, because the necessary fiscal resources do not exist. Today, farmers are the only ones who can deliver productivity gains and increased savings, but they can do so only if the huge resources they transfer to the rest of the economy go back to them.

Table 9.5
Uzbekistan: Taxation (-) of Agricultural Production:
1992
(US$ million)

PRODUCT	PRODUCTION (1000 tons)	TAXATION *
White Rice	334.75	(81)
Cotton Fiber	1440.57	(1,193)
Wheat (Grain crops)	1908	(219)
Maize	431	(27)
Barley		
TOTAL		(1,520)

* taxation measured at 1992 prices

Source: Bank staff estimates.

9.39   To support reform in this area, the Government should create the necessary enabling structures for private initiatives to develop the country's opportunities.

- **Market Information.** Developing a market-oriented economy successfully is predicated on a continuous flow of information prices, stock levels, and product movements in both domestic and foreign markets.

- **Legal Framework.** This must be adapted to the new economic circumstances and should focus on commercial contracts; the liability of specific professions, such as brokers, and commission agents; licensing; and regulation and supervision of organized marketplaces, including commodity exchanges.

- **Water and Land Pricing.** Government revenue, and the corresponding transfers, can be obtained more efficiently by pricing water and land. Water could be priced according to its opportunity cost, and land could be leased to farmers. Under a generalized program of land leasing, the Government could obtain revenue of approximately US$0.6 billion, if, for example, farmers were to pay an annual rent of roughly US$160 per hectare.[4] Trying to obtain all the revenue from land rental is not efficient in terms of resource allocation. The most efficient outcome would be to price both water and land. Pricing

---

[4] This would be equivalent to 16 percent of the gross value of farm income on a hectare of land that produces 800 kgs of lint cotton per year with cotton valued at $1,200 per ton.

water according to its scarcity value would eliminate wastage of water and would reduce the problems of land salinity. The pricing of water would reduce the rental price of land because land values incorporate the value of water when it is free.

- *Wholesale and Retail Marketing*. Facilitating commerce and trade by providing the physical means and locales to operate markets would help reduce marketing costs. In collaboration with local authorities, the Government should consider developing a network of agricultural wholesale markets, and creating retail shops by making credit for both investment and working capital available.

Box 9.2: Water Resource Management

Water allocation in Central Asia is governed by well-established criteria, initially based on decrees from Moscow but more recently confirmed by agreements between the riparian republics. Coordination is effected through the Inter-Ministerial Coordination Committee, and implemented by two river basin commissions (BVOs), one each for the Amu Darya and Syr Darya. The BVOs control all river and canal off takes that affect more than one country, manage inter-republic and inter-sectoral allocations, and monitor water use and water quality. The Syr Darya BVO is supported by a strong analytical and monitoring capability, and proposals are being developed both for strengthening this and for extending it to the Amu Darya BVO.

Although these arrangements have worked satisfactorily to date, the Aral Sea mission urged that a legally binding treaty be signed--also involving riparians other than the republics of the FSU--so as to guard against the dangers of future water disputes. Uzbekistan, as a downstream riparian on the Amu Darya and a mid-stream riparian on the Syr Darya, and a principle beneficiary of the present arrangements, would appear to have a strong interest in reaching such agreement.

C. MEDIUM AND LONG-TERM ISSUES:
REFORM TO SUSTAIN OUTPUT EXPANSION

9.40   In agriculture, as in other sectors, the next few years will be critical to reform and transition to a market-based economy, but for sustained development this must be complemented by longer-term strategies to exploit Uzbekistan's comparative advantage in the sector.

- Because water resources of Central Asia have been exploited fully, production strategy must thus focus on increasing value-added from land and water that have already been developed.

- Continued growth in value-added will depend crucially on crop diversification and agro-industrial development in line with Uzbekistan's comparative advantage. Liberalized markets and prices will provide the primary signals and incentives for attaining this objective, but Government support services will also play a crucial role.

- Irrigation expansion in Central Asia has been the primary cause of the environmental problems associated with the shrinking of the Aral Sea; any developmental path for Uzbekistan's agriculture must be consistent with measures that address environmental concerns.

A SUSTAINABLE ENVIRONMENT

9.41   Irrigation has created serious environmental problems and eroded the resource base. The most dramatic effect has been the shrinking of the Aral Sea, which has led directly to the destruction of transport, and related infrastructure. Other impacts have included (1) the loss of the fish resource of the Aral Sea, due to an increase in salinity and chemical pollution; (2) land degradation from the waterlogging and salinization of irrigated land; (3) crop diseases and insect infestation, due particularly to the cotton monoculture; (4) adverse health effects from the poor quality of water, and wind-blown chemicals; and (5) possible local climatic change.

THE ARAL SEA

9.42   According to a recent Bank mission, "reducing cotton areas, investing in water management, and other measures to save water for the sole purpose of increasing the flows to the Aral Sea is not a viable option." If so, modernizing irrigation and drainage must be evaluated in terms of releasing water for other domestic uses, rather than augmenting flows into the sea. Even so, the mission concluded that the sea should be stabilized at a "sustainable level," implying that, at best, Uzbekistan must live within its present water allocation. The mission also argued that priority should be given to assisting the "disaster" zone affected directly by the diminishing sea, including activities in health, water supply, employment, population planning, delta reclamation, and the stabilization of the exposed seabed.

9.43   Even if saving water to augment Aral Sea flows is "not a viable option," such programs may still--directly or indirectly--help alleviate regional problems. For instance, the reclamation of agricultural lands in the lower Amu Darya could, in conjunction with investments, alleviate water quality and health problems.

WATERLOGGING AND SALINITY

9.44   Salinization of land is a critical issue. About 2.1 million hectares--almost 50 percent of the irrigated area--is affected by salinization, of which 300,000 hectares are severely affected, 700,000 hectares are moderately affected, and 1.1 million hectares are only slightly affected. The primary method for control is leaching, which requires much water. Proper drainage could substantially reduce leaching requirements--by as much as 3,000 m3/ha (from 5,000 m3/ha to 2,000 m3/ha)--as could augmenting crop yields directly by controlling water levels and salinity. Moreover, drainage allows diversification out of high-water-using paddy, which may otherwise be the only viable crop in affected areas. For all these reasons, drainage programs have a strong prima facie justification. To date, subsurface and vertical drainage amounts cover only 1.5 million hectares.

9.45   Drainage water from the irrigated areas either returns to the rivers (ultimately to the Aral Sea) or collects in desert lakes. In the former case, flows may be reutilized repeatedly, deteriorating the quality of river water. In the lower Amu Darya, in particular, this practice has adversely affected agriculture and, more importantly, human health. A large right-bank collector drain is under construction, designed to pass through a long desert reach before outfalling in the Aral Sea. A broad study of drainage disposal should be undertaken to evaluate (1) preserving the desert lakes, (2) reutilizing water currently evaporated from their surface, and/or (3) collecting such waters to augment flows to the Aral Sea.

9.46   On top of salinization, some 500,000 hectares are affected by waterlogging. The loss of water through surface evaporation could be reduced through groundwater development, which would both add to irrigation supplies and contribute to yield increases in affected areas.

RESOURCE MANAGEMENT

9.47   Legally binding criteria for seasonal water allocation must be complemented by long-term water resource management of river basins. Responsibility for developing strategies could be assigned to the two BVOs (see Box 9.2), reflecting also regional agreements on the Aral Sea. Uzbekistan would need to develop a national water strategy within the context of the regional plan.

ENHANCING OUTPUT FROM LIMITED WATER AND ARABLE LAND

Water

9.48   To realize potential gains in agricultural output in Uzbekistan, Government policy and institutional changes must be supported by longer-term measures to improve the efficiency of land and water use (see Box 9.2) Such measures will involve a coordinated program of institutional support, incentives, investment, and technical progress. Priorities and linkages among them would be best established in the context of resource planning studies.

9.49   **Financing Irrigation**. Financial constraints have severely limited the funds available for maintaining, repairing, modernizing, and constructing irrigation and drainage systems. Since the early 1980s, new construction work has slowed rapidly, reflecting (1) increasing water constraints and a recognition of the problems that new development was posing for the Aral Sea; (2) the economic and financial crisis affecting the FSU and, more recently, Uzbekistan; and (3) since the beginning of 1992, the ending of subventions from the center. Table 9.6 summarizes expenditures in recent years by the Ministry of Melioration and Water Management (MMWM) and UZVODHSTROI (a Construction Agency) and the area developed in recent years by UZVODHSTROI (estimates for MMWM are unavailable).

9.50   **Water Use and Potential Savings**. Water use varies according to water availability, rainfall, cropping patterns, soils, leaching requirements, the design and condition of the irrigation network, and other factors (Table 9.7). SANIIRI estimates that average water use could be reduced to about 11,000 m³/ha, or by 17 percent of the 1991 figure. If crop evapo-transpiration ranges between 6,000 and 7,000 m³/ha depending on crop mix, if leaching requirements are 1,000 m³/ha, and if rainfall effectiveness is 50 percent, then target efficiency would be 55 - 60 percent. A savings

Table 9.6
Uzbekistan: Developmental Expenditures and Expansion of Irrigated Areas

	MMWM	UZVODHSTROI	
	M Rbls.	M Rbls	Ha
1988	na	1,310	22,300
1989	na	1,115	12,700
1990	1,120	1,240	11,500
1991	1,040	1,598	11,300
1992 (plan)	na	2,779	4,500

Source: Council of Ministers.

of 17 percent is equivalent to about 9 B m^3. Because irrigation losses and leaching water return to drainage and are extensively reused, net savings would be lower. Moreover, major drainage programs would also tend to reduce water reuse further, unless combined with expensive treatment works.

9.51   Achieving these water-saving objectives will involve complementary measures--in operations, investment, and incentives--many of which will have a positive impact on agricultural productivity.

Box 9.3: Irrigation

The Ministry of Melioration and Water Management (MMWM) has primary responsibility for policy, planning, development, and O&M of major irrigation and drainage works. It is funded from the state budget and, with the exception of vertical drainage, its responsibilities end at the boundary of the state or collective farm. However, few farms can do more than minor maintenance works, so that they normally have maintenance contracts with local offices of the MMWM. In principle, the state and collective farms are self-financing, with funding to support development works and to cover operating losses (if any) derived from the national budget for state farms and from the credit system for collective farms. Technical support and advice to farm management is provided by the Ministry of Agriculture.

In the past, new construction in designated areas was funded under the Union budget and carried out by the Central Asia Water Construction Committee. With independence, this was broken up, and its components transferred to the republics. Uzbekistan's Water Construction Committee (UZVOD) was amalgamated with the MMWM, but this was unworkable, and the two have again been separated. In principle, UZVOD will evolve into an autonomous construction agency, working on contract to the MMWM.

The research and development base is substantial and impressive, although it is being eroded by the loss of qualified staff and the impact of the country's financial crisis. Technical research and design, and the manufacturing of irrigation materials and equipment, are delegated to autonomous institutes and manufacturing entities, the most important of which are (1) the Central Asia Scientific Research Institute of Irrigation (SANIIRI) under MMWM, which previously had responsibility for all Central Asia and which, besides its design and research activities, manufactures a wide range of irrigation equipment; and (2) the Central Asia Design Institute for the Creation of Irrigated Cotton Areas within UZVOD, which has designed the massive irrigation and settlement projects undertaken over the past 30 years or so. Other important research institutes include the Institute of Water Problems in the Academy of Sciences and the Center for the Ecology of Water Management in the Ministry of Ecology.

Irrigation Water Management. Regional MMWM staff are responsible for distributing water received from the Basin Commission, or BVO, to the boundaries of the state and collective farms. Deliveries appear reasonably well-controlled, even if measurement at this level is often deficient and facilities have deteriorated due to inadequate O&M. Most controls are operated manually, although there has been some automation--for instance, of flow monitoring in the Fergana Valley. Water distribution within the state/collective farms is generally less systematic, and infrastructure is less well maintained.

Basin management follows well-tried procedures. Water demands of collective and state farms (including allowance for private land) are based on crop areas and water "norms," which are collated at the district (rayon), oblast, and national levels. In the past, crop areas were set by the state plan, but private, leasehold, and collective farmers are increasingly being given freedom to make their own choices. The initial water demands are adjusted by the BVOs in line with criteria governing national shares, and actual and projected water availability. The distribution plan is subsequently updated every 10 days to reflect river flows, rainfall, crop demands, etc. Similarly, planning for the noncrop season starts in September with leaching estimates based on soil tests and other factors.

Table 9.7
Uzbekistan: Water Use by Major Region in 1991
(averages weighted by irrigated area)

	Rainfall mm	Irrigated Area: 000ha	Water Use: m³/ha Norm	Crop	Non-Crop	Total
Fergana Valley	244	924.1	9.9	10.0	1.9	11.9
Mid-Syr Darya	424	957.5	10.5	9.7	1.2	10.9
Samarkand	500	407.1	10.6	7.9	0.7	8.6
Mid-Amu Darya	259	1,160.8	14.7	11.2	3.5	14.7
Lower-Amu Darya	112	750.1	19.3	14.2	3.8	18.0
Uzbekistan	290	4,199.6	13.1	10.8	1.4	13.2

Note: Fergana Valley - Andijan, Fergana and Namangan
      Mid-Syr Darya - Tashkent, Syr Darya, Djizak
      Mid-Amu Darya - Surhandarya, Karshi, Bhukara
      Lower-Amu Darya - Khorezm, Karalapak

Source: Ministry of Agriculture .

9.52   **Operational Improvements**. Operational improvements and water scheduling can be considered at each level of the system:

- *The Basin*. Basin operations are already systematic and well-established. The Amu Darya BVO is at an earlier stage in implementing water distribution based on sound analytical principles and should perhaps receive priority.

- *The Delivery System*. Present water-scheduling practices are effective in adjusting allocations to availability and--within limits--would allow reduced use over the longer term. This could hasten water savings through forced adjustments in cropping and other practices. However, such measures are limited with the present infrastructure, without reducing total cropped areas. Modernization would complement improved water distribution practices.

- *Within Farm*. A pilot Ministry of Agriculture program has shown that water indenting based on farm-level soil moisture measurements and centralized data analysis has the low-cost potential of reducing water use and enhancing crop yields. The present technology is adequate for areas with a water table at least 3 m below the surface and no salinity problems. Priority should be given to extending it to such areas (about 1 million ha) as well as to advancing program development to allow extension to less-favored areas. Rehabilitation and modernization of within-farm infrastructure would also help.

- *On-Farm*. Furrow irrigation (basin irrigation in paddy areas) dominates current on-farm practice and could be strengthened through improved land levelling, by the introduction of surge irrigation and other innovations, and, in particular, through on-farm field drainage.

9.53   **Investments**. Rehabilitating and modernizing the main and within-farm irrigation could include basic lining of canals but also some automation of measurement, monitoring, and control systems. However, a full modernization program that included extensive canal lining would be very expensive and would take years to complete. Careful planning work and feasibility studies are essential to prioritize areas to be modernized.

9.54   Experience of modern on-farm technologies (notably drip systems) has been mixed but the cost of drip systems is $3,500 - $4,000 per hectare and it seems unlikely that this can be justified other than for intensive horticultural and similar cropping systems. Subsurface irrigation is less expensive, although it is suited only to perennial cropping systems, whose scope is limited.

9.55   **Incentives**. The success and plausibility of operational improvements and investments will depend crucially on incentives. For the end-user, irrigation water is currently free, and, thus, neither state/collective farm managers nor private farmers have much incentive for saving water (although indirect incentives may exist where savings are associated with enhanced agricultural productivity). Subsidies on electricity and other inputs can also introduce serious distortions. As long as the water agency, MMWM, is funded from the state budget, incentives for improved performance will be independent of the irrigation service.

9.56   In 1989, a pilot scheme was introduced as a precursor for general water charges throughout the irrigated area. This scheme was a sort of dual tariff, based on the irrigated area and on the volume of water supplied. The objective was (1) to establish contractual relationships between the customers and the MMWM, so that the charge was seen as payment for delivery of service, and (2) to place the reimbursed monies into a special fund intended ultimately for financing O&M. Without any supportive constituency, the scheme collapsed, even though there are said to have been signs that it was having a positive effect on water use wherever the fee was collected. It seems that water measurement was a problem, and no resolution could be reached on how the monies collected to finance system O&M could be transferred.

9.57   The debate about whether or not a water charge should be introduced is continuing. One promising suggestion made by SANIIRI would be to link the fee to the irrigation norm established for that area. The basic fee could be set to cover O&M costs, with heavy penalties imposed if the norm was exceeded and rebates made if use was below the norm. Any scheme would also have to resolve how the monies collected to meet system O&M costs would be retained. Unless accurate control and measurement can be ensured at the point at which payment is made, however, no scheme will last.

9.58   Until it is in the interest of end-users and the delivery agency to save water, progress in water savings will be slow. Clearly, charges should cover at least O&M costs, with these costs reflecting the true cost of other inputs, notably electricity. Only if the charge is sufficiently high to ensure financial accountability by the irrigation agency will it begin to have a real influence on performance.

Land

9.59   In land privatization, some *qualitatively* significant steps have been taken. Land has been transferred to rural households, which can grow the products they wish, and leasing agreements have been developed between CS farms and members. These reforms have been implemented during the last two years, and small agroindustrial enterprises and private farms have begun to emerge.

9.60   **Land Leasing**. The Government views leasing within CS farms as preparation for the regime of private property. To lease land, farmers present an application to a village committee, with the power to approve or deny. The maximum lease is 25 years, and the CS farm is the lessor. Subleasing is allowed to children and relatives of lessees only, but the Government seems to be open to extending subleasing to third parties. The leasing price is agreed by the CS farm and the farmer, and payment is included in the price at which farmers sell produce to the CS farm. Because leasing fees are not known, the first element for developing an efficient land market--the transparency of transactions and prices--is absent. One alternative solution could be that farmers deliver an agreed-in-advance share of their output to the CS farm (share-cropping agreement). This solution would link the rental price of the land directly to its quality and would let farmers share the risk with the CS farm. Even so, staff in the Ministry of Agriculture claim that up to 100,000 hectares have been leased through 1992.

9.61   Farmers will exploit land fully only when property rights have been well defined. One option (full privatization) has been ruled out by the Government for now. An alternative is a generalized land leasing. For this to be successful, farmers must have full rights over the use of land and the freedom to organize their productive activities. This would generate revenue for the Government, thus compensating for the revenue loss from the elimination of the state order system. The system is also economically efficient. Moreover, if farmers perceive that the security of tenure on leased land is less than the security on the land where their houses and garden plots are located, investments will be biased towards housing. Providing the correct incentives to maintain and improve land quality is crucial to promote agricultural growth in Uzbekistan and a well-defined property rights system for land-use should contribute effectively to improved land quality. It should also expand output and lead to a better use of resources.

9.62   Land-use rights have to be defined and protected. The strongest protection against the arbitrary modification of those rights would be a clear definition of those rights, the recording of those rights in a public institution, and the establishment of a legal mechanism for protecting those rights. A clear definition of the property rights of farm households would reduce the power and authority of local authorities and farm managers, who are likely to resist change. A decision by the Government to maintain anything similar to the present system will discourage agricultural growth and gains in productivity. Such action, however, will discredit reform and weaken the support of the population for other urgent and necessary reforms.

9.63   **Land Distribution**. The Government claims that, during 1990-92, it distributed 350,000 hectares to rural households. Although, in theory, the household plot is given permanently to the farmer, the state can reclaim it if land is not used for the first three years. The size of the plot varies between 600 (in the cities) and 2,500 square meters in regions where the population density is low. The average size is 2,000 m2.

9.64   **Farm Reorganization**. While collective farms (CFs) are classified as cooperatives that do not qualify for budgetary allocations, state farms (SFs) are corporations that do qualify. CFs have already begun to be reorganized with land leasing, made on an individual basis or for groups of farmers. In other words, the Government is seeking to create true cooperatives or associations of farms within the present CFs. In the longer term, it is hoped that farm management will revert increasingly to the members of the association and that the CF managers will be retained only as cooperative managers at the discretion of the members.

9.65   As for the SFs, the Government has ceased giving them budgetary allocations and is moving towards converting them into CFs. Thus, 300 SFs have changed into cooperatives, and the Government expects to achieve its goal to convert all within three to four years.

CROP DIVERSIFICATION AND INCREASING PRODUCTIVITY IN COTTON

9.66   In the FSU, regional specialization was promoted. Uzbekistan's responsibility was cotton production to ensure Union self-sufficiency. The heavy reliance of Uzbek agriculture on cotton had many detrimental effects: (1) inadequate crop rotations, which drained soil fertility; and (2) inadequate attention to food production and/or processing infrastructure, promoting extensive dependence on imported food.

9.67   In response to these problems, the FSU planned to reduce the cotton-growing area gradually to around 1.6 million hectares, while maintaining production by increasing yields. Under this policy, the cotton area fell from 2.1 million hectares in 1987 to 1.72 million hectares in 1991; the 1992 area is estimated at over 1.6 million hectares. Yields of cottonseed increased from 2.3 tons/hectare in 1987 to 2.7 tons/hectare in 1991, while output fell from 4.9 million to 4.6 million tons.

9.68   If the Government so desires, it now has an opportunity to reduce the area planted in cotton. This strategy may have undesirable fiscal and foreign exchange consequences, but increases in productivity can accommodate the negative foreign exchange impact of reductions in the planted area. So, what are the potential sources of productivity gains in the cotton sector that could reduce cropped area while increasing output?

Competitiveness in World Markets

9.69   At current exchange rates and distorted input prices, Uzbek cotton seems to be able to compete in international markets. The sector, however, seems to be overextended as is indicated by the large differential between yields in high and low yield collective farms (10 to 1), and by the large subsidies to inputs. Because input prices must be increased to international levels, some of the cost advantages of cotton will disappear. Although the cost of inputs is a big slice of production costs (53 percent), the competitive edge of the cotton subsector in Uzbekistan could still be maintained as the increase in cotton prices, the increase in yields, and the higher efficiency of input use partly offset the increase in input prices. However, it may be that some low-yield cotton-producing regions may no longer be competitive when input prices are set at international levels.

Low Productivity

9.70   Cotton production is supported by a well-trained and experienced workforce. Quick gains in productivity are feasible. Gains in the production-to-marketing chain can be obtained if gains accumulate in each stage of production. These gains would come from the use of new, higher-yielding seeds and improved cleaning of seeds for planting; the removal of constraints on farmers' access to modern inputs; and more effective cotton marketing.

Increasing Yields

9.71   In recent years, the entire cotton crop has averaged a fiber yield of 850 - 890 kg/hectare, lower than other regions with similar growing conditions. Some irrigated areas in China have achieved yields of 900 to 1,100 kg/hectare and Australia's national yields averaged 1,554 kg/hectare. Thus, Uzbekistan can increase the productivity of its cotton growing by applying present agronomic technology judiciously. The efficient use of inputs is key to achieving increased cotton yields in Uzbekistan. The

Box 9.4: Agricultural Reform in China

Prior to reform, China was like Uzbekistan. Almost all land was collectively owned, over which farmers had no rights. The center dictated everything from the crops to be produced to the amount of land to be used to produce them. Pursuing self-sufficiency in grain, the Government expanded the sown acreage of grain without considering any comparative regional advantage. Consequently, the production of other crops and poultry contracted. Production was organized and carried out by the collectives. Production that exceeded the state procurement quota and the funds that could be retained for reproduction was distributed among farmers at the end of each year. Under the doctrine of egalitarianism and due to the difficulty of measuring and supervising farmers' work in agriculture, the earnings of farmers rarely matched their performance. Therefore, the work incentives of farmers were heavily distorted.

A small portion of land, about 5% of total land, comprised private plots, even before the land reform began. Private plots, though small, yielded about twice as much as collective land. Ideological constraints, however, precluded converting the land to some kind of private ownership until 1978. Land reform emerged. The so-called household responsibility system was introduced. The HRS contracts out land and other resources that had been collectively owned to individual households. These contracts specify quotas on the proportion of a household's production that it must submit to the government as an in-kind tax and to the collectives as funds for investment or community facilities. The residual production is at the disposal of the farmers. Land was leased initially for 3 to 5 years, but was later extended to 15 years. Households have rights to use the land but cannot sell these rights. Land is usually distributed according to the number of people in a household. Incentives have been greatly stimulated. Two studies estimated that this land reform alone accounts for 50 percent or more of the agriculture growth in 1978-84.

Efforts were also made to give farmers more autonomy and to reduce government intervention in production, which has become more responsive to price signals. Crops have been diversified, and cropping patterns and cropping intensity have been greatly reshaped since 1978. Land decollectivization also makes government interventions more difficult because the collectives through which the government used to control production have been weakened.

The institutional change from collective to HRS in China was a bottom-up process. It started in one of the poorest areas in Anhui province, where the Government had difficulty in promoting agricultural productivity under institutional constraints. Even so, within a couple of years, HRS spread throughout China. At the beginning of 1979, only 1 percent of farming institutions in China had adopted HRS; by 1981, this figure had risen to 45 percent, and it had reached 98 percent in 1983.

As in Uzbekistan a two-tier price system existed in China before 1978: quota prices and above-quota prices. Quota prices pertain to crops sold to fulfill state procurement orders. Above-quota prices apply to crops sold in excess of state order obligations. Both prices were determined by the government. These prices had been kept low and almost constant from 1952 to 1978. Farmers sold all their produce to the government through the state procurement system, and transactions at market prices were prohibited. As a result, agricultural production stagnated.

Among with institutional changes, China's policy on state prices and procurement has been amended to stimulate agricultural production. Specific measures include gradual reductions in quota levels and the number of crops subject to the quota. Moreover, prices for the major crops were raised significantly in the early 1980s. Between 1978 and 1984, above-quota prices were raised more than quota prices, with increases ranging from 30 percent to 50 percent. Therefore, the above-quota prices increased relative to quota prices, thus also increasing the share of sales at above-quota prices to the state.

Although procurement prices rose substantially in the early 1980s, retail prices in urban areas remained unchanged, and they were still lower than pre-reform quota prices. As agricultural production grew, the government budget was under pressure. To avoid a budgetary crisis, the government gradually replaced the two-tier price system with a unified price system beginning at the end of 1983, and extending to all main crops in 1985. The unified price is a weighted average between quota and above-quota prices, but since the constructed prices led to a lower marginal price than under the previous two-tier price system, agricultural production was discouraged.

Box 9.4 (cont.)

Problems

One of the problems in land reform lies in land ownership. The land is still owned by the state, and the absence of private land ownership discourages long-term investment in land improvements.

Another problem in land reform is the scale of land. Given the scarcity of land in China, the result of the distribution of land based on household size under HRS is that a household operates on less than half a hectare of land. The result of the "equal fertility" principle used to distribute land, so as to accommodate households for the differential quality of land, is that a household receives several plots of land. Consequently, land scale is far from optimal, and prevents farmers from taking advantage of modern technologies.

Despite these problems, agricultural production has increased dramatically, because these losses are minor compared with the gains from correcting its previously severe incentive distortions. The mechanization of China's agricultural production is very low.

present on-farm irrigation infrastructure leads to excessive water use and soil salinization, and the delivery of water to farms at no cost does not give them an incentive to use water efficiently.

9.72   In 1992, the use of pesticides declined sharply, because Uzbekistan lacked foreign exchange. An adequate supply of the appropriate pesticides should help increase productivity and the more intensive use of IPM methods. In addition, Uzbek cotton farms should test other agrochemicals, such as improved selections of growth regulators and defoliants.

9.73   Using fertilizers efficiently requires periodic soil testing to determine the optimal amount of fertilizer elements required for the particular crop that is being planted. This practice is seldom used in Uzbekistan, and it must be adopted to increase productivity.

Improving Ginning Quality

9.74   In cotton quality, the most pressing problem is the large amount of trash contained in machined-picked seedcotton. *Moisture control*, also inadequate, would permit efficient ginning and preserve the quality of cotton fiber throughout the process. The lower quality of Uzbek cotton from its outdated ginning technology has led to a 5 to 10 percent discount in its price relative to similar cotton from other countries.

Marketing Cotton

9.75   The sudden shift of responsibility for marketing cotton from Moscow to Tashkent, and at the same time having traditional buyers' contracts canceled, was accompanied by hesitation and disarray. The uncertainty about the quality of cotton contracted for and late deliveries hindered the marketing of Uzbek cotton. Until those problems are rectified, cotton exports can be expected to be discounted by around $88 per ton--a potential loss of $48 million in hard currency.

9.76   Another impediment to the efficient marketing of Uzbek cotton has been the *quality classification*, compared to international standards. A new unit (SIFHAT) has been organized to standardize the classification of Uzbek cotton consistent with international standards.

CHAPTER 10

ENERGY

10.1   Uzbekistan possesses substantial natural energy resources, including significant deposits of natural gas, oil, and coal, yet has become a net importer of energy. Natural gas is at the core of its energy supply base, providing two-thirds of its primary energy supply, and fueling the economic expansion of the last several decades. Uzbekistan is the third largest producer of natural gas in the former Soviet Union (FSU), after Russia and Turkmenistan. Production in 1992 was over 42 billion cubic meters (34 million tons of oil equivalent). It is also among the ten largest natural gas suppliers in the world, with marketable gas sales comparable to those of Indonesia. In contrast, although oil potential appears significant in the longer term, current production levels are minor. Uzbekistan imports over 60 percent of its oil consumption. Uzbekistan also plays a strategic role in electricity trade in Central Asia with the regional dispatching located in Tashkent. Electricity generation capacity expanded by two-thirds in the last decade, and current generation provides over one-half of the supply in the region.

10.2   Despite the significant expansion in the supply of natural gas and electricity in the last decade, rapidly escalating domestic energy consumption has eroded the surplus available for export, and Uzbekistan has become a net importer of energy. Imports of oil and hard coal more than offset exports of natural gas and electricity. Exports of natural gas have declined by over 50 percent between 1980 and 1990. During this time net energy imports increased fourfold. Based on world market pricing, the energy trade deficit in 1990 was US$1.1 billion. However, between 1990 and 1992, net energy imports declined by about 50 percent.

10.3   Yet the medium-term outlook in the energy sector looks promising, if effective reform policies are undertaken. Uzbekistan could be expected to shift the energy trade deficit into a surplus in the short term, and could again become a significant energy exporter in the longer term. The strongest influence is expected to come from oil and gas. Increasing domestic oil production to substitute for oil imports could have an immediate impact on the balance of payments during the economic transition. The greatest challenge in the medium to longer term, in addition to developing the country's oil potential, will be to secure export markets for excess natural gas supplies. The volume of natural gas available for export in the medium term is projected to be much greater than the Government currently envisions (projected at up to 30 billion cubic meters by 1996). This growing surplus is due to an expected decline in domestic demand. The Government needs to address this potential prominently in its reform agenda.

10.4   Effecting this medium-term outlook will require implementing three policy measures in the energy sector in the next 18 months. First, an investment framework would need to be developed to attract outside investment into the petroleum sector, including petroleum legislation and taxation. Second, energy pricing and taxation require reform to support one of the most critical elements of the economic transition process. This would also provide the incentive for improving energy end-use efficiency. Finally, institutional reform in the energy sector is essential; energy enterprises need to be restructured and corporatized to enhance the economic efficiency and development potential of this productive sector.

A. SECTORAL REFORM: THE CURRENT COMPOSITION OF THE SECTOR

ENERGY DEMAND

10.5   Uzbekistan's economy is highly energy intensive, with a per capita energy consumption similar to that of Greece, Italy, or Spain despite a far lower per capita GNP. It is the fourth largest consumer of energy among the former Soviet Republics. Similar to other countries in the FSU and Central and Eastern Europe, the energy intensity of the economy-- estimated at 1.7 toe/US$1,000 GDP-- is several times that of industrialized economies.   It is estimated that Uzbekistan has been using 35 to 50 percent more energy than might be expected based on its per capita income levels.   The low price of energy does not provide incentives for efficient energy use, including energy-efficient appliances or energy-efficient industrial processes. There is substantial potential for energy savings and end-use efficiency.

10.6   As shown in Table 10.1, natural gas accounts for the prominent share of primary energy supply, representing over two-thirds of the total in 1992. This share of natural gas used is one of the highest in any economy in the world, and reflects the fact that the amount of primary energy supply used to generate power and heat is more than one-half the total primary energy

Table 10.1
Uzbekistan: Energy Balance
(million tons of oil equivalent (MTOE))

	1980	1985	1990	1992
Total Production of which:	31.9	32.3	38.9	41.6
oil	1.3	2.0	2.8	3.3
gas	27.9	27.7	32.9	34.6
coal	2.3	2.1	2.6	3.2
primary electricity	0.4	0.5	0.6	0.5
Total Net Imports	1.9	3.6	8.3	3.8
Oil Exports	1.7	1.2	1.3	0.6
Imports	11.7	10.7	11.5	6.1
Net Imports	10.0	9.5	10.2	5.5
Gas Exports	59.6	61.9	62.5	
Imports	51.0	61.3	59.7	
Net Imports	-8.6	-6.6	-2.8	-2.6
Coal Exports	0.5	0.3	0.3	0.2
Imports	0.8	1.1	1.4	1.2
Net Imports	0.3	0.8	1.1	1.0
Electricity Exports	0.9	1.3	1.6	1.4
Imports	1.1	1.2	1.4	1.3
Net Imports	0.2	-0.1	-0.2	-0.1
Total Supply (TPES) of which:	33.8	35.9	47.2	45.4
oil	11.3	11.5	12.9	8.8
gas	19.3	21.1	30.1	32.0
coal	2.6	2.9	3.7	4.2
hydro	0.4	0.5	0.4	0.4
Fuel Shares				
oil	33%	32%	28%	19%
gas	57%	59%	64%	71%
coal	8%	8%	8%	9%
hydro/geothermal	1%	1%	1%	1%

Sources: Goskomprognostat. Bank staff calculations.

supplies, as well as the fact that the penetration of gas in household distribution accounts for almost 80 percent of natural gas consumed directly. The share of oil in the overall energy balance is comparatively low, at 19 percent. Coal and hydro account for a relatively minor share (9 percent and 1 percent, respectively).

10.7   Detailed energy balances showing consumption patterns are produced by the Government every five years, the last having been completed for 1990. As is indicated in Table 10.2, industry accounted for one-third of total energy consumption in 1990, agriculture just over 10 percent; the household sector 42 percent, and transport 15 percent. The agricultural sector, although accounting only for a relatively small percentage of total energy demand, consumes 30 percent of the country's electricity (largely for irrigation purposes) and 20 percent of the oil used outside the power sector. It also uses a large volume of natural gas as feedstock for fertilizer production.

10.8   Primary energy consumption grew at an average of 4 percent annually during the 1980s, with the largest increases in the agriculture and household sectors. Between 1985 and 1990, household demand for energy grew the most rapidly, increasing by nearly two-thirds. Agriculture demand for energy increased by one-fifth, while industrial and transport sector demand declined by 10 percent during this five-year period. Given the prominence of the residential sector in Uzbekistan's energy balance--comprising a higher share than in any of the other countries of the FSU--the pricing and subsidization of residential energy supplies will be the most critical issue associated with demand.

10.9   Energy demand in Uzbekistan and the neighboring CIS republics should be expected to decline substantially over the next few years. Initially, the decline will be driven by falling industrial output and economic retrenchment as the initial stages of the reform are undertaken. In the medium to long term, reduced energy demand will reflect the effect of higher relative energy prices, the restructuring of enterprises, and an increase in energy efficiency. Energy demand is expected to be affected prominently by the sharp declines in domestic demand in 1992 and 1993. Although oil and gas production continue to increase (4.4 percent and 2.7 percent, respectively, between 1990 and 1991), domestic consumption is expected to decline substantially. Projections of primary energy demand have been prepared based on the macroeconomic outlook included in this report (see Table 10.3).

Table 10.2
Uzbekistan Total Final Consumption (MTOE)

	1985	1990
Total Final Consumption	28.6	32.0
of which:		
oil	7.7	8.5
gas	9.8	11.0
coal	1.1	1.7
electricity	3.7	4.2
heat	6.1	6.5
other	0.2	0.1
Industry	11.5	10.5
oil	0.9	0.7
gas	4.5	3.7
coal	0.2	0.2
electricity	2.1	2.4
heat	3.7	3.2
other	0.1	0.1
Agriculture	3.0	3.6
oil	1.5	1.7
gas	0.3	0.2
coal	0.1	0.1
electricity	1.0	1.3
heat	0.1	0.3
other		
Transport	5.8	5.2
oil	4.5	5.0
gas	1.2	0.1
coal	1.2	0.1
electricity	0.1	0.1
Households	8.2	13.3
oil	0.8	1.5
gas	3.8	6.7
coal	0.8	1.5
electricity	0.4	0.4
heat	2.3	3.1
other	0.1	0.1
Fuel Shares		
oil	27%	27%
gas	34%	34%
coal	4%	5%
electricity	13%	13%
heat	21%	20%
other	1%	1%

Source: Goskomprognostat

ENERGY SUPPLY

Natural Gas

10.10   Natural gas is by far the most prominent resource in domestic energy production. In 1992, natural gas accounted for 83 percent of domestically produced energy supplies, with an output of 43 billion cubic meters. Production expanded by nearly 20 percent over the last decade, and has continued to grow during the past few years. However, production from the older fields is declining rapidly mainly owing to the advanced maturity of these fields and in one case, owing to the lack of appropriate compression facilities capable of operating in a high-sulfur environment. Under current plans, gas production is expected to reach 45 billion cubic meters in 1993, and 50 billion cubic meters by 1995.

Table 10.3
Projected Domestic Energy Consumption

	1990 Supply Volume (mtoe)	1992	1993	1994	1996	2000
			(Indices 1990=100)			
Electricity	10.7	93	84	74	59	52
Primary Energy						
Oil	13.0	77	68	59	46	42
Natural gas	30.1	96	86	76	60	51
Coal	3.7	93	85	70	50	42
Electricity and heat	0.4	120	130	140	160	200
Aggregate Primary Energy Demand	47.2	91	82	72	58	51
GDP (US$ billion)	27.8	75	70	66	71	93

Source: Goskomprognostat and Bank staff calculations.
Note: Primary energy demand projections are based on the macroeconomic outlook included in this report. It may be noted, however that individual sector agencies may be working on projections based on other assumptions, e.g. the Ministry of Electrification feels that domestic demand would drop by about 10% between 1990 and 1993 and stabilize thereafter.

10.11   Proven natural gas reserves have continued to increase and, as of early 1993, are estimated at 1,883 billion cubic meters, representing a reserves-to-production ratio of 44 years. The current constraint on increasing natural gas production is processing capacity. The newer fields have a higher sulfur content, and more than 90 percent of the new production now needs to be processed. Current processing capability is operating at full capacity.

10.12   Owing to the growing domestic demand for gas, and the large gas discoveries in Turkmenistan, Uzbekistan's exports of gas have fallen precipitously. Net exports have declined from 15.5 billion cubic meters in 1980, of which 13.3 billion cubic meters were supplied into the Russian system, to only 4.2 billion cubic meters by 1990, with the majority supplied to Central Asian countries. In 1990, the largest volume of gas exports went to Kazakhstan, followed by Kyrgyzstan and Tajikistan (see Table 10.4). Three-fourths of these exports was gas transited from Turkmenistan. Uzbekistan probably could negotiate foreign exchange earnings, or reach direct export contracts with European buyers, if exports into the Central supply system could be increased and agreements could be reached with Russia and the other transit countries of the gas transmission system.

10.13   An association, "Uztransgas," has been formed. The association operates the uniform gas supply system and sets transportation charges and transit fees. Transit fees should increase significantly in the future on the order of 5 to 10 percent of the volume of the gas, and could represent a substantial source of Government revenue. Turkmenistan currently transits 60 to 70 bcm across Uzbekistan for exports into the Russian system.

10.14   The gas pipeline system also depends heavily on imported steel tubulars from Russia and other countries in the FSU. The disruption in interrepublic trade has adversely affected the accessibility of these supplies. Furthermore, under the FSU, Uzbekistan's gas industry had been receiving $30 million a year in foreign exchange from Moscow to purchase the equipment necessary to maintain and continue operations. The lack of foreign exchange makes it difficult to acquire equipment and supplies to carry out a proper maintenance program.

10.15   Among the top three priority projects for attracting foreign investment into the country is the investment to develop the gas processing plant (currently under construction) at the giant Shutan gas field (a current production of 17 bcm). This plant would yield 300,000 tons of polyethylene and 50,000 tons of polypropylene.

Table 10.4
Natural Gas Trade in Uzbekistan
(BCM)

	1980	1985	1990	1991
Net export	15.6	6.4	4.2	3.8
Export	19.5	11.0	10.8	10.8
Russia	13.4	3.9	0.8	0.5
Turkmenistan	0.2	0.2	0.2	0.1
Kyrgyzstan	1.0	1.3	2.1	2.1
Tajikistan	1.1	1.4	1.8	1.9
Kazakhstan	3.8	4.2	5.9	6.2
Import	3.9	4.6	6.6	7.0
Afghanistan	2.4	2.4	0.0	0.0
Turkmenistan	0.0	0.0	3.3	3.4
Uniform gas supply system	1.4	2.2	3.3	3.6

Source: Uzbekneftgas.

Oil

10.16   Domestic oil production doubled between 1980 and 1990. However, it still contributes only a minor share to primary energy supplies, with a production of 3.3 million tons of oil in 1992. Production increased from 2.8 to 3.3 million tons per year between 1990 and 1992. This increase in production stems primarily from the increased output from natural gas condensates, which now contribute over one-half of total oil production. Oil is produced in the Fergana Valley, with production dating back to the 1880s, and from the natural gas-producing region in the south near the Turkmenistan border. While total oil production has continued to expand in the last few years, production from the older fields is declining by as much as 15 percent. The production decline in the maturing fields has been exacerbated by lack of production equipment and spare parts.

10.17   Oil reserves have grown substantially over the decade, increasing more than twofold to 244 million tons in 1993, supported by 294 billion rubles in exploration investment. In addition, a vast territory has been unexplored. Although hydrocarbon potential does not appear to be on the same order of magnitude as in some other countries in the region, including Kazakhstan, Azerbaijan, and Russia, the unexplored potential nonetheless seems significant. If sufficient investment is attracted, Uzbekistan could be expected to expand its oil production capacity, to become oil self-sufficient in the next few years, and to become a net exporter of oil in the longer term.

10.18   In 1992, Uzbekistan imported a net 5.5 million tons of oil (3.7 mt of crude oil and 1.9 mt of refined products). Uzbekistan also processes oil supplies from Kyrgyzstan and Tajikistan and supplies them with refined products. Since Uzbekistan is a landlocked country without other supply options, the only source of crude oil imports (beyond the crude processed for its neighbors) is from Russia. The prominent share of refined products is imported from Russia, although an important volume is also imported from Kazakhstan.

10.19   Two oil fields have been discovered--the Minbulak field in the Fergana Valley and the Kokdumulak oil and gas condensate field near the Turkmenistan border. If developed, these fields could increase oil production to 8 million tons within four years. Under present plans, the Kokdumulak field alone is expected to yield 4.3 million tons of oil and condensate within a period three years. These fields are both geologically and technically complex. Their development is critically dependent on imported equipment and would be greatly facilitated by the use of Western technology. Thus, the Government has placed priority on attracting foreign investment, to access both capital and Western technology and equipment. These two investment projects are the top priority of the Government. Besides helping to support Uzbekistan's balance of payments, developing these fields would also reduce Uzbekistan's critical dependence on Russian oil.

10.20   Investment requirements for developing the Kokdumulak field are estimated at US$200 million. Production could reach 4.3 million tons within three years. Developing the Minbulak field is estimated to require an investment of 15.9 billion rubles and US$210 million. Production is expected to reach 1.5 million tons within three years.

10.21   The Government is considering financing these projects from domestic resources. However, the Government should carefully assess whether internal financing for highly capital intensive projects is the best use of the limited domestic resources under the current economic conditions; instead, it should place priority on developing the necessary investment framework and institutional capacity to negotiate agreements with foreign investors, both for developing existing fields and for promoting further exploration. To this end, Uzbekneftegaz is attempting to involve foreign investors in development of the Mingbulak and Kokdumulak fields. It is also engaged in promoting oil and gas acreage for further exploration and development. Under an ongoing effort targeted at the international oil industry, the Government is offering for tender 11 blocks located in three of the major petroleum basins -- Fergana, Sarkhaindarya, and Ustyuirt in the Aral Sea zone. Promotion meetings are planned for Houston, London, and Tashkent.

Electricity

10.22   In 1991, Uzbekistan generated 54 terrawatt hours (TWh) of electricity, which is over one-half the total electricity generated in the Central Asian region. Of this total, 74 percent was from natural gas, 15 percent from hydroelectric power, and 7 percent each from fuel oil and coal. Owing to the high demand for natural gas combined with inadequate facilities for storing and processing natural gas, dual-fired power stations have had to burn fuel oil instead in winter months.

10.23   The plants are relatively well maintained, but serious concerns have been expressed about the availability and costs of spare parts, which are imported from over 300 suppliers. Most suppliers are in FSU countries, but some also exist in Bulgaria, Germany, Czechoslovakia, Hungary, and Poland. In 1991, the average capacity utilization factor of the plants was 57 percent, but power-supply conditions could quickly deteriorate if the access to capital for spare parts and equipment is not addressed urgently.

10.24   The financial situation in the power subsector is deteriorating given the increased costs of inputs and the cap that has been placed on tariffs. To prevent a financial crisis and a complete breakdown in the power supply, the Government must establish tariff increases immediately. In addition, the investment program in the power sector must be pruned and reduced to an affordable level, and must be directed primarily at investments for rehabilitation, retrofitting, and end-use efficiency.

10.25   A power station with four units has been planned at Talimarjan in the south. Natural gas supplies will not be restricted to the power station during the winter peak because the plant would be capable of utilizing untreated natural gas (0.5 percent sulfur content) from a nearby field. Given the dramatic increases in equipment costs, only the first unit is being constructed. The unit is about 90 percent complete, with most of the main equipment (boiler, turbine, generator, and transformer) already on-site. However, some critical equipment is lacking (high-pressure pipes and instrumentation). The Ministry of Electricity is seeking outside financing to complete the project. Financing requirements are estimated to be US$20.7 million and 1,140 million rubles, and completion is expected in 1994. The incremental cost for completing the construction of the first unit would be about US$40/kW. The project would be quite cost-attractive if the energy could be exported, or if the end product could displace fuel oil or, for environmental purposes, reduce emissions of the older coal-fired power plants.

10.26   All other major investments in the power sector would need to be curtailed (including the completion of the remaining three units of this plant) until domestic and regional demand for electricity in the future is assessed. Electricity demand is expected to decline over the next few years both in Uzbekistan and in neighboring republics as the restructuring process unfolds. Because generating capacity is expected to provide excess power over the medium term, Uzbekistan should pursue opportunities for promoting exports of electricity.

Coal

10.27   Uzbekistan is a relatively minor coal producer, with a domestic production of 6.5 million tons in 1992. Uzbekistan imports coal primarily from Russia and Kazakhstan, with smaller volumes exchanged with Kyrgyzstan and Tajikistan. The coal industry is in a period of transition, and is facing severe financial problems. There is scope for expanding production capacity, but financing requirements are substantial. The viability of coal operations must be reviewed and assessed, and activities should be restructured with a view toward creating joint stock companies for operational components that are viable.

10.28   Two primary coal deposits exist--brown coal deposits at Angren just east of Tashkent, and hard coal deposits near the Afghanistan border. Reserves of brown coal are estimated at 1.7 billion tons; hard coal deposits are estimated at 100 million tons.

10.29   The Government is considering developing a new mine with an initial capacity of 200,000 tons of high-quality coking coal that could have export potential. The project would be well suited for private joint venture participation.

ORGANIZATIONAL STRUCTURE

10.30   Energy sector activities are spread across several ministries, unions and concerns, and roles and responsibilities are not well defined. The concerns are large monopoly structures that, besides the core activities, operate many ancillary entities. The fragmented organizational structure is making the coordination of sectoral policies and activities very difficult.

10.31   The Ministry of Energy and Electrification (a total staff of 50,000) is responsible for the power sector. All other energy-producing concerns are organized in separate unions, which report directly to the Cabinet of Ministers. All oil and gas operations (except oil and gas exploration) have recently been merged into one concern (Uzbekneftegas) whose Chair is the Deputy Prime Minister and the Chairman of the Committee for the fuel and energy complex at the Cabinet of Ministers. Oil and gas exploration activities have remained under the jurisdiction of the National Committee on Geology.

10.32   The distribution of natural gas is handled by Uzbekgas, subordinated to the Ministry of Housing and Utilities. The coal subsector is under the responsibility of an integrated concern--Uzbekcoal--operating in Uzbekistan, Tajikistan, and Kyrgyzstan (with 30,000 staff in all three countries). Currently, operational and production decisions in the energy enterprises are not integrated adequately with the financial and investment strategies for the sector.

PRICING, SUBSIDIES, AND TAXATION

10.33   Similar to all FSU countries, the systemic underpricing of energy relative to other goods has led to a significant overuse of energy per unit of output relative to market economies. Reducing energy consumption and increasing energy efficiency will reduce energy imports and free up additional energy supplies for export. Increasing the price of energy to reflect costs of supply fully will provide an incentive for lowering the energy intensity of the economy. In addition, however, it will be necessary to install proper metering and to introduce energy efficient technologies.

10.34   Despite the steps taken to increase energy prices during 1992 and 1993, energy prices--particularly the price of natural gas and electricity in the domestic market--remain only at a small proportion of international prices (see Table 10.5). Energy-price subsidies are increasing rapidly. As of the fourth quarter of 1992, direct budgetary energy price subsidies were at an annualized level of 90 billion rubles.[1] Indirect subsidies have also increased significantly. Indirect energy price subsidies were estimated at an additional 52 billion rubles. Because the household and agricultural sectors in Uzbekistan consume a much larger share of total energy demand than in any other country of the FSU, the highly distorted energy pricing structure, which subsidizes these sectors to a greater degree, translates into a greater cost to the economy. Current domestic energy prices are not sustainable.

10.35   With the rapid escalation of input costs, energy enterprises subject to regulated energy prices are falling on extremely difficult financial times. They are finding it more difficult to acquire equipment and spare parts and to continue maintenance and routine operations. This pinch has placed increasing pressure on the Government budget. During the first nine months of 1992, the Ministry of Electricity received 4 billion rubles in credit--1 billion rubles for basic operations, 1 billion rubles as direct subsidies, and 2 billion rubles for new construction.

---

[1] The October 16, 1992, Cabinet Decree "On State Regulation of Energy Prices" increased subsidies to the household sector substantially. The direct budget subsidies to the energy producers to compensate for the difference between a measured production cost and the household energy tariffs are as follows; 1.89 Rb/kwh - electricity, 299.4 Rb/mcm - natural gas, 9.74 Rb/kg - LPG, 1589 Rb/ton - coal, and 1269.5 Rb/gcal - heat. The estimated budget allocation for the fourth quarter 1992 for coal, heat, and electricity was 35.8 billion rubles, or approximately 90 billion rubles on an annual basis, or $300 million at 300 Rb/US$.

Table 10.5
Uzbekistan - Energy Prices

	1991	Jan 92	Jun 92	Sep 92	Oct 92[1]	Jan 93	Jun 93	Jul 93	Russian Jul 93	As % Russian P	World Market $1=1020 Rb	As % World P
Crude Oil (Rb/mt)												
- producer[2]	80	350	824	824	8937	28415	46000	46000[1]	35000	131	112200[7]	41
- CIS import	80	448	2800	7600	15000	55463[3]	84825[3]	137020	110000	125	112200	122
						50600[4]	70700[4]	106500				
Refined Oil Products (Rb/mt)												
Ex Refinery[2]												
- gasoline	95	1057	4728	10066	52529	69738	101567	128491	70000	184	193800[8]	66
- diesel oil	154	932	4701	9803	40356	58897	90352	109085	45000	242	173400	63
- fuel oil	59	413	3204	5104	28760	43443	52927	64806	25000	259	81600	79
Retail (Rb/l.)												
- gasoline	0.30	0.85	6.0	10.0	40.0	40.0	100.0	120	125[2]	96	306	39
Natural Gas (Rb/1000m3)												
- producer	15	75	198	198	410	410	850	19200	na	91	91800	42
- export	50	75	960	1913	1913	19200	19200	38400	42000[3]			
- industry	45	325	325	325	602	610	1604	24054	12500[4]	192		
- residential	23.8	23.8	23.8	100	150	150	300	500	2000[5]	25		
Electricity (Rb/kwh)												
- industry	0.064	0.52	0.52	0.52	5.36	5.36	7.20	36	4.8	750	41.82	86
- budget supported						3.50	4.70	23.5		4375		
industry	0.064	0.34	0.34	0.34	3.50	2.06	2.80	14	0.32			
- agriculture	0.02	0.02	0.02	0.02	2.06	2.06	2.80	7				
irrigation	0.02	0.10	0.10	0.10	1.03	1.03	1.40	1	0.32	313	72.42	1
- residential	0.04	0.04	0.08	0.20	0.40	0.40	1.00	1	0.32			
Coal												
- producer	31	235	1400	2200	950	2883	4835	14880	4000[6]		20400	37
- industry	31	192	192	357	1211	2883	4835	6000			40800[10]	
- residential	11	30	30	500	700	200	4000					

Source: Uzbekistan Prices: Price Committee, Ministry of Finance
Russian Prices: Russian Federation World Bank Country Economic Memorandum
World Prices: IEA Energy Prices and Taxes, 1991

1/ Median calculated.
2/ Median calculated.
3/ Ukraine.
4/ Includes tax (9000 rubles net of tax).
5/ Excludes tax (2400 rubles including tax).

6/ Price before recent liberalization.
7/ Median calculated.
8/ Europe cif.
9/ West Europe Fob.
10/ Baltics.

10.36   Although moving energy prices to international levels will be a significant shock to the economy, the Government should immediately consider moving energy prices to reflect the costs of supply as rapidly as is politically feasible. Experience from other countries that have faced energy price shocks, such as the OECD countries during the 1970s and the Central and Eastern European countries during the past few years, suggests that economic restructuring has been most successful when the full level of increased energy prices has been passed onto industry and final consumers as rapidly as possible. Pricing energy to reflect the cost of supply and distribution will provide a signal to industry that it should restructure itself more efficiently.

10.37   All energy prices remain controlled. The degree of control varies greatly within the sector. The price of energy supplies to households, public enterprises, and the agriculture sector and all natural gas prices are set by the Cabinet of Ministers (upon recommendations from the Price Setting Committee of the Ministry of Finance) and by the energy-sector concerns. These prices are generally set below operating or import costs. Natural gas prices are set significantly below the opportunity cost of exports.

10.38   Price ceilings for electricity and heat in the industrial sector were established in an attempt to allow full recovery of electric utility operating costs, taking into account the cross-subsidies to the household sector. In practice, however, the industrial price ceilings have been unsuccessful, and budgetary subsidies were increased substantially in 1992.

10.39   The ex-refinery price of oil products is determined on the basis of the cost of crude oil (including transportation),[2] plus refining costs and a refining margin of up to 30 percent. Wholesale and retail prices for oil products are determined on the basis of oil product costs plus distributional costs and a profit margin of up to 40 percent (excluding the oil product costs). The retail price of gasoline is an exception; as of July 1993, it was controlled at 100 rubles/liter.

10.40   Oil and natural gas producer prices have been kept significantly below interrepublic trade prices in an attempt to exert downward pressure on domestic oil and gas prices until October 1992. As of October 1992, producer prices of natural gas were less than one-half the producer price of Russia and only 20 percent of the export price. Oil producer prices were reported to have increased more than tenfold between September and October 1992 and another fivefold between October 1992 and July 1993. Even under this increase, oil producer prices represent only 34 percent of the average cost of imported crude oil. The most efficient signal and incentive to raise domestic oil and gas production is to allow the producer price to be competitive with other supplies. Petroleum taxation should be established for producers (above the corporate excise tax), which could contribute to Government revenue.

10.41   However, natural gas, heat, and electricity prices to the household and agriculture sectors remain at only a small proportion (0.5, 1.5, and 19 percent respectively) of economic cost and world-market prices. Natural gas supplies, which account for the bulk of domestic energy consumption, are lagging the price increases in Russia, as well as in most neighboring countries. Pricing distortions and cross-subsidization among industry, agriculture, and households are severe. In general, it is much less expensive to supply energy to industrial users than households, owing to economies of scale and a higher load factor and utilization rate. In market-based economies, energy prices to households are typically 1.5

---

[2] Based on the volume of crude oil received from domestic supplies plus the cost of crude-oil imports.

to 2 times that of industrial users. In Uzbekistan, the structure is just the opposite, with energy prices to households only about 12 to 14 percent of industrial prices.

10.42   To reach comparable international price levels would require that industrial prices be increased 1.2 times for electricity and about 4 times for natural gas. In contrast, residential prices would need to increase about 70 times for electricity and 185 times for natural gas.[3]

TRADE

10.43   Energy plays a significant role in the overall trade balance of Uzbekistan. Based on world-market pricing and 1990 trade volumes, energy accounted for 21 percent of imports and 23 percent of exports. Based on world-market pricing, the energy trade deficit in 1990 was approximately US$1.1 billion. Oil is the single largest import commodity, representing 11 percent of total imports. Uzbekistan currently imports over 60 percent of its oil needs. As a landlocked country without other supply options, it has depended on Russia for most of its supplies. Thus, along with cotton, oil has been the focal point of the trade agreements with Russia.

10.44   The cost of oil imports increased by over 3,000 percent during 1992. By the end of the year, crude oil was reported to cost 15,000 rubles metric per ton, or about 40 percent of world-market pricing based on an exchange rate of R300/US$. Because oil was underpriced compared with cotton in interrepublic trade in early 1992, Uzbekistan was to face a significant terms-of-trade shock when the cost of oil increased to international prices. This terms-of-trade shock has largely been realized, as the relative price of cotton and oil in interrepublic trade reached the same level by the end of the year.

10.45   Significant oil discoveries have been made that, if developed, could triple the current domestic oil production of 3.3 million tons per year (67,000 barrels per day), and replace oil imports by 1996. The Government has placed top priority on attracting foreign investment for developing these fields. Development is highly capital-intensive, is dependent on the deployment of imported equipment and water, and would be greatly facilitated by the use of Western technology. The Government has estimated that required investments would cost US$500 million over the next four years.

10.46   Despite a general interest from the international oil industry, no concrete investment agreements have been reached. A clear and stable petroleum investment framework needs to be established to serve as the primary catalyst for attracting foreign investment. However, the lack of an export route, as well as the limited production potential compared with neighboring countries, is also expected to constrain potential financing. Financing from the international financial institutions may be a catalyst for spurring private-sector investment.

10.47   Natural gas exports could also increase significantly in the medium term. Owing primarily to an expected reduction in consumption, the supply of natural gas available for export could be projected to grow from the current level of 7.5 billion cubic meters to up to 30 billion cubic meters per year by 1996. Securing export markets for these supplies should be another top priority, given that natural gas exports will be a key determinant of success in the sector in the medium term. If a viable export market were to be established and if prices reached international market levels (adjusted for

---

[3] Based on domestic prices in July 1993, an exchange rate of 1020 Rb/US$ and comparable international energy prices, as shown in Table 10.5.

transportation costs), these exports could represent US$1.1 billion in export earnings. It may not be expected that natural gas exports could reach 30 billion cubic meters by 1996, but the volume of gas which could be available for export is much greater than the Government currently envisions. An adequate reflection of this potential in the reform agenda should be established. The priority in the near term should be negotiating export contracts, and continuing to work closely with Russia and Turkmenistan to agree on the accessibility and tariff structure of the gas transmission system, which carries gas to Western European markets. A longer-term strategy might entail participating in alternate oil and gas export routes from Central Asia to reach international markets.

10.48   While the medium-term prospects of the oil and gas sectors appear promising, Uzbekistan's energy strategy should also include the other energy sources. Investments in the electricity subsector to complete the gas-fired generation unit already under construction may be economically justified. This capacity could replace fuel oil, which is used to generate power in the winter months, or could displace electricity from the coal-fired power generation capacity, which would be desirable environmentally. In light of a reduction in demand and the absence of easy access to international markets, the future of coal activity is problematic. Selective hard-coal production could be expanded if foreign investment could be attracted into this subsector. However, future investment in the coal and power subsectors must balance domestic and regional demand with least-cost investment planning.

B. SECTORAL REFORM: MEDIUM-TERM OUTLOOK

10.49   Two medium-term scenarios have been prepared for the energy sector. Both are based on the macroeconomic reform projections discussed in Chapter 3. They differ in their assumptions about (1) the speed of development of oil and gas fields, (2) the impact of pipeline and other constraints on exports, and (3) the effect of higher energy prices on domestic demand for energy. Since these assumptions depend upon the Government's policy choices, the two scenarios illustrate the scope for influencing the development of the energy sector in a way that enhances its contribution to economic recovery and growth.

10.50   Scenario A (Table 10.6) is the "optimistic" outcome. It assumes that domestic or foreign investment is available to finance the development of the two recently discovered oil fields and that higher energy prices accompanied by vigorous energy conservation lead to a steady decline in energy demand. As a consequence, Uzbekistan would become self-sufficient in oil by 1995 and would have a substantial exportable surplus of oil from 1996 onwards. The amount of natural gas available for export would also grow rapidly, increasing from 2.6 mtoe in 1992 to 21.7 mote in 1996. Under this scenario, the country could earn a net annual surplus on its energy trade of US$1.7 billion at 1992 prices by 1996.

Table 10.6
Uzbekistan Energy Outlook - Scenario A

	1990	1992	1993	1994	1995	1996	1999	2002
OIL (mtoe)								
Production	2.8	3.3	4.6	5.6	6.5	8.0	9.6	11.3
Net Imports								
- Crude Oil	5.4	3.6	3.4	2.4	1.0	-	-4.2	-5.9
- Refined Oil Products	4.7	1.9	0.9	-0.4	-1.0	-2.1		
Total Net Oil Imports	10.1	5.5	4.3	2.0	—	-2.1	-4.2[a]	-5.9[a]
Apparent Consumption	12.9	8.8	8.9	7.6	6.5	5.9	5.4	5.4
NATURAL GAS (mtoe)								
Production	32.9	34.6	36.0	37.6	40.0	40.0	48.0	56.4
Net Imports	-2.8	-2.6	-10.1	-19.1	-19.6	-21.7	-32.3	-41.8
Apparent Consumption	30.1	32.0	25.9	18.5	20.4	18.3	15.7	14.6
COAL (mtoe)								
Production	2.6	3.2	2.6	2.6	2.1	1.9		
Net Imports	1.1	1.0	0.2	-	-	-		
Apparent Consumption	3.7	4.2	2.8	2.6	2.1	1.9		
PRIMARY ELECTRICITY AND HEAT (mtoe)								
Production	0.6	0.5	1.0	1.1	1.2	1.3		
Net Imports	-0.2	-0.1	-0.2	-0.2	-0.2	-0.2		
Apparent Consumption	0.4	0.4	0.8	0.9	1.0	1.1		
AGGREGATE PRIMARY ENERGY BALANCE (mtoe)								
Production	38.9	41.6	44.2	46.9	49.8	51.2		
Net Imports	8.3	3.8	-5.8	-17.3	-19.8	-24.0		
Apparent Consumption	47.2	45.4	38.4	29.6	30.0	27.2		
GNP(% change 1990)		-25%	-30%	34%	-32%	-29%		

Source: Goskomprognostat, Energy Enterprises and Bank Staff Projections
a/ Crude oil only.

10.51   Scenario B (Table 10.7) is the "pessimistic" outcome. In this case the development of new oil fields is delayed and is spread out over a longer period. Energy demand falls less rapidly, while constraints on access to pipeline capacity limit the growth in the country's exports of natural gas. The deficit in energy trade would decline slowly before turning into a small surplus in 1996 as a result of the decline in net imports of oil and oil products.

Table 10.7
Uzbekistan Energy Outlook - Scenario B

	1990	1992	1993	1994	1995	1996	1999	2002
OIL (mtoe)								
Production	2.8	3.3	3.2	3.2	4.6	5.6	7.2	8.0
Net Imports								
- Crude Oil	5.4	3.6	4.0	3.5	3.0	1.9	0.5	0.0
- Refined Oil Products	4.7	1.9	2.3	2.1	0.7	0.7	0.5	0.2
Total Net Oil Imports	10.1	5.5	6.3	5.6	3.7	2.6	1.0	0.2
Apparent Consumption	12.9	8.8	9.5	8.8	8.3	8.2	8.2	8.2
NATURAL GAS (mtoe)								
Production	32.9	34.6	33.7	34.1	32.0	30.6	30.5	34.0
Net Imports	-2.8	-2.6	-6.3	-7.3	-8.0	-8.0	-9.5	-11.0
Apparent Consumption	30.1	32.0	27.4	26.8	24.0	22.6	21.0	24.0
COAL (mtoe)								
Production	2.6	3.2	2.6	2.6	2.6	2.6		
Net Imports	1.1	1.0	0.7	0.4	0.2	-		
Apparent Consumption	3.7	4.2	3.3	3.0	2.8	2.6		
PRIMARY ELECTRICITY AND HEAT (mtoe)								
Production	0.6	0.5	0.8	0.8	0.8	0.8		
Net Imports	-0.2	-0.1	—	0.1	0.2	0.3		
Apparent Consumption	0.4	0.4	0.8	0.9	1.0	1.1		
AGGREGATE PRIMARY ENERGY BALANCE (mtoe)								
Production	38.9	41.6	40.3	40.7	40.0	39.6		
Net Imports	-8.3	3.8	0.7	-1.2	-3.9	-5.1		
Apparent Consumption	47.2	45.4	41.0	39.5	36.1	34.5		

Source: Goskomprognostat, Energy Enterprises and Bank Staff Projections.

10.52   As Figure 10.1 shows, the growth in domestic oil production should ensure that the country is at least self-sufficient in oil by the end of the decade. With policies that encourage investment in the oil sector and the more efficient use of energy in industry, the country might be able to export 4-5 million tons of crude oil by the year 2000. In this case, the question of access to export pipeline capacity would be critical to realizing the full benefit of this exportable surplus.

10.53   Figure 10.2 shows that this issue is even more urgent for natural gas. If it were to follow appropriate policies, Uzbekistan could have an exportable surplus of 40-50 billion cubic meters of gas by the year 2000. Existing pipeline capacity in Central Asia is not sufficient to cope with such an increase in volume, especially as Kazakhstan may also have an increasing volume of gas for export. Further, the country would need to develop export markets for this gas in competition with other potential suppliers in Central Asia as well as Russia itself. The prospect of a rapid increase in the volume of gas that could be exported and of the benefits of the foreign earnings that such exports would generate means that the Government must give high priority to developing a strategy which would enable it to increase natural gas exports in the short and medium terms.

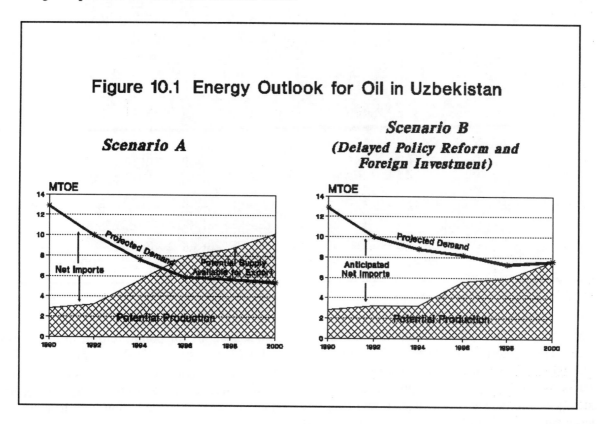

Figure 10.1 Energy Outlook for Oil in Uzbekistan

C. SECTORAL REFORM: ISSUES AND RECOMMENDATIONS

10.54   Uzbekistan's energy policy is torn between two exigencies, in some ways contradictory: how to manage the coming months of major dislocation by imposing the least damage on energy production capacity, and how to initiate policies that will increase the energy sector's contribution to the economy. Moreover, in view of the close relationship between the economies of Uzbekistan and the other FSU countries, but particularly countries in Central Asia, Uzbekistan cannot formulate its energy policies in isolation from what is happening beyond its borders.

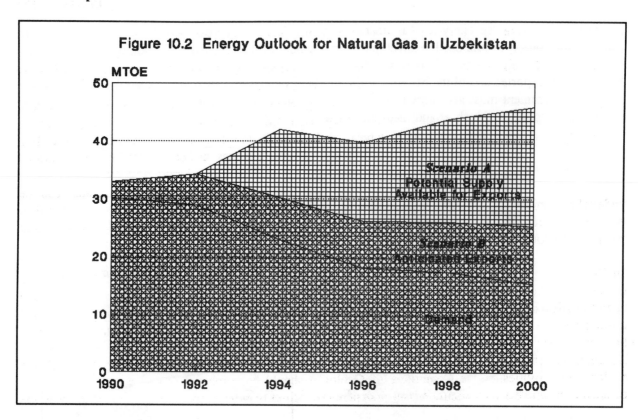

Figure 10.2 Energy Outlook for Natural Gas in Uzbekistan

10.55   This section summarizes the Bank's recommendations for policy reform in the energy sector. These reforms would need to be implemented quickly (that is, starting in the remainder of 1993) as an integral component of the macroeconomic program. An inherent part of these policy reforms focuses on expanding petroleum production. Moreover, a well-managed program of energy pricing and taxation, to promote energy efficiency and thus reduce domestic energy consumption, will increase the energy surplus available for export. Yet the policies proposed in these areas will not have their desired impact on production and consumption unless they are part of a much broader institutional reform in the energy sector.

INSTITUTIONAL ISSUES

10.56   The energy-sector institutions (ministries, concerns, and enterprises) have poorly defined mandates and lines of authorities. Overlapping responsibilities exist among institutions (particularly the oil exploration and production activities between the Committee of Geology and Uzbekneftegas), overstaffing is typical, and institutional activities cover more than core business responsibilities. Operational and production decisions are not integrated adequately with the financial and investment strategies of the sector.

10.57   Institutional reform in the energy sector is urgently required. The capacity of the Government to make the necessary reforms in the energy sector--managing the required foreign invest-ment, restructuring, commercializing and privatizing the energy enterprises, and implementing pricing taxation and legislative reform--will require substantial institutional strengthening.

10.58   In reforming the sector, the Government and the energy enterprises will require an energy strategy that clearly establishes the priorities and framework for the future. Effective institutions must be developed to formulate and implement energy sector policies and an investment strategy. An Energy Ministry needs to be established to carry out this function. The Ministry would be removed from the daily operational and financial decisions of the energy enterprises. An essential part of the move to a market economy is to establish economically independent and responsible economic enterprises that are accountable for their operational and financial decisions. In this regard, it is important that a clear distinction be made among political decision makers, regulatory bodies, and commercial entities. Parallel to creating an Energy Ministry for policy formulation, steps need to be taken to corporatize the energy enterprises, increasing financial and operational autonomy and accountability. This step can be undertaken rapidly. Ancillary activities should be divested and the number of employees reduced to economically efficient levels. Entities that are not natural monopolies (oil refining and distribution, and coal) can be considered for privatization.

10.59   In particular, a strategy for restructuring the petroleum sector would need to be developed in the near term. Experience has shown that making the oil and gas company financially and operationally distinct from the refining enterprise is generally more efficient economically and will introduce the necessary competition. Natural gas transportation can be separated from natural gas production, given the regulations that will be imposed on the natural gas transportation industry. Simultaneously, decisions should be made about whether the oil and gas production entities (together with the exploration activities of the Committee of Geology) should be combined into one state oil and gas company, or whether they should remain independent entities to support competition. Irrespective of the final structure adopted, individual profit centers need to be established for each business entity. Cross-subsidization from one highly profitable entity to support unsound investments in other entities will threaten the economic reform of the country.

10.60   For all natural monopolies (natural gas, electricity, and heat, and transmission and distribution), an independent arm's-length regulatory process among the Government, the enterprises, and the consumers could be created. It is recommended that the Government should establish a licensing/concession regime with rules that govern procedures for oil and gas exploration and development, new investments in the power sector, the operation of electricity, gas, and heat, and the transmission and distribution systems.

ENERGY PRICING AND TAXATION

10.61   As a general rule, energy prices need to be increased fully to reflect the economic costs of supply or the costs of importing energy from other FSU republics. For tradeable fuels not subject to monopoly powers (oil and coal), prices can and should be decontrolled immediately; the subsectors should be restructured and commercialized when possible. Producer and wholesale prices for oil and coal should be fully decontrolled. When sufficient competition exists in the retail market for these fuels, retail prices should also be decontrolled simultaneously and the system of state orders abolished for these commodities.

10.62   For the natural monopolies (natural gas, heat, and electricity transmission and distribution), the Government needs to develop pricing and tariff structures to regulate these industries. Tariff assessment studies must be undertaken to determine appropriate tariff structures and levels. For the natural gas sector, a cost assessment study needs to be undertaken in conjunction with a natural gas development study. Pricing of natural gas in the domestic market should be influenced by the assessed economic cost of gas. As long as production supersedes demand, true economic cost is determined on the basis of the marginal revenue that can be obtained on the export market. These studies should be initiated as rapidly as possible.

10.63   Prior to establishing a detailed tariff structure, natural gas, heat, and electricity prices should be determined on cost plus pricing principles, and increased to reflect import (or export parity), transportation, and distribution costs fully. A medium term program to eliminate household energy subsidies also needs to be adopted. At a minimum, the current (absolute) differences between the industrial and household prices of electricity, heat, and gas should not be allowed to increase.

10.64   Taxation from the energy sector (primarily on oil and gas) could provide a significant source of Government revenue. Taxation policy needs to balance the need for Government revenue against the retention needs of producers to continue and develop energy production. A profit-based petroleum taxation or an equivalent mechanism of licenses based on production-sharing contracts should be adopted. All existing oil and gas producers should be relicensed under the terms of the arrangement. These steps will ensure that the budget receives a reasonable share of Government rents while giving producers adequate revenue to maintain their operations and to support reinvestment.

FOREIGN INVESTMENT AND PRIVATE-SECTOR PARTICIPATION

10.65   Responsibility for managing existing assets, as well as for investing in new assets, should increasingly be transferred to the private sector, particularly for petroleum and coal. Doing so is essential for mobilizing the financing necessary to rehabilitate existing installations, develop new capacity, and introduce modern technology and management techniques. Where major foreign exchange financing is required (for example, for developing petroleum resources), the support of foreign investors will be necessary.

10.66   As a necessary but not sufficient condition, foreign participation and investment will require establishing an appropriate environment consisting of a framework of well-defined laws and fiscal terms. More generally, it will also require an outward orientation by the Government of Uzbekistan; an openness in dealing with foreign firms; and an understanding of what motivates an investor.

REGIONAL INTEGRATION

10.67   Despite the temptation to seek self-sufficiency, the Government must not lose sight of the reality of the outward orientation of the country's energy trade balance, and the fact that it will continue to be closely linked to its neighbors for the foreseeable future, given the configuration of pipelines and electricity transmission lines. In addition, much of Uzbekistan's installed equipment in the energy sector was manufactured in the FSU, and spares will inevitably come from this region.

TECHNICAL ASSISTANCE

10.68   Box 10.1 presents an estimate of Uzbekistan's basic technical assistance needs in the energy sector. The technical assistance activities proposed are a blend of policy advice and pre-investment work primarily aimed at promoting investment in the energy sector. The Government has requested donor assistance for these activities through the Consultative Group process. A number of donors have responded (notably the World Bank, EC and EBRD) and are in the process of initiating activities in critical areas including petroleum legislation, energy pricing and taxation, institutional strengthening and enterprise restructuring, advisors in petroleum negotiations, natural gas investment strategy, gas utilization and metering, heat and power supply rehabilitation, and petroleum products distribution.

Box 10.1: Technical Assistance

- Assist the Government in drafting petroleum legislation and in developing model contracts for petroleum agreement with foreign firms. $300,000

- Assist in projecting energy demand; assess and prioritize investments in energy supply. $550,000

- Assist in developing a comprehensive strategy for restructuring the oil sector and energy sector. $434,000

- Assist in structuring commercial petroleum arrangements to reflect an appropriate distribution of the benefits and risks between different investors in a venture. $245,000

- Assess energy intensity of the sector relative to international standards and estimate remedial capital required under appropriate energy-pricing policies. $246,000

- Assist in undertaking a cost-benefit analysis of oil pipeline investment options. $300,000

- Assist in prioritizing investment in the oil refining sector. $550,000

- Assist in preparing a program for restructuring the electric power and heating subsector and develop a comprehensive strategy for optimum investment in the power sector. $700,000

- Assist the Government of Uzbekistan in restructuring the coal concern. $500,000

- Assist in developing a comprehensive strategy for development and pricing policies for the natural-gas sector. $1,200,000

- Assist in formulating strategies for pricing gas exports; formulate a position on the sharing of CIS gas export revenues, and transportation prices, gas sales contracts, pricing, access, and tariffs in international trade agreements. $226,250

- Recommend a tariff structure for electricity and heat based on an assessment of long-run marginal costs. $250,000

                                    TOTAL $5,275,000

CHAPTER 11

MINING

11.1   The Government continues to be a direct participant in both planning activities and production in mining. The changes introduced since independence have not opened the sector, whose structure thus perpetuates state monopoly. All exploration continues to be undertaken by the state, and the Government continues to eschew the participation of private investment in exploration. As long as exploration is not opened to private investment, all investments for generating mining projects will continue to depend on budgetary allocations, and the contribution of private investment to the growth of mining in Uzbekistan will be severely limited.

11.2   The sector offers the possibility of increasing export earnings both in the short and medium terms--in particular with gold. However, the current pricing policies for mineral products distort incentives and resource allocation. A critical assessment of the competitivity and productivity of the different subsectors of the mining industry is needed to determine which mines can become competitive in a market-based economy. Investment decisions are made not according to an analysis of the rate of return of the project, but according to assessments about whether a specific commodity is needed or whether a geographic region is strategically important.

11.3   Against a scarcity of financial resources but with an urgent need for new technologies and modern management, the strategic plan for developing the mining industry must call for opening the sector. The Government would have to consider giving access to its mineral resources--to its own citizens and to private enterprises that can contribute the resources that are of greatest need--and would have to correct inefficiencies with the existing operations. Experience shows that countries whose mining industries are successful may implement different sectoral policies, but those policies contain some common ingredients: a framework for supporting the ability of public and private enterprises to conduct business, mechanisms for controlling costs, and a system for allowing investors to have access to foreign exchange. In implementing these policy ingredients, the Government would have to enact both mining-specific legislation to govern access to mineral rights and licensing issues (these are critical to opening exploration to private investment) and investment legislation to cover specific taxation issues, access to foreign exchange, and labor issues, as well as implement an institutional structure for administering the new policies.

11.4   Uzbekistan has two options for addressing the low productivity of state-owned mining enterprises (SOEs): privatization and commercialization. The Government has eschewed privatization. The commercialization option involves setting commercial goals, introducing firm budgetary constraints, and increasing the accountability and autonomy for managers. In addition, the Government would have to close its unprofitable mining operations, rationalize personnel and privatize ancillary services in those operations that can be competitive, and liberalize the prices of mineral commodities.

A. THE SETTING FOR SECTORAL REFORM

INSTITUTIONAL STRUCTURE OF THE SECTOR

11.5   The institutional structure of the sector consists of two State Committees (one for Geology and one for Precious Metals), one metallurgical concern, one coal company, and one gold-uranium complex. This structure is meant to perpetuate state monopoly, and is not conducive to private-sector growth. Private enterprise is limited to participation in joint ventures in previously known deposits, and private initiatives in exploration are effectively precluded by the absence of licenses to explore and mine; thus, the marginal role of the private sector will limit its possibilities for growth. Establishing a legal framework and an institutional structure to support developing private mining industry that can operate at the same level as existing SOEs is a major undertaking that the Government must consider in the short term if it intends to develop the sector to the extent that its mineral resources will permit.

THE COMPETITIVITY OF THE UZBEK MINING INDUSTRY

11.6   In much of the world, decisions about mining investment and sectoral restructuring are based increasingly on the relative competitivity of the country's industry rather than on projections of prices, which can be highly uncertain. However, assessing the relative competitivity of the mineral sector of Uzbekistan is difficult, in fact because the prices for all inputs, goods, and services are arbitrary and highly distorted, and do not refer to true production costs or to supply and demand. Thus, perhaps a more accurate assessment of the current competitivity of subsectors can be gleaned from productivity and physical parameters, rather than from a cost analysis of operations. The following assess the potential viability of the main subsectors of the minerals industry of Uzbekistan under free-market conditions:

- *Gold Subsector*. Gold production in Uzbekistan is generally competitive. Production is between 65 and 70 tons per year, of which 50 to 55[1] tons come from the Muruntau open pit. The operating parameters of Muruntau indicate that it would be competitive if operated under free-market conditions (see Box 11.1). However, Muruntau has far more personnel than it needs. It employs 5,000 personnel to operate all of its production facilities, including all maintenance and repair shops, but its workforce consists of 9,000 personnel, owing largely to the town-related functions in Zeravshan; a good proportion of these functions could be released from the responsibility of the enterprise. The remaining 15 to 20 tons per year (tpy) of gold are produced at the Almalyk complex, of

> **Box 11.1: The Muruntau Gold Operation**
>
>   The Muruntau open pit feeds the concentrator 20 million tons of ore per year with about 3 grs. Au per ton of ore. About 26 million m3 overburden and low-grade materials are removed yearly, in order to allow for the exploitation of the ore. The ore is subjected to gravimetric and cyanization processes, and the concentrates are then refined electrolytically. Overall recovery appears to be about 85 percent. As an order of magnitude, if this facility were operated under free-market conditions, production costs could be about $180 to $250 per ounce.

---

[1] These estimates and the others cited for gold in the text and box discussions are based on Bank staff estimates. The figures could not be confirmed because all information on gold, silver, and uranium production volumes, ore grades, and reserves is considered secret.

which more than 10 tpy are a by-product or co-product of copper ores. This production is competitive. The remaining 5 tpy come from several smaller underground gold mines. Some of these mines, operated by Uzbekzoloto (Uzbek Gold)--which exploits ores ranging from 3.5 to 10 grs. Au/ton--appear to be viable under market conditions, provided that personnel is reduced and operations are streamlined. Under free-market conditions, the amount of investment required by these small mines is on the order of US$30 million. The expansion of the Kryzl Alma mine and mill appears to be a profitable project that could interest private investors (especially considering the considerable sunk investment already made).

- **Copper Subsector**. Uzbek copper production can also be considered competitive. Production is projected at 83,000 tons in 1992. On the basis of ore grades, reserves, and physical parameters, copper operations appear to be capable of operating profitably under free-market conditions (see Box 11.2). Nevertheless, this subsector has considerable room for improvement; the productivity and yields of these operations fall substantially below international standards, equipment appears to be operating beyond normal operating life, and personnel is excessive. Streamlining this subsector will require improved, long-term focused management, improved technologies, and investments estimated under free market conditions on the order of US$200 million.

> **Box 11.2: Uzbek Copper Production**
>
> The bulk (about 85 percent) of the Uzbek copper production comes from the Kalmakir open pit mine, where 22 million tons/year of ore at 0.4 percent Cu with gold, molybdenum, and silver content are extracted. The Sari Checku open pit accounts for the remainder-- 4 million tons/year of ore at 0.4. percent Cu. Both mines appear to have serious difficulties with their equipment, reflecting the presently low level of investment in equipment replacement and the problems being experienced by the CIS suppliers.
>
> The ore from both mines is processed at the Almalyk concentrator, located 2 kilometers away from Kalmakir and 24 kilometers away from Sari Checku. Copper recovery is about 79 percent, and copper content in the concentrate is about 18 percent (both very low by Western standards). Gold is recovered in the copper concentrate. A molybdenum concentrate with about 37 percent Mo is also obtained.
>
> While copper mines at 0.4 Cu would be classified as marginal operations (a production cost of about $1.00 to $1.30 per pound of copper), the sizable credit for gold content (not disclosed) could well make Kalmakir competitive if operated under free-market conditions.

- **Lead and Zinc Subsectors**. The production of lead and zinc in Uzbekistan is not internationally competitive. Given the low grades and distance from the mines to the concentrator, the Altin Topkan mine and the Uch Kulach open pit are not economically viable (see Box 11.3). Under market-based conditions, they would not cover even their variable cash costs; thus, these mines should be closed to avoid a deficit of roughly US$50 million per year, which would have to be covered with budget allocations.

- **Coal Subsector**. Coal production in Uzbekistan can be considered an efficient import substitution industry (see Box 11.4). Its capacity to export profitably is limited by slope stability problems and the relatively low quality of coal produced at the Angrean pit, as well as by the existence of an ample supply of coal in Russia. Nevertheless, because coal is a low-value, high-volume commodity, freight provides the coal subsector with an important cost advantage in the internal market. Possibilities for coal self-sufficiency depend on the solution to the Angrean slope stability problem.

Box 11.3: Lead-Zinc Mining in Uzbekistan

The fine content of lead concentrates is estimated to be about 25,000 tons/year and zinc tons/year. The Almalyk zinc refinery is operating below capacity (115,000 tons/year) because Russian and Kazakh concentrates are no longer being processed there. Nevertheless, some 15,000 tons of foreign concentrates, supplied by the Marc Rich trading group, will be tolled in Almalyk during 1992. The local production of lead and zinc ores comes primarily from the Altin Topkan underground mine and the Uch Kulach open pit.

The Altin Topkan mine extracts 3,000 tons/day of ore, with 1.0 percent Pb and 1.2 percent Zn; 2/3 of the ore is mined by sublevel stopping and 1/3 by block caving. The ore is delivered to the Almalyk concentrator, located 17 kilometers away. The Uch Kulach mine extracts 2,000 tons/day of ore, with 2.1 percent Zn and 2.0 percent Pb. The ore is transported by railway to the Almalyk concentrator, which is 320 kilometers away. Mill recovery is about 65 percent on zinc and 80 percent on lead. Fine content of both zinc and lead concentrates is about 35 percent. All these figures are very low by Western standards. Under free-market conditions, the unit costs of these operations would be several times higher than the market price.

PRICES, STATE ORDERS, THE ALLOCATION OF FOREIGN EXCHANGE, AND BUDGETARY SUPPORT

11.7   The access of mineral producers to international markets is limited, and they supply the domestic market at prices that are only a fraction of the international price. Nevertheless, price treatment varies from metal to metal and, for gold, from producer to producer (see Box 11.5). Gold production is sold to the state and is not traded. Depending on the producer, the gold is sold for about 20 percent of the world-market price or simply turned in for free. The state then subsidizes the producers from budgetary allocations.

Box 11.4: Uzbek Coal Mining

Uzbekistan produces 5.4 million tons/year of coal to cover 65 percent of its internal demand, and imports about 3 million tons/year (a free-market value about US$80 to US$100 million) from Russia to cover the remaining 35 percent. The Angrean open pit accounts for almost 90 percent of the Uzbek production. It was projected to produce 4.75 million tons in 1992, at 3,500 Kcal/Kgr and 16 percent to 25 percent ash content. Since it suffered a disastrous slide in May 1991, and following the recommendation of Soviet scientists, the stripping ratio at Angrean has been increased from 4 m3/ton of coal to 8.8 m3/ton of coal. Nevertheless, slides are reported to continue, evidencing the persistence of the slope stability problem. The remaining 650,000 tons of local production comes from three small underground mines.

New investment projects (that is, Uchkuduk) are also funded from budget allocations (see "Existing Investment Projects" in this section). Copper is subject to quotas for internal and export markets (again see Box 11.5). In contrast to gold, copper production is traded, and producers do not receive budgetary support. Access to foreign exchange by the producer is limited to a fraction of the export revenues. Conversely, the state provides budgetary allocations to the enterprises to cover their expenses and investments.

Box 11.5: Prices and Allocation of Foreign Exchange for Mineral Products

- **Gold Subsector.** Uzbekzoloto and Almalyk were sell their 15 ton/yr production to the state for 450 rubles/gr in September 1992 (about US$2/gr), or about 20 percent of world-market price. The financial deficit is covered by budgetary allocations and borrowing from commercial banks. Muruntau turns in its 55 ton/yr production to the state at no cost, and subsequently receives funding through budgetary allocations.

- **Copper Subsector.** Internal and CIS price, applicable to 90 percent of the production, was 210,000 rubles per ton in September 1992 (US$1,000/ton), or about 40 percent of world market price.[1] Only 10 percent of the copper production is exported outside the CIS. Foreign exchange generated by export transactions outside the CIS, which fall within budgeted volumes, is allocated 60 percent to the state and 40 percent to the enterprise. If budget volume is exceeded, 80 percent of the excess foreign exchange goes to the enterprise and 20 percent to the state.

- **Lead and Zinc Subsectors.** All production is sold inside the CIS at prices estimated to be about 40 percent of world-market prices.

- **Coal Subsector.** All production is consumed internally. The internal price to the producer of "brown" coal (3,500 Kcal./Kgr) was 345 rubles/ton, or about US$1.60/ton in September 1992, roughly 5 percent of the price of the internationally traded coal (with 6,000 to 7,000 Kcal/Kgr).

---

[1] About 50 percent of total production is sold to CIS countries, as per the Inter Republic Agreement. About 14 percent is assigned to cover plant needs at Almalyk; this copper is also sold in the CIS to buy CIS-made equipment. The Uzbek internal consumption is about 26 percent of total production.

EXPLORATION

11.8   All exploration in Uzbekistan is undertaken by the state; more than 90 percent is undertaken by the State Committee for Geology, which transfers the projects to state mining enterprises only at the final feasibility stage. Thus, the state, with public funds, assumes the exploration risk while the state enterprises are not interested in the results of the prospecting and exploration activities. In fact, because projects change hands, neither the exploration entity nor the mining outfit can actually integrate the costs and the benefits of the mining cycle into one account. Under such circumstances, it will be extremely difficult to establish the required discipline to develop a profitable sector under market-based conditions (see Box 11.6). The responsibility and the full cost of exploration would have to be assumed by the mining enterprises.

EXISTING INVESTMENT PROJECTS

Projects Reserved for the State

11.9   The Kyzylkum Rare Metals and Gold enterprise, to which the Muruntau mine belongs, is currently developing and constructing the Uchkuduk gold-uranium project. The Government does not seem to have interest in private investment in the Kyzylkum desert area--an area with the most promising gold yields in Uzbekistan--and the project would be 100 percent state-owned. Uchkuduk is projected to start production in early 1994, feeding 5 million tons of ore annually to the mill. Neither the grade of the ore nor the projected production were disclosed to the Bank mission. Nevertheless, the considerable size of this undertaking must be pointed out--an investment of at least $500 million under market-based conditions, of which probably one half is still outstanding, to be invested during the next 18 to 24 months. The Uchkuduk project has faced delays owing to metallurgical-environmental problems caused by the high content of arsenic in the ore. For seven

---

Box 11.6: Exploration - Key to Developing the Sector

Exploration is the most critical phase of the mining cycle and also the riskiest one. Exploration technology is changing rapidly, with considerable advances made even in the past decade. Some private international companies have the resources and motivation to stay abreast of these advances. Given favorable geology, as appears to be the case in Uzbekistan, the exploration interests of international companies that possess state-of-the-art exploration technology will be determined by Government policy. However, the Government has not yet shown any interest in the participation of such firms in exploration in Uzbekistan. The only agreement for foreign investment in the mining sector that has been signed thus far, and those under negotiation, refer to deposits which had already been known and where the expertise sought from the foreign partner is related to the exploration phase. The enactment of a regulatory framework, discussed in this report, would provide the vehicle for opening the sector to private investment in exploration.

---

years, a pilot plant built to deal with this problem has treated the ore. The mission was informed that a satisfactory solution had been found and that the State Committee for the Protection of Nature will be responsible for controlling the emission and disposal of tailings. An opinion specifically about the competitivity of Uchkuduk cannot be presented, given the lack of information.

Projects Open for Joint Ventures

11.10   The Government has stated its intention to promote joint ventures as an instrument to allow private-sector participation in mining. Thus far, one joint venture has been signed, and conversations are being held with other groups for new projects. In effect, Newmont Mining (Colorado, USA) recently signed an agreement with the Government to extract gold from low-grade ore stock-piled at Muruntau, which the existing mill cannot treat. The project would use Newmont's heap-leach technology. The capital cost of the venture is estimated to be between US$80 million and $100 million, to be disbursed over 18 months beginning in March 1993. Production would start during the third quarter of 1994 and is projected to yield about 300,000 ounces per year for the first two years and then about 180,000 ounces annually for at least ten years. Discussions being held with other foreign groups pertain to known deposits that must be developed further and, as was mentioned in the previous paragraph, that are not located in the Kyzylkum Desert area. The mission was not informed of any project under consideration in which a private investor would carry out a full exploration program.

B. SECTORAL REFORM: AREAS AND RECOMMENDATIONS

DEVELOPING THE MINING SECTOR IN UZBEKISTAN: THE AVAILABLE OPTIONS

11.11   Given the need for modern management expertise and for improved mining technologies, the bulk of the effort to ignite and maintain growth in the mining sector should come from private investment, especially from companies that offer the required resources to develop the sector. In order to establish the foundation to support private investment, the Government must adopt a policy and institutional structure that support stable and transparent regulations to govern the rights and obligations of the investor and the Government, a competitive and well-structured fiscal regime, access to foreign exchange at market rates, and well-organized institutions to monitor and assist the producers effectively.

11.12   Thus far, the Government has addressed the private-sector participation in mining only by promoting joint venture agreements with selected foreign enterprises. This is a positive step, but it does not in essence open the sector, and thus does not ensure growth in accordance with the geological potential of Uzbekistan. In addition, the agreements would essentially preclude the possibility of creating and establishing local private mining enterprises. Although such enterprises might not make a significant economic contribution in the beginning, their creation and promotion would indicate the Government's commitment to undertake a thorough reform program.

11.13   Two options are available to improve the efficiency of the existing operations: (1) transferring the existing state-owned enterprises into the private sector, and (2) laying the foundations for a mixed sector, in which reformed SOEs, foreign investment, and local private companies can coexist in equal terms, under free market mechanisms and prices.

A MIXED MINING-SECTOR STRATEGY

11.14   As an initial step and as a precondition for any effort to develop the sector, it is important that excessive state control be relaxed in order to allow both public and private enterprises to be managed independently. Thus, the Ministries or State Committees must cease to be command organisms, and regulations must allow the SOEs to operate as if they were private enterprises.

The Regulatory Framework

11.15   Reforming the mining sector will require both mining-specific legislation and investment legislation to cover such critical issues as taxation, access to foreign exchange, dividend control, business registration, and labor and employment conditions. Although a detailed analysis of investment legislation is beyond the scope of this discussion, several mining-specific regulatory changes are recommended.[2]

---

[2] The discussion in the reminder of this section pertains to regulations applicable only to mining, not to hydrocarbons. Important differences in the technical aspects of their respective businesses make it imperative that regulations cover mining and oil/gas separately. The expected value of mineral (mining) deposits is far less certain than is the expected value of oil and gas deposits, particularly in the early stages of exploration. Thus, resource allocation on the basis of a market price determined in advance is seldom feasible in mining, while it is very common in oil and gas. This difference has important implications in the design of the minerals rights systems. Access to oil and gas deposits is often auctioned off as a concession after a relatively small investment by the state in geophysical information, an investment that is then promptly recovered in the auction. The high degree of uncertainty at the initial stages of mining exploration would almost certainly preclude the possibility of successful auctions and make the chance of recovering state investment remote. Thus, mining rights are best allocated through a first-come first-served priority system.

The Mining Code

11.16   Two general principles should guide the development of a mining code: that the investor has the right to explore for and mine minerals in return for specific, monitorable commitments, and that the investor should have secure and long-term title to mining rights. More specifically the code should:

- Apply equally to all investors--public and private, domestic and foreign, large and small: there is no reason to create differential access to mineral rights for different classes of investors

- Specify the ownership of mineral resources and vest a single authority with the power to grant exploration and mining rights

- Contain explicit criteria for allocating rights, and for allowing both exploration and mining rights to be transferred and sold

- Ensure that land under license is either actively explored and worked or relinquished; land rentals and/or minimum work requirements should be specified clearly

- Prescribe procedures for settling disputes, either in court or by arbitration

- Specify that mining companies have the right to market their product unencumbered by obligations to sell to the Central Bank or a state marketing corporation

- Be as clear as possible and leave minimal space for ministerial discretion.

Mineral Rights and Licenses

11.17   With the important exception of the Unites States, the most important mining countries assume public ownership over the subsoil (for example, Canada, Australia, Chile, and Mexico). Public ownership in this respect does not prevent secure titles from being allocated to private parties, nor does it imply that rights cannot be tradable. However, it does mean that the state can charge for the exploitation of natural resources and has a legitimate interest in how they are exploited.

11.18   *The security and continuity of tenure is essential*. The investor must be assured of its right to the minerals and of its rights to proceed from exploration to mining, provided that predefined criteria are met. The rights should be tradable. Companies must be able to buy or sell their mineral rights. Finally, the *power to grant mineral rights should reside with one authority* and not be subject to overlapping or concurrent jurisdictions (for example, national and provincial).

11.19   Most countries have adopted a dual licensing system: an exploration license, typically for 3 to 4 years with one or two renewals, and a mining license, for 25 to 30 years renewable. Other countries use a single licensing system, in which, after a defined period, the concession holder must prove that it is engaging in either construction or production. In both cases, minimum work requirements and/or land rentals are specified. These requirements and rentals are established at a level that, while providing a clear disincentive to holding land unnecessarily, does not act as a barrier to entry. The resources obtained from rentals should normally cover the full cost of administering the rights and licenses, but do not provide additional resources of major fiscal significance.

Investment Agreements

11.20   Investment agreements for projects are often a *sine qua non* for foreign investors in countries where sovereign risk (that is, unilateral changes by the Government to the investment rules) is great owing to political circumstances or the absence of experience. In the recommended context of a valid mining code, agreements can supplement the law or implement it. Furthermore, for Uzbekistan, many investors may fear interference by the ministries. Agreements may be used to guarantee in writing that the ministries will not interfere with any operation.

INSTITUTIONAL STRUCTURE

11.21   Implementing a mining strategy in which the private sector will play an important role requires an institutional framework that comprises four main building blocks: a Ministry of Mines, a Department of Mines, a Geological Survey, and a Promotional Agency. Normally, the Department of Mines and the Promotional Agency are located within the Ministry of Mines; the mining sector is frequently placed together with energy in a Ministry of Energy and Mines. This configuration is flexible; what is important is the existence of entities to assume the necessary functions.

The Ministry of Mines

11.22   This Ministry would be responsible for broad policy direction, effecting coordination with other ministries, organizing and leading the negotiation of mining agreements, and supervising other mining agencies. Specifically for Uzbekistan, the Government must ensure that the Ministry will not interfere with the operations of either the private or the state-owned enterprises. For the latter, supervision would be ex-post and based on results.

The Department of Mines

11.23   This department would be a sub-unit within the Ministry. Core duties would include licensing and administering exploration and mining rights, and monitoring compliance with work requirements, and health and safety standards. The department would also compile production statistics and general industry information. The administration of mining rights would normally call for implementing a Mining Cadastre (that is, a cartographic and registral control of the mineral land of the country) so as to avoid legal conflict in concessions management.

The Promotional Agency

11.24   This entity would be small agency that serves as point of contact for prospective foreign investors. It would not have decision-making authority; it would serve merely as a "one-stop shop" under which companies would seek all approvals and make all required reports. The agency could be located in the Ministry of Mines, depending on the relative importance of the sector for purposes of foreign investment.

The Geological Survey

11.25   This entity should be a separate, independent agency under the general supervision of the Ministry of Mines. Its role would be to provide the basic geological infrastructure of the country, including mineral reconnaissance, geological mapping, the publication and dissemination of maps, and the compilation of a modern and accessible geological and exploration data-base. It should be responsive to the needs of investors for geological data and maps, rather than setting a program of exploration work for its own purposes.

11.26   The survey should not undertake detailed exploration or feasibility work, nor should the Government finance detailed mineral exploration programs. If the state decides to remain a producer in the sector, the detailed exploration should be financed by the state mining companies and be counted as an expense or investment against their financial statements.

THE STRUCTURE OF STATE-OWNED ENTERPRISES

11.27   Should the Government preclude total or even partial privatization--placing the strategic and operational control of the company in the hands of a qualified partner--reform would have to be made within commercialization. Commercialization requires setting commercial goals, introducing firm budgetary constraints, and increasing the accountability and autonomy of managers, with rewards and sanctions limited to performance. The fundamental objectives must be to ensure that:

- Decisions are made according commercial, not political, criteria

- Companies are subject to the same regulatory and tax codes as private enterprises

- Senior management appointments are based on merit and experience

- Special treatments, such as subsidies or privileged access to mining rights, are avoided.

11.28   For Uzbekistan, the commercialization of the mining SOEs will also require the following adjustments:

- *Closing unprofitable operations*. Two operations--the lead-zinc mines Altin Topkan and Uch Kulach--may have to be closed. Other, less clear candidates for closure exist. A study should be undertaken to analyze the competitivity and the value added of the individual mining operations in Uzbekistan under market-based conditions. The closing of mines would be decided on the basis of the conclusions of the study.

- *Rationalizing personnel*. All operations visited by the Mission employed excess personnel. Overstaffing is due partly to the fact that mining enterprises in the FSU assume roles that Western companies do not; it is also due in part to the restrictions imposed on the management of the state enterprises. Management must be free to define its personnel needs and to implement them. A study of the personnel needs for individual mining operations according to efficiency criteria should be undertaken. Subsequent rationalization would implement the conclusions of the study.

- *Privatizing ancillary services*. Many mining-related services--such as transportation, hospitals, stores, and so forth--need not remain in the hands of the mining company, much less in those of the state. These ancillary services could be privatized, with a view toward creating the incentives necessary to encourage competition. A strategy paper to delineate the basis for transferring these services to the private sector could be proposed.

- *Incorporating responsibility for exploration.* In order to be held accountable for their results, the state mining companies must be given autonomy and control over all their activities, including prospecting and exploration. The SOE's would be free to undertake these activities directly or to contract the service with a state agency or a private group.

- *Freeing prices and providing access to foreign exchange by the mining SOEs.* In order to act as private enterprises and to be responsible for their economic results, the SOEs must have access to the market mechanisms. Otherwise, the incentives for these enterprises will be distorted, and they will not try to optimize their economic results. If the state is anxious to cash in its benefits as the owner of these companies, it should do so through dividends.

11.29   A word of caution about commercialization is in order. Many countries have attempted to commercialize public enterprises, and the results have not always been favorable. Many conflicting interests must be resolved to ensure successful commercialization, regardless of the extent of financial engineering. Yet all of the adjustments listed in this section must be carried out if commercialization is to have a chance to succeed. No easy alternatives exist; experience with management contracts as an intermediate way shows only mixed to poor results. The contractor remains dependent on the owner, since not enough is at stake to encourage the contractor to operate freely. *As has been mentioned, the only true alternative to commercialization is privatization, and this option has been precluded by Government.*

C. TECHNICAL ASSISTANCE NEEDS

11.30   A technical assistance program recommended to support the proposed reform of the mining sector would consist of five components:[3]

1.   *Minerals Development Strategy Policy Statement.* This component calls for preparing an agenda and conducting dialogue among the relevant agencies in Uzbekistan to define sectoral policies. It would also provide assistance for preparing a policy statement, and for summarizing the conclusions of the dialogue.

2.   *Mining Legislation and Taxation Policies.* The program would include a specialized lawyer and a taxation specialist for three months to support efforts to prepare a mining code, related mining regulations, model investment agreements, and a competitive fiscal regime for the sector. The consultants would assist a Government-appointed commission with representatives from the sectoral institutions, the management of the state-owned enterprises, and institutions responsible for promoting foreign investment.

---

[3] The Bank may consider participation in assisting Uzbekistan's mining sector. A critical element for the Bank would be whether the Minerals Development Strategy Policy Statement is prepared.

3.   ***Institutional Structure Design and Implementation***. The program would include a team of four specialists for three months to assist in preparing a detailed design for a new sectoral-institution structure. A subsequent implementation support phase would be included to support the new cadastral system and the new Department of Mines (two persons for one year). The program component would be tied and conditioned to the enactment of the new mining code. The Government would appoint a local counterpart to work with the proposed specialists.

4.   ***Sector Restructuring Strategy and Organization***. The program would include two components:

   - The execution of five base-study documents to guide the process of commercializing the SOEs: (1) a competitivity/cost analysis of existing mines--to define which of the existing mines would or would not be profitable under free-market conditions, and under what conditions; (2) a personnel rationalization study for profitable mines--to prepare a plan, including manning tables and implementation timetables, for releasing excess personnel in mines that would be competitive under free-market conditions; (3) a lay-off plan to serve displaced workers; (4) a strategy paper for privatizing or otherwise divesting ancillary services at profitable mines--to plan for transferring such services as transportation, health, repair shops, and so forth to the private sector, and provide the appropriate incentives for encouraging competition.

   - Support the Government and SOEs in devising a strategy for implementing the recommendations of the base studies.

5.   ***Environmental Baseline Study***. The program would include a study of the environmental problems caused by mining and metallurgical operations, culminating in mining-specific standards and controls for environmental protection.

CHAPTER 12

THE INFRASTRUCTURE FOR PRODUCTION: TRANSPORT AND TELECOMMUNICATIONS

12.1   The cornerstone of any market-based economy is an efficient system for supplying production and business inputs and distributing output to customers. This support infrastructure in Uzbekistan consists of two sectors: transport and telecommunications. This chapter discusses each of these sectors and how they can best be configured to support the production and marketing needs of the emerging Uzbekistan economy.

I. TRANSPORT SECTOR

12.2   Uzbekistan has a relatively well developed transport system well adapted to its geography. However, the sector faces serious problems. Its need for the rehabilitation and replacement of assets is immense. Transport demand is also likely to change substantially in the near future. Furthermore, as in the other sectors of the economy, inadequate pricing systems, incentive structures, and regulations create institutional inefficiencies. These are primary, immediate challenges facing the sector. They will require Government action at many different levels.

A. THE SETTING FOR SECTORAL REFORM

INSTITUTIONAL STRUCTURE

12.3   An unusual disaggregation of responsibilities exists in the transport sector. Five Government agencies hold primary sectoral responsibility at the ministerial level: the Ministry of Highways, the Joint Stock Corporation of Automobile Transport, the Railway Board, the Civil Aviation Agency (which includes Uzbekistan Airways), and the Tashkent Association of Passenger Transport Companies. These ministries are coordinated by a deputy prime minister and the Department of Construction, Communication, and Transport in the Cabinet of Ministers.

CURRENT INDICATORS AND PROBLEMS

Facilities and Equipment

12.4   Given its level of development, Uzbekistan has adequate facilities and equipment for road, rail, and air transport. Uzbekistan contains 42,000 km of main roads, and about 90,000 km of local roads (serving cities, villages, state farms, and industries). The road network reaches most parts of the country and is particularly dense in the populated areas. Overall road density is 0.3 km/sq km, about half that of Eastern Europe, and 6km/1,000 inhabitants, about the same as Eastern Europe's. The rail system primary serves the country's major corridors. It includes 3,500 km of rail line (of which about 270 km are electrified) and a fleet of more than 600 mainline locomotives. Given the withdrawal of Turkmenistan from the Central Asia rail system, the main east-west rail line that connects Uzbekistan to the Black Sea through Kazakhstan and Russia is now split into various sections, each of which is under the control of either the Turkmen or the Uzbek railway. Air transport is also well served by nine main civil airports, including four that can accommodate 747s, and a vast fleet of aircraft.

12.5   Despite the adequate transport structure, one of the primary problems facing the sector is the deterioration and relative inefficiency of many transport assets. For example, about 1,000 kilometers of railtrack must be rehabilitated; about 40 percent of the locomotive fleet and about a third of the truck fleet of the Ministry of Road Transport have exceeded their service life. Most equipment-application technologies also date back to the 1950s and 1960s.

Transport Demand

12.6   As in all FSU countries, the economy of Uzbekistan is unusually transport-intensive. There were approximately 2.8 tons x km of freight transport for each US$ of GDP in 1991, or about 3.5 times more than in the United States and 10 times more than in Western Europe. Rail transport is the most extensively used mode, with 60 billion tons x km carried in 1991, or about 75 percent of all freight transport (excluding pipelines), and about 4.5 billion passengers x km, or about 50 percent of intercity surface passenger transport. Air passenger transport (primarily to and from other parts of the FSU) was comparatively important, with 10.5 billion passengers x km in 1991.

12.7   In the next few years, however, transport demand is likely to change substantially. Total demand can be expected to decline because transport prices will be tied more closely to costs, and will thus increase in relative terms; moreover, the reform process will create a less specialized and monopolistic structure, thus diversifying trade patterns, and, in general, shortening distances between buyers and suppliers. Overall, the current decline of about 30 percent may last over the long term. In addition, the structure of demand (and thus the shares of various transport modes) should be expected to change considerably, given the diversification of customer requirements, greater flexibility and responsiveness by transport operators, and changes in relative costs. Consequently, for example, interregional road transport and the use of containers are likely to grow substantially. Conversely, the modal share of rail transport may be expected to decline. Air transport is likely to remain at its current depressed level.

International Transport

12.8   Being landlocked is a major geographic determinant of the Uzbekistan transport sector. Distances to many of its current and potential export/import markets are very far (for example, about 3,000 kilometers to the Black Sea, 3,500 kilometers to Moscow, and about 5,000 kilometers to the main Chinese ports). Thus, transport adds substantially to the cost of traded goods (for example, about US$150-175 to the cost of one ton of cotton to Western Europe, which is currently valued at about US$1,100 CIF). Because all land transport routes include transit through several countries, the Uzbekistan economy also depends highly on the political stability and the performance of the transport systems of these countries. In addition, temporary or permanent-capacity bottlenecks such as those that currently exist at the Kazakhstan/China border may affect the availability of certain routes. Being landlocked is an especially key factor given Uzbekistan's close economic ties to the FSU and its relatively high share of foreign trade relative to total output. The Government is thus correctly concerned about its international transport and has made it a priority to ensure that the country has access to several alternative routes (rail, road, and multimodel). The national airline has recently signed intergovernmental agreements on air travel with China, England, Egypt, Germany, India, Israel, Pakistan, and Turkey. Currently, however, the existing rail (and, in a few cases, road) systems of other FSU countries and

China appear to be fulfilling international transport satisfactorily and at a reasonable cost, and this scenario is likely to remain in the short to medium term. Expensive new investments thus seem premature. Yet long-term needs should be addressed. In particular, economic studies should be undertaken immediately to assess the benefits and costs of various alternatives--for example, the road connection to Karachi (Pakistan) and the railway link to the Iranian network. These studies would provide an objective basis for policy dialogue and long-term action.

B. SECTORAL REFORM: AREAS AND RECOMMENDATIONS

12.9   As in other sectors of the economy, the economic strength of the transport sector depends on whether several structural changes can be made, and on how these measures are introduced. The overriding priority is to create an appropriate incentive structure for the sector: pricing must reflect the diversity of transport services; taxes and fees must be based on sounder, more equitable criteria; and the environment for meeting supply and demand must be opened up, encouraging competition. Accompanying these changes in incentives should be an improved institutional structure for formulating policy, regulations, and operations effectively. Only when an effective incentive and institutional structure is developed can the Government target funding and investment priorities efficiently.

IMPROVING THE INCENTIVE STRUCTURE

Pricing

12.10   The Government controls the price of almost all transport services (except road transport at the intraregional level and outside the FSU). Although, in practice, price adjustment has been flexible, the pricing system creates numerous difficulties that cannot be managed adequately by the Government. In any economy, a large diversity of transport services must be offered to satisfy the needs of customers. All of these services should be priced separately; moreover, in countries that are undergoing the types of economic changes that are being experienced in Uzbekistan (which create considerably variable transport-input prices in both absolute and relative terms), adjustments must be made frequently and promptly. Given the sheer volume of work and the absence of administrative capability, it is unlikely that Uzbekistan can currently respond adequately to those necessary adjustments. Thus, distortions are bound to appear, preventing the most effective use of assets, discouraging innovation and investment, and creating an inefficient modal allocation. Thus, the Government should free transport prices progressively for all services that can be made competitive (primarily road and inter-urban passenger transport). It should also establish mechanisms to allow regular price increases based on the actual costs of rail and air transport and of public transport.

12.11   Another concern about Government control over pricing is that enterprises use poor cost accounting systems and practices, often not taking their full costs into account (particularly the costs of depreciation and personnel). Consequently, prices are generally below costs. In addition, some enterprises are cross-subsidized; for example, the cheap suburban fares of passenger transport are obtained at the expense of intercity transport. Subsidies for urban and suburban passenger transport, which may currently be estimated at around 60 percent to 90 percent of actual costs (depending on transport mode), should be removed at least partly. Remaining subsidies, if deemed necessary for social reasons, should be made transparent by their incorporation into the federal budget.

Road User Taxation

12.12   In countries with an efficient road infrastructure, road users (trucking fleets, bus companies, and individual car users) must be charged for the marginal costs they impose on society (road deterioration, congestion, and environmental costs). In most such countries, the primary instruments for this purpose are an annual vehicle registration tax and, most important, a diesel and gasoline tax that is tied directly to the quantity of road use. However, no such taxes exist in Uzbekistan. The current road taxes are a tax on company turnover and a tax on transport expenditures that is only very indirectly related to road use. Thus, for instance, even if the price of petroleum products reflected their opportunity costs (which they currently do not), road users would not pay adequately for using the road. A modern system of road user taxation must be introduced in Uzbekistan to improve economic efficiency in the transport sector and to raise the additional critical revenue necessary to maintain and rehabilitate the road system. Moreover, a fuel tax could be established. A Road Fund Law is under preparation, addressing some of these necessities.

Competitive Environment

12.13   Although the Government has already taken steps to encourage competition in road transport by opening road freight transport at the intraregional level and outside the FSU, interregional and inter-FSU road freight transport, which may be expected to grow substantially in the near future, are still submitted to a licensing system. Under the system, freight is allocated administratively to available truckers; moreover, the licensing company, Uzvneshavtotrans, is itself a major trucking company. This system makes it difficult to allocate freight efficiently according to the needs and constraints of both the customers and the transport companies.

12.14   A competitive environment in which demand and supply can interact freely is now in place in many countries (for example, in Western Europe) and has shown that it can promote flexibility and the most efficient allocation of all resources. The Government should establish this environment for road transport. Already existing are several dozens of competent, almost independent road transport companies that are currently state-owned but are inefficiently grouped under monopolistic regional associations; they can, and appear to be keen to, take advantage of new opportunities. New private companies are also likely to emerge. A competitive market can thus develop very quickly. If necessary, the market information could be disseminated through a network of independent, probably private freight forwarders, and should in fact be encouraged by the Government.

12.15   More competition should also be introduced into passenger transport. Intercity passenger transport is successfully competitive in many countries, and, provided that bus terminal operations are adequately organized, could easily become competitive in Uzbekistan. Urban passenger transport could also be competitive; if the Government intends to continue subsidizing it, it should also introduce special procedures that have proved successful in other countries--for example, tendering bus routes. In general, improving competition and efficiency in passenger transport would also increase competition between road and rail transport, thus forcing rail to restructure and adjust to the changing market.

Privatization

12.16   The potential for privatization in the transport sector is substantial, particularly in road transport and in the construction industry. Improving the efficiency of these subsectors requires adapting to many different market demands and special circumstances, responding rapidly to change, and creating a highly flexible organization and personnel--characteristics that, in most cases, are exhibited only by active private entrepreneurs. Moreover, as was discussed earlier, a competitive business environment, appropriate for private-sector operations, could easily be introduced in road transport. Competition could also be encouraged readily in the construction industry, provided that appropriate contractual arrangements and supervisory procedures are developed for Government civil works contracts. The Government should thus give priority to privatizing these two subsectors. In particular, the restrictions that apparently apply to international road transport and "services" (including maintenance) for highways[1] which were included in the July 2, 1992, regulation on privatization, do not seem justified on the basis of other countries' experience and could usefully be removed. The privatization of Uzbekistan Airways could be a longer-term objective. However, beforehand, competition and efficiency in the air transport subsector should be encouraged by opening it up to private companies (as in most Western countries), with minimal regulatory constraints.

DEVELOPING THE INSTITUTIONS

Organizational Structure

12.17   The allocation of Government functions should be improved substantially. A major feature of the current institutional structure is that the regulatory, policymaking, and infrastructural responsibilities are entwined with the operations of Government companies. For example, in civil aviation, one entity operates Uzbekistan Airways, regulates air transport, and provides airports; similarly, the Ministry of Automobile before its recent transformation into a joint stock corporation assumed part of the regulatory function, operates most common carrier road transport services, and provides bus terminals. This structure precludes transparent and objective decisionmaking. In particular, the interests of Government companies are likely to have a pervasive influence on how regulations are formulated and infrastructure or common-use facilities are provided. Yet such companies should be made to conform to established rules applied similarly to all public and private companies. It is imperative that the Government separate organizational functions that are not compatible.

12.18   In addition, the Government could also organize its policy formulation, regulation, and sectoral coordination functions more effectively. It should especially strengthen its ability to analyze trends and emerging problems in the sector, and to monitor how transport policies are implemented, most likely under the lead of the Cabinet of Ministers. It must also devote more attention to multimodal transport and international transport routes, which are key to the transport needs of Uzbekistan in the future. For this purpose, the information system must be upgraded, more staff are required, and consultants should be relied on systematically to provide in-depth analyses. In addition, a unit should be created to prepare and monitor the enforcement of regulations for vehicle weights and dimensions.

Government Enterprises

12.19   The relations between Government and its enterprises must also be rationalized. All companies that can perform on a self-financing and commercial basis should be autonomous. Most should have the status of private enterprises, even if they remain under public ownership. For the natural monopolies, such as the railways or airports, and for a few large companies, such as the airline, the

---

[1] According to this regulation, the privatization of international road transport is prohibited, and "services" for highway can be privatized only through management contracts.

Government should establish "performance plans" or "contract plans," delineating financial and operational objectives for the companies (including productivity targets and investment need) and providing a framework for revising tariffs. They would enable companies to function autonomously while ensuring effective Government supervision at regular intervals.

ROAD SUBSECTOR

12.20   In general, the subsector is characterized by an unusual degree of decentralization: responsibilities for both tax collection and road management have been delegated fully to the lowest administrative level (the district's). If complementary measures are taken, this organization could create strong accountabilities. Yet, even though other capabilities are quite developed in the road subsector (particularly at a technical level), substantial progress could be achieved in some key areas. In particular, roadworks and road policies could be improved, as illustrated by the following:

- The quality of road materials and the execution of civil works are generally quite poor, primarily because real contractual relationships between the project owners and the construction companies did not traditionally exist in FSU, nor did adequate quality control procedures. Thus, despite generally sound designs and good natural materials (river gravels, for example), the quality of road pavements is usually much inferior to what should be expected; in turn, poor quality translates into unnecessary vehicle operating costs and increased maintenance and rehabilitation expenditures. Given the scarcity of funding, this infrastructural problem should be improved immediately, by establishing detailed supervising procedures at each stage of construction, as well as organizational arrangements for carrying them out.

- Competition among construction companies must be encouraged and a fair and efficient relationship established between them and the Government (in the road subsector, as well as in any sector that requires construction). For this purpose, the Government must establish standard but specific tendering and contract documents for civil works, and procedures and organizational arrangements for selecting contractors and administering contracts.

- Given the broad decentralization measures and the current lack of data flowing back to central institutions, the Government cannot readily monitor and control the implementation of its road policies. A road management information system (MIS) is imperative; it should contain data on road conditions, traffic, road safety, and work programs. Simultaneously, planning systems should be improved. Already familiar with computers and mathematical models, engineers and technicians could easily use the more modern and accurate systems now widely available to determine optimal maintenance and rehabilitation expenditures. For this purpose, as well as for building the MIS, the central level should also be provided with modern equipment for road condition surveys.

- Road research must be encouraged to promote local standards and road techniques adapted to the climate, available materials, and traffic specificities. Realistic objectives should guide construction and maintenance standards, always in recognition of the implementation and control capabilities of the different levels of Government and the contractors.

- For the longer term, most maintenance activities could be contracted out to the private sector. However, as the experience of such countries as Great Britain shows, the Government should (1) ensure that the public sector retains a capability for maintaining and patrolling roads routinely, and (2) address all considerations that may affect the productivity of workers.

- The qualifications and efficiency of personnel should be enhanced with in-house training and performance-based promotions.

Road Maintenance Expenditures

12.21   In addition to increasing the efficiency of the Ministry of Highways, the Government must urgently increase funding for maintaining the road network. From 1990 on, the lack of funding has led decisionmakers to give priority to salaries, and then to routine maintenance works. The wearing course has not been reconstructed, deteriorating the roads prematurely and increasing vehicle operating costs. Periodic road maintenance was carried out on 5,000 to 6,000 kilometers each year until 1990. In 1991, only 3,700 kilometers were covered, and, based on observations in the Tashkent region, less than 600 kilometers will have been treated in 1992. The reduction in maintenance activity could have dramatic results in the longer term. Nothing is presently irreversible, however, and the network can be saved if at least 6,000 kilometers of periodic maintenance are undertaken yearly from 1993 on. Despite some sections in newly irrigated (and thus badly drained) areas, bearing capacity seems to be adequate; thus, some thinner types of wearing course could be tried--for example, surface dressing over possible cold asphalt reshaping. This process could substantially lower the cost of maintenance.

Investments

12.22   Given the likely decline in transport demand and the relative overcapacity of the transport system, investment in the transport sector should be targeted at replacing equipment, rehabilitating the infrastructure (roads and railtrack), and eliminating specific bottlenecks. In any case, maintenance should be top priority. Investment proposals should be subjected to a rigorous economic and financial analysis according to sound international practices. In particular, equipment replacement should be considered only if transport demand cannot be satisfied at a reasonable cost by improving operations and/or increasing the productivity of existing assets. To the largest possible extent, investment decisions should be left with transport enterprises, and they should bear the full cost of these decisions.

TECHNICAL ASSISTANCE

12.23   The sector could be improved more rapidly if technical assistance could be obtained from abroad. Box 12.1 presents the areas where assistance could be beneficial.

Box 12.1: Technical Assistance and Training

A well-targeted technical assistance program would support Government efforts to:

• Establish better cost-accounting systems in transport companies

• Develop planning systems for road and rail transport

• Improve the capacity of the Ministry of Highways to supervise civil works and to establish adequate procurement and contract administration procedures for civil works

• Improve railway operational management, particularly to meet the needs of customers more effectively

• Analyze the economic and technical aspects of the various international transport routes

• Improve the Government's sectoral organization--particularly formulating and monitoring Government policies, and preparing performance plans for large state-owned enterprises.

II. TELECOMMUNICATIONS

12.24   All FSU countries have inherited a telecommunications network organized centrally with international routing via Moscow, and with a low priority for investment, leading to obsolete equipment that provides poor-quality service and coverage and which is deteriorating further. Because recent economic difficulties and traditionally low tariffs have failed to generate enough revenue to maintain and extend the system, the rate of new line installation has dropped sharply. The Government has recognized that these sectoral shortcomings must be overcome if the telecommunications infrastructure is to make its essential contribution to a market-based economy. The network cannot be modernized without a substantial influx of foreign investment. The Government recognizes this investment need, and has addressed it as one of its top priorities.

12.25   Many countries are now recognizing the vital role of high-quality telecommunications in supporting modern economic activity and in attracting external companies both as contributors and as users of the telecommunications sector. Thus, the competition for external telecommunications expertise and investment is intense worldwide, and those countries that create the most favorable circumstances for modern developments in the sector will be able to attract the highest-quality consultants and investors.

A. THE SETTING FOR REFORM

12.26   The main challenge in the telecommunications sector is to avail itself of new technical opportunities to meet the demands of customers for new and improved international, long distance, and local services. This challenge will rest on major financing and funding decisions in a range of planning and operational strategies, appropriate tariff policies, and cost-effective and organizational approaches to modernization. The sector must pursue one key reform to support the most effective responses to its overriding challenge: reorganizing the institutional structure of the sector so that the Government creates a framework for encouraging service improvements, privatizing sectoral enterprises, commercializing the sector, and upgrading existing facilities. Only when a strong institutional structure is created to take these steps will the sector be prepared to attract investment.

B. ISSUES AND RECOMMENDATIONS

SPECIFYING INSTITUTIONAL ROLES

12.27   The current institutional structure is inadequate for four reasons: the Ministry combines policy and operational responsibilities without a commercial orientation; it does not have the resources necessary to develop and administer policies, including those pertaining to the scope of liberalization and some elements of privatization in the sector; the entities that provide services are not organized in the most appropriate way at the regional or national level; and the required underlying disciplines, such as accounting, planning, training, marketing, and legal skills, are not developed enough to support a market-based approach. (Box 12.2 describes the institutional structure of the sector.)

12.28   The Ministry recognizes that it must reduce its involvement in the daily management of the sector, and has thus established concerns that should become responsible for their own financial viability, including financing some activities at the center for such areas as research and development, national planning, and training. Hence, over time, the Ministry should become involved less directly in detailed progress measures, including the financial performance of the concerns and their constituent enterprises. The Ministry has also had to absorb activities that until recently had been carried out under the control of central planners for the FSU as a whole, without a corresponding transfer of all the necessary resources.

> **Box 12.2: Institutional Structure**
>
> Only since the recent granting of independence to the country has the Ministry of Communications had responsibility for Telecommunications, Posts, and Media Distribution, including broadcasting and newspapers, and related activities, including construction and some manufacturing. It has moved quickly to establish three concerns--one for Telecommunications (Uzbektelecom, 14 enterprises), consisting of one enterprise in each of the 13 regions of the country and one in Tashkent city; one for Posts (Uzbekistan Pocktosy, 17 enterprises); and a Planning, Construction and Industry concern (Uzbekalokainvest, 22 enterprises). It also controls another 26 enterprises directly, including local, long distance, interregional, and international telecommunications services in Tashkent city. As with other FSU countries, Uzbekistan has had to adapt the elements of the former USSR structure, such as the allocation of the USSR-wide transmission facilities to the individual countries, to be organized in Uzbekistan by a new enterprise called TPO. Planning institutes had previously been organized to meet the needs of the Soviet Union within regions, and some functions, such as Frequency Control and International Service, were controlled in Moscow. The absorption of these arrangements without the capabilities necessary to cope with the enlarged technical and operational responsibilities in the absence of the former central resources has exacerbated the difficulties facing the Ministry.

12.29   The Ministry must now formulate a sectoral policy that defines sectoral responsibilities, including service obligations, coverage requirements, and objectives. Again, it must separate itself from the operational provision of services, clarify the responsibilities for and conditions of ownership among the various current and potential participants in the sector, and balance commercial and public utility considerations. The Ministry has made a start by separating Posts from Telecommunications, and by planning to reduce its involvement in the operational activities of the sector (although for the time being it remains deeply involved in both the concerns that it has established and the enterprises that report directly to the Ministry).

12.30   These enterprises that have emerged from the division of the Soviet Union are unlikely to provide the best structure for addressing the overriding challenge to the sector: to provide technologically sound international long-distance and local services cost-effectively to customers. Thus, the Government should review existing enterprises to assess whether they should and can be reorganized and their responsibilities coordinated effectively to enhance services (for example, in Tashkent City, five enterprises are involved in providing basic services). In addition to providing a framework for improving service arrangements, the review can also serve as a guideline for coordinating funding and responsibility for upgrading service facilities, and for structuring privatization and commercialization efforts to encourage competition. When combined with an updated assessment of sectoral requirements, capabilities, and current resources, the review should culminate in the emergence of the preferred sectoral structure. Only when this structure is in place will the telecommunications sector create an environment to attract external investors.

12.31   The existing service arrangements are typical of the FSU countries (see Box 12.3). The quality, spread, and range of services are inadequate compared with those required to support a modern market-based economy. Under the old system, plans for basic services had been decided centrally, with would-be customers waiting years for service; hence, the Government made little effort to differentiate among customers on the basis of need or their ability to pay, or to determine whether targets were being met.

12.32   Improving the quality and cost-effectiveness of basic services is paramount. Beyond establishing a more effective institutional structure, the Ministry should concentrate on developing a more comprehensive strategy of implementation, which will require a more detailed telecommunications act than the general one recently passed. The initial emphasis should be on two tasks: setting up an effective service company, and introducing some elements of competition in the sector.

12.33   The service company would be separated from the Ministry, which, while still initially a state enterprise, would eventually become commercially oriented and operating under a license that defined its rights and obligations. The terms of the license would reflect the objectives of national policy, both of which would be defined and implemented by an act of Parliament. The Government should also specify the extent of competition to be introduced, which would also be sanctioned by the Parliament. Currently, new services, products, and networks are available only from the monopoly service provider or through joint ventures that it chooses to establish with external partners. These arrangements simplify introducing new capabilities because they remain under the control of one organization. Yet they fail to take full advantage of the potential for new suppliers to respond more dynamically to needs without being inhibited by links with the established provider. Appropriate areas for the introduction of competition would be value-added services (for example, information and data services) and products attached to the network (such as private branch exchanges and telephones), provided that they conform to interface standards. Alternative networks, such as cellular networks for mobile applications, may be authorized, provided that operational conditions are defined, such as the number of providers allowed, the role of the PTT, and the relationships among the companies that provide the cellular and basic networks.

12.34   Establishing a more independent service organization and introducing competition into the sector will necessitate a regulatory function operating on behalf of the Ministry to oversee the monopoly service company and encourage it to improve performance. Other countries in Eastern Europe

Box 12.3: Existing Service Arrangements

There are about 1.46 million telephone customers (just over 7 for every 100 of the population, which is low even compared with some of the other CIS countries--for example, Kazakhstan has 13), of which 1.12 million are in urban areas and 0.34 million in rural areas.   There are 380,000 business and 1.08 million residential customers.   The official waiting list is 360,000, with an estimated 1 million additional prospective customers who have not registered.   The average waiting time for installing a telephone is three to five years.   The total installed capacity is 1.65 million lines, almost all analog from the FSU and Eastern Europe. Twenty percent of urban capacity (or about 300,000 exchange lines) uses switching equipment that is no longer in production, with about half of this capacity at least 20 years old. The lack of spare parts has led to growing customer complaints about service quality. Fifteen percent of the urban and 73% of rural stations have no access to the automatic intercity and international telephone network. Only half of urban and 14% of rural lines have the numbering registering facilities required for automatic trunk and international services. The capital investment by the Ministry between 1987 and 1992 for all purposes increased from 67 to 123 billion rubles in nominal terms. A more indicative figure is the number of lines installed in Tashkent city in 1987 (42,500, compared with a target of 37,000), in 1990 (9,000 against a target of 50,000), and in 1992 (a projected 10,800 against a target of 46,000). Hence, the projected growth for the 1991-95 period of 750,000 urban and 350,000 rural lines, as well as 12,000 channels from 5 switches for intercity traffic, can be regarded as the hoped-for expansion, rather than solid plans, for which the Ministry has neither the resources nor the technical and planning capabilities to introduce modern digital technology.

The current traffic patterns for intercity, FSU, and international traffic are dominated by Tashkent city (24.8 million of 77 million calls in 1991). Within these totals, the city had 162,500 of 180,000 international calls, which is a very large proportion of a very small part of total calls. Recently, the facilities for international traffic have been upgraded when the Ministry purchased an Intelsat standard A satellite earth station and collaborated with KDD and others to provide 4 channels to Japan and South East Asia, 4 to Pakistan, 8 to the United States (with ATT), 8 to Western Europe (under discussion with Deutsche Bundespost), and 6 channels spare. These facilities are available in targeted locations such as major hotels with bills in foreign currency and in selected government offices. Additional satellite facilities are under discussion with Turkey to enhance international and transit capabilities via Ankara.   These improvements will also further the distribution of TV programs.

Financial Aspects. Five of the 13 regional enterprises were operating at a loss for the quarter prior to a recent tariff increase. Tariff levels are decided by the Government (rental and call charges), by the Ministry (125 elements), and by the enterprises (400 elements).   The result is that political pressures and traditionally low levels keep telecommunication tariffs well below the appropriate levels either to cover costs or to contribute to reinvestment, despite a threefold increase in early 1992 and a further threefold increase now under consideration for 1993.   The telecommunications enterprises are required to pay the following taxes to the federal government: profit tax (18%), VAT (30%), property tax (0.5%), pension fund and social insurance (37%), and employment fund (3%).

In addition, a significant subsidy must be made from telecommunications to the postal business when these two entities are combined, although the amount is not known. The combined effect is that the telecommunications business has been taxed by the Government at a higher level than is normal in Western countries, at a time when more money must be retained for reinvestment in the infrastructure.

have faced similar problems for a longer period of time (as described in Box 12.4).[2] Two lessons from other countries are informative--that improving the structure and performance of the major operating entity is a priority task, and that it is time consuming and difficult for the Ministry to build up the resources necessary to support its policy and regulatory roles effectively and for the legislature to enact

---

[2] Detailed terms of reference for appropriate studies have been tested--for example, in Bulgaria--and can be adapted for Uzbekistan.

the necessary legal structures. Nevertheless, building this framework to support liberalization is essential for attracting foreign expertise and financing to improve the sector.

Box 12.4: Experience in Countries with Similar Backgrounds

　　　　All of the Eastern European countries face the same challenges--to invest in modernizing the infrastructure, to restructure the Ministry so that it concentrates on policy development and regulatory oversight, and to improve the structure and effectiveness of the operating entities providing services. In Bulgaria, a cooperative investment program costing $232 million is being supported by EIB, EBRD, and IBRD for the 1993-1995 period. In parallel with project preparation, consultancy studies costing 2 million ECU have been carried out during 1992. These have addressed four themes: (1) policy, creating, the role of the Ministry, a regulatory function, and liberalization and privatization; (2) establishing a commercially oriented entity to provide telecommunications services more independently from the Ministry and separated from Posts, with particular attention to human resource development issues; (3) improving financial aspects, including tariff policy, accounting systems, and revenue-generating strategies; and (4) building management information systems and computerization within the new telecommunications entity. During 1993, the first stages of the project and the recommendations of the studies will be implemented, with a follow-up program of studies being planned. This systematic approach provides a framework to encourage additional investment in the sector and a more coherent consideration of such topics as joint venture partnerships and the implementation of new policy initiatives. In Ukraine, the approach has been different. Joint ventures have been negotiated in such key areas as international and long distance basic service and in cellular service. These will lead to service improvements but uncertainty exists about whether the terms of the deals will enable Ukraine to meet all its objectives, including the expansion of local networks and the introduction of liberalization to the extent deemed appropriate. The issues addressed by the studies in Bulgaria are still important for establishing a framework to encourage investment, although the realization of recommendations must take into account the major policy decisions that have been taken. Discussions are proceeding with IBRD on the investment needs that should have priority for early funding, and on the studies program that would best contribute to achieving sectoral objectives. In other Eastern European countries that have been addressing these issues for a longer period, there have been difficulties in agreeing to effective laws that are necessary for implementing the most recent policies (e.g., in Hungary, a modernization law for telecommunications has just been passed, but without a mechanism for its implementation). The controversy raised by the proposals has been resolved in a way that enables each side to claim victory but does not provide a satisfactory basis for progressing with the intentions. In Poland, the impact of most of the liberalization measures remains to be seen, but the intention to promote local independence has been affected by the competitive responses of the PTT to the requests for interconnection from prospective new local telephone companies (i.e., the ability to make fair competition work in these environments must still be demonstrated).

UPGRADING NETWORK FACILITIES

12.35   Along with creating a framework for encouraging service improvements, the second major challenge is to upgrade the existing network facilities to provide improved services. Yet, in Uzbekistan, the existing arrangements for developing telecommunications are problematic. First, financial policies do not generate nearly enough investment support in either local or foreign currencies. Second, the responsibility for organizing a major modernization program is diffused over the Ministry, various concerns, and enterprises. Third, the sector has limited experience with new technologies. Several Eastern European countries have had unrealistic hopes that they could produce modern telecommunications technology competitively and market the output to neighboring countries--thus reducing their demands on foreign currency for imports. However, the great difficulty in achieving this ambition raises the likelihood that many service companies face higher costs for equipment from local suppliers or are tied into deals with foreign manufacturers. And, fourth, the sector lacks experience with procedures for developmental planning, procurement, and project implementation.

12.36   The Government has focused thus far on developing international facilities that do not rely on Moscow, and on the regional companies to develop responsive service at the local level.   The Government lacks a satisfactory developmental plan that is comprehensive, technically adequate, and coordinated with the purpose of a cost-effective transition to new technologies, and which accounts properly for customer needs and their willingness to pay.   However, it is widely recognized that networks at international, long distance, and local levels must be rehabilitated, modernized, and expanded.   The current systems are obsolete, contain old large parts, and cannot be maintained satisfactorily, causing severe disruptions of service.   In addition, Uzbekistan must assess and establish its participation in international projects involving the networks of neighboring countries.   Outside assistance will be required to advise on how to strengthen the planning, procurement, and implementation capabilities within the enterprises, concerns, and the Ministry.

12.37   Several immediate contributions to maintain and rehabilitate the existing service have been proposed by planners in Uzbekistan and must be reviewed by the Bank.   They cover spare parts required between now and the end of 1993 for switching, transmission, and radio relay equipment, plus energy equipment, cables, measuring instruments, computer techniques, and equipment for teletype and facsimile service--with hard-currency costs (including the provision of equipment from FSU republics and Eastern European countries) estimated to be $9.4 million.

12.38   The priority of network improvements should be on servicing higher revenue-generating targets--primarily business subscribers for international, transnational with other FSU countries, and national and local services.   Any capacity previously allocated to other departments of government which becomes surplus to requirements should also be reallocated to help meet emerging business needs.

PROMOTING PRIVATIZATION

12.39   As a follow-up to the recent Privatization Law, a Ministry Committee has been considering privatization in the sector.   It has specified enterprises that should not be privatized, those which should be privatized immediately, and those which should follow in a second wave.   The recommendations are awaiting a decision from the Committee for State Property.   The first wave of proposals for privatization, such as newspaper distribution, are welcomed.

12.40   The Ministry Committee has proposed that the 13 enterprises responsible for telephone service in each of the provinces be privatized, allowing their staff to have a major say in the form of privatization adopted.   This policy proposal is not advisable for three main reasons.   First, it is very unlikely that an enterprise that is influenced strongly by workers will satisfactorily and aggressively pursue the necessary changes in technology, levels, and workplace behavior.   Second, long-distance service should be organized by the entity that is responsible for providing this service, not by 13 distributed contributors (even if the intention is to coordinate their activities through a central committee).   And, third, the external financing essential for realizing an early modernization program would not be attracted by a structure of divided responsibilities for providing services.

12.41   Earlier in chapter 6 of this report, it was recommended that staff retain not more than 30 percent of preemptive acquisition rights.   One of the major reasons for the pioneering privatization of British Telecommunication was to weaken the power of the unions to impede the process of modernizing and commercializing the new company by giving staff a balanced work incentive--up to 10 percent of the shares made available to staff but distributed according to performance.   The same considerations should apply in Uzbekistan.   Yet other forms of privatization at the local level have been attempted (for example, in Poland). The Government should give some consideration to involving communities and other customers more fully in the financing and oversight arrangements for investments where appropriate, and for contracting out ancillary activities, such as construction and maintenance, to a greater number of private enterprises in addition to those within the existing concerns.

Commercializing the Service Sector

12.42   Whatever service structure emerges from the sectoral review must be reinforced in the disciplines that will facilitate providing services more responsively and commercially. The relevant disciplines include management, organizational structures, finance, accounting, information systems, human resource development and personnel policies, corporate and technical planning, technical operation and management, and marketing and customer service procedures.

12.43   Current responsibility for telecommunications tariffs is spread among the Government, the Ministry, and enterprises. Tariffs have been insufficient to generate revenue for investment and have not kept pace with inflation, despite a recent threefold increase. Before this increase, 5 of the 13 provincial telephone enterprises were operating at a loss in the most recent quarter. The objective should be to increase tariffs in stages (most likely over one or two years), so as to ensure not only a suitable return on existing assets, but also an appropriate contribution to future investment. When tariffs have been stabilized, they should be adjusted regularly in line with inflation. Such increases are likely to lead to some reduction in demand, but the enterprises emerging from the Structural Review should devote more effort to measuring demand patterns for existing and new services from different types of customers. Proposed tariff levels should be correlated with costs and should emphasize the ability to contribute revenue (especially in hard currency) while striving to maintain affordable access for all customers (for example, through public callboxes if necessary). This is the direction of the initial improvements of international service in Tashkent. The organizations that offer monopoly services should propose tariff levels within guidelines set by the regulatory authority; the guidelines should establish incentives for good performance by the operating companies and should meet state objectives. The Ministry or the regulatory authority must also decide on revenue-sharing arrangements and transfer payments among the enterprises when more than one is involved in processing a call. The terms of payment, as well as technical considerations for all forms of interconnection, must be established, as must revenue sharing for traffic (which becomes more complicated as the number of enterprises that are involved grows). Fees must also be agreed upon for services that benefit several enterprises and are carried out at the headquarters level of a concern or at the Ministry.

12.44   The studies program proposed earlier would address each of the areas outlined above-- Ministerial policy and regulatory roles, including liberalization, restructuring, and commercialization of the service sector by strengthening the underlying disciplines and improvement in financial assessments, including a review of tariff policies. Each of the studies in these areas would require the transfer of knowhow from consultants to counterparts, as well as more general training to prepare key staff to operate within a market economy.

INVESTMENT CONSIDERATIONS

12.45   Several measures to stimulate foreign economic activities, and to attract and retain foreign investment, are relevant to improving the telecommunications sector. They include loans on property, enterprises, private business, external economic activity, foreign investments, renting, denationalization, and privatization and more directly the law on telecommunications. In general, these improvements are steps in the right direction, but are not specific enough to encourage investment. In particular, the telecommunications law is a broadbrush outline that does not empower the scope of liberalization that should be introduced. When proposals are developed at the more specific level, the experience of other countries suggests that legal changes become more controversial and difficult to pass because those with a priority interest in the nationwide provision of basic service hesitate to approve new arrangements that they believe will threaten that goal. Thus, a full understanding of the improvements in other countries that have modernized their approaches but have maintained the safeguard of interest should be conveyed to relevant parties, particularly to rural legislators.

12.46   Improving tariff policies will be a particularly essential step in attracting foreign investment support for service provision and network upgrades. Foreign capital and expertise will also be more forthcoming if sectoral liberalization creates new opportunities with satisfactory returns on investment. Improved sectoral policy, regulatory mechanisms, and a tax regime that treats restructured telecommunications enterprises llike other commercial companies will also attract investment.

12.47   The streamlining of organizational responsibilities for basic services will also attract foreign capital and expertise. The modernization of a network--replacing analog with digital equipment-- is an expensive task, costing at a current replacement value of existing facilities at least US$1.6 to 2.0 billion spread over many years. The task would have to be combined coherently and cost-effectively with the provision of new services, and similar actions taken by neighboring countries to modernize the regional interstate system and provide adequate access and routing to the worldwide international network. This strategy will require a combination of profit reinvestment and major loans and investments from external services in the face of growing competition for investment capital.

12.48   Improvements in the telecommunications infrastructure significantly enhance economic progress in all countries. The Government of Uzbekistan recognizes this need and has declared this sector a high-priority investment area. The present policies, structures, and financial performance of the sector will attract investment by multilateral organizations or by commercial interests, except possibly for tied deals, which may not be in the long-term interests of the country. Policy and structural changes that will improve investment opportunities in a manner consistent with the general economic reform program of the country are needed. This assistance will be most needed in the short and intermediate time frame--up to five years--by which time the expected changes are likely to have created a more self-sufficient and profitable sector. The sector's strength will be enough to attract wide-ranging financial support, although the extent of the investment requirements (particularly at the local level) could still leave a significant role for continued long-term financial contributions.

C. TECHNICAL ASSISTANCE NEEDS AND FACILITIES

TECHNICAL ASSISTANCE

12.49   Experienced international consultants should be selected in a competitive bidding process to provide action-oriented proposals and transfer knowhow to counterparts in Uzbekistan. (Box 12.5 provides a summary of the areas for technical assistance and for studies to modernize the network.) Several key areas require technical assistance:

- Improving sectoral policy and strategy, and the role of the Ministry, by
  establishing an appropriate organizational structure, a supporting legal

structure, a regulatory function and its responsibilities, and training for staff to undertake their new responsibilities.

- Regrouping and restructuring the service operating enterprises into an improved allocation of responsibilities and devolved powers.

- Improving the organizational structure and management of services, including finance, accounting, and information systems, human resource development and personnel policies, corporate and technical planning, technical operations planning, and marketing and customer service procedures. Each topic area would require training--some at central and some at local levels.

- Establishing tariff policy and demand assessment.

Box 12.5: Technical Assistance

- Develop policies and legal structures, and establish a regulatory function

- Restructure the service responsibilities within the sector--create new organizational units with assigned responsibilities and structures, and with development paths to realize changes

- Develop financial and accounting disciplines within the sector

- Address tariff policy and demand analysis

- Address human resource development issues and training arrangements for key personnel to respond to the needs of a market-based economy

- Develop planning procedures and information flows

- Prepare a development strategy to maintain the network and improve service via modernization and new procedures

- Estimated total cost of $2.6 million.

REHABILITATION

12.50   The priority list of the most-needed equipment proposed by Uzbekistan should be the basis for further discussion on immediate improvements.

NETWORK MODERNIZATION

12.51   A more comprehensive review of network modernization should be undertaken, incorporating the work of consultants to assess needs, financing options and viability, appropriate mechanisms for coordinated technical planning across all relevant groups, and technical options to meet requirements. Proposals would be implemented by the sectoral structure that emerges from the studies proposed above. The output should culminate in a strategy for modernization and new services and a plan of action for implementing the priority steps in the most cost-effective manner. The extent of local supply in equipment provision would be one factor that would affect the cost-effectiveness of service provision. The suitability of and justification for such a local manufacturing industry for the sector, as well as the modernization of the existing capabilities, should thus also be reviewed and assessed.

CHAPTER 13

HEALTH, EDUCATION AND TRAINING

I. HEALTH

13.1   Uzbekistan faces significant constraints as it redefines its economic and social system. The demise of the FSU could have serious consequences for the health status of the population. In 1991, approximately 3.7 billion rubles were spent on health care, representing 11.3 percent of the federal budgetary expenditures and 5.9 percent of GDP. In 1992, health expenditures reached 26.4 billion rubles, representing 14 percent of the federal budgetary expenditures and 6.3 percent of GDP.[1] The population views health care as a right, but the fiscal situation will soon force the government to reduce health expenditure. In the face of severe economic constraints, an unstable financial base, shortages of vaccines, medical supplies, and equipment, and indications that the health status of some groups is deteriorating, a review of the health sector is needed.

A. THE SETTING FOR REFORM

DEMOGRAPHY

13.2   With a population of 21.7 million, Uzbekistan is the largest country in Central Asia. The population is young (about 41 percent are younger than 15 years) with a dependency ratio of .9. Large regional variation exists for many statistics. Reportedly, the better educated, wealthier citizens live in large cities, and rural populations (about 60 percent) experience higher rates of disease incidence and mortality. The national birth rate is high, at 3.5 percent. However, it ranges from 2 percent in Tashkent city to 4.5 percent in Qashqa Darya. (Box 13.1 provides a profile of selected demographic characteristics.)

MORBIDITY

13.3   The health characteristics of the population are typical of those in both developing and industrialized countries. Many rural poor, with large families, suffer from acute, infectious diseases, such as respiratory infections and diarrheal diseases. Richer urban populations tend to have chronic illnesses related to lifestyles (being sedentary, and smoking) and diets (animal fat consumption), such as circulatory heart and cerebrovascular diseases. Nationally, the major causes of mortality are circulatory (42.1 percent), respiratory (16.5 percent), and injuries (9.6 percent). Poor-quality drinking water, the lack of sanitation, and improper clinical management partly explain the higher mortality rates in rural areas. Death rates from circulatory diseases are the fourth highest in FSU countries. (Box 13.2 provides a profile of morbidity rates from selected diseases, by age group.)

---

[1] In 1991 off-budgetary expenditures represented one-third of total health expenditures. Preliminary figures on the off-budgetary expenditures for 1992 suggest that they may have substantially reduced.

NUTRITION

13.4   Rapid inflation for foodstuffs has prompted the population to substitute bread for both vegetables and meat products. Table 13.1, also presented in Chapter 8, shows the changing patterns of the consumption of selected food products between 1991 and 1992, with shifts attributed to price increases.[2]

13.5   Incidence of micronutrient deficiencies, such as Vitamin A and iron, are likely to occur in the next 2 years. The lag period between significant price rises and changes in the nutritional status of children reportedly takes 3 months or longer. However, open markets, barter, and hoarding could affect this time estimate.

13.6   Currently, 80 percent of mothers breastfeed for 2 months, of which 50 percent do so for 3 to 4 months, and only 20 to 30 percent for 8 to 10 months. Thereafter, infants require baby food and food

Box 13.1: Demographics[1]	
Population (in million, 1992)	21.7
Percent of former USSR	7%
Number of regions	12
Autonomous regions (Karakalpakstan)	1
Percent male and female:	
female	50.1%
male	49.4%
Percent of population living in urban areas	40%
Ethnic groups	
Uzbek	71.4%
Russian	8.3%
others	20%
Population distribution by age:	
0 to 14 years old	41%
older than 14 years	59%
Life expectancy (years, 1990):	
female	72
male	66

Source: Health Care in the Republic of Uzbekistan, Department of Health Statistics, Statistics Office, Ministry of Health, 1992 and Goskomprognostat.
1/ 1991 estimates unless otherwise noted

supplements (dry milk), which introduces health complications because supplements are frequently mixed with contaminated water, causing diarrhea and other potentially fatal enteric disorders. Reportedly, only 25 percent of demand for supplements is being met.

THE HEALTH OF WOMEN AND CHILDREN

Women's Health

13.7   Women--especially rural women--face a difficult, strenuous life due to physically demanding work, poverty, and large families.[3] Maternal mortality is high, at a national average rate of 65.3 per 100,000 live births. However, this rate masks the very high rates seen in some regions, such as Tashkent City, where the rate is 141 per 100,000 live births. Approximately 5 million women are between age 15 and 49; however, family planning services are limited to induced abortions. The average woman has five children, and 200,000 women have ten or more. Families tend to be large; more than

---

[2] Meat, poultry, canned meat, fish, egg, and animal fat consumption dropped by between 19 and 67 percent. Concurrently, the consumption of beans, vegetables, fruits, berries, and melons dropped by 16 percent to 69 percent. Flour consumption rose by 46 percent, indicating that people are increasing their consumption of inexpensive (subsidized) breads and flour products.

[3] However, UNICEF and WHO report that this is a myth concocted under a government policy that discourages breastfeeding.

700,000 families have at least four children. In addition, births are closely spaced.[4] Approximately 70 percent of women do not use contraceptives.[5]

Children's Health

13.8   The health status of infants and children is affected directly by the health and education of mothers and by family size. The infant mortality rate (IMR) is high, at 35.5 per 1,000 live births.[6]

13.9   In 1991, the prevalence of major childhood diseases (1 to 14 years old) was 55 percent for respiratory infections and 15 percent for digestive and parasitic infections.

	Age Groupings:		
Diseases	Age 0-14	Age 15-19	Age 19+
Respiratory system	54.55	30.27	30.51
Infectious and parasitic	8.15	4.49	3.38
Digestive system	6.94	15.21	11.10
Injury and poisonings	6.37	12.82	11.37
Skin and subcutaneous tissue	6.14	10.04	7.27
Nervous system disorders	6.02	11.04	11.05
Blood and blood-forming organs	3.99	4.87	4.24
Endocrine and metabolic	3.41	1.92	0.71
Genitourinary system	1.13	3.02	6.29
Musculoskeletal system	0.47	1.49	2.95
Circulatory system	0.35	2.54	4.24
Complications of pregnancy	-	0.01	5.06
Congenital anomalies	0.29	0.29	0.05
Mental disorders	0.23	1.41	0.89
Neoplasms	0.07	0.13	0.67

Box 13.2: Morbidity: Annual Prevalence of Diseases Registered at Health Delivery Facilities (1991) (% of morbidity)

Source: Health Care in the Republic of Uzbekistan, Department of Health Statistics, Statistics Office, Ministry of Health, 1992.

However, diarrhea is probably under reported.   Care for ill children is hampered by a chronic shortage of drugs; only half of the necessary drugs are available.

13.10   Vaccination programs to prevent childhood diseases have been a success. Historically, vaccination coverage has been high; however, coverage rates are dropping (see Box 13.3).[7] Some immunization protocols are not in line with WHO guidelines.

13.11   In the FSU, BCG and DPT vaccines were produced at the Tashkent Institute of Serum and Vaccines. However, their quality was so poor that Union approval was withdrawn. In 1992,

---

[4] Approximately 8 percent of women have two deliveries per year, 70 percent wait 1.5 to 2 years between deliveries, and only 18 percent wait longer than 2 years.

[5] A comprehensive program for health improvement was implemented in 1991. Since the inception of the program approximately 576,000 IUDs were inserted. It is estimated that about 4.7 percent of IUDs were inserted improperly, causing failures and adverse health effects. The total number of IUDs amount to almost 1.2 million users. Utilization of oral contraceptives is small, with only 85,000 women using them. Around 80,000 couples use condoms, but a shortage of latex and condoms exists. Sterilization is not provided by the health care system.

[6] The IMR ranges from 24.8 in Tashkent City to 51.4 in the Republic of Karakalpakstan (Aral Sea area). This figure could be underestimated.

[7] BCG is provided at birth to 93 percent of children born in maternity facilities. Other children have had good access to immunization in the 7,000 centers around the country.

production of BCG vaccines has resumed in Uzbekistan. However, the other vaccines must be purchased from other FSU republics, in particular Russia and other foreign manufacturers. In 1992, virtually no vaccines were purchased. In May 1992, UNICEF contributed 350,000 doses of measles vaccine and USAID contributed 200,000 doses, yet the supply met less than half the demand. All childhood vaccines are either in short supply or completely finished.

13.12   The cost of immunizing children is rising rapidly, and the integrity of the immunization program is being threatened.[8] The cold

Table 13.1
Changes In the Consumption of Foodstuffs
(average per capita in kilograms)

Food Item	1991	1992	Percent Change
Meat and Poultry	5.3	4.3	-19%
Canned Meat	1.3	0.6	-54%
Fish	1.2	0.4	-67%
Vegetable Oil	5.3	5.1	- 4%
Animal Fat	1.0	0.5	-50%
Eggs	30	23	-23%
Sugar	6.4	5.6	-13%
Flour	34.9	50.8	+46%
Beans	8.9	7.5	-16%
Potatoes	3.3	3.3	--
Vegetables	7.7	4.0	-48%
Fruits, Berries, Melons	1.6	0.5	-69%
Tea	0.9	0.9	--

Source: Goskomprognostat, Uzbekistan

chain, required for certain vaccines, has significant shortcomings and needs to be refurbished.[9] One result of the breakdown of the cold chain is the waste of vaccines. Unofficial reports note that wastage rates range from 30 to 50 percent as in some rural areas, temperatures can rise to over 50 degrees centigrade during the summer. While temperatures are 20 to 30 degrees cooler than the air, both measles and polio vaccines would be inactivated. Children who receive these vaccines would not be immunized.

PHARMACEUTICALS

13.13   Curative care depends heavily on the use of pharmaceuticals, and a substantial amount of the limited foreign borrowing is being used to purchase them (see Box 13.4). The Government is concerned about how the foreign credits would be repaid. Since 1992, 65 percent of drugs are distributed free, while others are sold in pharmacies at prices below cost. Thus, the long-term outlook for a sustainable drug procurement program is not good. Farmatsia would like to meet long-term needs by building drug plants in different regions of the country, thereby freeing itself from foreign drug firms. Staff have not analyzed the feasibility of this option, but experience from other countries suggest that the prices from national production will not be competitive with transnational.

---

[8] In 1991, 55.7 million rubles were allocated for vaccines. This figure rose to 520 million rubles in 1992, due primarily to inflation. The price of disposable syringes has risen by a factor of 15 during 1992.

[9] Existing refrigerators and coolers are typically 35 to 40 years old. Even large, central refrigerator facilities are reportedly susceptible to breakdown. Vaccination equipment, including refrigerators (200), sterilizers (3,000), syringes (800,000 to 1 million), and needles, is required.

ENVIRONMENTAL HEALTH

Human Health Issues

13.14   This section discusses environmental health issues in a brief, schematic way.   A more complete analysis of environmental issues is provided in Chapter 14 of this report. This section focuses on the impacts of biological and chemical contaminants in water and air on human health.   Health effects from exposure to radioactive contaminants and contaminated foodstuffs are not discussed.

13.15   Uzbekistan and the other Central Asian republics face uncertain health   risks   from   environmental influences.   Analyzing   the   effect   of environmental pollutants requires specific data on the identity of pollutants, their concentration levels by source, routes of exposure, dose per exposure, and the number of exposures, and their duration

Box 13.3: Coverage of Childhood Vaccinations
(percent of eligible children, 0 to 1 year of age)

Vaccine	1990	1991
Diphtheria		
--average	87.1	84.1
--regional range	(76-94)	(71-93)
Pertussis		
--average	79.4	79.6
--regional range	(55-89)	(65-92)
Polio		
--average	90.0	89.1
--regional range	(77-99)	(76-99)
Measles		
--average	85.1	83.9
--regional range	(13-107)	(73-96)

Source: Health Care in the Republic of Uzbekistan, Department of Health Statistics, Statistics Office, Ministry of Health, 1992.

(acute or chronic).   While a large number of potential environmental hazards have been reported in Uzbekistan, little data are available to substantiate the claims, except for problems with drinking water (see below).   Most likely, environmental "hot spots" exist in site-specific locations.

Drinking Water

13.16   The supply and quality of drinking water are deficient in Uzbekistan.   The Ministry of Health has documented examples of the biological contamination of water supplies based on samples taken throughout the country and on the reported incidence of diseases.   Of 3,009 rural communities, 1,184 have no access to potable water.   Many of the remaining 1,825 have serious problems, including the use of open reservoirs without sanitary zones, the lack of chlorine, and the lack of filtration equipment. Heavy dependence on surface water often contaminated with industrial and agricultural chemicals (fertilizers and pesticides) is reportedly a major problem.   In some areas, animal excreta are a major source of coliform bacteria.   In 1991, 15 percent of water systems that were tested violated Uzbekistan's guidelines for coliform bacteria, and 36 percent violated them for chemical pollution (based on former USSR standards, which reportedly differ from international standards).   Much of the water supply infrastructure was built in the 1950s and needs repair.   Only 230 of 8,000 industrial enterprises are classified by the Government as nonpolluters.   Epidemiological data on pollutants, concentrations in water supplies, human exposure, and doses are lacking.   In 1989, a State Committee of the Environment was established to investigate environmental pollution; little has been accomplished.

Sanitation

13.17   Sanitation and sewerage are a source of drinking-water-related health problems. Approximately 43 percent of urban populations have sewer pipes--18 percent of the national population. In rural areas, only 6 percent have sewer pipes. Even in Tashkent City, only 64 percent of the population has access to sewer pipes. Health effects related to poor sanitation are associated primarily with gastro-intestinal disorders from bacterial, viral, or parasitic infections.

Box 13.4: Uzbekistan Pharmaceuticals

Uzbekistan's drug list contains 3,000 drugs, which is 10 to 20 times greater than what is suggested by WHO guidelines. Responsibility for production and distribution of drugs is divided between two ministries. The Ministry of Health controls drug procurement and distribution through Farmatsia (Research and Production Association). There is also a drug production facility, Chemico-pharmacological plan under Farmatsia. It is managed by the Ministry of Industry. Currently, Chemico cannot operate competitively Thus, it would seek participation in a joint venture with a foreign drug firm.

In 1991, at least 50% of demand was met for selected antibiotics, blood sugar control tablets, hormonal injections, and cancer treatment. For many drugs, the 1992 order was less than for 1991, based on MOH's funding expectations. In 1992 there was a significant unmet demand, with only selected antibiotics and dysbacteriosis treatment receiving above 50% of what was demanded.

Farmatsia estimates that $148 million are needed annually to satisfy demand. In 1992, The Government reported an urgent need for $65 million of drugs. The Government is negotiating with Turkey ($30 million credit), Hungary ($2.5 million barter), and India ($2.1 million barter) for pharmaceuticals.

Air Pollution

13.18   Reportedly, 2.6 million tons of pollutants are emitted from motor vehicles. Carbon monoxide, nitrogen oxides, lead, particulate, and other pollutants contribute to this load. The lack of lead-free fuels and catalytic converters and the use of heavy diesel fuels contribute to the problem. Point-sources of air pollution contribute one-third of air pollution loads. The main fixed sources comprise sulfur dioxide from power plants, hydrocarbons from natural-gas facilities and petroleum refineries, heavy metals from metallurgical facilities, and aerosolized particles from the construction industry.

13.19   Health effects from either fixed or point sources of air pollution are not well documented. Digestive conditions are frequently noted among the population who reside in the Aral Sea area. These conditions are hypothesized to stem from aerosolized salts and agricultural chemicals.

HEALTH BUDGET AND FINANCE

13.20   Health services are funded by the central Government through the federal budget and by local governments. (Box 13.5 provides a detailed description of the organization, infrastructure, and personnel of the health care system in Uzbekistan.) The health care financing system consists of three major components: the federal health budget, which funds health-service provision and is the largest source of finance to the Ministry of Health; local budgets (at regional, city and district levels), which fund the administrative costs of the respective institutions; and a newly emerging revenue source, which comprises charges and fees for some drugs and selected services.

13.21   Table 13.2 shows the sources of finance for 1991 and 1992 for health care delivery. In 1991, the total was 3.7 billion rubles, of which 65 percent was financed through the federal budget. In 1992, total health expenditures are estimated to be approximately 26.4 billion rubles, of which 80 percent was financed through the federal budget. Although the share of budgetary financing increased in real terms, health spending declined.

13.22   User fees comprise a small proportion of the health care budget. In 1991 and 1992, some oblasts charged for selected procedures-- abortions, ultrasound, and physical exams. About 76 million rubles were raised in 1991 from the sale of drugs and user fees. In 1991, 32 outpatient clinics, 26 diagnostic exam clinics, and 3 consultation clinics were already financially self-sufficient. Service-charge policy varies across regions and oblasts. Individual oblasts are experimenting with fee-for-service systems for selected procedures. However, it was noted that services would not be withheld from those unwilling or unable to pay.

Table 13.2
Uzbekistan: Sources of Finance for Health Care Delivery
(in billion rubles)

Budget Area	1991	1992 (estimated)
Federal Budget	2.4	21.1
Local Budgets	1.20	5.10
Charges, Fees	0.08	0.20
Total	3.7	26.4

Expenditures

13.23   As shown in Table 13.3, the distribution of expenditures from the state budget changed between 1991 and 1992 and is expected to change again in 1993. Over half of the annual budget comprises salary and salary insurance tax. General operating costs (undefined) are expected to double from 7 to 15 percent between 1992 and 1993. Nutrition, which accounted for 11 percent of the budget for 1991 and 1992, is expected to drop to 6 percent in 1993. This drop reportedly reflects a reduction in the availability of food supplements for pregnant women and infants.

13.24   Expenditures for the Ministry of Health budget are also shown in Table 13.3. The share of salary and salary-related expenditures increased in 1992 to 88 percent. Table 13.4 summarizes social expenditures and highlights the portion allocated to the health sector. Health care and physical culture account for almost 12 percent of the federal expenditures.[10]

13.25   Table 13.5 shows health expenditures as a percentage of GDP for Uzbekistan and several other countries. At 5.1 percent, Uzbekistan is the highest of the FSU countries, which, for the seven FSU countries shown, range from 2.0 to 4.4 percent. In comparison, the OECD average is 7.6 percent while for the United States it increases to 12.1 percent.

B. SECTORAL REFORM: RECOMMENDATIONS

STRENGTHEN THE CHILDHOOD IMMUNIZATION PROGRAM

13.26   The immunization program needs to be stabilized, reversing the current declining trend. The program should include systems for monitoring the potency and quality of vaccines. Childhood

---

[10] This is less than the 22.6 percent reported for Kyrghyzstan.

vaccinations made according to WHO guidelines would reduce the number of children who receive unnecessary vaccinations, ensure that the Ministry of Health's contraindication protocols are eliminated, and reduce the likelihood that services are limited during summer months. The effectiveness and efficiency of the cold chain must be analyzed, especially in rural areas. Temperature-sensitive color indicators should be used to identify vaccines that have been exposed to inactivating levels of heat. Estimates should be made of essential supplies, including syringes, needles, sterilizers, and fuel. Internal and external sources of funds for the immunization program should be identified and pursued to ensure the financial integrity of the program.

RATIONALIZE DRUG USE AND BEGIN COST RECOVERY

13.27   The Ministry of Health urgently needs to develop an essential-drugs list, to reduce overall drug utilization, and to streamline operations, which will include developing a coherent logistical distribution system. An essential-drugs supply list should be created on the basis of WHO's list of approximately 200 drugs, replacing the current list of 3,000 drugs. This measure would reduce drug expenditures and the need for foreign exchange. Selected, high-priority drugs should be purchased, including antibiotics and drugs to treat tuberculosis. The Government should expand the local production of oral rehydration salts for diarrheal diseases, and avoid the expensive and less desirable use of intravenous infusion of rehydration salts.

Table 13.3
Composition of Health Expenditures
(in percent)

	1991	September 1992	Projection 1993
I. Health Care Sector			
Salary	41	44	37
Insurance tax (37%)	10	13	16
Operating costs	7	7	15
Business trips	0	0	0
Education	0	0	0
Nutrition	11	11	6
Drugs	8	4	6
Equipment	6	1	6
Pillows, sheets, etc.	3	1	6
Capital construction	6	3	4
Capital repair	4	1	6
Other expenses	3	14	0
Total	100	100	100
II. Ministry of Health			
Salary	70	65	
Insurance tax (37%)	15	23	
Operation costs	14	11	
Business trips	2	0	
Total	100	100	

Source: Ministry of Health, September 1992, Uzbekistan.

13.28   In the longer run, a plan must be developed to address cost-recovery and to establish a reasonable pricing policy. During 1993 and 1994, cost recovery should focus on large-volume drugs for curative, noninfectious diseases.

DEVELOP A WOMEN'S HEALTH STRATEGY

13.29   A women's health strategy should be developed, including a safe motherhood initiative. At the current rate of growth, the population of Uzbekistan will double in less than 25 years, increasing the demand for social services whose provision is already strained. The goal should be to reduce maternal mortality, increase the spacing of childbirth, stabilize fertility rates, reduce anemia in pregnant women, and reduce the number of abortions. Indicators are required for detecting changes in the health status of women.

13.30   The Indonesian family planning program (BKKN) could serve as a model, whereby a predominantly Muslim country has successfully implemented a program for stabilizing its birth rate. The BKKN is a government-funded family program which has strong political support from the president of the country. It is integrated from the national to the village levels through an extensive network of kaders who monitor and follow-up with accepting couples. Reportedly, initial discussions with Indonesia have been made. Such a program would have both health and budgetary benefits. Maternal mortality rates would be reduced by 20 to 25 percent, the health status of fertile women would improve, family size would stabilize, and the number of abortions probably would be reduced. These health benefits would translate into savings associated with a reduction in curative care.

Table 13.4:
Expenditures for Social, Cultural, and Social Safety Net

Category	1992 (bln rbl)	%
Health Care and Physical Culture	21.1	12.1
Social Safety Net[a]	64.9	37.3
Education	45.0	25.8
Pensions	43.1	24.8
Total	174.1	100.0

[a] Includes family allowances, consumer and children goods subsidies, social insurance and unemployment benefits.

TARGET VULNERABLE GROUPS

13.31   The Government should establish a system for monitoring the health status of vulnerable groups. The health status of population subgroups in Uzbekistan varies considerably. In Uzbekistan, there are 700,000 families with four or more children, 37,000 single elderly persons, and a significant amount of people in remote and poor rural areas, and their health status is likely to be lower than average. Recent research in Africa indicates that user charges for maternity and perinatal services can substantially reduce attendance--18 percent increase in babies born outside of maternity houses, and an 80 percent increase in neonatal tetanus. Fees equivalent to 1.5 percent of nonfood household budgets were found to reduce service utilization by two-thirds. Thus, vulnerable groups with low incomes should be exempted from user fees.

13.32   It is possible to use the Government's extensive health information network to identify vulnerable groups. Children and single elderly persons could be monitored to note changes in their nutritional status due to substitution among food groups. For children, monthly growth increments are a sensitive indicator of nutritional problems. Communities that show an increase in the incidence of nutritional problems could be targeted for

Table 13.5
Composition of Health Expenditures (as percent of GDP)

Countries	%
Uzbekistan, 1992	5.1
Other FSU countries, 1990	
Azerbaijan	3.8
Estonia	2.6
Kazakhstan	3.3
Kyrgyzstan	4.4
Russia	3.0
Ukraine	2.7
OECD average, 1990	7.6
United States, 1990	12.1

assistance. The protection of vulnerable groups should be integrated with national social protection programs.

Box 13.5: Organization, Infrastructure, and Personnel

Organization

Health care delivery is within the competence of the Ministry of Health (MOH). It remains a blueprint of what existed in the former Soviet Union: centralization, emphasis on collecting health statistics, poor maintenance and refurbishment of capital, overstaffing, underbudgeting, and low-quality care. The Government lost Union transfers, reducing an important source of financing of health care services. However, the system also has several strengths: most people have access to some level of care even if its quality is not optimal (universal coverage); financing is equitable; an information network extends down to the village level, which facilitates identifying those in need; immunization rates for childhood vaccinations are high and nutritional supplements are available for deficient populations.

The Ministry has responsibilities in the areas of health, sanitation, and environmental health protection that conflict with the responsibilities of other ministries. Consumers have very limited choice about service delivery, and little is known about consumer satisfaction.

Laws are slowly changing to allow physicians to establish private medical practices, but privatization remains virtually non-existent. Administratively, it is unclear how a privatized system would work. The Government is hesitant to allow physicians to build practices outside the Government sector and to set charges for services. The idea of a physician potentially earning more in private practice than as a Government employee is causing concern among some administrators. One view is that physicians were trained by the state and thus owe their livelihood to the "people." There are also likely to be problems with patients. However, illegal fees are already being paid for drugs and services. Other problems faced by clinicians trying to establish practices include an inability to purchase equipment, drugs, and supplies.

Infrastructure

Uzbekistan contains 1,370 medical institutions. Each of the 12 regions has a large hospital, and there are 158 district hospitals. Nationally, there are 256,600 hospital beds. Few health facilities were originally constructed for health purposes. The MOH inherited older buildings that were converted into health facilities. At 12.1 hospital beds per 1,000 people, Uzbekistan's ratio is more than twice that of other middle-income countries. In 1992, it is estimated that hospital beds were reduced 12 percent.Buildings are old (20 to 50 years old) and medical equipment and supplies are lacking (especially surgical equipment), a severe shortage of drugs exists, an apparent surplus of beds and staff exists, and the surgical operating capacity is around 50%. In rural areas, water and sewer systems are frequently located outside the wards, requiring that patients physically leave the wards. In-patient stays are long, ranging between 1 and 40 days, with an average of 10 to 15 days in hospitals and 10 to 15 days in rural facilities.

Personnel and Wages

Uzbekistan has 71,100 physicians (3.4 per 1,000) and 226,600 nurses (10.9 per 1,000). These rates are much higher than for other middle-income countries. General practitioners, pediatricians, and surgeons comprise over 50% of all physicians. Reportedly, the level of training and competence of physicians is sub-optimal. A lack of equipment, the variety of schools of medicine (Western, Oriental, and homeopathic), a lack of standardized treatment protocols, and low wages, have contributed to a low technical competence.

Box 13.6: Comparison of Selected Health Indicators with Other Countries

Table 1 presents a comparison of Uzbekistan with Russia, lower-middle income countries, and high-income countries. Overall, Russia has a better health profile. Uzbekistan's birth rate is high, its infant mortality rate is 75% higher than Russia's, its fertility is twice Russia's, and its maternal mortality is 30% higher. In comparison with lower-middle-income countries, Uzbekistan rates fairly well. It has a higher birth rate, a lower death rate, and lower infant mortality rate (70% of the average country group average). Each physician and nurse in Uzbekistan is responsible for fewer than 10% of the number of people noted for other lower-middle-income countries, excluding Russia. In high-income countries, each physician in Uzbekistan is responsible for less than 60% of the population per physician of these countries. However, even with a large number of health professionals, Uzbekistan's health profile is that of a poorer country. The potential explanations are that physicians and nurses are less well trained and have limited access to medical equipment, medicines, and supplies, and medical staff.

When selected health status indicators for Uzbekistan are compared with a subset of other FSU countries, Uzbekistan has a higher birth rate, and about the same life expectancy. The fertility and infant mortality rates in the three Asian Republics, including Uzbekistan, are higher than those for Belarus, Moldova, and Armenia. Uzbekistan's maternal mortality rate is relatively high--50% to 260% higher than in other countries. Overall, the Central Asian republics have a lower health status than other CIS countries. These figures must be interpreted cautiously.

Table 1
Selected Demographic and Health Statistics:
Comparison of Uzbekistan with Other Countries, 1990

Indicator	Uzbekistan	Russia	Turkey	Thailand	Average for Low-mid-Income Countries	Average for High-Income Countries
Birth rate (per 1,000)	34.5 (1991)	13.4	38.0	22.0	30.0	13.0
Life expectancy at birth (years)	69.5 (1991)	69.4	67.0	66.0	65.0	77.0
Total fertility rate	4.1 (1991)	2.0	3.5	2.5	4.0	1.7
Infant mortality rate	35.5 (1991)	19.4	60.0	27.0	51.0	8.0
Maternal mortality rate	65.3 (1991)	49.0	207	270.0	-	5-18
Population per:						
Physician	297 (1990)	217 (1990)	1390 (1984)	6290 (1984)	3000 (1984)	470 (1984)
nurse	93 (1990)	74 (1990)	1030 (1984)	710 (1984)	1050 (1984)	150 (1984)
% urban population	39.9% (1991)	73.6%	61%	23%	52%	77%

Sources: World Development Report 1992, World Bank, Washington, D.C.
Uzbekistan, USAID Health Profile (selected data) April 24, 1992, Center of International Health Information, Arlington, Virginia, USA
Russia, USAID Health Profile (selected data) April 24, 1992, Center for International Health Information, Arlington, Virginia, USA
Health care in the Republic of Uzbekistan, Department of Health Statistics, Statistics Office, Ministry of Health, 1992.

ELIMINATE UNNECESSARY SERVICES AND USE INPUTS MORE EFFICIENTLY

13.33   In the medium term many services should be privatized or eliminated--for example, "rest sanatoriums" are vacation retreats and should not be subsidized.   If possible, the Chemico-pharmacological plant should be privatized.   The Government must use health care inputs more efficiently.   Uzbekistan contains too many hospital beds.   Infectious-disease hospitals (occupancy rates of 61 to 66 percent) and tuberculosis hospitals (occupancy rates of 48 to 79 percent) could be eliminated. At 12.1 beds per 1,000 population, a 50 percent cut in beds would still leave Uzbekistan with a higher ratio than most middle-income countries.   Beds could be eliminated by reducing in-patient stays.   Excess medical staff throughout the country should be reduced by laying off about 40 percent of doctors. Uzbekistan's ratio of physicians/nurses to the total population is several factors higher than for typical lower-middle-income and some high-income countries.

13.34   Owing to an excess of staff and inflation, salaries have begun to comprise an increasingly larger proportion of the Ministry of Health's budget.   In 1991, salaries and the salary tax were 51 percent of the budget.   This share rose to 57 percent for the planned 1992 budget.   A reduction in staff would free-up resources for other uses without adversely affecting the health status of the population, and would bring Uzbekistan in line with other lower-middle income countries.   Higher salaries for doctors could be implemented for those who perform better.   While the number of medical staff should be reduced, it is important that the effect of increased unemployment on social expenditure requirements be evaluated. Retraining programs will be required for unemployed health personnel in the transition.

13.35   Lay-off physicians might be encouraged to offer services within the context of private practices, in which prices are not set by the state.   In addition, private practices could compete with each other for services and prices, thereby providing consumers with more choices.

13.36   Using WHO's clinical management guidelines could reduce the number of injections, reduce drug demand, shorten in-patient lengths of stay, increase the efficiency of inputs, and improve the quality of care.   Many drugs are unnecessarily delivered parenterally, sharply increasing the demand for needles and syringes.

REDEFINE THE MINISTRY OF HEALTH BUDGET ALLOCATION

13.37   The Government must decide who should set priorities for health care, choose criteria for setting priorities, and decide how resources should be allocated.   A core strategy should be developed and given funding priority, which is especially important in the face of rapid inflation and uncertain budgets.   Successful prevention programs that reduce the demand for expensive curative services should receive priority funding.   The Government should re-allocate funds to its priority areas to ensure that they are supported.   Protection against inflation and potential cuts should be provided for priority programs.

ASSESS ENVIRONMENTAL HEALTH

13.38   In the longer run, the effect of the environment on health must be evaluated.   While it is sensible to address issues associated with drinking water, it is not sensible to take dramatic action in limiting most environmental pollution until a risk assessment analysis is undertaken.   Only then can priorities be set and decisions taken to limit pollutants in a cost-effective way.   Existing stringent contaminant standards should not be enforced rigorously until the risk and costs of meeting the standards are assessed.   Remedial actions should be targeted at environmental "hot spots."

13.39   Policy decisions must be supported by data on the types of risks and their potential impacts. A comparative human health risk analysis would be a useful start. A risk analysis would identify contaminants by media, assess concentrations, estimate human exposure and doses, and characterize the potential human health risks. Surrogate measures could be used when field data are unavailable. Output would be used to develop a baseline analysis to understand the dimension of problems, to establish clean-up priorities, and to develop targeted environmental health regulations.[11]

DEVELOP A SUSTAINABLE FINANCE MECHANISM

13.40   The Government must develop schemes for increasing income for the health sector. However, central funds are required until plans for alternative financing mechanisms can be developed and implemented. In the next 18 months, the Government should begin a program to allow health delivery facilities to charge for selected procedures and drugs at prices that at least cover production costs. Individual facilities should have discretion about how funds should be used as they seek to improve the quality of service and replenish stocks.

13.41   Charges could have the dual benefit of increasing efficiency and augmenting resource bases. As experience with charging fees accumulates, differential fees could be determined for curative procedures. This process should be phased-in over two to three years to limit the "shock" factor. Infectious disease treatment, such as drugs for tuberculosis, should be subsidized to limit the onset of epidemics.

13.42   Selected case studies of self-sufficient clinics should be undertaken to better understand how they set prices, introduce the schemes, and manage their resources. The Government plans to develop a health insurance system to ensure that a stable financial base is supported.

13.43   Russia is developing a health insurance program and has already generated several useful insights. The benefits and costs of the Russian experience should be reviewed to provide useful guidance to the Government in creating its program. The models of social security from Costa Rica and the experience or privatization from Chile should be analyzed. Aspects that deserve specific review include the following: insuring mechanisms, premiums, insurance provision, the role of the Government, medical services provision, incentives to providers and consumers, the timing of implementation, monitoring procedures, review mechanisms, and reprogramming.[12]

13.44   Care must be given to identifying sources of funds. The transition to an insurance scheme should build on one of the strengths of the existing system--that is, money collection from employees and employers. Subsequently, funds could be distributed under an insurance scheme. However, the Government should not require employers to shoulder the majority of health insurance costs. Such costs would place a significant burden on firms just as they are trying to enter cost-competitive world markets.

---

[11] A potential collaborative partner is the U.S. Environmental Protection Agency's Office of International Activities. It has developed training materials to assist countries in Eastern Europe and the FSU in undertaking comparative human health-risk analysis, to understand how economic analysis should be applied, and to develop policy analyses pertaining to environmental health. Output could be used to decide how to balance competing developmental needs and health-risk factors associated with drinking water systems and the agricultural sector.

[12] International agencies, such as the International Labor Organization, could also provide technical advice on many aspects of insurance schemes.

Both firms and individuals should contribute. Insurance should be compulsory for all citizens to ensure an adequate source of funds. Compulsory insurance would also reduce the risk that the healthy would opt out, leaving a high-risk pool who would be unattractive to private insurers. The state should cover the insurance premiums of the poor, the elderly, and the unemployed.

C. TECHNICAL ASSISTANCE NEEDS

SHORT-TERM: 6 TO 12 MONTHS

Strengthening the Childhood Immunization Program

13.45   Assistance to help project vaccine needs and to assess the existing immunization program, including an evaluation of the cold chain, is urgently required. Approximately 1,400,000 doses of measles vaccine are required for 1993. In addition, the other five childhood vaccines are in very short supply or have been exhausted. The cold chain in rural areas has reportedly broken down, and thus cold boxes and vaccine carriers are urgently needed. Other equipment in short supply includes sterilizers, syringes, and needles. The goal should be to maintain relatively high vaccination coverage in areas where it is currently high, and to increase it in other regions, such as the Area Sea area. Collaborative partners include USAID, UNICEF, and WHO.

Strengthening the Pharmaceutical System

13.46   The Ministry of Health urgently requires assistance to develop an essential-drugs list, reduce overall drug needs, and streamline operations, including a coherent plan to purchase and distribute drugs. Government estimates indicate that over $100 million of pharmaceuticals would be required in 1993.

13.47   Assistance is needed in evaluating the existing system, recommending options, developing a long-term strategic plan, and teaching analytical methods. A cost-recovery system focused initially on drugs for curative, noninfectious diseases. Assistance is required in negotiations with international drug manufacturers and distributors to ensure that high-quality generic drugs are purchased. These should include antibiotics and drugs for treating tuberculosis. However, drug purchases must be limited, owing to the existence of other significant needs in the health sector. Some projections of drug need would consume more than the entire annual budget for the Ministry of Health. Collaborative efforts could be considered with the Drug Action Program, WHO, and UNICEF.

MEDIUM-TERM: 12 TO 18 MONTHS

Women's Health Project

13.48   Consultants could help analyze the system of existing services for women, develop indicators for monitoring progress, develop programs to encourage breastfeeding, and train trainers for the long-term development of programs. Training workshops should be organized, as should visits to countries that have successfully implemented women's health programs, especially countries such as Indonesia. The UN Family Planning Agency (New York) is a potential collaborative partner, as are UNICEF, WHO, EEC, and USAID.

Vulnerable Populations

13.49   Methodologies are required for monitoring the health status of such population subgroups as children in large families (four or more children), rural women, and single elderly persons. This activity should be integrated carefully with national social protection programs. Consultants could help develop survey instruments and methodologies, and could develop indicators and analytical methods. Potential collaborative partners include the UN Administrative Committee Coordination/Subcommittee on Nutrition (Geneva), the International Food Policy Research Institute (Washington, D.C), and UNICEF and USAID. All efforts should be integrated closely with the national social protection program.

Health Sector Needs and Priorities

13.50   The Government requires assistance in identifying health care priorities, projecting the demand for services, estimating costs and budgets, and identifying potential sources of funding. A resident adviser is required to examine broad resource allocation questions across many programs, including the prevention of childhood and infectious diseases, curative care, the provision of drugs, infrastructure support, and the organization of health service delivery. Assistance would also be required to develop strategic plans for the medium and long terms. Training abroad would help decisionmakers learn the necessary analytical tools and methodologies more rapidly. Workshops and training seminars are required to provide decisionmakers with an understanding of basic economics, policy analyses, and finance. Potential collaborators include the World Bank, WHO, EEC and USAID.

Environmental Health

13.51   Technical assistance is required for establishing a baseline for environmental health policy development. Consultants could help teach and apply risk assessment and economic analyses that already exist and have been tested and used in Eastern European countries. Doing so would save a significant amount of time and money and give Uzbekistan the benefit of the experience gained in other countries. In-country workshops would provide an excellent educational forum. A potential collaborator is the U.S. Environmental Protection Agency, which has developed an integrated set of training materials that cover risk assessment, economic analysis, and environmental policy analysis.

Health Sector Finance

13.52   Technical assistance is required for identifying, evaluating, and recommending options for financing health care. This assistance includes teaching the basic principles of health care financing, organizational structure, and evaluation methods.

II. EDUCATION AND TRAINING[13]

13.53   The process of economic transformation will rely on a human capital base that needs to be expanded and reoriented. In order to expand and reorient this base, the Government should enhance the capacity of the education and training system, particularly the capacity to transmit new knowledge, skills, and attitudes and to adapt existing knowledge to the needs of Uzbekistan. The ability to impart values to sustain the transformed economy and the new political status will require that the population as a whole be reoriented considerably. The process of transformation will require considerable interface with the ideas and techniques of other countries, and the generation and dissemination of new knowledge in Uzbekistan. Much of this interface is the task of the education system. Changes will be required in the education and training sector to cope with the increased monetizing of the economy, the application of principles of profitability and the laws of supply and demand to most undertakings, the widespread expansion of private ownership of goods, skills and intellectual property, the fostering of personal initiative and the reconciliation of individual and group rights with those of society as a whole. This would mean investing in new curricular orientation and programs, expanding the reach of the education and training system, and strengthening its management.

13.54   This section discusses the principal developmental issues facing the education and training system. It proposes both short-term and long-term measures to modernize the management (administration and planning) of the system, without seeking to preempt the country's control of the specific institutional development measures required. It examines the key weaknesses in the school system--deteriorating physical facilities, curricular problems, and a the issue of high staff/student ratios-- and makes a few recommendations in each of these areas. It addresses the costs and financing of the sector and the importance of an early start on certain essential cost-reduction measures, as well as some diversification of financing sources. This, however, must be seen as a preliminary survey of the sector and not an exhaustive treatment of its achievements and problems. A full sector study will be necessary to provide a basis for any intensive dialogue between the Bank and the Government.

13.55   The education sector in Uzbekistan has suffered prolonged under-investment in physical plant. However, it does have a large number of motivated and well-educated staff at all levels who have coped well with some of the deficiencies in the system. (Box 13.7 provides a detailed overview of the educational system in Uzbekistan; Box 13.8 discusses a new law passed in 1992 which creates a useful developmental framework for the education sector.)

---

[13] This review was not able to cover training outside the educational system, and the coverage of the sector contains some gaps, especially on the technicums (Grades 10-14)--due largely to the limited time available and the difficulty of obtaining information readily. Further work is required in several areas to facilitate informed dialogue between the Bank and the Government on this vast and complex sector. An essential basis is detailed work by the Government on elaborating its developmental priorities and detailed sectoral work by the Bank, particularly on management, testing, textbook production, vocational training, technical education, and costs and financing.

A. MAIN ISSUES AND RECOMMENDATIONS

13.56   Three main areas must be addressed by the Government:

- *Organization and Management*. Ensuring adequate funding and staffing of sector management and its strengthening to cope with the development of the sector, and the need for a comprehensive developmental strategy.

- *The Physical Base, Curricula, and Teachers*. Formulating a strategy (1) to overcome the deteriorating physical plant (schools and instructional equipment) and the shortage of supplies at all levels of the system, (2) to expedite the on-going reform of curricula and programs, and for preparation and production of the necessary textbooks and examinations; and (3) to adjust the low student staff ratio and the unnecessarily long and expensive teacher training program.

- *Financing Arrangements*. Considering ways of increasing the relatively low direct participation by households in the financing of the system.

ORGANIZATION AND MANAGEMENT

13.57   The budget for central administration is only 0.32 percent of the total sectoral budget in the Ministry of Higher Education (MOHE) and the Ministry of People's Education (MOPE).[14] The offices are ill-equipped and lack up-to-date machines, computers, and supplies (even paper). The staffing of central administration has also been reduced considerably in recent years in response to the financial crisis. This reduction of central management, frequently undertaken in countries during periods of austerity, represents a false economy, since it weakens the capacity of the center to lead the system toward greater overall efficiency.

13.58   In the past, Uzbekistan had three education ministries (general, vocational, and higher) which were later merged into one. Then, in an effort to reduce the span of control, the Government split the Ministry into the MOPE and the MOHE. The current issue is whether two ministries are required. The ministries of education believe that the present arrangement is a good one; however, higher education ministries often manage relatively small staffs in the institutions under their control--largely self-managing institutions that encompass high internal management costs. Several MOPE and MOHE functions could advantageously be merged, regardless of whether the two ministries are merged.[15] The reorganization effort proposed below should examine this question thoroughly.

---

[14] This comparison refers only to the central administration budgets for MOHE/MOPE and their MCs (salaries of head office staff, office supplies, and travel). It does not include provincial and district administrative costs.

[15] These functions include for example planning and the procurement of civil works and instructional equipment and supplies.

Box 13.7: The Educational System

The educational system is managed by two Ministries of Education (MOEs)--the Ministry of Peoples Education (MOPE) and the Ministry of Higher Education (MOHE).

Sectoral management is shared among various partners. Under the Cabinet of Ministers, MOPE and MOHE control overall policy, sector development, and curricula. MOPE deals with pre-school institutions, regular schools (grades 1-11) and out-of-school education and directly administers vocational schools, which are seen as "republic-wide" institutions. MOHE directly administers secondary specialized schools (technicums) and higher education institutions, both of which are seen as "republic wide."[1] Day-to-day administration of pre-schools and regular schools is the responsibility of departments of education in the provincial and district and Tashkent municipal governments, reporting administratively to the local authority and professionally to MOHE/MOPE. Schools are also operated by enterprises and non-education ministries, the latter to an extent that is unusually large and unnecessary.[2]

Each of the two ministries has a unit responsible for procuring and distributing school supplies, and a Methodology Center (MC), to prepare curricula (including syllabi, textbooks, teachers' guides, and examinations). The school supply units manufacture or purchase furniture, equipment, and supplies and sell them to the schools at a profit. They have a monopoly of the supply role, and how much they supply depends on the budget of the school system for these items--a situation devoid of incentives for efficiency. Preparation of curricula rests with the MCs, but implementation rests with the two ministries and the local government.

Leadership in educational thought was formerly exercised largely from Moscow. Since independence, the central MOEs have been weakened, rather than the gaps being filled. With the recession, MOPE staff were reduced from 385 in 1989 to 103 by September 1992, and MOHE staff to 52. These staffing measures sought to reduce absolute management costs, whereas the pre-eminent need was to improve management capacity to promote overall sectoral efficiency in coping with economic and educational challenges. Boards and departments in MOPE/MOHE are small (about four or five persons each), generally lacking a critical mass, and have precisely demarcated areas of responsibility. Units for finance (MOPE) and personnel (MOHE/MOPE) fall directly under the ministers. Library and documentation services to inform staff about educational practices worldwide do not exist. Staff should be increased in strategic areas--in particular, planning, textbook preparation and production, educational testing, vocational training--and the auditing of management testing.

---

[1] MOPE administers all purely teacher training institutions at the technicum or higher-education level and some boarding schools (for children who are disturbed, handicapped, or from very remote or nomadic families). MOHE administers some pre-schools and boarding schools attached to higher education institutions.

[2] Seven ministries have higher education institutions--Agriculture, Health, Culture, Communications, Railways, Tourism and Water Resources. Two more operate technicums. Enterprises conduct preschool centers, regular schools, and vocational training. The respective MOEs control the curricula of these schools.

13.59   There is a need to strengthen the school inspectorate, especially in view of the fact that principals have been saddled with more authority under the new Education Law (see Box 13.7) and require more guidance and support. The other concern about the management of the education system relates to the role of the provinces and districts and how they can best be supported in their administration of schools. The long-range development strategy should, therefore, address issues of school management at the local level, including what functions should be handled at that level and how corresponding resources can be secured.

13.60   The Government has taken many measures to improve and reorient the school system to the needs of Uzbekistan. However, a comprehensive strategy or long-range perspective plan to guide the growth, programming, and changes that are occurring in the system was not available to the mission. The Government states that, with the economic instability and the absence of a firm economic forecast, it is difficult to undertake comprehensive educational planning. In each MOE, the planning unit forecasts enrollments, the Board for Personnel projects the need for teachers, and the Board for Capital Construction prepares rolling capital expenditure programs. These exercises are based on data originating in the districts and collated and analyzed at the center. Qualitative aspects of development are addressed in the Methodology Centers. The recession and the ongoing emigration of Russians have, among other things, invalidated the long-term forecasts of enrollment prepared by MOPE in 1991, and the unit has abandoned such forecasting given the lack of staff. With several quantitative and qualitative issues facing the sector and the necessity for decisions about prioritizing them, a long-range, integral, developmental strategy is urgently required to guide the balanced development of the sector.

RECOMMENDATIONS

13.61   Strengthening sector management is the first and most urgent measure for building a sector that can respond to the demands of nation building and the market economy. Good central leadership is the starting point of any reform in the sector. To improve provincial and district management, the central Government would need to be equipped to play the key role. The specific needs are to:

> **Box 13.8: New Education Law**
>
> The new education law (July 1992) creates a useful developmental framework. It breaks new ground in allowing individuals time for self-education; securing the right to paid leave for part-time education and training; defining management functions; identifying the competencies of government agencies and branches; protecting children and their rights; establishing some independence of schools in matters of finance; and sanctioning international cooperation in education.
>
> The law allows private schools to exist and obtain state aid under certain conditions, and public schools to levy fees on terms prescribed by the legislature, and to contract with firms to train persons for them. It lets schools keep (1) bank accounts for funds that are raised by them; (2) budget funds unspent at the end of the year; and (3) foreign currency accounts when they cooperate with a foreign institution. School principals are empowered to select and enter into job contracts with teachers and pay them extra amounts for good performance.
>
> The law upholds (1) the right to lifelong education and to present oneself for examinations if one feels ready for them, even if through private study; (2) the rights and duties of students, teachers, and parents, including participation in school management, such as through a School Council; and (3) state duty to fund education adequately--an obligation that officials take to mean at least 20% of the state recurrent budget.

- Prepare, on as wide a basis of participation and discussion as possible, a long-range, integral education development strategy at the national level, including all necessary institutional development for administration and planning

- Strengthen the central administration of MOHE/MOPE as needed by:

- Establishing larger, more viable units and ensuring the coordination of functions

- Increasing the number of adequately trained specialized staff

- Ensuring that the budget allocation for administration represents an adequate share of the sectoral budget

- Providing better information services to staff both on the sector nationally and on practices in other parts of the world

● As progress is made towards a market economy, re-examine the current arrangement for supplying the schools with materials and equipment, with a view toward an arrangement that promotes competition

● Place all publicly funded schools under the admiistration of the central education sector ministries,[16] provided that the ministries of education have been suitably strengthened.

PHYSICAL BASE, CURRICULA AND TEACHERS

The Physical Base

13.62   The "material technical base" of the system--namely, buildings, instructional equipment, and supplies--has deteriorated over the years. The system is now confronting acute shortages of (1) school places and suitable buildings; (2) textbooks; (3) furniture and instructional equipment and supplies; (4) audiovisual aids; (5) recurrent funding; and (6) good school libraries and science laboratories. Some of this erosion originated in the recent recession; the rest began several years ago. The physical development strategy necessary to overcome these material shortages, which are becoming more acute each day, has not yet been designed. Each sub-sector has its own peculiar combination of problems and needs (as shown in Box 13.9).

13.63   **Pre-School**. Elaborating a developmental strategy for this sub-sector requires addressing such questions as: (1) the optimal cost-sharing arrangements (see Box 13.11); (2) the viability of the family preschool; (3) the educational benefits of the system (which must be evaluated even in a preliminary way); and (4) the developmental potential of the fledgling local toy industry. The management of the sub-sector should also be strengthened, which includes exposing staff to pre-school experiences elsewhere. The short-term focus (1993-94) should be on planning, evaluation, and institutional development, with major investment in expansion coming at a later stage.

13.64   **Regular Schools**. A massive construction and reconstruction program is urgently needed. The modest ongoing Government efforts can hold the situation until 1995, when, following the development of a comprehensive strategy, large-scale investment would be required for qualitative and

---

[16] The Law provides adequately for School Councils on which interested ministries can be represented, in addition to the normal interaction between employer and trainer that exists with vocational training.

quantitative improvement.   MOPE estimates that 500,000 new places are required annually for replacements and population growth. At this rate, the system would catch up in a reasonable period of 10 years.[17] Normal construction capacity was formerly about 225,000 places annually, but officials state that with the recession, among other factors, it has dropped to 90,000. Thus, a major expansion in construction capacity is also required.

13.65   **Vocational Schools**. In vocational education, the system operates pragmatically as it attempts to adjust to the dissolution of the Moscow links. It functions in close contact with employers. With 260 trades on its list, management recognizes that some consolidation is necessary. For each school a list of trades relevant to the particular region is agreed with the local administration. The schools admit students on the basis of agreements with enterprises. Two types of programs are offered--three-year combined vocational and secondary courses for the brighter students, and two-year, purely craft courses. The system has moved somewhat away from the rigidly organized USSR set of trades based on certain industries that remained in force even after the economy of Uzbekistan had broadened. Today, programs are being modified in line with the boom in light industry and the slump in construction and heavy industry. At its current size, however, the system is said to be inadequate for the training needs of the economy. With the transition to a market-based economy, many issues must be resolved--the optimal size of the system (little labor-market data seem to exist to determine optimal size), program consolidation and orientation to national needs, and stronger management arrangements--as a basis for designing a developmental strategy to be incorporated into the proposed plan.

13.66   **Higher Education**. In this sub-sector, the first priority is to consolidate and improve quality. In view of the plethora of problems, it would be unrealistic to try to improve all institutions at once. It would be advisable instead to identify specific institutions, each covering particular disciplines, to be upgraded into *centers of excellence* that would help develop local sister institutions. In this context, the needs of the selected institutions (buildings, equipment, staff training, and library resources) can be identified. Some of the key disciplines are agriculture; architecture and physical planning (including the environment); business/public management; economics; education; engineering; law; library, documentation, and information sciences; foreign languages; mathematics; medical and health sciences; natural sciences; and social sciences. Senior university staff from various disciplines should visit institutions abroad to familiarize themselves with current developments and to establish links with potential partner institutions.

13.67   **General**. The management of civil-works procurement is weak. The Boards of Capital Construction of both MOEs are understaffed and need architects. The Boards survey needs, prepare budget requests, and commission design and construction for works financed by the central Government. Buildings are designed by the State Institute of Design, which also supervises construction. For many years, one standard design has been used for regular schools. State firms (from the Irrigation,

---

[17] Bank staff estimate that the annual population increase in the age group 6-16 (grades 1-11) will be about 140,000 and, in the age group 6-14 (grades 1-9), about 120,000. The deficit over the next 10 years would be as follows:

(a) Existing shortage (reflected in shift system)	1.140 m
(b) Existing places considered unsuitable	1.750 m
(c) Depreciation of suitable places (3% per year, excluding (b)) .	0.650 m
(d) Growth in enrollment	1.300 m
TOTAL	4.84 m

Box 13.9: Uzbekistan: The School System

Pre-School. MOPE estimates the enrollment ratio at about 35% of the age group 1-6, with about 1.34 million children in 9,834 pre-school centers. Access to such schools is unevenly distributed. Some 65% of children entering Grade 1 have not been to a pre-school, and most of these are rural children. Enterprises are disbanding these schools, and the Government is being pressed to take over their operation. In 1992, 221 were closed, and another 100 were taken over by MOPE. Facing a deficit of 2.0 million places, the construction program produces about 50,000-60,000 places per year, whereas for full enrollment in 10 years' time the annual need is about 300,000. Most of the schools are short of teaching apparatus, toys, and instructional games. Many are deficient in furniture, equipment, plumbing, and heating, and in many rural centers the children are underfed by state standards. Only a small minority are in good shape. Despite the problems, these schools serve a useful purpose and deserve to be encouraged. In an effort to expand access, MOPE is sponsoring the innovative "family pre-school," which is worth pursuing.[1] The Government regards the pre-school as essential (since both parents often work), as supporting the nutrition, health, and intellectual development of the child, and as an integral part of the social safety net.

Regular Schools. Enrollment in regular and vocational schools (Grades 1-11) in 1992 amounted to 4.9 million out of a mission estimated 6+ to 16+ age group of 5.7 million--an enrollment ratio of 84%.[2] The recent reduction of compulsory schooling from 11 to 9 years was a correct decision taken in light of financial realities, and eases the pressure on the school system (since only about 50% are expected to pass from Grade 9 to Grade 10). Nonetheless, the problem of places for Grades 1-11 is serious. Some 50% of the school buildings are considered unsuitable, many were originally built for other purposes, and many substandard ones have been provided by the poorer collectives. Both district and central repair budgets fall far below need.[3] Some 10% of the schools are dilapidated and deemed unsafe. Because some schools lack canteens and others have space limitations, only 50% of the students receive a hot meal, and, due to budget limitations, the level of nutritional support falls below state standards in some parts of the country. As of 1992, 5,300 of the 8,500 schools worked on two shifts, affecting 1,137,900 (or 25%) of the students, and 26 on three shifts.

Vocational Schools.   Vocational training covers about 220,000 students with an annual output of about 100,000.[4] Training equipment needs to be increased in quantity and modernized. According to MOPE, of the 440 vocational schools in the country, about 190 are located in suitable buildings but need to be provided with educational production workshops and other facilities.

---

[1] This school is a family home serving the children of that home and a few relatives; the mother of the home (the teacher) receives basic training and supervisory support.

[2] Because the Government has not provided population statistics broken down by individual year age groups, this figure is not definitive.

[3] For instance, the 1992 budget gave MOPE 10% of the amount needed; sponsors thus contributed 80 million rubles. In Bukhara, the budget provided 1.2 million rubles to cope with 120 schools (about US$50 per school).

[4] Remarks here pertain to the training of persons in trades and crafts in the two-year and three-year vocational training programs, not to the training of technicians and others in the technicums. The mission was able to visit only one of these technicums, which was housed in a well-adapted building, and is thus unable to comment on the physical facilities generally.

Box 13.9 (cont.)

Higher Education. In 1992, the higher education enrollment of 321,682 students (including 138,223 in evening or correspondence courses) in 53 institutions represented about 19% of the 17+ to 20+ age group, compared to the level of 23.6% reported in 1990 for the USSR. The quality of the facilities varies by and within institutions. Rectors report serious shortfalls in classrooms and laboratories, instructional equipment and supplies, library facilities and collections (including up-to-date journals), computers and access to foreign data banks, and textbooks (especially in Uzbek) and publishing facilities to disseminate research findings. These institutions are striving to attain world standards. Some have done excellent research work despite their equipment shortages. Several of their inventions and innovative techniques have considerable potential to assist economic development especially in agriculture and industry. However, these advances in technology cannot be operationalized because of the lack of funds for the necessary equipment and supplies with which to produce the necessary prototypes. Higher education admissions declined in 1992 because an entrance test was introduced, the demand for graduates declined, the emigration of Russians increased, and good physical facilities remained in short supply. This decline seems only temporary; there is no shortage of candidates. However, because the Government is reluctant to admit more persons than can reasonably expect jobs, growth should be controlled for the next two years while sub-sector planning is continuing.

Curricula. Language is a sensitive area, requiring time to build consensus. A major step has been taken in making Uzbek and five Central Asian languages the languages of instruction.[5] Uzbek history and culture and Arabic script (for Uzbek) are being introduced. Effort is under way to produce a sufficient number of competent teachers and supporting reading material. Some schools have added French, Arabic, and English to the already overloaded curriculum.

Teachers: (i) Salary. By September 1992, the Government had introduced several recent improvements in salaries and benefits for teachers. However, in the mission's view, the salary question should be kept in view. Many of the better vocational teachers are being lost to industry, although these staff can earn additional money by selling the products they make at the schools. In higher education, easing restrictions on staff earnings from research contracts was a positive step; however, while salaries at this level compare favorably in the country, they do not compare favorably in the international market (for which many local staff are qualified). As Uzbekistan opens up to the world and the market-based economy takes shape, there will be some "brain drain" both locally and abroad.

(ii) Surplus. The official staff:student ratio for regular schools is 1:30 for the higher grades and 1:35 for the lower. At the higher education level the standard ratios vary according to the type of institution, but a rough guide is 1:8. At all levels, the actual ratios exceed these standards. The actual 1992 MOPE ratios were as follows: preschool, 1:12; regular school, 1:11.5;[6] vocational schools, 1:12, and higher education, 1:6.8. At MOHE, the actual higher education ratios were roughly 1:10.3 on the average; 1:9.8 in teacher training; 1:6 in foreign languages; and 1:4.5 in architecture and construction. These ratios are well above the Government's standards and even international norms. Comparisons with much wealthier countries illustrate the problem--Ireland, with US$11,120 GNP per capita, had 27 pupils per teacher at the primary level and 15.8 at the secondary level. For the United Kingdom, the corresponding figures were $16,550, 20 and 13.4 and for the Netherlands, $18,780, 17 and 12.9. For Uzbekistan, the figures are $1,350 and 11.5. [Figures taken from the World Bank's World Development Report 1993, UNESCO's Statistical Yearbook 1992 and data supplied to the mission by MOPE]. Thus, there is scope (and need) to apply more realistic ratios. MOPE targets regarding new teachers should be more modest.[7] As Technical Annex 13.4 shows, holding staff numbers steady to the year 2000 would improve the ratio to only 1:14, with about 18,000 new staff merely compensating for attrition. The high

---

[5] All schools teach Uzbek and Russian. However, the language of instruction may be Uzbek, Russian, or any of five Central Asian languages.

[6] This figure is based on data given to the mission--school enrollment of 4.6 million and a teaching staff of 403,000 (or 504,000 if non-teachers are included).

[7] At MOHE the problem is less serious because the current surplus was due partly to a decline in enrollment in 1992 without a parallel reduction in staff, which can be corrected over a short time.

Box 13.9 (cont.)

number of non-teaching staff should also be reviewed. The MOPE projections of preschool teacher needs should also
be revised. Applying more realistic ratios would release the resources necessary to improve administration, school
supervision, supplies of textbooks and equipment, in-service training, and teachers' salaries, and would effect an
improvement in the quality of teachers, as admissions to training and recruitment into teaching become more selective.

(iii) **Training**. Teachers are trained at technicums for the pre-school and primary levels (Grades 1-4), and
at the university level for Grades 5-11. The courses offered are of five years' duration post-Grade 9 in the technicums
and four years post-Grade 11 in the higher education institutions. Both programs involve pedagogical training and
general education. With stipends payable to trainees at the technicums and given the fact that the MOPE unit costs
at the higher education level are above those of MOHE, it would be more economical to transfer most of the general
education component of the training programs to the general system and shorten the training program to three years
post-Grade 11 or one year post-BA equivalent at the university. This measure would be more in line with international
practice, provide more flexibility in responding to changing needs, and concentrate scarce higher education teacher
trainers and specialists at a few excellent centers of research and training. The proposals presented imply a severe
reduction in the teacher training program. The MOPE teacher training institutions (36 technicums and 6 colleges)
produce about 20,000 teachers annually, and MOHE institutions about as many more. The annual need is less than
18,000. This would mean closing several training programs. The spare training capacity thus created could be used
temporarily to retrain existing teachers for new curricula and for teaching in the Uzbek language.

Agriculture, or Construction Ministries) construct the schools under fixed-price contracts that liberally
allow price increases during construction--a system that does not encourage efficiency. Building
construction by the provinces and districts, cooperatives, and collectives is not under the control of these
Boards. Some of these local projects have been left uncompleted as financing dried up. Years sometimes
elapse between design and construction, during which time needs change. The procurement process needs
to be coordinated at the central and local levels, along with a review of overall design and construction
capacity. MOEs must strengthen their facilities planning.

Recommendations

13.68   The deteriorating "technical-material base" of the education system requires urgent
attention. However, at each level of the system, questions of policy, institutional strengthening, and
detailed planning must be addressed as a basis for any large-scale physical investment. In this process,
priority should be given to:

- Improving institutional arrangements for pre-school education (including
increasing and training management staff) and evaluating the educational
effectiveness of the pre-schooling program

- Examining the constraints on construction capacity in the country and adopting
measures to promote expansion

- Considering ways to strengthen the facilities-planning capacity of MOHE/MOPE

- Identifying higher education institutions as potential centers of excellence and determining what is required to raise them to that standard

- Providing emergency funding for (1) equipment needs of higher education institutions (US$10 million) and (2) equipment and teaching-aids needs of the pre-school system (US$3 million).

CURRICULA

13.69   Immense and complex problems face curricular change. This crucial transitional period demands substantially new curricula to support (1) nation building; (2) new international relations (with Central Asia and the world); (3) a market-based economy; and (4) the promotion of world standards at all levels. The technical challenge is to elaborate and carry out these aspirations practically and efficiently. With regard to the market-based economy, the education and training system has two responsibilities: (1) to inform its students and trainees (both in school and out-of-school) about the economy and society and the promise and opportunities inherent in these, and (2) to equip persons with the necessary abilities, skills and attitudes to help them to earn their living and contribute to the welfare of society. These are the normal responsibilities of an education/training system; however, over the next generation Uzbekistan will be undergoing such rapid economic and social change in ways which are not all predictable (since they involve political and social choice and international realities) that the education and training system will be under immense pressure to adapt and to respond to the demands placed upon it. Although the market economy will not emerge overnight, the changes in education should have been begun already and will need to be expanded as the economy becomes more market-based.

13.70   The leaderships of the sector and of the Methodology Centers (MCs) recognize the shortage of staff competent to pilot this curricular adjustment process in regard to the transition to a market-based economy. The MCs do not fully understand the scope of the profound changes required in the next 10 to 15 years. The task is not one of the normal curriculum revision; it calls for a fundamental rethinking of many values and assumptions. In some areas--improving the social relevance of what is taught in history, geography, and language, or individual and social responsibility for the environment, or in economics (particularly the relationship between capital and labor), or in political science--the needs are obvious. In others, such as arithmetic, where a more commercial emphasis will be required, the needs are less evident to educators who are not aware of the demands of a market-based economy. The qualitative change required is profound. New fields of study will be required, such as business management, as will substantial new bodies of additional knowledge in such fields as law, commerce, social work and finance. Textbooks at all levels and in all fields will need to accommodate the new language and thinking of the marketplace (including economic competition at the individual and national levels) and, in order to meet the myriad demands by firms and individuals for information, a different approach toward making information readily and publicly available will be needed. Libraries and high technology information services with international links will need to become part of a strong outreach (or extension) program of the sector. The emphasis in an era of rapid change will need to be placed on the adaptability of the school leaver to further education and work, hence on a thorough and broad general education for all. The management of the sector will need to focus attention on the search for and judicious use of resources to bring about maximum educational benefits, keeping the public dialogue open on the changes required--so that maximum possible consensus accompanies these extensive changes--and adjusting programs and curricula as rapidly as possible as the labor market and the society evolve. Thus the next few years will need to see a very forward looking and dynamic leadership in the sector, not one that has all the answers but one that is eagerly searching for answers, evaluating performance and commissioning research into problems. Whatever strategies are adopted will have to be tailor-made for Uzbekistan and there is no model that can be imposed or designed by outsiders; the adaptation has to be done by persons fully conversant with national culture and traditions as well as the goals of the country. Hence a high-level independent research institute, free to undertake incisive work on educational and socioeconomic issues associated with educational change should be established, along with a forum such as a National Council on Education.

13.71   Specific needs in the areas of curriculum, textbooks, and examinations are:

- The staff of the MCs, to the extent that they are drawn from the teaching service, should receive some salary premium that recognizes their special talents.

- The process of curriculum renewal should be accelerated; knowledge is expanding rapidly in some fields, especially at the higher education level (for example, molecular biology, informatics, and medicine).

- The preparation of textbooks and supplementary reading materials should be managed separately from curriculum development, even though good liaison with curriculum and examination policy is required.

- The management of educational testing and examinations should also be separated from curriculum development although some considerable liaison is needed; further, the results of material examinations should be analyzed and disseminated to assist teachers, students and school administrators in diagnosing and addressing problem areas.[18]

- The testing and examination system needs to be developed. Two efforts are being made to develop testing that should be encouraged.[19]

- The curriculum of the regular schools contains too many subjects (25), and should be streamlined and consolidated; in vocational training, where the proliferation and orientation of trades owe much to the needs of the former USSR, these trades (now down to 260) should be consolidated further and orientated toward national needs.

- As much leeway as possible should be given to the schools in interpreting and applying the curriculum.

---

[18] Analysis of the results of the traditional General Certificate of Education examination--given at the end of grade 11--consists primarily of identifying common errors of grammar and spelling and showing how to avoid them.

[19] Experimental work has begun in the MOPE MC on multiple-choice tests. A Testing Center has just been established to conduct admissions tests for higher education, owing primarily to the poor performance of those being admitted. The report of the 1992 pilot test was not made available to the mission. With Turkish technical assistance, the Government plans to expand this unit of 8 staff to 100, and to buy US$2 million worth of equipment.

13.72   Some dissatisfaction with student performance does exist, although specific indices of student performance, such as examination results, were not available to the mission. Some positive steps worthy of support have been taken or are being considered to try to raise standards in the school system. Plans have been made to establish schools for gifted children, attached to higher-education institutions in some cases. In line with the change to a compulsory 9- rather than 11-year period of education, the aim is to introduce two new types of schools--the gymnasium (grades 1-9) and the lyceum (grades 10-11)--and to provide ongoing assessments of students. At the technicum level, the aim is to move to a 2- or 3-year post-Grade 11 program; this would be more economical than the present 4- to 5-year post-Grade 9 program.

13.73   In vocational schools, a dropout rate of 5 percent per year was cited, as was a failure rate of less than 1 percent. In the technicum visited, the few students who fail the final examination are given a make-up test, which they usually pass, and the technicum thus did not have a failure rate. Some officials complain, however, that students in technicums and higher education institutions are allowed too many opportunities to repeat, but precise figures were not available to the mission. Conversely, the proposal to conduct vocational training at the post-Grade 6 level appears to be ill-advised, since it involves persons that are too young and have too slender a general-education base to meet the challenge of technology today and tomorrow.[20] At the higher-education level, sensible changes have been introduced to raise standards, rationalize resources, and align the system more effectively with international practices. Following their admission through the new entrance test for *all* applicants, students will all pursue a two-year basic course, followed by an examination. Those who pass will proceed to the next level--a two-year program leading to the BA equivalent (with a further two years for the MA equivalent). Those who fail, however, must leave the system, but are given a chance to take a make-up examination and receive the junior specialist's diploma if they succeed.

13.74   The system of managing (1) curriculum design, (2) textbook preparation and production, and (3) testing and examinations should be reconsidered, in particular the advantage of separating them and ensuring that each has the specialists, resources, and mandate required to conduct its task efficiently. Consideration should also be given to establishing an independent high-level research institute that would analyze major issues of relevance to education, and that would help shape curricular thought and influence qualitative development perspectives (para. 13.73).

TEACHERS

13.75   Uzbekistan has a large body of dedicated, qualified, and competent teachers at all levels. Yet, with the system in transition, issues pertaining to teachers are deep and interwoven. First, the mission noted the steps taken by the Government in 1992 to improve significantly the pay and benefits of teachers, but this matter should be kept under review. Second, there are more teachers being trained than the system can absorb, and their training, given the level of available resources, may be too long.

---

[20] The motive is to increase the numbers going into vocational training and reduce those going into secondary education, but this justification is insufficient for such a retrograde step.

Box 13.10: Out-of-School Education

Out-of-school (non-formal) education for adults and youth is given a prominent place in the system. The responsible Board in MOPE, working with NGOs which are organized at the national, provincial, and district levels, lends support to a wide range of activities, such as food production, hiking, creative arts, women's groups, and so on. The Board identifies ways to help these groups and to facilitate their access to education and training in line with their objectives. Specifically, the Board helps them find meeting places, train personnel, and obtain instructional equipment. The courses cover such areas as child care, small-scale earning activities, safety, and avoidance of anti-social behavior. One senior official stated that there is need for a kind of adult education center to correct attitudes toward work.

The constraints are of qualified staff, funding, and awareness of what goes on elsewhere. The number of staff in MOPE is inadequate for a country and task of this size. In 1991-92 there were 598 organizations and 367,681 persons enrolled. Funding for direct assistance to groups in 1992 was only 3 million rubles. The staff would benefit from training and exposure to non-formal programs elsewhere in the world, such as in Indonesia and Thailand. The Bank has given extensive support to non-formal education in Indonesia, both for institutional strengthening and for the expansion of learning opportunities. The innovative "learning groups" financed in the three Indonesia projects foster small-scale enterprise in ways that can easily be adapted to Uzbekistan. This activity has great potential to transmit the ethos and principles of the market economy quickly to youths and adults and thus accelerate and support the economic transformation.

COSTS AND FINANCING

13.76   For 1992, central Government funding for public education amounted to 46.9 billion rubles, representing 24 percent of total Government budgetary expenditures and approximately 11 percent of GDP.[21]   However, the real costs and financing of the sector are difficult to establish primarily because the available data on financing the system cover only central and local governments and do not include financing by families and enterprises. MOPE calculations of the cost per student at the various types of school give a recurrent cost ratio of 1.0 for regular schools (at 2,503 rubles per student) to 1.7 for pre-school, 3.4 for vocational schools, 4.3 for teacher training technicums, and 4.5 for teacher training colleges.

13.77   In the context of the proposed preparation of a comprehensive long-range plan, the Government should consider the following:

- Measures to stimulate wider financial participation by parents and enterprises, chiefly in preschool education (see Box 13.11)

- The gradual elimination of stipends to students younger than age 16 in any but higher education institutions (see Box 13.11)

- The adoption of a means test for all awards of stipends

---

[21] A breakdown by the Ministry is not available.

- The institution of a modest tax on the salaries of all university graduates as a contribution to higher education costs, payable only when their salaries rise above a certain level

- The possibility of a levy on employers to assist in financing vocational and technical education, with exemptions for those employers who contribute satisfactorily to the support of education and training.

B. PRIORITY INVESTMENT NEEDS AND TECHNICAL ASSISTANCE

13.78   The absence of a comprehensive sectoral strategy and the incomplete nature of our knowledge of the sector make it difficult to identify priorities in any but a preliminary way. Some of the needs that arose in discussions with officials are so urgent and widespread that some difficult decisions of phasing will have to be made. The strategy adopted in listing these needs is twofold (1) to give the highest priority to strengthening the capacity of Uzbekistan to design its developmental policies and thus coordinate and order its dialogue with donor agencies, and (2) to support the balanced development of the system, rather than the selection of isolated elements that are presumed to have the greatest isolated impact. This explains the emphasis upon institutional strengthening and planning. The outcome of these initial investments would thus help shape future investments by a variety of donors.

PHASE I: IMMEDIATE INVESTMENTS, 1993-94

Technical Assistance

- *Preparation of a long-range (10- to 15-year) integral developmental strategy for the sector, including its institutional development needs*. This can be prepared in 24 months with technical assistance (expert services) and training (through such sources as the UNESCO International Institute for Education Planning) establishing the nucleus of the planning machinery, elaborating a developmental program, and identifying projects for Phase II.

- *Strengthening of sectoral management*. This measure should be approached in stages over a 10-year period.   The initial phase, which would involve reorganization, staff training, and equipment, would require two years and a technical assistance program.

PHASE II: THE DEVELOPMENT PROGRAM, 1995-99

Technical Assistance

- *Continued strengthening of management*. Staff development, expert services (local and foreign), and office equipment and supplies at central and provincial levels.

Box 13.11: Uzbekistan: Costs and Financing of Education

For the **pre-school** system, it is widely accepted that the parents should contribute. MOPE is the dominant provider--587,000 (44% of total) enrolled in its pre-schools in 1992. About 2,000 centers are conducted by Local Executive Committees (LECs), which fix the fee level--usually about 12 rubles monthly, compared with operating costs of about 800 rubles. The mission has no data on what would be a reasonable levy on parents, but, at full cost as of September 1992 (say 800 rubles each), two children would consume the salary of a teacher. Enterprises conduct several centers and parental contributions vary. In the current recession, and with the emergence of a market economy and enterprises becoming more profit-conscious, there is a trend among the enterprises to cast off these centers. The central Government is therefore under increasing pressure to enlarge its support and to find more economical ways to operate; hence its interest in the new family pre-school.

For the **regular** schools, serving the compulsory age group, the principle is that the costs should be met by the government, particularly the local government. The "local budget," which is chiefly for the regular schools, was 19.2 billion rubles; however, as neither the breakdown of this budget nor the extrabudgetary contribution to the financing is available, unit costs cannot be calculated. No tuition fees are charged. Children in Grades 1-5 receive free meals, while those above that level pay half-price. Pre-inflation prices are retained for school uniforms. Textbooks are bought by the LEC and supplied free on loan to the student for the year; where the LEC cannot afford to buy them, the provincial and finally the central Government would pay. Officials feel that the parents cannot afford to pay for textbooks, since their price has risen much faster than wages. In order to test the feasibility of the idea of private education, one regular private school has been established in each province.

MOHE and MOPE are the main financiers of **vocational, secondary specialized and higher education**. The related 1992 budget for these three sub-sectors was allocated in percentage terms as follows:

ITEM	MOHE %	MOPE %
Salaries/Soc. security payments	42	31.0
Student subsidies (food, stipends)	43	56.2
Miscellaneous (incl. some subsidies)	11.5	9.6
Repairs	3.5	3.2
TOTAL	100.0	100.0

Thus, roughly half the budget is for student subsidies. Officials deem them essential, since some post-secondary students support families. Higher education monthly stipends barely cover boarding and lodging. It is not clear to the mission why persons enrolled in vocational schools (as distinct from any other students at the same grade level) need to receive a stipend. There is no clear means test in the granting of subsidies.

Employers help vocational schools through donations of (sometimes obsolete) equipment and contributions to capital repair and construction--but this source, for reasons indicated above, is now less reliable and its scale and potential are unknown. There is no training levy; on the contrary, MOPE signs agreements with employers to train students and pays the firms for this. The net cost to MOPE of the vocational schools (about 11,000 rubles per student year) is low by any international standards.

In higher education, the average net cost to MOHE (for its various types of institutions) is estimated at about 14,560 rubles and to MOPE (for its teacher training institutions) is about 28,000 rubles.[1] The real average cost may be significantly higher. Enterprises sponsor students in fields of direct interest to them.

---

[1] These are mission estimates based on the 1992 budget figures of R. 2.035 billion for MOHE and R. 393.74 million (adjusted by 70%) for MOPE for their respective higher education institutions. The enrollment figures assume that evening students cost 50% of full-time students and correspondence students, 25%. This assumption gives MOHE a full-time equivalent student body of 139,798 and MOPE 23,788 in higher education.

- *Assistance toward qualitative improvement in education*. Staff development, expert services, and office equipment and supplies for curricular design, educational testing and examinations, and textbook preparation and manufacture.

Capital Investment

This component would comprise the items identified in the plan as the most urgent. It would probably include:

- A *construction program* for regular schools, vocational training, and technicums

- A tranche of a *higher education development program aiming at centers of excellence* (including education)

- Pilot projects in *pre-school and out-of-school education*

- *Textbook development and manufacturing* components.

CHAPTER 14

ENVIRONMENT

14.1   Uzbekistan has inherited an economic structure and obsolete technologies that generate excessive pollution and use resources wastefully. The cost of remedying the country's environmental problems will be high. Thus, the Government must set priorities carefully and develop a strategy for addressing those priorities over time in a least-cost framework. This chapter discusses the major environmental concerns, analyzes both the contributing factors and previous achievements, and, based on an evaluation of alternative options, recommends a priority program of action.

A. MAIN ENVIRONMENTAL CONCERNS

14.2   The most important environmental problems facing Uzbekistan are linked to the management of water resources and water quality in the Aral Sea Basin. The development of large-scale irrigation projects has led to wide-scale land and water degradation.[1] Among the causes and symptoms of the country's environmental problems are: the orientation of industry and agriculture to cotton-growing, a high population growth rate and its concentration in the basin area, limited water resources, an intensive use of water in irrigation, and the lack of controls and effective monitoring.

14.3   The primary environmental damage is caused by agricultural runoff and discharges of industrial wastewater. Much of the contaminated water is treated inadequately (if at all). The widespread use of pesticides and mineral fertilizers and the absence of modern irrigation and drainage systems exacerbates these problems.

LAND

14.4   In 1987, Uzbekistan had the highest level of irrigated land within the FSU under cotton and cash crops (see Table 14.1). The consequent environmental damage is evident. Crop rotation, which is used to protect the soil, was not practiced, and livestock development absorbed much of the organic fertilizers, which were already in short supply; it was thus necessary to use a large quantity of mineral fertilizers and pesticides (see Boxes 14.1 and 14.2). In the end, their use destroyed the natural biological processes taking place in the soils, and degraded the natural regulating mechanisms. (Box 14.1 discusses the environmental concerns associated with land degradation.)

WATER

14.5   Discharge of untreated or insufficiently treated water containing chemicals and pesticides into rivers has damaged water quality. This, in turn, has affected both human health and agriculture (see Box 14.2, which discusses the environmental concerns associated with water contamination). For

---

[1] This problem, considered to be one of the greatest manmade environmental disasters of this century, is discussed more fully in Annex 3 (Aral Sea Issues) in this Volume. The intensive use of the waters of the Amu Darya and Syr Darya for irrigated agriculture in the Republics of Central Asia and Kazakhstan has caused an irreversible drying of the Aral Sea and devastation of the Basin area. In the past 30 years, the area of the Aral Sea has shrunk from 68,000 to 39,000 square kilometers, its volume of water declining to less than one-third of its original (from 1,005 km3 to 280 km3), and salt concentration has increased from 10 to 28 grams per liter of sea water.

example, the Amu Darya River is the primary source of drinking water in the Basin area. In certain months, the mineralization of water in the Amu Darya is 0.54 to 0.75 grams per liter of water, compared with 7 milligrams per liter, its normal level. Water hardness exceeds 1 gram per liter.

14.6   An examination of the data available suggests that the most serious environmental health problems in the Amu Darya and Syr Darya Basin result from exposure to nitrates and pesticide residues. These findings are consistent with the widely held belief that excessive and careless use of pesticides and fertilizers is the main issue of concern.

Table 14.1
Crop Types on Irrigated Lands in the FSU and the new Republics (1987)
(in percentage)

Total	Total	Grain	Cotton and Cash Crops	Vegetables	Fodder - Pasture Animals
FSU	100	23	23	7	47
Russia	100	24	2	8	66
Ukraine	100	35	5	11	49
Uzbekistan	*100*	*12*	*60*	*5*	*23*
Kazakhstan	100	28	12	6	54
Georgia	100	30	4	16	50
Azerbaijan	100	30	32	3	35
Moldova	100	32	11	19	38
Kyrgyzstan	100	33	8	4	55
Tajikistan	100	12	57	5	26
Armenia	100	27	5	12	56
Turkmenistan	100	15	53	6	26

Source: Uzbekistan Ministry of Environment.

AIR

14.7   The drying of the sea has exposed vast salt beds to the winds, creating occasional salt and dust storms. It is generally believed that these storms damage both agriculture and human health. Particularly affected are areas immediately southeast of the Aral Sea. However, the correlation between exposure to salt and dust in this manner and health impacts is still inconclusive.

14.8   The dominant role of gas in power generation and domestic heating means that the main air quality problems are associated with industrial emissions and automobile transport. Exposure to lead dust from non-ferrous metal plants and leaded gasoline, hydrogen fluoride from the Tajik aluminum plant, and a variety of organic compounds including chlorinated hydrocarbons seem to be the main threat to health.

WASTE

14.9   The country lacks a proper system for the disposal of solid and hazardous industrial waste. Industrial conglomerates formed of smaller industries are not required to report data on waste treatment and disposal. This is a major flaw, together with the absence of appropriate regulatory requirements and their enforcement in the area of waste disposal.

Box 14.1: Environmental Concerns: Land Degradation

More than 90% of the irrigated land has been contaminated heavily by an <u>excessive use of pesticides</u>; some estimates indicate that their use is atypically higher, exceeding six times the average required per hectare (Table 1). Laboratory tests of foodstuffs in 1988 showed that 19.5% did not meet the sanitary norms, and that 2.9% contained pesticides that exceeded the permitted concentration levels.   Despite the fact that mineral-fertilizer use per hectare of irrigated land is much higher than the average for the FSU, it is not as high as generally believed. (Mineral fertilizer use per hectare of irrigated land is compared for different countries in Table 2, which shows that its use in the Netherlands is the highest among all countries compared.)

Table 1: Application of Pesticides In the Republic of Uzbekistan
(in preparation form)

Indexes		1989	1990	1991
Total Pesticide Use:	thousand tons	84.2	85.9	59.8
compared with 1989	%		102.0	71.0
of which sulfuric chemicals in use	thousand tons	35.6	37.2	20.9
compared with 1989	%		104.5	58.7
Area of Irrigated Agricultural Fields	thousand ha	100.0	104.5	58.7
Area Treated by Pesticides of All Types	thousand ha	3,809.0	3,762.0	3,762.0
Among Them by Sulfur Chemicals	thousand ha	837.7	802.7	430.6
Total Pesticide Use/Hectare: kg/ha	36.0	43.2	41.6	
including sulphur chemicals kg/ha	42.7	46.3	48.5	
Higher Specific Norms of Pesticides Application in the Republic (Surkhndarya, Kashkadarya provinces)	kg/ha of treated area	65.8	90.9	85.8
Lowest Specific Norms of Pesticides Application in the Republic (Tashkent, Khoresm provinces)	kg/ha of treated area	21.1	19.8	20.4

Source: Uzbekistan, Ministry of Environment.

The quantity of <u>terminal DDT</u>, prohibited since 1983, exceeds concentration limits in more than half of the analyzed soil samples.   Over-limit concentrations of magnesium chlorate have been registered in more than 80% of the irrigated lands. The accumulation of benzene hexachloride isomers is less apparent because they are more water soluble and can be removed in successive rinsing of the land. Other herbicides and insecticides are rarely found (Table 3, see Technical Annex). Storehouses containing nearly 12,000 tons of <u>forbidden or expired pesticides</u> are stored and managed by the Republican Industrial and Scientific Amalgamation, but remain a source of soil pollution.

Despite efforts to reduce pesticide use in the country, its level of application remains high. Between 1989 and 1991, the gross area under pesticide use declined from 2.3 to 1.4 million hectares, but pesticide use per hectare of cultivated land rose in the same period, from 36 to 42 kg/hectare. Despite the intensive application of pesticides, mineral fertilizers, and chemicals, crop capacity and animal <u>productivity remain low</u>, because the ecological requirements of the soils are not being met. Besides the low efficiency of chemical preparations, more than 30% of potash phosphate and more than 50% of nitric fertilizers cannot be assimilated by plants. They are washed out of the irrigated area but contribute to the pollution of soils and surface and underground waters.

All irrigated land is salinized to some extent, of which more than 50% is <u>heavily salinized</u> (with 90-95% salinity) and eroded (Table 3), particularly in the Karakalpakstan, Bukhara, and Syrdarya regions. In Kashkadarya and Khorezm, land salinity is 60-70%. The level of <u>humus</u> (a major index of soil fertility) has declined by 30 to 50%, and soils with low and very low humus content (from 0.4 to 1%) occupy about 40% of the irrigated area. Water and wind erosion (<u>deflation</u>) threatens 20% of the irrigated land; the majority of deflation-affected soils are situated in the Fergana, Surkhandarya, Kashkadarya, and Bukhara regions. The accelerated process of water erosion can be observed in the adyr zone of the Fergana and Andidjan regions and in the foothills of the Tashkent region. Excessive pasturing and the neglect of pasture circulation have degraded the pasture land.

Box 14.1 (cont.)

Of 22 million hectares used in pastures, 6 million hectares suffer from deflation and 3 million hectares from water erosion.

A high content of heavy metals in the soils has been noticed in the Tashkent, Almalyk, and Bekabad (Chirchik) regions.

Table 2: Mean Consumption of Mineral Fertilizers
(kg per hectare)
Evaluated in 100% of Nutrient Substance

	1980	1987	Nitrogen Fertilizers		Phosphorus Fertilizers		Calcium Fertilizers	
			1980	1987	1980	1987	1980	1987
FSU	84	122	35.8	50.8	24.2	36.9	21.2	30.4
Uzbekistan	416	438	243	240	131	136	42	6.2
Yugoslavia	105	134	53	61.0[a]	27.0	34.0[a]	25.0	33.0[a]
Romania	113	125	58	66.0[a]	45.3	42.0[a]	9.6	21.0[a]
GDR	325	339	149.4	158.5	77.2	65.6	98.6	114.9
Czechoslovakia	335	303	130.5	114.7	95.8	88.1	108.3	100.4
Canada	44	51	20	27	15	15	8	9
United States	113	106	56	57	27	22	31	27
Finland	191	234	76	88	58	66	56	63
Netherlands	844	782	565	566	98	98	144	118
Japan	429	378	142	129	152	139	135	111

a/ 1985
Source: Ministry of Environment.

Table 3: Irrigated Low-Productivity Land
(thousand hectares)

Low-Productivity Land	Total Irrigated Areas	Cotton Irrigated Areas
High-salinity Lands	238.4	196.0
Wetlands	24.7	21.7
Moderately and Highly Stony Lands	50.6	41.8
Water-eroded Lands	50.5	34.9
Gypsum Land	200.0	108.0
Total	564.2	
Physical Area	494.4	388.2

Source: Ministry of Environment.

B. OVERVIEW OF CURRENT ENVIRONMENTAL POLICY

14.10   Current environmental pollution and natural-resource degradation in Uzbekistan are due to past economic policies that promoted quantitative production targets at the cost of environmental quality. These policies were accompanied by pricing systems under which natural resources were undervalued and the environment as a whole was treated as a free good. Lacking were sound

Box 14.2: Environmental Concerns: Water Contamination

The indiscriminate use of water in agricultural activities along the river basin, and its collection and drainage into the rivers, contaminates the drinking water and creates the single most *crucial* environmental problem in the country. Poor quality of water is associated with significant health problems in the region, and has an impact on agricultural productivity for downstream users.

Water scarcity is also a problem in certain regions of Uzbekistan and is likely to be a significant issue if present inefficiencies continue and the demand for water continues to grow with the increasing population.

Nearly 85 percent of the urban population and 52% of the rural population have access to centralized piped water, but it is of variable quality. The quality of water for each user for irrigated areas decreases as it flows downriver, and the most severely affected are the populations and agriculture nearest to the Sea. The most severely affected areas in drinking-water quality are the Karakalpak, Khorezm, Bukhara, and Navoi regions. Nearly one-third of the delivered water in the cities and over half of that provided to the villages does not meet Government standards.

The unpiped and ground water used by the remaining population is often worse, particularly in the Bukhara and Navoi regions, where their underground waters are drawn from the Damhodzin underground water reservoir situated in the vicinity of industrial Samarkand. In Fergana Valley, underground water is heavily contaminated with oil. While leakages from piping are common (accepted up to 3% of volume of products in Uzbekistan), they have gone largely unnoticed due to the underground construction of pipes carrying the products. Approximately one million tons of oil have collected in the underground waters, covering an area of approximately 10 square kilometers. Because these leakages could not be observed in the past, the Government is now insisting that the pipes carrying the products be elevated to 3-5 meters above ground.

The economical use of water resources in both industrial and agricultural sectors is required. The Government plans to reduce specific water consumption in agriculture by 15% by 1995 and another 20% through the reconstruction of irrigation systems and other measures by 2005. It plans to eliminate the discharge of waste waters to surface and underground sources, reduce water losses in the transportation of water over long distances through more effective demand planning, set-up higher standards for discharge water quality for all water users, promote better technology in agriculture, improve sewerage systems, and construct collectors to drain salted and drainage waters.

However, these measures are likely to be unsustainable unless incentives for adhering to the more efficient use of water are established. In this context, the appropriate pricing of water and other inputs will play a role, together with the measures already planned for pollution fees, and fines for indiscriminate dumping.

---

environmental policies and regulations, realistic standards, and an environmental management system capable of enforcing these standards. Such policies have led to severe environmental consequences, with increasingly adverse effects on the health of the population.

14.11   The movement from a centrally planned to a market-based economy, with the attendant realignment of prices, changes in ownership, and tighter budgetary control, will have a major effect on the efficiency of resource use and on the structure of the economy, and on the future state of the environment. However, as the experience of OECD countries has shown, the market alone cannot resolve all environmental problems. The market's positive impact on the environment will be reflected by the decisions of both individuals and economic agents who seek to maximize the benefits of developing scarce resources, both natural and financial. Macroeconomic reforms must be coupled with efforts to develop institutions, regulatory instruments, and economic incentives that discourage behavior that damages the environment--for example, through price reforms that reflect not only the full costs of production but also a reasonable estimate of the costs of resource use on environment and health.

14.12   Environmental protection must be treated as an integral part of the entire macroeconomic reform process.   Therefore, before heavy spending starts within the market sector, the existing environmental infrastructure must be upgraded, environmental standards and regulations revised and amended, monitoring systems for compliance strengthened, and a self-financing system for the sector established.

14.13   Effective legislation requires an environmental strategy that is closely linked to the economic reform strategy.   Many of the environmental laws of the FSU appear to be strong on paper, but are not tied to realities.   A transition must be made from largely uncontrolled environmental risks to risks that are controllable to the extent found acceptable to the Uzbek society.   Thus, a system in which environmental laws represent a statement of goals must be transformed into a system in which those laws provide operational requirements for controlling the sources of environmental risk.

14.14   Environmental liability for past pollution will become an important issue during the privatization process.   A lack of clarity about this issue could cause unnecessary delays in concluding privatization contracts.   In practice the burden of any clean-up will fall, in one way or another, on the state.   However, it is critical that a clear division of responsibilities is established and inventories of contaminated land are prepared as privatization proceeds.   Privatized enterprises must, therefore, be subject to strict monitoring so that they can be held accountable for current emissions.

14.15   Uzbekistan uses the air and water standards of the FSU, with the addition of a limited number of its own national standards.   The Soviet standards were more stringent than European Community (EC) or U.S. standards.   Using standards as a basis for enforcing compliance was quite rare in the FSU; in fact, the standards were used most frequently as a reference point for describing air and water-quality conditions at a specific location.   The practice of setting unrealistic standards that cannot be enforced contributed to the general disregard for environmental laws and regulations, and should thus be avoided in the future.

14.16   Funds available to the State Committee through its budgetary sources are quite modest (less than 0.5 percent of total Government expenditures).   They are clearly inadequate for addressing the environmental agenda (described in Box 14.3) and for meeting urgent environmental needs.   Almost all of the Government budget allocated to the environmental ministries is spent on wages and "apparatus" maintenance, including buildings, recurring expenses, travel, and limited staff training.   No funds are available for special environmental programs, although a small portion of the Ministries of Science and Education funds are allocated for such purposes as research and environmental education.   Owing to inflation, the Government would require an additional 25 to 30 percent or more of its budget this year just to maintain the current level of activity.

C. RECOMMENDATIONS

LEGISLATIVE AND REGULATORY REFORMS

14.17   The complexity of environmental problems requires clear lines of authority with well-articulated roles and responsibilities.   Regional and local institutions can play a significant role in negotiating environmental standards for local industry, which in the future can be held more accountable for environmental damage, and more closely involve the local populations. While all documents related to the local environment are maintained by the local institutions, the human and technical capacity of

Box 14.3: Status of Current Efforts

The Uzbekistan Government has been working to define a comprehensive environmental program through its Ministry of Environment (also referred to as the State Committee for Nature Protection) which would address many of the concerns outlined in this chapter. It has prepared a set of standards and limits for the use of natural resources, allowable emission levels, and fees, fines, and taxes for pollution. In addition, it recognizes the necessity for economic incentives for the preservation of nature, innovative financing mechanisms, credit provisions for nature-protection measures, and investment policies to address environmental concerns.

Government plans call for the following measures by 1995: reducing areas for cotton by up to 45%; increasing areas for vegetables, potatoes, and melons from 4.9 to 6-7%; increasing fodder areas; increasing the production of some perennial plants and enlarging personal plots; halting the construction of large irrigation systems without state approval and expert input; reducing the application of highly toxic pesticides by 50% and substituting them with others that decompose relatively rapidly; banning the use of these toxic pesticides (by the years 2000 to 2005); and increasing the organic farming share to 90-95%. Other objectives are to complete the planned construction of landfills, storage facilities, and eventual disposal of forbidden pesticides, and of toxic industrial and residential waste, as well as the construction of waste processing plants in cities by 2005. Further objectives include reconstructing the existing system of drainage and irrigation channels, and constructing new ones; introducing progressive methods of irrigation; the salt-cleaning of irrigated land; new irrigation technologies; and reducing present water consumption in irrigation by 25%. Still other objectives are to reduce soil erosion by various means and to recultivate deserted land, control water logging and promote contour agriculture on slope and erosion-prone land, establish larger pasture lands, and provide water for desert and semi-desert pastures by use of underground water.

these institutions is very limited. The absence of trained and capable individuals at this level will continue to pose a major constraint on local-level participation unless training is provided and unless incentives are offered to attract and retain well-qualified individuals.

Short-Term Reform

14.18   Reform measures must be complemented with an effective regulatory and legislative framework for environmental concerns. Establishing this framework will likely require that standards be revised to reflect the country's administrative, technical, and financial capacity. Since resource requirements are likely to exceed what can be provided, it is imperative that a strategy be developed to establish priorities that can be used readily by decisionmakers. An environmental strategy could serve as a framework for facilitating the coordination of international assistance to the sector.

14.19   Land leasing must be planned carefully so that water allocation and ownership interests do not impede water management. To prevent the excessive use of pesticides (and mineral fertilizers in some cases), water waste, indiscriminate dumping, and end-of-pipe pollution from all sources, the Government must introduce a system of economic incentives to accompany effective regulation and its enforcement. A more comprehensive infrastructure for treating and discharging waste water is needed. An appropriate range of economic and policy instruments must be chosen to address the environmental concerns in Uzbekistan.

14.20   A mechanism for resolving interministerial conflicts should be established. The Ministers of Agriculture, Mining, Industry, and Environment have significant control over aspects of environmental management and regulation. Yet an integrated, national environmental policy does not exist, nor do mechanisms for resolving disputes, owing to overlapping lines of authority. An institutional framework is required to foster the resolution of conflicts whereby they are consistent with national policies for economic development and environmental concerns.

Medium-Term Reform

14.21   The ecological value of existing protected areas may be affected adversely by changes in use as land is leased. Important wetlands may also be affected. An adequate mechanism for protecting these lands has yet to be developed. A significant obstacle is the current inadequacy of compensation for landholders to maintain private lands for conservation purposes. Procedures that provide proper compensation to holders, and enforceable restrictions on land use in conservation areas, must be developed. The issue should be addressed as an element of the new land ownership and nature protection legislation. In the meantime, environmental education programs should be implemented for landowners.

14.22   The Ministry should consider adopting more realistic ambient standards, and establish interim standards that will permit the transparent transition of existing industry and municipalities to the new standards in a reasonable time period (over 10 to 15 years). New sources of pollution should be required to meet these standards immediately. Local authorities should be permitted to apply standards more stringently than the national minimum in environmentally sensitive areas.

PRICING REFORMS

Short-Term Reform

14.23   Energy and natural-resource prices are generally still very low in Uzbekistan and must be rationalized. In particular, the increases in energy prices recommended in chapter 10 will reduce the environmental damage associated with wasteful use of energy. Consideration should also be given to raising and rationalizing charges for all forms of water use so as to encourage water conservation. This could also be linked to discharge fees for wastewater discharges to rivers. Finally, subsidies for fertilizers and pesticides should be eliminated as rapidly as is feasible.

Fees and Fines

14.24   In July 1992, the State Committee for Nature Protection considerably revised an existing system of payments and fees for polluting the environment, and fines for exceeding the required standards. The level of funds available from this system has been highly uncertain and quite insignificant in the past. It is unlikely that the system can raise the higher amounts expected. The laws governing these fines are still new, and enforcement has not yet caught up with intentions.

14.25   Fees and fines are a source of extrabudgetary funds available to the State Committee for Nature Protection and its regional governments, and are used to finance direct environmental measures by the Committee. The State Committee has control of 15 percent of the funds raised from this system, while the rest are spent by local authorities according to established guidelines. Because the National Fund is an extrabudgetary account, it is very important that it be operated transparently, and disclosed fully to the public. Clear criteria must be established for using revenue, based on the principle that the "polluter pays" (that is, that the funds finance only a part of abatement costs) and on cost-effectiveness measures (that is, the highest benefits per unit of investment costs have priority). In addition, a council of representatives from ministries, academic institutions, and nongovernmental organizations should be formed with the task of governing the operation of the Fund, and to support a system of economic incentives. Similar considerations apply to the local environmental funds operated by local authorities using their share of the revenue from fees and fines.

14.26   Since the purpose of fines is to ensure compliance with permits, rather than to generate revenue, using fines as the sole source of revenue for the National Fund appears to be inappropriate. Moreover, the level of fines is inadequate to effect significant changes in practices by polluters. Thus, the relationship between fees and fines should be modified; natural-resource taxes (royalties) should be revised to more fully reflect the relationship between extraction costs and market prices.

STRENGTHENING MONITORING AND ENFORCEMENT

Medium-Term Reform

14.27   Monitoring and enforcement are significant impediments to the regulatory reform process, both of which must be strengthened, particularly the monitoring capacity of the Ministry of Environment at both the national and regional levels.

14.28   The following are recommendations for improving the efficiency of the existing monitoring systems: (1) designing an efficient information management system on emission and discharge and ambient monitoring for the Ministry for Environment, especially for the most polluted areas; (2) identifying and obtaining the necessary equipment, spare parts, and software; (3) training personnel at the ministerial and regional levels to monitor and integrate information management; and (4) reducing the number of pollutants currently covered by the monitoring system. Again, these recommendations can be implemented effectively only when the legal framework clarifies the enforcement of responsibilities and authority of the Ministry and its branches.

14.29   Much of the monitoring equipment in Uzbekistan is either outdated, ineffective, or simply inoperative, and must be replaced. Air and water pollution and land contamination levels must be monitored as input for a risk analysis. The output from risk analyses can be used for several purposes, such as siting and developing pollution control guidelines.

Long-Term Reform

14.30   Many countries apply a system whereby major enterprises monitor their own emissions, subject to review by the government. This system saves scarce administrative resources. However, it assumes that the government has the capability to control the monitoring activities of the enterprises, and that enforcement is carried out uncompromisingly. In Uzbekistan, regulations should be established for self-monitoring and reporting by enterprises, and making the reporting of false information a criminal violation. The purchase of necessary equipment will not be an overwhelming burden; the application of stack-gas analysis instruments would provide many enterprises with a mechanism for improving energy efficiency.

ENVIRONMENTAL AUDITING

Medium-Term Reform

14.31   Environmental auditing of industrial plants, municipal utilities, and mining facilities is an immediate necessity, and would be undertaken most effectively during the transitional years, in conjunction with analyses of the long-term economic viability of industries, mines, or municipalities. The purpose of these audits would be to identify the environmental problems associated with the facilities or sites in question and to recommend low cost solutions to these problems. Investigations of waste minimization and/or pollution prevention measures are an essential part of these audits. In some OECD countries, audits are carried out by private consulting firms paid by companies. It will be essential to provide early training in this area to ministry and branch staff, as well as to representatives of industry. Whereas industry should ultimately bear the full cost of environmental audits, they could be made available to industry as a service in the early years of the transition to a market-based economy--with some level of cost sharing.

D. TECHNICAL ASSISTANCE

14.32   Technical assistance will be required in preparing an institutional framework that will govern local-level environmental management. A full study should be undertaken to provide specific recommendations and an implementation schedule, detailed guidelines, financing criteria, operational procedures, and an accounting system for an Environmental Protection Fund and municipal governments. These efforts should be supported by a legal department, with attendant regional offices for strengthening the enforcement structure. Revision of water and air quality standards and the development of a institutions to manage river basins should be included in this exercise.

14.33   Training needs: priority should go to providing ongoing training to Ministry of Environment staff and the staff of other government agencies and enterprises, both locally and abroad, especially in adapting previous regulatory practices to a market-based economy.

14.34   The second training priority is to support institutional strengthening and human resource development in environmental planning and nature protection, including training for implementing environmental audits of industrial enterprises, applying risk management techniques, and studying environmental and natural resource economics and management. Scientific staff must be exposed to modern monitoring methods, as well as training in new technology. Fellowship training programs would be useful.

14.35   Technical assistance will also be required to develop a management system for the Ministry of Environment and its regional offices, simultaneously with a financial management and accounting system. These efforts should also focus on strengthening the EIA system and the process of public participation.

ANNEX 1

GOVERNMENT OF UZBEKISTAN - ORGANIZATIONAL STRUCTURE

PRESIDENT & CHAIRMAN OF THE CABINET OF MINISTERS

State Committee of Control
Ministry of Defense
Ministry of Foreign Affairs
Ministry of Internal Affairs
Ministry of Justice
National Security Service

SUPREME COUNCIL

Prosecutor's Office
State Committee on State Control
Central Bank
Sectoral Banks
Sixteen Committees of the Supreme Council
Supreme Court
Supreme Economic Court

PRIME MINISTER

DEPUTY PRIME MINISTER (FOREIGN ECONOMIC RELATIONS)

Ministries	State Committees	Central Services	Associations, Concerns & Companies
Foreign Economic Relations	External Assistance Management Department at Cabinet of Ministers		

DEPUTY PRIME MINISTER (ECONOMIC AFFAIRS)

Ministries	State Committees	Central Services	Associations, Concerns & Companies
Finance	Forecasting & Statistics	Tax Inspection	National Company for Tourism
Labor	State Property and Privatization		Association of Public Services
	Customs		Association of Leasing Enterprises

DEPUTY PRIME MINISTER (AGRICULTURE)

Ministries	State Committees	Central Services	Associations, Concerns & Companies
Agriculture	Construction of Water Systems	State-Cooperative Production and Construction Association	Fruit, Vegetable & Wine Concern
Land Reclamation & Water Management			Forestry Production Concern
State Customs Committee			Water Resources Construction
State Committee for Material & Agro-Industrial Equipment Maintenance			Fish Industry Concern
State Forestry Committee			Collective Farm Association

DEPUTY PRIME MINISTER (TRADE AND CONSUMER GOODS PRODUCTION)

Ministries	State Committees	Central Services	Associations, Concerns & Companies
			Union of Consumers' Cooperatives
			State Makhalliy Sanoat Corporation
			State Association for the Production of Light Industry Goods
			Savdo State Joint-Stock Association
			Union of Consumer Service Enterprises and Organization

DEPUTY PRIME MINISTER (INDUSTRY - ENERGY)

Ministries	State Committees	Central Services	Associations, Concerns & Companies
Automobile Transport	Precious Metals	Board for Light Industry	Association of Trade in Uzbekistan
Communications	Security of Mining Works	Board for Wood	Association of Contract and Trade
Energy/electrification		Processing	National Air Company
		Standards	State Concern - Bakery Products
		Metrology & Certification Ctr.	Uzbekistan Gas & Oil Concern
			Precious Metals Concern
			Association for the Production of Light Industrial Goods
			Corporation of Local Industry
			Furniture Industry Association
			Consumer Corporation
			Chemical Industry Concern
			Metallurgical Industry Concern
			Mechanical Engineering Concern
			Radio Electronics Concern
			Coal Mining Production Concern
			Central Asian Board of Railways
			Agricultural Machinery & Equipment,
			Motor Vehicles & Components Concern
			Research & Technical Support for Cotton Processing Industry
			Petroleum Products
			Petroleum and Gas
			Machinery Manufacturing
			Electronic/Electrical Equipment

DEPUTY PRIME MINISTER (CONSTRUCTION AND TRANSPORT)

Ministries	State Committees	Central Services	Associations, Concerns & Companies
Construction Materials	Research & Design Institution	Construction Board of	State Automobile Transport Joint-Stock
State Construction Committee	Construction	Tashkent	Corporation
Equipment Installation		Central Asia Railroads	State Industrial & Civil Construction
& Special Construction Works		Administration	Material Production
Automobile Roads		Administration for	Motor Road Construction & Operation
Municipal Services		Logging Production of	Contracts and Trade
Communications		of Structural Elements	Installation & Special Construction Work
			National Airline

DEPUTY PRIME MINISTER (SCIENCE AND CULTURE)

Ministries	State Committees	Central Services	Associations, Concerns & Companies
Public Education	Science & Technology	Archives	TV & Radio Broadcasting Company
Secondary & Higher Education	Environmental Protection	Information Agency	Cinematography Company
	Meteorology		
Culture	Sport		
	Publishing & Printing		

DEPUTY PRIME MINISTER (SOCIAL SECURITY & HEALTH)

Ministries	State Committees	Central Services	Association, Concerns & Companies
Housing	Science & Technology	Religious Affairs	State Television & Radio Broadcasting Company
Medical Care	Physical Culture & Sports	National Information	State Film Company
Social Security			
Labor			
Public Health			
Cultural Affairs			
Public Education			
State Press Committee			

ANNEX 2

ISSUES ASSOCIATED WITH THE INDUSTRIAL SECTOR

2.1　　　The industrial sector of Uzbekistan has depended heavily on the FSU production network. Enterprises in the FSU accounted for more that 80 percent of the sector's inputs and more than 60 percent of its outputs for industrial products and intermediates. The consumer and end-user goods-oriented subsectors, such as light industry, agro-industry, forest products & woodworking, and building materials, have been somewhat less dependent on the FSU, with 30 to 45 percent of their inputs and outputs being traded with the FSU. This dependency of the industrial sector of Uzbekistan for inputs and outputs is illustrated in Table 1.

Table 1
FSU Dependence of Uzbekistan's Industrial Sector on the FSU

	Inputs: % from FSU	Outputs: % to FSU	Share of Capacity Utilization (%)
All Industry	75	60	70
Metallurgy			
Ferrous metallurgy	55	50	65
Non-ferrous metallurgy	50	70	45
Metalworking & Machine Building			
Agro-machinery	80	60-65	41
Machine building	90	90	80-85
Cotton machinery	90	80	80
Radio electronics	70	70	81
Forestry Woodworking, Pulp & Paper	95	5	90
Building Materials	30	45	80
Chemical & Petrochemical	70	70	88
Light Industry	30-35	30-35	n.a
Agro-Industry	35	45	65-70
Other Industry	n.a.	n.a.	n.a

Source: Bank staff estimates.

2.2　　　The central question facing the industrial sector of Uzbekistan is how it can make the transition from being an integral component of the FSU production network to responding to the new market-based signals in Uzbekistan should the Government decide to pursue in structural reform.

2.3　　　In order to ensure the future viability of the industrial sector as new patterns of trade evolve and the sector begins to rely increasingly on international markets and sources of supply, the Government should implement the following priority policies:

- Policies to *increase the flexibility of enterprises to adjust to* market signals and to the context of international input and output prices; and

- Policies to reach *product standards and quality* to international levels as soon as possible.

2.4　　　The impact of the economic reform program on the industrial sector will be significant. It is important that the impact of the proposed reform scenario on the industrial subsectors be assessed and then a set of priorities be developed for formulating sectoral and subsector-specific policies.[1]

2.5   Even though most of the subsectors and their enterprises that are reviewed here reported that they were profitable under the 1991 cost and price structures, it is impossible to ascertain whether the enterprises were intrinsically viable and whether the enterprises can remain viable as the prices of inputs and outputs continue to shift in the FSU. This uncertainty is due mainly to the fact that such a high proportion of inputs and outputs are procured from and shipped to the FSU, where resources had been allocated centrally under artificial transfer-pricing mechanisms.

2.6   The degree of transfer-pricing subsidy can be inferred to some extent by

Table 2
Profitability (percent) Based on Value Added at Domestic and World Prices

Subsector	at Domestic Prices[1]	at World Prices[2]	Variance
Fuel Industry	34	46	12
Metallurgy	61	39	-22
Metal Working & Machine Building	29	-3	-32
Woodworking		-16	
Pulp and Paper	31	30	
Building Materials	27		
Chemicals	20	9	-11
Light Industry	17	-1	-18
Agro Industry	17	-88	-105

Sources: Goskomprognostat.
Senik-Leygonie C. and Hughes G. (1992), "Industrial Profitability and Trade among Former Soviet Republics."

Notes: The significant negativity of the value added at world prices for Agro-Industry is due to the fact that in compiling the source data the researchers have included losses at the farm level as inputs to the Agro-Processing subsector. Excluding farm losses, which are often as high as 40% in many cases, the value added for Agro-Industry is likely to be comparable to Light Industry, whose capital and labor and energy intensities are similar.

comparing the domestic value added (DVA) with world value added (WVA), defined for this section as the percentage of value added at world price. This measure would be somewhat more practical for the industrial sector, since most of its enterprises produce tradables. To assess the degree of adjustment required by the subsectors during the transition, Table 2 shows the profitability of the subsectors according to DVA and WVA in a steady-state situation. This comparison supports assessing the present impact (the DVA) and the future implications (the WVA) of the changes that are taking place.[2]

2.7   The variances between DVA and WVA in Table 2 indicate the extent to which a subsector might have been subsidized through the FSU transfer pricing mechanisms. The greater the variance, the more difficult the adjustment period will be for the subsector. The likelihood of survival of the subsector will be determined by the value added at world prices. Thus, these data provide some direction for

---

[1] Cost and other data were not available in sufficient detail to support full analyses of these issues. However, based on the information that was obtained, certain hypotheses about the issues could be formed. Despite distortions due to transfer pricing and reporting deficiencies, the available figures provide valuable clues about the degree of subsidization and the likely internal efficiency among the subsectors, and help support some of the initial hypotheses and formulate additional ones.

[2] A recent study by Senik-Leygonie and Hughes (1992) is helpful in providing some estimates of value added at world prices in the steady state and provides an indicative basis for comparison as illustrated in Table 2.

developing hypotheses; however, this analysis is merely a starting point for further studies to support decisionmaking of any kind, and should be treated only as such.

PRELIMINARY SUBSECTOR ASSESSMENT AND OUTLOOK

2.8   Certain conceptual hypotheses might be formulated to evaluate each subsector. For example:

- The subsectors that depend less on the FSU for inputs and outputs are likely to be more responsive to domestic reform measures.

- The subsectors whose value added at world prices is negative are not likely to be viable at world prices unless restructured to become more competitive.

- The likelihood of domestic supply response by the subsectors will depend on the degree to which they serve the domestic market and on the capital intensity of the subsector. The contribution to the economy will be greater among subsectors whose value added at world prices is higher and which can lend themselves more readily to the adjustments required by the reform program. This ease of adjustment can be inferred in some measure from the structural flexibility of the subsector, indicated by its lower capital and energy intensities.

- The impact (positive) on external trade is likely to be greater for those subsectors whose value added at world prices is higher and which serve external markets more.

2.9   The following is a brief assessment of each of the subsectors in terms of its ability to adjust to the changing conditions and its likely response to the adjustments under the reform program being proposed. (Table 3 summarizes this assessment.)

Fuel and Power

2.10   The higher profitability projected for the fuel industry at world prices is due to the fact that low fuel prices have historically been used to subsidize the economy and higher priority industries. Thus, at world prices, the value added by this subsector is expected to be higher. The subsector is not likely to require operating subsidies if prices are liberalized. However, given its high capital intensity, any increase in output will require a significant amount of capital. Thus, given the likely capital constraints in the future, the supply response of this subsector to the reform program may only be significant in the medium term.

Metallurgy

2.11   The large economies of scale used in metallurgy would make it the most competitive of the industrial subsectors of Uzbekistan. These economies of scale are reflected in the lower labor intensity and the capital intensity of the subsector and apparently compensate the high energy intensity of the sector.[3]

2.12   Most of the output in this subsector serves external markets. Despite its high value added in world prices, the variance from value added at domestic prices is the highest for this sector (after machine building). Thus, it is likely that adjustment will be difficult for this sector. However, owing to its high value added, its likelihood of survival is high, but its contribution to external trade under the reform program, while positive because of its export profile, is likely to be undermined in the long run by its high energy intensity. However, because it can reach its world export potential almost immediately, it should make a significant contribution to the economy during the transition process.

2.13   Even though metallurgy is highly profitable at world prices and depends less on the FSU than do chemicals or machine building, it has suffered the greatest drop in output (other than chemicals) in the first half of 1992, and the greatest decline in labor productivity. While some of this decline was in the ferrous segment due to a shortage of steel scrap,[4] ferrous metallurgy alone cannot explain all of the decline, since it comprises only 8 percent of metallurgy overall. It is likely that some of the changes might have occurred in the gold and uranium operations.

Machine Building

2.14   Machine building, which largely served the military industrial complex, was a high-priority subsector. Because it depends highly on the FSU for inputs and markets,[5] it is unlikely to provide a domestic supply response to the reform programs. Owing to the high variance between the value added at domestic prices and at world prices, it will have great difficulty in making the required adjustments. Furthermore, its negative value added at world prices and its inordinately high labor intensity will make its survival unlikely without external support or major restructuring. Given its size and the fact that it imports more than it exports, the impact on external trade under the reform program will be moderately negative.

2.15   However, this subsector enjoyed the highest average new investment rate (as a percentage of net fixed assets) over the past 15 years. In addition to its high investment level, it also enjoyed the highest levels of investment in new technology. Thus, it has the most modern equipment and technology among the subsectors (see Table 4). For some of its segments, the subsector could have a dominant position in the world markets they serve--for example, cotton-picking machines.

---

[3] The low capital intensity of the subsector might actually be an anomaly in the data, since energy intensity generally correlates with capital intensity. The capital intensity of this subsector should be at least as high as the building materials subsector, if not more.

[4] It is interesting to note that the shortage of scrap is reportedly being caused by the recent liberalization, the transfer to collectives, and the autonomous management of enterprises. Most organizations, now tend to conserve materials and equipment and repair and use them longer, as well as generating less scrap in production.

[5] Its capacity far exceeds domestic demand present and projectable.

Table 3
Subsectoral Analysis

	Fuel & Power	Metallurgy	Machine Building	Forestry Woodworking, Pulp & Paper	Material	Building Chemical	Light Industry	Agro-Industry
Share of Sector (%)								
Output	6.6	10.8	10.4	1.5	3.3	4.4	42.8	18.1
Employment	5.1	6.4	22.8	2.8	7.6	4.8	36.7	10.8
Assets	27.5	8.4	16.7	1.6	7.8	14.6	13.3	6.4
Index of:[a]								
Capital Intensity	4.17	0.78	1.61	1.07	2.36	3.32	0.31	0.35
Energy Intensity	2.86	2.32	0.62	0.57	2.24	6.16	0.25	0.23
Labor Intensity	12	9	33	28	35	16	13	9
Dependence on FSU								
For Inputs (%)	n.a.	50	80	95	30	70	35	35
For Outputs (%)	n.a.	70	70	5	45	70	35	45
Value Added (%)								
Domestic Prices	34	61	29	31	27	20	17	17
World Prices	46	39	-3	7	n.a.	9	-1	-88

Sources: Goskomprognostat; Energy data: Ministry of Power; various enterprises.

Note: The analysis in this table should be regarded as indicative; rather than prescriptive, several possible distortions are likely to be present in the data (for example, as mentioned earlier, transfer pricing makes the domestic financial data inconsistent with what they might be under free-market pricing). The world price data, as described in the source information, seemed to have been based on rigorous calculations by Soviet planners to track "shadow prices" for their planned economy and thus to evaluate the opportunity cost of their allocation decisions. However, these data impute world prices only for FSU markets and, as such, assume freight costs, albeit at world prices, to and from FSU locations. Export freight is not accounted for.

[a]   Capital Intensity = % of Assets in Subsector/% of Output in Subsector; Energy Intensity = % Energy Consumed by Subsector/% of Output in Subsector Labor; and Intensity = # of employees per 1 million rubles of output.

Chemicals

2.16   The chemicals subsector is highly capital and energy intensive. The positive world profitability indicated can be explained by its lower-than-average labor intensity. Moreover, its profitability might possibly have been higher had it not suffered the greatest reduction in new investment throughout the 1980s.

2.17   The Chemicals subsector is also more vulnerable to the impending changes. While this subsector is profitable at world prices and slightly less dependent than machine building on the FSU, its product mix is skewed more towards commodity items, such as acids, ammonia, and fertilizers, for which international prices often fluctuate widely and margins are generally very thin. Competitive advantage in this capital and energy-intensive business requires consistently high levels of investment.

Table 4
New Investment in Fixed Assets
(as a percent of net fixed assets)

	1976-80	1981-85	1986-89	Percentage Decline: 1980-89
All Industry	**35.10**	**32.30**	**23.70**	**32.48**
Fuel and Power Industry	28.70	24.40	21.80	24.04
Metallurgy	35.30	31.10	26.20	25.78
Metalworking and Machine Building	39.30	37.00	29.00	26.21
Forestry Woodworking, Pulp and Paper	32.20	29.40	21.60	32.92
Building Materials	31.60	23.70	21.50	31.96
Chemical and Petrochemical	46.80	38.60	19.20	58.97
Light Industry	37.00	45.30	24.60	33.51
Agro-Industry	32.30	30.10	22.80	29.41

Source: Goskomprognostat.

2.18   Because the subsector is highly integrated with the FSU, and given its high capital intensity, the domestic supply response to the reform program will be slight. In this connection it should be noted that, if the domestic prices of fertilizers and pesticides are liberalized, imports should also immediately be allowed.

Light Industry

2.19   Light industry has traditionally been a low-priority subsector and thus received little or no transfer pricing support, and controls on consumer prices were generally more rigid. Because a large proportion of its inputs and markets are local, and given its low capital and labor intensity, it is likely to generate a significant supply response to the reform program. Not counting textiles and yarn (80 percent of output), the value added at world prices might in fact be higher than indicated. Thus, given the reform programs, including the privatization of the smaller enterprises in this subsector, the subsector is likely to become self-supporting during the reform period. Given its potentially negative value added and its low level of exports,[6] the subsector overall will probably make a negative contribution to external trade under the reform program. The contribution of the subsector to the overall economy would be positive.

2.20   Output from light industry increased in the first six months of 1992, and its labor productivity, which is above the sectoral average, showed an almost negligible decline over this period. The subsector had a very high investment rate in the first half of the last decade and one of the two

---

[6] Even though cotton is the largest export commodity for the country, processed cotton exports, including yarn and textiles, constitute only 44 percent of the output of the sector. Processed cotton exports to the FSU are only 26 percent of the output of the sector. The majority of the cotton exported by Uzbekistan is raw cotton and is counted as an agricultural export. Of the 1.5 million tons of cotton produced in Uzbekistan, only about 150,000 tons are processed in Uzbekistan at 120 cotton processing plants. The rest is sold as raw cotton. Cotton processing accounts for 80 percent of the output of the light industry subsector.

highest investment rates in the sector over the last 10 years, most probably in cotton and textiles. Spinning and weaving plants seemed to be running at capacity, and the equipment, while somewhat dated, seems to be in good operating condition.

Agro-Industry

2.21   The significant negativity of the world profitability of agro-industry is due to the fact that the losses at the farm level are treated as inputs consumed by the industry itself. While this situation does truly reflect the efficiency of the subsector (whose profile is likely to be slightly better than the profits for light industry, due to similar capital intensity and lower labor intensity), it is indicative of the degree of waste at the farm level. As with light industry, widespread privatization in agro-industry is possible in the short term and would help to ensure that the subsector becomes viable.

2.22   Thus, reform is also likely to generate a significant supply response from this subsector. The sector is also likely to become self-supporting if the reform measures are implemented, especially those aspects of the reform package that would allow the food enterprises, which are leased or privatized, to procure inputs on a competitive basis and to sell their products in a free market. This subsector is also likely to make a positive contribution to external trade.

POLICY FOCUS

2.23   Sector-specific policy for the industrial sector should focus on (1) procurement of inputs, (2) energy intensity, and (3) capital intensity.

Procurement of Inputs

2.24   Materials, including raw materials and purchased parts but excluding energy, account for as much as 69 percent of the total operating costs of the industrial sector. In some subsectors, such as light industry and agro-industry, materials account for as much as 88 percent of total costs. Thus, this component of the cost structure of the sector is the one that requires the most attention. The challenge is not only to keep production going but also to procure an adequate amount of raw materials while also minimizing the cost of those materials. Thus, procurement is a critical function for which policy support, training, and technical assistance are necessary.

2.25   The central problem with material costs is that most items must reportedly be procured from single-source suppliers. Up to 80 percent of all material inputs must be procured from suppliers that are apparently monopolies within the FSU for the particular input required for production.

2.26   Some possible policy options include (1) phasing out the state order system not only for agricultural produce but also for other industry related inputs-outputs, (2) enhancing the ability of enterprises to procure more outside the FSU, (3) motivating enterprises to strengthen their procurement skills and procedures, and (4) providing technical and other assistance to enable enterprises to do so. The desired policy changes and approaches are as follows:

> • The ability of the enterprise to procure and diversify outside the FSU can be improved by (1) reducing the role of the state in commercial activities, (2) allowing the enterprise to retain more of its foreign exchange earnings, (3)

promoting trade and transport links with other countries,[7] (4) developing information management, and (5) providing training.

- Enterprise managers must also become more motivated to reduce material costs. This can be accomplished by appropriate changes in accountability and enterprise governance (see chapter 6).

2.27   In addition to reducing material costs, enterprises must be pushed to use materials more efficiently. They can do so by rationalizing products and processes; programs to institute such projects should be established and adequate provisions made for them in the medium term in the capital budgets of the enterprises. Material use should also be tracked more efficiently and made one of the performance criteria for measuring managerial performance.

Energy Intensity

2.28   Energy intensity (see Table 5) is particularly relevant for the process-oriented subsectors, such as chemicals, metallurgy, and building materials, where the plant and equipment are relatively old and the cost impact of energy at world prices might be severe. Even though profitability at world prices should be positive for the chemical and metallurgy subsectors, competitiveness could be enhanced significantly by managing this factor. Chemicals, which is the most energy intensive, needs particular attention.

2.29   One way to generate the appropriate operational priorities for energy conservation at the enterprise level is to establish an appropriate energy-pricing policy (see chapter 10). The energy intensity of the various products of the critical sectors must be monitored carefully, and appropriate conservation measures taken to control any further increase in energy intensity. Companies in many industrialized countries have achieved significant marginal reductions in energy intensity by implementing such conservation measures as improved scheduling and line balancing. The performance indicators in the management contract must include specific goals for reducing energy intensity. In process-oriented industries, any major reduction in energy intensity generally requires a significant amount of capital for modifying process. A study should to be undertaken immediately to identify and prioritize the required investments for yielding the greatest reduction in energy intensity at the least cost in the shortest possible time.

Capital Intensity

2.30   The competitiveness of the sector could be severely undermined if capital intensity is not managed adequately. Policy measures are required at the enterprise level to manage this factor more effectively. Two components of capital require attention in this regard: (1) working capital, and (2) fixed capital.

---

[7] Some progress has already been made in this regard with new rail links between Uzbekistan and China (links with Pakistan and Iran are under construction). Trade and transport agreements are also being negotiated with these and other countries. These initiatives should receive high priority as part of the trade policy of the country.

2.31   The *working capital intensity*[8] of the sector is somewhat high compared with a group of Western companies[9] whose aggregate product profile is similar to that of the sector (see Table 6).

2.32   Thus, even though the amount of current assets employed increased dramatically in 1992 owing to inflation, working capital intensity appears to have increased only slightly. At world prices, this gap could translate into a significant competitive disadvantage. Actual working capital employed (current assets minus current liabilities) has increased by about R130 billion, which has been financed by short-term bank loans at 8 to 14 percent interest in most cases.

2.33   *Fixed capital intensity* is somewhat more difficult to measure because the costs have historically been based on the transfer prices of the central planning system and are probably not very meaningful because the prices do not reflect the

Table 5
Energy Intensity of Certain Products in Critical Subsectors

Subsectors	Products	Typical Western Co. kwhr/ton
Chemical	Urea	180
	Kaprolactam (Nylon)	2,300
	Ammonia	1,400
Metallurgy	Steel (Electric)	623
Building Materials	Cement (Dry)	160
	Cement (Wet)	116

Source: Uzbek Enterprises.

present replacement costs even within the FSU. However, almost 70 percent of the equipment in the sector might be less than 10 years old (Table 7). The anomaly in the valuation must be corrected immediately, since pricing policies based on this valuation (that is, the level of depreciation) might significantly decapitalize the sector. Normally, such revaluation should be made according to prevailing and generally accepted accounting procedures. However, until such standards become available in the country, the urgency of the situation demands that plant and equipment be revalued to appropriate levels according to accounting and control mechanisms presently available to the enterprises. Some enterprises have already begun such projects.

2.34   Revaluing the fixed-asset base will necessitate that management take adequate actions to maintain or increase utilization levels. While much of the recent decline in utilization may have been due to inadequate supplies of raw materials, many other areas might be addressed so as to maintain utilization levels. For example, the enterprises in the sector do not seem to maintain inventories of machine-repair parts on site.

2.35   Appropriate capital budgeting functions should be incorporated into the organizations of the enterprises and concerns and required training should be provided. Such measures would provide a

---

[8] This is generally the current assets (less liquid assets such as cash or marketable securities) required to generate a unit of revenue. However, in this case, a surrogate (accounts receivable + inventory/revenues) has been used owing to the paucity of data.

[9] The companies are ABB (machine building), RhonePoulenc (chemicals), St. Gobain (building materials), Nestle (agro-industry and consumer products), and Champion International (forest products).

disciplined and efficient allocation of resources to projects that are most viable, and avoid the likelihood of inordinate increases in the fixed-capital intensities of the enterprises.

PRODUCT STANDARDS AND QUALITY

2.36   Pro forma viability in terms of world prices might not be very meaningful if the enterprises cannot ultimately sell their products in world markets or against world competitors in domestic or FSU markets. This could easily happen if the sector reaches parity with world prices but not with world product standards. Under those circumstances, the sector would not only be unable to export to hard currency markets, but it would also be retrenched from its traditional FSU markets. Thus, the sector must make additional efforts to increase the pace at which its products are being upgraded to meet international standards.

2.37   While several activities and programs are under way to upgrade product standards to international levels (for example, a packaging machinery enterprise in the machine building subsector is in the final stages of having its products certified to ISO 9000 standards), the level of activity and emphasis does not reflect the urgency of the situation. A sectorwide effort must be undertaken immediately to upgrade products comprehensively to international standards. The basic technical capability to accomplish this goal clearly exists. What is lacking is (1) an adequate understanding of the specific technical requirements that must be met (these can be met through technical assistance) and (2) priorities at the policy and enterprise level for implementing the required level of activity.

Table 6
Working Capital Intensity

	Uzbek Industry	Western Companies
1991	0.40	0.35
1992	0.41	n.a.

Source: Goskomprognostat, Bank Staff estimates, and Annual Reports.

Note: The 1992 figure could be grossly understated due to insufficient accounting standards. Actual inventory receivable levels could be substantially higher. Thus, these figures should be considered only approximate and as notional.

Table 7
Age of Equipment
(As of 1989)

Age	Distribution
1 to 5 years	40%
6 to 10 years	29%
11 to 20 years	20%
Over 20 years old	11%

Source: Goskomprognostat.

Technical Assistance

2.38   Technical assistance for defining and setting goals for product and process modifications that are required to meet international standards would support the substantial technical talent available in these subsectors. Since the industrial sector comprises a large number of enterprises, disseminating the required knowhow in a centralized fashion might not be feasible. However, other options might be worth considering.

- A technical assistance fund could be set up for the enterprises, to be accessed directly on a competitive basis for specific projects. The proceeds could be used to retain the necessary experts in the respective industries to provide the required knowhow and guidance not only for upgrading products and processes to international standards but also for penetrating international markets.

- The enterprises could also seek out joint venture partners who could provide the required technological guidance and access to markets. Important in this regard is that the current joint-venture trend in the sector--where the foreign partner provides the technology or capital and takes his return in kind through countertrade or barter agreements--should be considered carefully. While capital, technology, and market access are the positive aspects of this relationship, barter agreements often require surrendering more value than would be the case if cash were rendered. In the long run, these agreements may tend to decapitalize the enterprise. A better alternative is to have an attractive environment for direct foreign investment, which would obviate the need for most such arrangements.

ANNEX 3

ARAL SEA ISSUES

BACKGROUND[1]

The Aral Sea lies between Kazakhstan and Uzbekistan in a vast geological depression in the Kyzylkum and Karakum deserts. In 1960, the Aral Sea was the fourth largest inland lake in the world. Since then, however, it has shrunk significantly due to the nearly total cutoff of river inflow from the Amu Dar'ya (river) and Syr Dar'ya as a result of heavy withdrawals for irrigation. By 1989 the sea level had fallen by 14.3 meters, and the surface area had shrunk from 68,000 km2 to 37,000 km2. The salinity of the sea had increased to 2.8 times its 1960 level.

The Aral Sea basin extends over 690,000 km2, including the republics of Kazakhstan, Kyrgyzstan, Tajikistan, Turkmenistan, and Uzbekistan. A small portion of its headwaters is located in Afghanistan, Iran and China. The basin is formed by two of the largest rivers of Central Asia--Amu Dar'ya and Syr Dar'ya--both fed by the snow melts and glaciers from the mountains. The Amu Dar'ya sources are located primarily in Tajikistan, with a few watercourses originating in northeastern Afghanistan. The Syr Dar'ya originates mainly in Kyrgyzstan. It runs across small portions of Tajikistan and Uzbekistan and through the Kazakh provinces of Chimkent and Kzyl-Orda.

The total population of the Aral basin is estimated at 35 million, based on the 1989 census. Uzbekistan, with 21.7 million in 1992, is the most populated among the countries in the region; Kazakhstan has a population of 16.5 million, 2.48 million of whom live in the Aral basin. The rate of natural population increase in the region averaged 2.54 percent in the period 1979-89, compared with a national (FSU) rate of 0.87 percent.

The Aral basin has three distinctive ecological zones: the mountains, the deserts, and the Aral, with its deltas. The Tian Shan and Pamir Mountains in the south and southwest are characterized by high altitudes (with peaks over 7,000 m) and by high moisture coefficients, with average annual precipitation ranging from 800 to 1,600 mm. The mountains host large forest reserves and some national parks. In their foothills and valleys, soil and temperature conditions are favorable for agriculture. The lowland deserts of Karakum and Kyzylkum cover most of the basin area, and are characterized by low precipitation (less than 100 mm/year) and high evaporation rates. Both the rivers' banks and deltas and the Aral Sea islands are characterized by a variety of vegetation and wildlife resources. For example, the Barsakelmes Island, in the main part of the Aral Sea, is a natural reserve for endangered species such as the Kulan (Asiatic wild burro) and Siagak, an ancient variety of antelope. The sea itself was the habitat for more than 24 species of fish, and for several other aquatic organisms.

---

[1] For reference, the issues surrounding the Aral Sea Basin have been studied by several individuals and organizations; in particular, UNEP has produced the Diagnostic Study for the Development of an Action Plan for the Aral Sea, which was issued in July 1992. This report presents a comprehensive analysis of the causes of the Aral Sea crisis and provides a basis for elaboration and analysis of the strategies for future activities for mitigating the ecological disaster.

ISSUES

The main issues pertaining to the Aral Sea basin area are as follows: the reduction of the sea, the destruction of its aquatic ecosystem, the lowering of soil quality in the Aral Sea basin, the pollution of surface and groundwater of the delta draining into the Aral Sea, the depressed economy, and the adverse health impact on the population due to the absence of potable water and inadequate sanitation.

Both the causes and regional effects of the Aral Sea shrinkage can be enumerated. Inefficient irrigation practices coupled with heavy chemical applications, cultivation of cotton and rice, and inappropriate development policies are among the important causes. For the last three decades, Soviet policy in the region focused on massive irrigation projects along the Amu Dar'ya and Syr Dar'ya, with the primary goal of creating a Central Asian cotton belt. Urban and industrial water use, though still a small proportion of total water use, has also risen. The irrigation techniques have led to high rates of leakage and evaporation, as well as to waterlogging and salinity build-up. As a result, the two river flows that feed the Aral Sea are nearly completely expended before they ever reach the Sea.

During the past decade numerous reports and articles have been written by experts, both national and foreign, on this crisis, attracting worldwide attention. Environmental experts, scientists, engineers, and economists from all over the world have joined their counterparts from the FSU. Their findings have been presented in several publications during the past decade and discussed in many international seminars. Recently, in June 1992, the Stockholm Environment Institute, Boston Center, published the results of a microcomputer model for simulating current water balances and evaluating water management strategies in the Aral Sea region. The study presented a picture of an unfolding and deepening crisis situation and concluded that, in the absence of an action plan to save the Aral Sea, its surface areas would decrease from its 1987 level of 41,000 square kilometers to 9,000 square kilometers by the year 2015, and that the Sea would turn into several small residual brine lakes.

The United Nations Environment Program (UNEP) considers that, in terms of its ecological, economic, and social consequences, the Aral Sea is one of the most staggering ecological disasters of the twentieth century. Recognizing the crucial need to save the disappearing Aral Sea and the need to provide an overall perspective of the Aral region, the UNEP issued a diagnostic study of the state of its environment, its population, and its economics in July 1992. The report presents a comprehensive analysis of the causes of the Aral Sea crisis, but it does not recommend a specific action plan. It provides, however, a basis for an elaboration and analysis of the strategies for future activities for mitigating the ecological disaster.

THE BANK'S ASSESSMENT OF THE ARAL SEA CRISIS[2]

Despite a decade of studies by national and international experts, a viable plan for addressing the Aral Sea problems has not been formulated. Ideas and suggestions abound, but their technical, economic, financial, and political feasibility has not been examined. The studies indicate that the solutions may be extremely expensive and difficult to finance, and would take decades to implement. Thirty major action programs suggested in these reports broadly cover the following categories of action:

---

[2] This assessment is based on numerous reports written by experts, and on the findings of the Aral Sea Reconnaissance Mission, which visited the Aral Sea basin in September 1992.

- Actions proposed to increase the inflows to the Aral Sea (4 major projects and programs)

- Actions proposed to save a part of the water currently used for irrigation and other purposes and use the saved water to increase the inflows to the Aral Sea (14 major projects and programs)

- Measures to improve the health and environment of the population in the Aral Sea region (8 major projects and programs)

- Rationalization of water rights in the Aral Sea basin across Central Asia and Kazakhstan (4 major projects and programs)

The technical, economic, financial, and political feasibility these programs has not been determined. They seem to constitute a master program, costing around $US30 to 50 billion and requiring a period of 40 to 50 years to implement. The authors of these programs have not considered how essential these projects are, who will finance them, and whether the republics are willing to share such large costs.

The proposed projects and programs underline one overriding objective: to increase the inflows to the Aral Sea and restore it to its pre-disaster conditions, or to some level that would save the sea. The rationale of this objective is not clear.

The feasibility of some grand schemes for increasing the inflows to the Aral Sea--such as diverting the rivers flowing north to the Arctic Sea, or transferring water from the Caspian Sea, is questionable. Aside from their huge costs, these schemes could involve serious political and environmental issues.

The feasibility and sustainability of some proposals for increasing the inflows to the Aral Sea by reducing the existing uses is also questionable. They include, for example, limiting water deliveries from the Amu and Syr Rivers for irrigation and other purposes, and reducing the area of cotton and rice crops. It may be necessary to take these actions for other economic reasons, but it seems unrealistic to expect that the water saved from these actions would be available for increasing the inflows to the Aral Sea on a sustainable long-term basis.

The Bank's assessment of the Aral Sea crisis is classified under three categories: (1) Aral Sea and Aral Sea-related issues; (2) regional issues; and (3) developmental issues that should receive high priority, although they are not directly related to the Aral Sea problems.

Aral Sea and Aral Sea - Related Issues

- Views differ and uncertainty exists about the extent of the existing and future adverse effects of the Aral Sea crisis. The problems appear to be more manageable than has been indicated by previous reports.

- The proposals to divert water from outside the basin (from the Arctic rivers and Caspian Sea) to fill the Aral Sea do not appear to be viable.

- Conserving the water resources of the basin by reducing waste, improving water management, diversifying crops, and other measures are important measures and should receive priority. However, the political feasibility and economic justification of diverting the saved water to fill the Aral Sea is questionable.

- The available information indicates that it is not possible to restore the Sea to its predisaster conditions. However, it may be necessary to stabilize the Sea at a sustainable level based on available flows.

- The living conditions of the people in the zone around the Aral Sea that has been seriously affected by the changes in the Sea are deplorable. The absence of potable water, water-borne diseases, inadequate health facilities, the depressed economy, the absence of employment opportunities, the adverse effects of sand and salt storms, and the deteriorating ecosystem are some of the major problems. This disaster zone covers parts of Kazakhstan, Uzbekistan, and Turkmenistan. Improving the living conditions and environment of the people in this area should receive high priority. The suggestions made in some reports to shift the most severely affected population appear to be unrealistic. The people need developmental assistance, not migration assistance.

Regional Issues

- The Agreement signed on February 15, 1992, among the Aral Sea Basin republics and the Protocol and Resolutions established from April to August 1992 for cooperation on management, utilization, and protection of water resources, and for joint measures for the solution of the Aral Sea problems, are commendable. However, a preliminary review indicates that they are not adequate enough to constitute binding legal treaties. Some subdued complaints about the fairness of allocations are already simmering, and other riparian countries (China, Afghanistan, and Iran) have not been consulted. It is advisable that these agreements be improved to internationally accepted standards to avoid possible conflicts in the future.

- The republics have established an Interministerial Committee and two River Basin Commissions (BVOs) for allocating water, monitoring water use and quality, and undertaking data collection, analysis, management, and forecasting. These arrangements are working satisfactorily and are commendable. However, the capacity and effectiveness of these institutions should be enhanced by increasing their decisionmaking and regulatory powers and providing them with advanced equipment, facilities, and technologies to play their role most effectively.

- The need for comprehensive planning and the management of water resources, both quantity and quality, and for the short and long terms, was stressed at some meetings. Given the scarcity of water resources, increasing demands, and the fact that the river flows have been almost fully diverted for irrigation and other purposes at present, the need and importance of developing strategies for comprehensive management of the water resources should be underscored.

- The high caliber of researchers and scientists from research institutes and academies of sciences dealing with water resources, ecology, and pollution control is impressive. However, talent continues to be depleted owing to the lack of funds, advanced equipment and facilities, and career development opportunities. These problems require urgent attention.

- The Central Asian Research Institute of the region has now become an institute of the republic in which it was located. The need for a regional institution to address regional and Aral Sea research requirements and to provide research support to the BVOs should be considered a high priority.

Developmental Issues

The republics' concern about their country-specific development issues and the high priority they attach to water supply and sanitation, health, ecology, population, salinity and waterlogging, drainage, pollution control, and food self-sufficiency programs in their respective countries is overwhelming. These programs should receive high priority for external assistance.

Statistical Appendix

Statistical Appendix - Contents

---

[1]   It is assumed that GNP is identical to GDP.

Uzbekistan
Table 1.1: Population and Employment - Summary Table

	1985	1989	1990	1991
		(in thousands)		
Total Population	17868.0	19785.2	20227.3	20613.3
Males	8808.9	9773.9	9992.3	10183.0
Females	9059.1	10011.3	10235.0	10430.3
Urban	7200.8	8032.8	8212.3	8265.9
Rural	10667.2	11752.4	12015.0	12347.4
Under 16	7611.5	8496.7	8686.7	8886.1
Active Age/1.	8813.5	9716.0	9948.3	10125.2
Over Active Age	1443.0	1572.5	1592.3	1601.9
		(in percent)		
Total Population	100.0	100.0	100.0	100.0
Males	49.3	49.4	49.4	49.4
Females	50.7	50.6	50.6	50.6
Urban	40.3	40.6	40.6	40.1
Rural	59.7	59.4	59.4	59.9
Under 16	42.6	42.9	42.9	43.1
Active Age/1.	49.3	49.1	49.2	49.1
Over Active Age	8.1	7.9	7.9	7.8
		(in percent)		
Total Employment	100.0	100.0	100.0	100.0
Material Sphere	73.7	74.1	74.1	74.6
Industry and construction	23.1	24.6	24.1	22.6
agriculture and forestry	37.9	38.5	39.3	41.5
transport & communication	4.4	3.2	3.1	3.0
other material sectors	8.2	7.8	7.6	7.4
Non-Material Sphere	26.3	25.9	25.9	25.4
Employment by enterprise type	100.0	100.0	100.0	100.0
state sector	71.8	67.0	65.6	64.6
collective farms	15.4	13.8	13.7	14.2
private sector	9.9	13.8	14.9	16.9
cooperatives & other	2.9	5.4	5.8	4.2

Source: State Statistical and Forecasting Committee of Uzbekistan (Goskomprognostat)
1/ women:16-55, men:16-60

UZBEKISTAN
Table 1.2: Employment by Sector and by Enterprise

	1985	1989	1990	1991
	(in thousands)			
Total Employment	**6619.1**	**7624.1**	**7940.8**	**8322.7**
Material Sphere	**4875.5**	**5647.0**	**5884.0**	**6208.3**
Industry	1015.1	1183.8	1201.4	1202.1
construction	516.7	689.5	710.0	680.0
agriculture	2505.4	2932.8	3115.3	3451.4
forestry	5.5	5.3	4.9	5.0
transport & communication	293.1	242.0	250.0	250.8
trade & public catering	443.6	453.6	458.6	470.0
other material sector	96.1	140.0	143.8	149.0
Non-Material Sphere	**1743.6**	**1977.1**	**2056.8**	**2114.4**
communal service	149.4	197.0	193.9	191.7
science and research	120.2	99.8	103.4	99.3
education, culture and art	792.3	948.7	997.8	1038.3
health & public security	376.5	445.8	468.0	492.7
banking & finance	21.8	23.2	23.3	24.7
administration	111.6	114.1	118.9	118.6
other non-material services	171.8	148.5	151.5	149.1
Employment by enterprise type				
state sector	4753.5	5109.3	5211.1	5379.1
collective farms	1019.0	1055.8	1085.4	1185.6
private sector	657.8	1050.2	1184.3	1405.9
cooperatives & other	188.8	408.8	460.0	352.1
	(in percent)			
Total Employment	100.0	100.0	100.0	100.0
Material Sphere	73.7	74.1	74.1	74.6
Industry	15.3	15.5	15.1	14.4
construction	7.8	9.0	8.9	8.2
agriculture	37.9	38.5	39.2	41.5
forestry	0.1	0.1	0.1	0.1
transport & communication	4.4	3.2	3.1	3.0
trade & public catering	6.7	5.9	5.8	5.6
other material sector	1.5	1.8	1.8	1.8
Non-Material Sphere	26.3	25.9	25.9	25.4
communal service	2.3	2.6	2.4	2.3
science and research	1.8	1.3	1.3	1.2
education, culture and art	12.0	12.4	12.6	12.5
health & public security	5.7	5.8	5.9	5.9
banking & finance	0.3	0.3	0.3	0.3
administration	1.7	1.5	1.5	1.4
other non-material services	2.6	1.9	1.9	1.8
Employment by enterprise type				
state sector	71.8	67.0	65.6	64.6
collective farms	15.4	13.8	13.7	14.2
private sector	9.9	13.8	14.9	16.9
cooperatives & other	2.9	5.4	5.8	4.2

Source: State Statistical and Forecasting Committee of Uzbekistan

UZBEKISTAN

Table 1.3: Empoyment in State Sector by Profession

(As of September of 1990, in thousands)

	Managment	Specialists	Other Employees	Workers
Total	**362.3**	**1266.4**	**103.2**	**3496.4**
Material Sphere	**207.7**	**326.4**	**47.5**	**2817.2**
Industry	68.4	91.2	11.2	922.6
construction	51.9	62.7	7.0	435.3
agriculture	27.4	91.8	12.6	946.8
forestry	0.4	0.9	0.1	3.5
transport	10.7	19.8	5.7	183.0
communication	1.4	2.0	0.1	8.9
trade & public catering	43.9	47.0	10.0	305.9
other material sector	3.5	11.1	0.8	11.1
Non-Material Sphere	**154.6**	**939.9**	**55.7**	**679.2**
communal service	9.3	16.1	3.5	101.8
science and research	10.1	43.9	1.5	28.9
education	58.9	499.5	13.9	181.2
culture and art	11.2	45.0	3.7	22.5
health & public security	23.2	276.7	11.5	154.1
banking & finance	4.2	8.5	9.4	2.4
administration	25.9	32.4	7.2	9.1
other non-material services	11.8	18.0	5.0	179.2

Source: Uzbek State Statistical and Forecasting Committee

UZBEKISTAN
Table 2.1: Gross National Product at Current Prices

(million Rubles)

	1987	1988	1989	1990	1991
GNP	**27269**	**29372**	**30698**	**32430**	**61549**
of which					
Consumption	21372	22546	23976	26258	46685
by Households	15876	17141	18117	19914	37263
By State enterprises	5496	5405	5859	6345	9423
Government Expenditure	375	649	1058	1890	2253
Investment	7786	8002	9721	10433	15860
Resource Balance	-2263	-1825	-4056	-6150	-3250

In percent

	1987	1988	1989	1990	1991
GNP	100	100	100	100	100
of which					
Consumption	78.37	76.76	78.10	80.97	75.85
by Households	58.22	58.36	59.01	61.40	60.54
By State enterprises	20.16	18.40	19.09	19.56	15.31
Government Expenditure	1.37	2.21	3.45	5.83	3.66
Investment	28.55	27.24	31.66	32.17	25.77
Resource Balance	-8.30	-6.21	-13.21	-18.96	-5.28

Souces: State Statistical and Forecasting Committee of Uzbekistan

UZBEKISTAN

Table 2.1a: Gross National Product on the Basis of Value Added

(at current prices, in billions Rubles)

	1991	1991 (in percent)	1992	1992 (in percent)
Gross national product	61.5	100.0	416.9	100.0
Industry	15.6	25.4	119	28.5
Agriculture	22.9	37.2	149.5	35.9
Construction	6.4	10.4	54.4	13.0
Services	16.6	27.0	94	22.5
Trade	2.4	3.9	10.3	2.5
Transport and comm.	2.6	4.2	20.2	4.8
Other sectors	11.6	18.9	63.5	15.2

Source: State Statistical and Forecasting Committee of Uzbekistan

UZBEKISTAN
Table 2.2: Gross National Product on the Basis of Value Added
(In million rubles, at current prices)

	1987	1988	1989	1990	1991
Material Sphere					
Gross Social Product	46218	48232.5	49747.2	53487.1	108882.3
Intermed. Cons.	24809.3	25346.4	26016.3	28104.1	61393
of which:					
material expenses /1.	23357.2	23925.8	24572.9	26407.7	59189.5
business trav. exp.	292.5	328.6	242.4	267.2	425.5
social-cultural					
services exp /2.	281	238.4	436.3	553.3	815.3
mineral resources					
exploration exp.	103	103.1	105.6	102	150.1
R&D	29.3	42.5	253.9	237.8	350.6
inter. payments on loans	464.4	423.2	1.5	0.9	2.7
other services	48.8	48.8	3.5	6.1	9.3
losses in stocks	233.1	236	400.2	529.1	450
Value added mat.sph.	21408.7	22886.1	23730.9	25383	47489.3
Non-material sphere					
Gross output services	7874.8	8627.1	9168	9556.4	11947.3
of which:					
wages & salaries	3671.7	4102.3	4126.7	5153.9	6919.6
social security					
contributions	234.9	252.3	278.8	296.6	369.9
profits	130	130	-80.1	20.8	157.8
purchase of					
non-material service	558.7	590	559.8	591.6	854.5
material expenditures/3.	1455.5	1551.2	1640.9	1917.4	2275.5
depreciation	1403	1556.3	1364.9	396.7	400
rent payments	217	241	181.8	144.3	170
other expenditures	204	204	1095.2	1035.1	800
Intermed.Cons.	2014.2	2141.2	2200.7	2509	3130
of which:					
non-material serv.					
& bus.travel	558.7	590	559.8	591.6	854.5
material exp.	1455.5	1551.2	1640.9	1917.4	2275.5
Value added					
in non-mat.sphere	5860.6	6485.9	6967.3	7047.4	8817.3
Gross National Product	27269.3	29372	30698.2	32430.4	56306.6

1.minus depreciation

2.including education, health, social welfare

3.minus depreciation

Source: State Statistical and Forecasting Committee of Uzbekistan

UZBEKISTAN
Table 2.3: Conversion from MPS to SNA Accounts
(million Rubles, at current prices)

A# = MPS indicator

B# = SNA indicator

	1987	1988	1989	1990
A1.Gross Social Product/1	46218	48232.5	49747.2	53487.1
plus: gross output non-mat.sph/2	7874.8	8627.1	9168	9556.4
B1. equals: Gross volume output	54092.8	56859.6	58915.2	63043.5
A2.Material expenditures	26864.2	27489.5	28189.1	30085
minus: depreciation	3507	3563.7	3616.2	3677.3
plus: expenditures on non- material & other serv.	1219	1184.6	1043.2	1167.3
of which:				
bus.travel	292.5	328.6	242.4	267.2
social-cultural serv.	281	238.4	436.3	553.3
R&D	29.3	42.5	253.9	237.8
mineral resources expl.	103	103.1	105.6	102
interest payments on loans	464.4	423.2	1.5	0.9
other services	48.8	48.8	3.5	6.1
plus: losses in stocks	233.1	236	400.2	529.1
plus: material exp. in non-material sphere/3.	1455.5	1551.2	1640.9	1917.4
plus: services & other exp. in non-material sph.	558.7	590	559.8	591.6
B2. equals Intermed.Cons.	26823.5	27487.6	28217	30613.1
A1-A2 equals A: National Income/4.	19353.8	20743	21558.1	23402.1
B1-B2 equals B: Gross National Product	27269.3	29372	30698.2	32430.4

1/ Also Gross Material Product
2/ Also Gross output services
3/ minus depreciation
4/ Also Net Material Product

Source: State Statistical and Forecasting Committee of Uzbekistan and Bank staff estimates

UZBEKISTAN

Table 2.4: Gross Social Product, Material Expenses and Net Material Product

(in millions of Rubles, at current prices)

	1987	1988	1989	1990	1991
Industry					
Gross product	25955.4	25817.2	25623.9	26719.9	62236.6
Material input	18986.7	19296.3	20013.9	21155.2	46990.4
Net product	6968.7	6520.9	5610	5564.7	15246.2
Agriculture					
Gross product	9799.1	11245.6	12404.1	14028.9	28261
Material input	3286.1	3431	3285	3667.4	8382
Net product	6513	7814.6	9119.1	10361.5	19879
Forestry					
Gross product	12.1	11.9	11.7	12.6	12.6
Material input	3.8	3.7	2.6	3.7	3.7
Net product	8.3	8.2	9.1	8.9	8.9
Construction					
Gross product	5896.5	6270.7	6265.7	6940.2	9751.4
Material input	3141.9	3218.6	3203.4	3463.2	4845.7
Net product	2754.6	3052.1	3062.3	3477	4905.7
Transport					
Gross product	1829.4	1910.3	2007	2314.3	3471.5
Material input	902.8	929.3	979.4	1047.9	1541
Net product	926.6	981	1027.6	1266.4	1930.5
Communications					
Gross product	81.3	85.5	93.2	95.5	
Material input	18.1	18.9	20.4	21.8	
Net product	63.2	66.6	72.8	73.7	
Trade					
Gross product	1374.4	1527.2	1686.6	1776.3	3008.5
Material input	340.3	360.9	392.3	447.8	758.4
Net product	1034.1	1166.3	1294.3	1328.5	2250.1
Other branches					
Gross product	1269.8	1364.1	1655	1599.4	2140.7
Material input	184.5	230.8	292.1	278	398
Net product	1085.3	1133.3	1362.9	1321.4	1742.7
Total Material Sphere					
Gross social product	46218	48232.5	49747.2	53487.1	108882.3
Material input	26864.2	27489.5	28189.1	30085	62919.2
Net material product	19353.8	20743	21558.1	23402.1	45963.1

Source: State Statistical and Forecasting Committee of Uzbekistan
Notes:

1/ In 1991, figures of transport represent the sum of gransport and communication.

UZBEKISTAN

Table 2.5: Gross Social Product, Material Expenses and Net Material Product
(billion Rubles, at current prices)

	1990	1991	92.01	92.02	92.03	92.04	92.05	92.06	92.07	92.08	92.09	92.10	92.11	92.12
Total														
Gross product	53.5	108.9	20.3	25.8	34.5	34.4	38.6	49.8	48.8	52	74.4	179.8	156.9	185.7
Material Input	30.1	62.9	15	18.7	22.4	24.6	25.8	34.5	33.7	29.9	39.6	72.5	95.4	113.2
Net product	23.4	46	5.3	7.1	12.1	9.8	12.8	15.3	15.1	22.1	34.8	107.3	61.5	72.5
Industry														
Gross product	26.7	62.2	18.2	22.4	26.5	28	28.7	35.8	31	33.6	41.6	58.3	101.3	429.8
Material input	21.2	47	14	17.2	20.4	21.5	22.1	27.7	23.9	23.8	33.2	44.8	77.7	406.2
Net product	5.6	15.3	4.2	5.2	6.1	6.5	6.6	8.1	7.1	9.8	8.4	13.5	23.6	23.6
Agriculture														
Gross product	14	28.3	0.3	0.4	0.5	1.6	2.5	6.5	10.5	7.6	14.7	103	29	21.5
Material Input	3.7	8.4	0.2	0.3	0.1	1.6	1.6	4	7	3.2	0.2	21.8	6.4	5.7
Net product	10.4	19.9	0.1	0.1	0.4	0	0.9	2.5	3.5	4.4	14.5	81.2	22.6	15.8
Construction														
Gross product	6.9	9.8	0.9	1.7	2.3	1.9	3.4	3.2	3.9	3.4	6.8	6.3	8.4	58.6
Material input	3.5	4.8	0.5	0.8	1.1	0.9	1.6	1.6	1.8	1.6	3.4	2.6	4.4	26.7
Net product	3.5	4.9	0.4	0.9	1.2	1	1.8	1.6	2.1	1.8	3.4	3.7	4	31.9
Transport and Comm.														
Gross product	2.4	3.5	0.4	0.7	1.2	1	0.8	1.8	1.6	1.2	6.2	5.7	12.4	1.9
Material Input	1.1	1.5	0.2	0.3	0.5	0.5	0.3	0.8	0.7	0.5	2.3	2.2	6	1.2
Net product	1.3	1.9	0.2	0.4	0.7	0.5	0.5	1	0.9	0.7	3.9	3.5	6.4	0.7
Trade and Others														
Gross product	3.4	5.1	0.5	0.6	4	1.9	3.2	2.5	1.8	6.2	5.1	6.5	5.8	2.5
Material input	0.7	1.2	0.1	0.1	0.3	0.1	0.2	0.4	0.3	0.8	0.5	1.1	0.9	2
Net product	2.6	4	0.4	0.5	3.7	1.8	3	2.1	1.5	5.4	4.6	5.4	4.9	0.5

Source: State Statistical and Forecasting Committee of Uzbekistan.

UZBEKISTAN
Table 2.6: Net Material Product Implicit Deflators By Sector

	1987	1988	1989	1990	1991
Net Material Product	100	97.85	98.63	102.57	203.30
Industry ·	100	86.00	65.79	63.03	154.92
Agriculture	100	108.47	130.49	138.46	280.51
Construction	100	98.82	103.76	114.24	162.68
Transport and Communication	100	100.00	104.10	119.92	173.17
Trade and Others	100	101.29	107.57	110.15	184.07

Source: State Statistical and Forecasting Committee of Uzbekistan

UZBEKISTAN

Table 2.7: Net Material Product Implicit Deflator, Monthly by Sector

Date	Total	Industry	Agriculture	Construction	Transport & Commun.	Other
91.01	100.0	100.0	100.0	100.0	100.0	100.0
91.02	102.4	101.8	99.5	101.5	106.6	101.8
91.03	103.0	102.3	100.7	102.3	108.3	102.0
91.04	113.1	104.5	100.5	113.4	109.1	143.5
91.05	114.3	109.2	99.6	105.6	126.8	145.4
91.06	113.6	108.7	100.1	104.3	125.6	146.7
91.07	108.5	105.2	100.5	108.7	120.7	116.4
91.08	107.4	103.3	101.1	111.5	125.4	114.6
91.09	124.3	132.0	141.0	113.2	128.0	129.1
91.10	123.2	149.5	122.8	107.2	180.1	128.1
91.11	121.5	142.6	123.3	109.2	182.3	128.4
91.12	141.0	140.5	176.1	109.0	166.3	156.8
92.01	488.4	504.0	210.5	829.6	371.3	1236.9
92.02	565.4	579.9	236.7	951.2	447.2	1422.6
92.03	711.2	729.0	299.6	1199.9	568.4	1783.6
92.04	802.0	764.8	307.1	1365.5	588.3	2576.6
92.05	808.2	797.1	303.4	1268.4	681.4	2604.3
92.06	710.3	701.8	269.7	1108.6	597.2	2324.5
92.07	680.5	680.6	271.7	1157.6	575.1	1848.8
92.08	708.4	702.6	287.4	1249.0	628.6	1914.3
92.09	769.8	907.5	411.5	1275.7	952.9	2478.2
92.10	916.7	1084.6	744.1	1605.2	1203.1	2833.6
92.11	1021.0	1190.2	893.2	1062.7	1987.1	1873.4
92.12	1224.6	1333.5	1240.5	1667.6	1787.3	2366.2

Source: State Statistical and Forecasting Committee of Uzbekistan and Staff Calculation

Notes: Data after August of 1992 should be considered with caution.

It does not appear consistent with trends of other price indices.

Uzbekistan
Table 3.1: Balance of Payments 1992

	in rubles (billion)	in covertible currency (in million US dollars)	Total
Current account	-39	-170	-369
Non-interest current account		-160	-359
Trade balance			-259
Interrepublic balance	-39		-199
Exports 1/	123		
Imports 1/	162		
Foreign trade balance		-60	-60
Exports		869	
Imports		929	
Factor services (net)		-110	-110
Interest component		-10	-10
Capital account		165	165
Foreign direct investment		40	40
Net increse in foreign credits		125	125
Errors and omissions	19		97
Overall balance			
	-20	-5	-107
Financing			
Interepublic arrears	-40		-204
Correspondent accounts	60		306
increase in reserves(-)			5

1/ Converted from the ruble figures using an average market exchange rate over 1992.
2/ Average exchange rate in 1992 (rubles/$) is 196.

Source: Goskomprognostat and Bank Staff Calculations

UZBEKISTAN
Table 3.2: Exchange Rates
(at end of period, rubles/per dollar)

Month	Year	Official Exchange Rate	Market Exchange Rate
September	1991	0.60	..
October	1991	0.58	..
November	1991	0.59	..
December	1991	0.57	..
January	1992	1.67	90
February	1992	1.67	120
March	1992	1.67	120
April	1992	1.67	150
May	1992	1.67	155
June	1992	1.67	140
July	1992	1.67	140
August	1992	1.67	145
September	1992	1.67	200
October	1992	1.67	395
November	1992	1.67	450
December	1992	1.67	450
January	1993	572	625
February	1993	593	700
March	1993	684	750
April	1993	823	851
May	1993	994	1028
June	1993	1116	1200

Source: National Bank of Uzbekistan

UZBEKISTAN
Table 3.3: Trade by Commodity Groups At Current Prices for 1987-1990
(In million rubles)

	1987 Exports	1987 Imports	1988 Exports	1988 Imports	1989 Exports	1989 Imports	1990 Exports	1990 Imports
Total Trade	8974.0	12973.6	10486.9	12327.1	10169.3	14158.3	9351.5	14661.8
Foreign	1515.8	1599.9	1529.7	1703.4	1627.7	2112.3	1182.4	2798.0
Interrepublic	7458.2	11373.7	8957.2	10623.7	8541.6	12046.0	8169.1	11863.8
Oil and Gas	601.8	990.1	641.6	1000.4	645.6	1031.6	598.4	888.4
Foreign	21.0	40.5	22.4	32.1	21.2	1.9	5.9	2.4
Interrepublic	580.8	949.6	619.2	968.3	624.4	1029.7	592.5	886.0
Electric Energy	201.9	151.8	180.7	191.6	213.9	186.8	207.1	172.1
Foreign	0.4	0.0	0.4	0.0	1.1	0.0	0.0	0.0
Interrepublic	201.5	151.8	180.3	191.6	212.8	186.8	207.1	172.1
Coal	13.8	47.8	14.5	37.6	8.1	41.9	8.1	47.9
Foreign	0.0	0.0	0.0	0.0	0.0	0.0	0.0	0.0
Interrepublic	13.8	47.8	14.5	37.6	8.1	41.9	8.1	47.9
Other Energy (Peat)	0.0	0.2	0.0	0.2	0.0	0.2	0.0	0.2
Foreign	0.0	0.0	0.0	0.0	0.0	0.0	0.0	0.0
Interrepublic	0.0	0.2	0.0	0.2	0.0	0.2	0.0	0.2
Ferrous Metals	111.3	671.8	111.4	676.2	111.5	676.1	98.9	661.3
Foreign	0.0	28.3	0.0	23.4	0.0	20.4	0.1	13.9
Interrepublic	111.3	643.5	111.4	652.8	111.5	655.7	98.8	647.4
Nonferrous Metals	347.4	387.0	468.2	374.1	468.1	424.5	446.7	409.1
Foreign	0.1	13.3	0.1	9.8	3.6	11.0	18.0	0.4
Interrepublic	347.3	373.7	468.1	364.3	464.5	413.5	428.7	408.7
Chemicals & Products	736.1	979.5	853.7	1012.2	893.7	1110.6	852.7	1147.3
Foreign	39.2	40.9	40.2	35.8	60.3	136.9	60.0	174.2
Interrepublic	696.9	938.6	813.5	976.4	833.4	973.7	792.7	973.1
Machine Building	1127.5	3292.0	1302.2	3292.5	1190.1	3552.6	1230.9	3625.3
Foreign	73.2	123.9	99.6	140.3	85.9	228.9	180.2	333.1
Interrepublic	1054.3	3168.1	1203.2	3152.2	1140.2	3323.7	1050.7	3292.2
Wood & Paper Prod.	32.7	741.5	31.7	601.2	35.0	724.9	14.9	559.7
Foreign	2.2	85.2	0.2	86.9	0.0	58.3	0.0	47.2
Interrepublic	30.5	656.3	31.5	514.3	35	666.6	14.9	512.5
Construction Mat.	82.4	235.8	82.7	213.1	69.0	227.6	71.6	205.2
Foreign	0.3	22.5	0.1	25.1	0.0	11.4	0.2	13.6
Interrepublic	82.1	213.3	82.6	188.0	69.0	216.2	71.4	191.6
Light Industry	4279.6	2616.7	4575.2	2205.1	4658.9	2757.3	4241.7	2963.1
Foreign	1347.3	739.8	1296.6	712.3	1358.4	905.4	857.6	1024.8
Interrepublic	2932.3	1876.9	3278.6	1492.8	3300.5	1855.9	3384.1	1939.3
Food Industry	789.3	1961.1	847.0	1875.0	795.3	2155.5	824.3	1982.6
Foreign	7.8	406.0	14.1	393.5	33.0	486.1	14.4	735.3
Interrepublic	781.5	1555.1	832.9	1481.5	762.3	1669.4	809.9	1247.3
Oth. Industrial Branches	34.9	231.4	64.7	203.0	65.5	246.6	75.4	409.0
Foreign	0.0	2.5	0.0	5.7	9.0	4.5	2.2	74.8
Interrepublic	34.9	225.6	64.7	197.3	56.5	242.1	73.2	334.2
Agric. Prod. (Unprcsd)	589.4	610.8	871.9	587.7	757.2	661.1	447.4	1309.2
Foreign	22.6	93.7	58.9	238.5	53.6	247.4	42.8	377.2
Interrepublic	566.8	517.1	818.0	348.6	703.2	413.7	404.6	932.0
Mat. (Comm., Trans., Svcs.)	25.9	56.1	440.8	57.8	257.4	357.0	233.4	281.4
Foreign	1.7	0.0	2.1	0.0	1.6	0.1	1.0	1.1
Interrepublic	24.2	56.1	438.1	57.8	255.8	356.9	232.4	280.3

Source: Statistical and Forecasting Committee of Uzbekistan

UZBEKISTAN
Table 3.4: Inter-Republic Trade: Geographical Distribution
(in million rubles)

	1990	1990	1991	1991	1992	1992	1993	1993
							The first three months	
	Exports	Imports	Exports	Imports	Exports	Imports	Exports	Imports
Armenia	82	156	67	231 1/	208	198	24	1
Azerbaijan	67	198	220	277	1192	671	199	251
Belarus	177	582	603	965	4259	9347	3678	3155
Estonia	49	43	114	87	1063	179	41	88
Georgia	65	167	120	249 1/	340	466	109	2
Kazakhstan	784	1453	1259	1795	13786	19822	41856	43593
Kyrghystan	365	323	662	613	4527	5462	12834	1975
Latvia	33	157	64	128	698	375	3	63
Lithuania	47	150	169	198	1665	769	81	328
Moldova	110	89	307	199	2474	484	450	70
Russia	4840	5937	10972	7840	65387	85818	73533	139252
Tajikistan	503	330	644	237	3708	5126	31252	14676
Turkmenistan	216	620	475	2701	6560	11395	14345	51640
Ukraine	833	1659	1664	2247	17291	22137	12695	10287
Total	8169	11864	17339	17766	123157	162248	191099	265382

(in percent)

Armenia	1.00	1.32	0.38	1.30	0.17	0.12	0.01	0.00
Azerbaijan	0.81	1.67	1.27	1.56	0.97	0.41	0.10	0.09
Belarus	2.16	4.90	3.48	5.43	3.46	5.76	1.92	1.19
Estonia	0.60	0.36	0.66	0.49	0.86	0.11	0.02	0.03
Georgia	0.80	1.41	0.69	1.40	0.28	0.29	0.06	0.00
Kazakhstan	9.60	12.25	7.26	10.10	11.19	12.22	21.90	16.43
Kyrghystan	4.46	2.72	3.82	3.45	3.68	3.37	6.72	0.74
Latvia	0.40	1.32	0.37	0.72	0.57	0.23	0.00	0.02
Lithuania	0.58	1.26	0.98	1.11	1.35	0.47	0.04	0.12
Moldova	1.35	0.75	1.77	1.12	2.01	0.30	0.24	0.03
Russia	59.25	50.04	63.28	44.13	53.09	52.89	38.48	52.47
Tajikistan	6.15	2.78	3.72	1.33	3.01	3.16	16.35	5.53
Turkmenistan	2.64	5.23	2.74	15.21	5.33	7.02	7.51	19.46
Ukraine	10.20	13.99	9.60	12.65	14.04	13.64	6.64	3.88
Total	100	100	100	100	100	100	100	100

Source: State Statistical and Forecasting Committee, Intelligent Decision System
Notes: 1/ Estimate based on its import share of 1990.

UZBEKISTAN

TABLE 3.4a: Geographical Distribution of Foreign Trade

(in million US dollars)

	1992 Exports	1992 Imports	1993 Exports	1993 Imports
Total	869	929	164	271
Australia	3.47	5.01	1.37	0.45
Austria	29.29	14.60	0.37	1.24
Argentina	24.50	0.00	0.00	0.00
Afghanistan	40.26	32.34	0.47	1.68
Bangladesh	0.11	39.59	0.00	0.00
Belgium	112.23	1.24	14.29	3.20
Bulgaria	12.67	12.37	0.41	0.30
Hungary	51.81	13.96	5.38	9.97
United Kingdom	117.32	0.14	8.50	3.07
Viet Nam	0.94	21.63	0.08	0.12
Germany	94.02	0.12	9.22	6.70
Greece	0.48	0.02	0.00	0.08
Denmark	1.25	1.01	0.00	0.00
India	1.09	16.67	3.00	0.32
Indonesia	22.39	0.78	19.08	9.68
Israel	13.81	0.00	2.50	0.00
Ireland	5.73	0.00	0.00	0.75
Iran	2.39	0.21	0.01	0.00
Spain	11.40	8.06	0.03	0.00
Italy	2.13	2.41	0.85	4.93
Korea PDR	0.18	0.04	0.49	0.95
Canada	3.91	1.42	0.00	0.00
Cyprus	39.53	67.63	0.00	0.00
China	3.25	1.36	6.01	5.78
Korea	0.11	0.00	8.21	4.60
Cuba	0.12	0.00	0.00	0.00
Lebanon	0.09	0.06	0.03	0.00
Liechtestein	1.82	0.04	2.50	0.14
Malyasia	0.03	0.09	0.00	0.00
Mongolia	20.20	0.00	0.05	0.00
Nigeria	0.16	2.40	20.85	0.00
Netherlands	3.45	0.08	0.03	30.50
UAE	47.80	0.79	0.01	0.14
pakistan	2.18	15.16	7.36	0.00
Poland	0.00	0.16	1.12	2.04
Romania	1.10	0.00	0.03	0.18
Saudi arabia	4.32	0.98	0.00	0.00
Singapour	37.64	0.78	0.34	1.07
Syria	3.21	0.00	0.00	0.00
Slovakia	0.30	0.00	0.30	0.12
Slovenia	0.06	21.33	17.35	0.00
USA	77.32	1.02	3.64	6.21
Hong Kong	0.02	0.00	0.72	3.76
Thailand	0.23	0.00	0.00	0.00
Taiwan	39.33	35.06	23.34	0.30
Turkey	8.06	0.00	0.00	46.38
Uruguay	15.93	0.16	0.00	0.00
Finland	0.00	5.06	0.00	0.00
France	7.10	16.88	0.71	2.09
Chechoslavakia	4.57	198.17	4.19	1.17
Switzerlnd	0.00	7.12	0.00	120.76
Sweden	0.00	7.25	0.00	0.00
Yugslavia	0.00	5.69	1.21	2.02
Unidentified	0.00	370.46	0.00	0.00

Source: State Statistical and Forecasting Committee of Uzbekistan

UZBEKISTAN
Table 3.5: Compositions of Foreign Trade for 1992
(in million dollars)

	Unit	Quantity	Value	Percent
Total Exports			869.3	100
Cotton- Fibre	1000 tons	600.7	673.3	77.5
Non-ferrous metals	1000 tons	21.8	40.5	4.7
Ferrous Metals	1000 tons	76.7	17.7	2.0
Mineral Fertilizers	1000 tons	317.3	39.3	4.5
Electrical-energy	mln. kwh	131.2	13.1	1.5
Oil Refinary Products	1000 tons	136.6	8.4	1.0
Others			77.0	8.9
Total Imports			929.3	100
Wheat	1000 tons	3734.8	535.8	57.7
Meat,Food and Poultry	tons	29797.1	45.0	4.8
Sugar	1000 tons	144.6	43.7	4.7
Textile & Clothes			31.9	3.4
Foot-Ware	th. pairs	889.4	14.2	1.5
Rice	1000 tons	51.3	14.8	1.6
Tea	tons	6036.7	9.7	1.0
Fresh Potatoes	tons	40600	4.6	0.5
Butter, Other Milk Fats	tons	5910	8.8	0.9
TV & Radio Sets	unit	16094	1.8	0.2
Silk Fabric	1000 meters	189	1.3	0.1
Cotton Fabric	1000 meters	1370.5	2.5	0.3
Cigarettes	1000 pieces	43732	0.6	0.1
Sedan Cars	unit	63	0.9	0.1
Fertilizers	1000 tons	0.3	2.7	0.3
Aluminium Wares	1000 tons	..	0.0	0.0
Cereal crops (excluding wheat and rice)	1000 tons	218.9	22.4	2.4
Others			188.6	20.3

Source: State Statistical and Forecasting Committee of Uzbekistan

UZBEKISTAN

Table 3.5a: Compositions of Foreign Trade for the First Three Months of 1993

(in million dollars)

	Unit	Quantity	Value	Percent
Total Exports			**164.0**	100
Cotton- Fibre	1000 tons	140.1	138.8	84.6
Non-ferrus metal &	1000 tons	6.9	8.8	5.3
Ferrous Metals	1000 tons	45.9	5.1	3.1
Mineral Fertilizers	1000 tons	1.2	0.3	0.2
Electrical-energy	mln. kwh	..	..	
Oil Refinary Products	1000 tons	..	..	
Others			11.0	6.7
Total Imports			**270.8**	100
Grain	1000 tons	1026.7	151.5	56.0
Meat,Food and Poultry	tons			
Sugar	1000 tons	60	18.2	6.7
Textile & Clothes	na		3.3	1.2
Foot-Ware	th. pairs	359.8	4.6	1.7
Rice	1000 tons	4	1.1	0.4
Tea	tons	15640	27.8	10.3
Fresh Potatoes	tons			
Butter, Other Milk Fats	tons	335	0.5	0.2
TV & Radio Sets	unit	225	0.1	0.0
Silk Fabrics	1000 meters	250	0.9	0.3
Cotton Fabrics	1000 meters			
Cigarettes	1000 pieces			
Sedan Cars	unit	6	0.1	0.0
Mineral Fertilizers	1000 tons			
Aluminium Wares	1000 tons			
Ferrous Metal	1000 tons	4.3	5.6	2.1
Other Cereals	1000 tons	4	0.5	0.2
Other Cereal Products	1000 tons	1150	0.2	0.1
Others			56.4	20.8

Source: State Statistical and Forecasting Committee of Uzbekistan

UZBEKISTAN
Table 3.6: Trade by Commodity Groups at Current Domestic and World Prices in 1990
(in million Rubles)

	Inter-republic Trade				Foreign Trade				Total Trade			
	Domestic Prices		World Prices		Domestic Prices		World Prices		Domestic Prices		World Prices	
	Export	Import	Export	Import	Export	Import	Export	Import	Export	Import	Export	Import
INDUSTRY	7532.1	10651.5	6481.6	10172.9	1138.6	2419.7	804.2	1004.2	8670.7	13071.2	7285.8	11177.1
POWER	207.1	172.1	310.7	258.2	0	0	0	0	207.1	172.1	310.7	258.2
OIL AND GAS	592.5	886	1424.9	2288.7	5.9	2.4	12.4	2.7	598.4	888.4	1437.3	2291.4
Oil Products	0	171.7	0	607.8	0	0	0	0	0	171.7	0	607.8
Refineries	140.1	327.6	312	729.6	5.9	2.4	12.4	2.7	146	330	324.4	732.3
Gas Products	452.4	386.7	1112.9	951.3	0	0	0	0	452.4	386.7	1112.9	951.3
COAL	8.1	47.9	7.6	44.8	0	0	0	0	8.1	47.9	7.6	44.8
OTHER FUELS	0	0.2	0	0.1	0	0	0	0	0	0.2	0	0.1
Combustible Shales	0	0.2	0	0.1	0	0	0	0	0	0.2	0	0.1
Peat	0	0	0	0	0	0	0	0	0	0	0	0
FERROUS	98.8	647.4	120.7	750.6	0.1	13.9	0.1	18.1	98.9	661.3	120.8	768.7
Ferrous Ores	0	1.4	0	1.3	0	0.2	0	0.2	0	1.6	0	1.5
Ferrous Metals	96.8	502.9	119.3	619.6	0.1	10.5	0.1	14.1	96.9	513.4	119.4	633.7
Coking Products	0	22.7	0	33.7	0	1.1	0	1.6	0	23.8	0	35.3
Fire Resistant	0	9.3	0	17.8	0	0.3	0	0.5	0	9.6	0	18.3
Metal Products	2	111.1	1.4	78.2	0	1.8	0	1.7	2	112.9	1.4	79.9
NON-FERR.	428.7	408.7	711.3	678.9	18	0.4	30.1	0.3	446.7	409.1	741.4	679.2
Non-ferrous Ores	45.9	35.9	71.6	56	0	0	0	0	45.9	35.9	71.6	56
Non-ferr. Metals	382.8	372.8	639.7	622.9	18	0.4	30.1	0.3	400.8	373.2	669.8	623.2
CHEMICALS	792.7	973.1	605.7	805.7	60	174.2	44.2	123.7	852.7	1147.3	649.9	929.4
Mineral Chemistry	0	21.9	0	28.1	0	0.3	0	0.3	0	22.2	0	28.4
Basic Chemicals	290.2	279.8	209.5	202	44	40.8	31.8	31.1	334.2	320.6	241.3	233.1
Chemical Fibers	176.6	79.1	125.9	56.4	9.4	1.8	6.7	1.2	186	80.9	132.6	57.6
Synthetic Resins	.90.5	69.6	69.3	53.3	1.4	1.5	1.1	1.2	91.9	71.1	70.4	54.5
Plastic Products	50	35.9	39.9	28.6	0	0.3	0	0.2	50	36.2	39.9	28.8
Paints & Laquers	38.6	35.8	29	26.9	0.3	4.1	0.2	3.8	38.9	39.9	29.2	30.7
Synthetic Paints	0	13.3	0	11.3	0	5.3	0	3.9	0	18.6	0	15.2
Synthetic Rubber	0	9.7	0	7.2	0	1.5	0	0.9	0	11.2	0	8.1
Organic Chemicals	80.9	120.7	71.8	107.1	4.6	1.1	4.1	0.7	85.5	121.8	75.9	107.8
Tires	2.4	115.6	2.4	113.3	0	0.1	0	0.1	2.4	115.7	2.4	113.4

Part 1 of Table 3.6

UZBEKISTAN
Table 3.6: Trade by Commodity Groups at Current Domestic and World Prices in 1990
(in million Rubles)

	Inter-republic Trade				Foreign Trade				Total Trade			
	Domestic Prices		World Prices		Domestic Prices		World Prices		Domestic Prices		World Prices	
	Export	Import	Export	Import	Export	Import	Export	Import	Export	Import	Export	Import
Rubber & Asbestos	11.2	90.4	9.6	77.8	0.3	24.6	0.3	13.1	11.5	115	9.9	90.9
Other Products	12.7	24.4	12.5	24.1	0	29.3	0	12.3	12.7	53.7	12.5	36.4
Pharmaceuticals	39.6	76.9	35.8	69.6	0	63.5	0	54.9	39.6	140.4	35.8	124.5
MACHINERY	1050.7	3292.2	1324.7	3438	180.2	333.1	245.5	273.3	1230.9	3625.3	1570.2	3711.3
Energy & power	0.5	25.2	0.5	22.9	0	1.7	0	1.7	0.5	26.9	0.5	24.6
Technology	0	7.4	0	7.6	0	0	0	0	0	7.4	0	7.6
Mining	1	13	1.6	20.3	0.1	0.2	0.2	0.2	1.1	13.2	1.8	20.5
Transportation	41.2	34.9	55.9	47.3	26	8	35.3	7.9	67.2	42.9	91.2	55.2
Railway Equipment	1	34.1	0.7	24.6	0	5	0	5	1	39.1	0.7	29.6
Electro-technical	143.9	237.1	132	217.4	11.5	2	10.5	1.7	155.4	239.1	142.5	219.1
Cables	82.2	26.7	82.2	26.7	1.7	0.1	1.7	0.1	83.9	26.8	83.9	26.8
Pumps	54.9	124.4	62.8	142.3	3.1	14.1	3.5	12.4	58	138.5	66.3	154.7
Machine Tools	8.3	45.5	9.5	51.9	0	43.6	0	39.4	8.3	89.1	9.5	91.3
Forging/Pressing	0.4	11.2	0.3	9.8	0	0.1	0	0.1	0.4	11.3	0.3	9.9
Casting Equipment	0	2	0	2.2	0	0.6	0	0.5	0	2.6	0	2.7
Precision Instr.	12.1	19.3	7.4	11.7	5.7	0.1	3.5	0.1	17.8	19.4	10.9	11.8
Synthetic Diamonds	25.8	19.2	24.7	18.4	0.6	0	0.6	0	26.4	19.2	25.3	18.4
Tools and Dies	38.7	179.4	34.8	125.9	0.1	86.7	0.1	79.3	38.8	266.1	34.9	205.2
Autos & Parts	10.7	813.4	18.1	640.1	0.1	18.9	0.1	18.7	10.8	832.3	18.2	658.8
Bearings	2.5	21.8	2	17	0	0	0	0	2.5	21.8	2	17
Tractors & Agri.Eq.	142.1	223.7	192.4	302.9	3.3	9.7	4.5	9.7	145.4	233.4	196.9	312.6
Construction M&E	31.2	112.5	43.9	158.4	0.3	17.1	0.4	15.6	31.5	129.6	44.3	174
Communal M&E	0.5	14.5	0.7	19.5	0	0.5	0	0.5	0.5	15	0.7	20
Light Ind. M&E	51.5	89.5	58.9	102.3	43.3	22.9	49.5	17.7	94.8	112.4	108.4	120
Food M&E	1.2	15.7	1.6	20.4	0	18.3	0	13.8	1.2	34	1.6	34.2
Trade M&E	0.5	20.7	0.7	30.4	0	0.3	0	0.3	0.5	21	0.7	30.7
Printing M&E	0	7.1	0	5.9	0	6.5	0	5.8	0	13.6	0	11.7
Appliances	40.5	119.3	16.1	58	13.4	12.5	7.5	3.9	53.9	131.8	23.6	61.9
Sanitary Eng.	21	40.2	11.3	21.6	0	0.7	0	0.7	21	40.9	11.3	22.3
Shipbuilding	0.6	36.8	0.7	42.7	0	0	0	0	0.6	36.8	0.7	42.7

Part 2 of Table 3.6

UZBEKISTAN
Table 3.6: Trade by Commodity Groups at Current Domestic and World Prices in 1990
(in million Rubles)

	Inter-republic Trade				Foreign Trade				Total Trade			
	Domestic Prices		World Prices		Domestic Prices		World Prices		Domestic Prices		World Prices	
	Export	Import	Export	Import	Export	Import	Export	Import	Export	Import	Export	Import
Radio Electronics	61.2	402.8	70.4	271.9	1.7	26.3	2	13.4	62.9	429.1	72.4	285.3
Other Ind. M&E	223.4	470.3	424.7	894	64.7	4	122.5	5.3	288.1	474.3	547.2	899.3
Metal Construction	0.5	8.5	0.5	9.1	0	0.8	0	0.8	0.5	9.3	0.5	9.9
Metal Products	30.9	82	24.2	64.3	4.6	14.7	3.6	3.2	35.5	96.7	27.8	67.5
M&E Repair	21.6	14.6	45.3	30.6	0	0	0	0	21.6	14.6	45.3	30.6
Medical Equipment	0.8	19.4	0.8	19.9	0	17.7	0	15.5	0.8	37.1	0.8	35.4
WOOD & PAPER	14.9	512.5	11.6	367.6	0	47.2	0	26.6	14.9	559.7	11.6	394.2
Logging	0	42.2	0	27	0	0.1	0	0.1	0	42.3	0	27.1
Sawmill	1.5	290.7	1.1	218.3	0	0.7	0	0.5	1.5	291.4	1.1	218.8
Plywood	0	13.6	0	10.9	0	0.8	0	0.6	0	14.4	0	11.5
Furniture	1	43.7	0.4	19.1	0	41.8	0	22.5	1	85.5	0.4	41.6
Paper & Pulp	12.4	110.8	10.1	90.1	0	3.8	0	2.9	12.4	114.6	10.1	93
Chemistry Prod.	0	11.5	0	2.2	0	0	0	0	0	11.5	0	2.2
CONSTR. MAT.	71.4	191.6	68.6	192.5	0.2	13.6	0.2	4.5	71.6	205.2	68.8	197
Cement	8.6	9.4	6.9	7.5	0	0.3	0	0.2	8.6	9.7	6.9	7.7
Asbestos Products	7.3	34.7	9.9	47.1	0	0	0	0	7.3	34.7	9.9	47.1
Roofing	10.3	0.8	10.9	0.8	0	0	0	0	10.3	0.8	10.9	0.8
Precast Concrete	12.1	8.5	12.9	9.1	0	0	0	0	12.1	8.5	12.9	9.1
Wall Materials	0	2.4	0	0.9	0	0	0	0	0	2.4	0	0.9
Ceramics	1.3	2.5	1.1	2.2	0	0.2	0	0.1	1.3	2.7	1.1	2.3
Constr. Products	5.8	7.2	3.8	4.8	0	0.9	0	0.7	5.8	8.1	3.8	5.5
Other	8.2	33	10.6	42.6	0	0.3	0	0.2	8.2	33.3	10.6	42.8
Glass & Porcelain	17.8	89.4	12.5	73.8	0.2	11.7	0.2	3.1	18	101.1	12.7	76.9
Medical Products	0	3.7	0	3.7	0	0.2	0	0.2	0	3.9	0	3.9
LIGHT INDUSTRY	3384.1	1938.3	1542.1	580	857.6	1024.8	464.7	252.5	4241.7	2963.1	2006.8	832.5
Cotton Products	2537	349.6	1288.8	107.7	816.2	70.9	448.9	24.2	3353.2	420.5	1737.7	131.9
Flax Products	0	43.7	0	18.1	0	2.4	0	1.9	0	46.1	0	20
Wool Products	138.7	416.8	35.5	108.4	0.2	36.6	0.2	7.9	138.9	453.4	35.7	116.3
Silk Products	377.6	440.9	72.9	76.3	38.3	189.4	14.2	53.7	415.9	630.3	87.1	130
Hosiery/Knitwear	20.5	180.1	6.9	61.1	0	195.5	0	34.4	20.5	375.6	6.9	95.5

Part 3 of Table 3.6

UZBEKISTAN

Table 3.6: Trade by Commodity Groups at Current Domestic and World Prices in 1990
(in million Rubles)

	Inter-republic Trade				Foreign Trade				Total Trade			
	Domestic Prices		World Prices		Domestic Prices		World Prices		Domestic Prices		World Prices	
	Export	Import	Export	Import	Export	Import	Export	Import	Export	Import	Export	Import
Other Textiles	107.4	112.6	65.8	63.7	1.4	43.7	0.8	7.1	108.8	156.3	66.6	70.8
Sewn Goods	126.8	158.3	41.3	51.6	0.4	268.8	0.1	62.6	127.2	427.1	41.4	114.2
Leather	76.1	236.3	30.9	93.1	1.1	217.5	0.5	60.7	77.2	453.8	31.4	153.8
FOOD PROD.	809.9	1247.3	306.4	570.7	14.4	735.3	5.2	279.9	824.3	1982.6	311.6	850.6
Sugar	0	373.6	0	147.2	0	0.6	0	0.5	0	374.2	0	147.7
Bread Products	0.1	1.1	0.1	0.6	0	2.1	0	1.1	0.1	3.2	0.1	1.7
Confections	1.1	71	0.5	32.3	0	3.1	0	0.7	1.1	74.1	0.5	33
Vegetable Oils	285.8	27.2	106.6	9.8	4.3	0.8	1.1	0.4	290.1	28	107.7	10.2
Perfume Oils	83.4	48.1	59	34.1	0.7	83.3	0.5	29.4	84.1	131.4	59.5	63.5
Distilleries	15.6	2.8	1.3	0.2	0	0	0	0	15.6	2.8	1.3	0.2
Wines	26.6	3.4	3.4	0.4	0	0	0	0	26.6	3.4	3.4	0.4
Fruit/Vegetables	184.2	2	59.9	0.6	3.5	7.7	1.1	5	187.7	9.7	61	5.6
Tabacco	168.2	75.4	58.9	23.1	2.2	86.9	0	27.8	168.2	162.3	58.9	50.9
Other Food	2.3	38.2	0.6	29.5	2.2	204.1	0.8	64.5	4.5	242.3	1.4	94
Meat Products	0	251.5	0	119.2	3.1	174	1.4	91.8	3.1	425.5	1.4	211
Dairy Products	0	114.9	0	59.5	0	165.6	0	55.7	0	280.5	0	115.2
Fish Products	6.9	101.2	2.8	41.8	0	0.8	0	0.5	6.9	102	2.8	42.3
Flour & Cereals	35.7	136.9	13.3	72.4	0.6	6.3	0.3	2.5	36.3	143.2	13.6	74.9
OTHER IND.	73.2	334.2	47.3	197.1	2.2	74.8	1.8	22.6	75.4	409	49.1	219.7
Microbiology	9	33.5	7.5	27.9	0	0	0	0	9	33.5	7.5	27.9
Animal Feed	1.3	2.5	1.1	2.2	0	0	0	0	1.3	2.5	1.1	2.2
Other Products	62.9	298.2	38.7	167	2.2	74.8	1.8	22.6	65.1	373	40.5	189.6
AGRICULTURE	404.6	932	146.7	510.6	42.8	377.2	7.6	290.9	447.4	1309.2	154.3	801.5
Crops	292.9	829.9	111	483.8	0.9	375.5	0.2	290	293.8	1205.4	111.2	773.8
Animal Husbandry	111.7	102.1	35.7	26.8	41.9	1.7	7.4	0.9	153.6	103.8	43.1	27.7
OTHER PROD.	232.4	280.3	260.8	309.3	1	1.1	1	0.9	233.4	281.4	261.8	310.2
Info. Services	0	0	0	0	0	0	0	0	0	0	0	0
Other Services	24.6	60.2	23.9	58.4	1	1.1	1	0.9	25.6	61.3	24.9	59.3
Transport Expenses	207.8	220.1	236.9	250.9	0	0	0	0	207.8	220.1	236.9	250.9
TOTAL	8169.1	11863.8	6889.1	10992.8	1182.4	2798	812.8	1296	9351.5	14661.8	7701.9	12288.8

Part 4 of Table 3.6

Source: Intelligent Decision System.

UZBEKISTAN
Table 3.7: Foreign Trade by Means of Payments for 1992
(in millions US dollars)

Total Exports	**869.3**
Of which	
in convertable currencies	448.1
on clearings basis	7.3
barter	413.9
Total Imports	**929.3**
Of which	
in convertable currencies	473
on clearings basis	17.9
barter	438.4
transfers	
Resources Balance	**-60**

Source: State Statistical and Forecasting Committee of Uzbekistan

UZBEKISTAN
Table 3.8: Interrepublic Trade by Commodity Groups at Current Prices
(in million Rubles, at current domestic prices)

	1990	1990	1992	1992
	Exports	Imports	Exports	Imports
POWER	207.1	172	140	12894
OIL AND GAS	592.5	886	4358	34747
Oil Products	0	172	..	..
Refineries	140.1	328	..	..
Gas Products	452.4	387	..	..
COAL	8.1	48	127	1342
OTHER FUELS	0	0	..	..
FERROUS	98.8	647	2003	25922
NON-FERR.	428.7	409	14253	6142
CHEMICALS	792.7	973	10462	20231
MACHINERY	1050.7	3292	22131	18585
WOOD & PAPER	14.9	513	417	8162
CONSTR. MAT.	71.4	192	1106	2176
LIGHT INDUSTRY	3384.1	1938	49070	10514
Cotton Products	2537	350	..	..
FOOD PROD.	809.9	1247	5640	14199
OTHER IND.	73.2	334	66	1453
AGRICULTURE	404.6	932	1510	4642
OTHER PROD. *	232.4	280	11874	937
TOTAL	8169.1	11864	123157	161946

Notes:
  * an estimate.
  Data for 1991 are not available

Source: Statistical and Forecasting Committee of Uzbekistan

UZBEKISTAN

Table 4.1: Summary of Fiscal Operations for 1987-1991

(in billion rubles)

	1987	1988	1989	1990	1991
Total revenue and grants	9.1	9.7	10.8	14.6	28.0
Corporate income tax	1.9	1.7	1.5	1.9	3.5
Individual tax income	1.0	1.1	1.3	0.9	1.6
Turnover taxes	3.1	3.3	3.7	4.0	5.8
Value-added tax(VAT)	--	--	--	--	--
Excise tax	--	--	--	--	--
Social security tax	0.8	0.8	0.9	1.1	--
Price differential tax	--	--	--	--	--
Revenue from privatization	--	--	--	--	--
Other tax and nontax revenue	1.8	1.1	0.9	0.9	5.1
Union grants	1.9	2.3	2.9	6.3	12.0
revenue from reevaluation	--	--	--	--	--
revenus from selling rep. bonds	--	--	--	--	--
Total expenditure	9.2	10.1	11.0	14.9	31.1
National economy	4.3	4.6	5.0	8.1	11.1
Social and cultural	4.6	5.2	5.5	6.2	11.0
Subsidies	--	--	--	--	5.3
Othe current	0.2	0.2	0.5	0.6	3.7
Capital expenditure	--	--	--	--	--
Administration & legislature	--	--	--	--	--
Overall balance	-0.1	-0.4	-0.3	-0.4	-3.1
(In Percent of GDP)					
Total revenue and grants	33.4	32.9	35.0	44.9	45.5
Corporate income tax	7.0	5.7	5.0	5.9	5.7
Individual tax income	3.8	3.8	4.3	2.7	2.6
Turnover taxes 1/	11.3	11.3	12.2	12.3	9.4
Value-added tax(VAT)	--	--	--	--	--
Excise tax	--	--	--	--	--
Social security tax	2.8	2.8	3.0	3.3	--
Price differential tax	--	--	--	--	--
Revenue from privatization	--	--	--	--	--
Other tax and nontax revenue	2.9	3.6	3.0	2.6	8.3
Union grants	7.0	8.0	9.4	19.4	19.5
Total expenditure	33.7	34.2	35.9	46.1	50.5
National economy	15.9	15.7	16.4	25.0	18.0
Social and cultural	17.0	17.7	17.8	19.2	17.9
Subsidies	--	--	--	--	8.6
Othe current	0.8	0.8	1.8	1.9	6.0
Capital expenditure	--	--	--	--	--
Overall balance	-0.3	-1.4	-0.9	-1.1	-5.0

Source: Ministry of Finance and IMF

Notes: 1/ includes sales tax in 1991.

UZBEKISTAN
Table 4.2: Budgetary Compensation in Goods and Services
(Million Rubles)

	1991	1992
Flour	2102.9	4580.4
Meat	919.8	1620
Milk	524	980
Sugar	NA	1673
Tea	56.3	565
Soap	NA	200
Children Clothes	NA	72.1
Fuel	62	3000
Natural Gas	NA	348.7
House Heating	140	634
Urban Transportation	NA	567.9
Total	3805	14241.1

Source: Ministry of Finance

Table 4.3: General Government Budget for 1992
(billions rubles)

	1992 (Actual)	1992 As % GNP
Total Revenue of which	142.7	34.2
1. VAT	38.5	9.2
2. Excise	35.2	8.4
3. Export tax	8	1.9
4. Enterprise profit tax	24.6	5.9
5. Personal income tax	10.8	2.6
Total expenditure of which	188.4	45.2
1. Expenditure on social-cultural projects including:	69.5	16.7
Education	45	10.8
Health and physical culture	21.1	5.1
Culture	2.1	0.5
Science	1	0.2
Social security	0.3	0.1
2. Expenditure on social saftey net including	49.1	11.8
Budgetary compensation on consumer goods		
Compensation on children goods		
Other		
3. Expenditure on national economy	15.5	3.7
4. Expenditure on financing of the centralized state capital investment	12.1	2.9
5. State Administrations		
6. Defence, security service and law enforcements		
7. Subsidy to precious metal production		
8. Others	42.2	10.1
Surplus	-45.7	-11.0

Source: Ministry of Finance

UZBEKISTAN

Table 5.1: Monetary Balance

(millions rubles)

Monetary Income	As of April 1st (1992)	As of June 1st (1992)	As of July 1st (1992)	As of Sep. 1st (1992)	As of Jan. 1st (1993)	As of Apr. 1st (1993)	As of Jun. 1st (1993)
1. Cash held by population	14450	21178	26080	39523	96784	207637	341767
2. Personal deposits	18775	19513	20412	21109	23882	45425	50405
3. interests on deposits	3182	3182	3182	3182	3182	3182	3782
4. Deffered payments of Bonds	5495	5224	5155	8609	5910	2860	2114
(USSR bonds to be paid by the issue of Uzbek bonds)							
5 Certificates	1180	1046	1016	649	1206	509	478
6. Deposits in other banks	334	391	470	297	572	2107	2350
7. Insurance	280	280	280	280			
Total	43696	50814	56595	73649	131536	261720	400896
Assets of National Economy							
1. Total deposits of enterprises and organizations	21856	29007	30277	37806	141003	183388	
of which:							
Deposits	839	1085	1153	1334	2588	5488	
Capital investment account	5598	7881	7537	6838	13475	39690	
2. Deposits of government, trade unions, public and other organizations	4763	3173	3197	5444	14377	22440	
3. Banks' profits	4702	5685	7395	10600	27750	130204	
4. Other liabilities	6992	5194	3432	19930	360059	317318	
5 Total bank assetes used for settlements	17775	29859	47990	102639	391556	667823	
Of which:							
Correspondent accounts	6448	4179	7620	65277	72118	96820	
Accounts of branch banks	11327	25680	40370	37362	319438	571003	
Total assets of economy	56088	72918	92291	176419	934745	1321173	
Funds for credit resources regulation	3838	4692	5072	5135	11093	38814	
Total amount of money	103622	128424	153958	255203	1077374	1621707	

Source: Central Bank of Uzbekistan

Table 5.2: Enterprises Past Dues on Supplier's Accounts
(in millions of rubles as of beginning of the month)

Organizations	92.01	92.02	92.03	92.04	92.05	92.06	92.07	92.08	92.09	92.10
State construction	11.4	17.6	32.3	59.2	80.6	121.1	134.3	167.1	114.4	145
Association of Uzbek furniture	1.7	7.2	13.5	47	109.5	206.2	111.4	144.1	121.4	71.4
Uzbek special construction	7	30.5	59	78.9	161.1	339.4	431.5	568.6	280.8	310.4
Ministry of construction	52	183.7	399.8	706.1	1227.7	1852.9	2434.9	3689.4	1731.5	2371.2
Association of light industry	51.7	125.2	633.2	1628.8	1672.9	3266.7	6444.3	8642.7	4500.5	5199
Ministry of local industry	30.3	93.1	403.7	587.2	816.7	1205.3	1507.1	1878.6	1898	1310.8
Uzbek grain production	5.7	27.2	73.6	216.7	176.8	381.8	863.3	1521.1	1176	1153.9
Ministry of water	360.3	576.2	1128.9	1888.2	2139	2919	4040.6	5051.5	4289.9	4867.5
Collective farms	15.4	34.1	198.2	391.9	524	850.5	1243	2591.3	2481.5	3299.7
Ministry of agriculture	566.9	930.1	2225.8	6867.5	4771.3	7974.4	11999.1	19569	35090.9	17802
Ministry of transportation	26.9	38.8	69.6	125.2	176.5	300	493.7	745.2	590	649.9
Ministry of communications	10.4	17.5	35.2	35.3	82.7	138	154.2	167.7	76.7	98
Uzbekbrashu	29.8	47.4	474.6	1090.6	1091.1	3039.8	4853.5	7437.6	6204.8	7250.9
Ministry of trade	6.9	26.5	184.4	1287.3	2231.7	5475.5	7642.7	8649.9	3889.8	3960.9
Uzbek service center	23.2	25.4	60	103.8	289.7	413.9	581.4	573.7	475	312
Ministry of housing	88.9	171.5	531.7	653.5	880.5	1258.8	1439.1	1682	1090.2	1257
Ministry of highways	19.2	32.3	56.4	79.6	109.5	146.6	189.2	257.6	196	256.1
Uzbek contract trade	18.4	42.8	153.6	1141.4	2272.7	3455.5	5529.8	7938.4	3255.7	1900
State committee of oil production	11	171.8	41.2	43	77.1	300	651.5	2373.4	1975.8	2660.2
Ministry of construction materials	14.7	29.7	171	357.9	452.7	932.9	1405.4	1998.9	1106.1	1330.5
Tashkent construction	9.5	52.7	244.3	293.4	649.5	1037.4	1471.9	1881.2	958.9	1451.3
State committee of forest	0.7	0.6	1.3	1.6	131.4	3.9	11.7	1073	217.8	263.2
Ministry of energy	na	5.7	34.2	104.4	174.8	296.2	304.5	250.5	240.9	175.9
Cooperatives	38.6	39.3	43.9	72	99.9	144.4	210.7	223.6	367.1	175.5
Other organizations	171.2	1200.1	3040.1	6170.5	11089.5	20732.6	26677	33774.5	2639.5	21925.6
Departments of FSU	384.1	na	na	na	na	na	na	na	na	na
Total	1955.9	3927	10309.5	24031	31488.9	56792.8	80825.8	112850.6	74969.2	80197.9

Source: Ministry of Finance

UZBEKISTAN

Table 5.3: Enterprises Past Dues on Bank Short-Term Loans

(in millions of rubles as of beginning of the month)

Organizations	92.01	92.02	92.03	92.04	92.05	92.06	92.07	92.08	92.09	92.10
State construction	na	na	na	0.5	0.2	0.2	0.2	0.1	na	0.1
Association of Uzbek furniture	na	na	na	0.2	0.2	0.2	0.4	0.2	7.5	0.5
Uzbek special construction	na	0.7	1.6	1.4	1.7	4.5	5.1	6	2.2	14.6
Ministry of construction	5.6	9.1	7.8	13	3.3	9.6	12.8	9.2	8.5	21.2
Association of light industry	na	na	1.4	18.4	0.5	2.7	8.6	19	1231.7	286.9
Ministry of local industry	2.2	0.9	1.1	2.6	2.2	4.6	32	8.2	20.2	16.9
Uzbek grain production	na	0.1	0.7	na	na	na	11.2	11.2	na	1.3
Ministry of water	5.4	6.8	6.9	10.4	10.1	9.9	13.3	14.4	22.5	14
Collective farms	na	0.4	0.9	2.4	0.8	0.2	1.5	1.3	3.1	9.4
Ministry of agriculture	13	60.8	122	53.4	32.7	36.5	39.6	49.7	82.2	116.8
Ministry of transportation	0.6	1.1	1.5	0.9	3.2	5.4	6	5.7	4.9	9.2
Ministry of communications	0.4	0.7	2.3	2.9	1.9	0.5	0.9	0.3	0.8	2.4
Uzbekbrashu	0.3	1.3	12.9	4.8	3.9	5.6	7.1	5.4	14.6	11.9
Ministry of trade	0.1	0.3	0.8	2.8	18.5	5.7	17.2	7.9	4	63.7
Uzbek service center	1.5	1.4	1	0.6	0.1	0.3	4.2	0.9	5.1	4.4
Ministry of housing	1.8	2	2.4	2.1	15.7	5.8	3.7	14.6	8.8	12.2
Ministry of highways	0.4	0.6	0.5	0.7	0.8	0.8	0.9	1	1	2.1
Uzbek contract trade	0.1	na	0.1	1.4	1.1	0.5	1.9	1.2	2	3.7
State committee of oil production	na	na	na	na	na	0.5	na	0.1	na	na
Ministry of construction materials	0.1	0.3	0.3	1.4	0.7	6.7	4.3	18	7.3	6.6
Tashkent construction	0.4	4.7	4.3	0.3	1.5	17.3	19.7	37.2	27.6	14.4
State committee of forest	na	na	0.1	0.1	na	na	3.2	1.4	na	4.8
Ministry of energy	na	na	na	na	0.8	0.7	na	na	na	na
Cooperatives	4.9	5.3	5.3	4.8	4.3	4.9	5.1	5.8	7.2	7.9
Other organizations	24	37.4	49.6	51.6	93.9	129.5	158.9	350.5	229.2	459.4
Departments of FSU	12.9	na	na	na	na	na	na	na	na	na
Total	73.7	133.9	223.5	176.7	198.1	252.6	357.8	569.3	1690.4	1084.4

Source: Ministry of Finance

UZBEKISTAN

Table 6.1: Agricultural Production

(In million rubles, at constant 1983 prices)

	1986	1987	1988	1989	1990	1991	1992 est
Total of which:	10014.3	10048.8	10031.2	10456.2	1113.7	10993.6	11047.8
Grains	251.5	339.7	400.6	316.9	363.5	367.7	401.9
Potatos	59.0	50.0	59	62.1	64.3	67.1	83.6
Vegetables & melons	857.7	898.9	967.4	938.3	998.5	1102.5	1169.8
Fruits *	750.9	700.8	705.5	534.8	748.4	547.5	737.0
Cotton	4210.2	3983.1	4462.9	4170.9	4240.3	3854.3	3569.2
Livestock for slaughter of which:							
Cattle	3218.9	3417.6	3641.8	3764.3	4070.1	4321.7	4313.0
Pigs	na	na	na	na	143.9	125.7	121.7
Sheep & goats	221.3	226.0	242.2	252.8	294.5	299.0	306.0
Poultry	132.2	159.4	169.8	216.2	198.5	167.8	147.9
Milk	993.3	1050.3	1124.6	1161.5	1203.4	1321.4	1363.6
Eggs	195.5	214.4	223.5	232.6	234.9	224.8	191.4
Wools	201.5	208.4	215.7	208.9	220.7	216.9	217.7

Source: State Statistical and Forecasting Committee of Uzbekistan
* include grapes and berries.

UZBEKISTAN

Table 6.2: Summary Agricultural Production
(in million rubles, at constant prices of 1983)

	1986	1987	1988	1989	1990	1991	1992 est
Total agriculture	10014.3	10048.8	10931.2	10456.2	11113.7	10993.6	11047.8
Crops	6795.4	6631.2	7289.4	6691.9	7043.6	6671.9	6737.8
Animal husbandry	3218.9	3417.6	3641.8	3764.3	4070.1	4321.7	4313.0
Collective farms							
Total agriculture	3588.1	3469.8	3802.1	3670.2	3681.6	3389.6	3358.0
Crops	3036.4	2896.5	3199.1	3091.9	3083.7	2818.7	2792.0
Animal husbandry	551.7	573.3	603.0	578.3	597.9	570.9	566.0
State farms							
Total agriculture	3768.2	3894.1	4305.7	3920.8	4120.9	3741.5	3700.0
Crops	2883.8	2921.8	3258.7	2874.0	3068.4	2828.9	2797.0
Animal husbandry	884.4	972.3	1047.0	1046.8	1052.5	912.6	903.0
Other state enterprises							
Total agriculture	210.4	194.0	186.3	162.1	185.7	144.7	141.0
Crops	124.9	123.6	116.8	117.0	119.8	90.2	88.0
Animal husbandry	85.5	70.4	69.5	45.1	65.9	54.5	53
Private plots							
Total agriculture	2396.9	2436.6	2577.2	2642.3	3064.3	3667.8	3800.8
Crops	1620.8	1710.6	1833.7	1975.9	2253.7	2712.1	2763.2
Animal husbandry	776.1	726.0	743.5	666.4	810.6	955.7	1037.6
Semicollective & semistate farms							
Total agriculture	50.7	54.3	59.9	60.8	61.2	50.0	48.0
Crops	13.6	16.5	18.6	14.5	15	14.1	14
Animal husbandry	37.1	37.8	41.3	46.3	46.2	35.9	34

Source: State Statistical and Forecasting Committee of Uzbekistan

UZBEKISTAN
Table 6.3: Production and Average Yield of Major Agricultural Crops

	Production (1000 tons)						Cultivated area (1000 hectares)						Average yield (tons per ha.)					
	1986	1987	1988	1989	1990	1991	1986	1987	1988	1989	1990	1991	1986	1987	1988	1989	1990	1991
Grains	2061	2776	3337	2627	3073	2854	944	1277	1333	1154	1259	1348	2.2	2.2	2.5	2.3	2.4	2.1
Corn	389	421	520	461	430	431	117	118	116	111	108	108	3.3	3.6	4.5	4.2	4.0	4.0
Rice	1248	1822	2200	1641	2096	1908	700	1004	1050	882	1004	1080	1.8	1.8	2.1	1.9	2.1	1.8
Grain crops	424	533	617	525	547	515	127	155	167	161	147	160	3.3	3.4	3.7	3.3	3.7	3.2
Cotton	4989	4858	5365	5292	5058	4647	2054	2108	2017	1970	1830	1721	2.4	2.4	2.7	2.7	2.8	2.7
Cotton fiber	1622	1505	1732	1656	1623													
Potatoes	309	262	308	325	336	351	30	31	31	30	42	40	10.3	8.6	10.0	10.9	8.0	8.8
Fruits	1982	2032	2211	1896	2405	1918	393	405	411	444	310	459	5.0	5.0	5.4	4.3	7.7	4.2
Fruits & Berries	660	604	627	548	660	512	208	214	212	221	231	242	3.2	2.8	3.0	2.5	2.9	2.1
Grapes	696	652	655	416	745	480	131	127	128	132		134	5.3	5.1	5.1	3.2		3.6
Mellons	626	776	929	932	1000	926	54	64	71	91	79	83	11.7	12.2	13.0	10.2	12.6	11.1
Vegetables	2491	2558	2760	2585	2843	3348	113	117	123	123	141	166	22.1	21.8	22.4	21.1	20.2	20.2
Tobacco	28	33	30	33	31	41	10	10	8	8	8	9	2.7	3.3	3.6	4.1	3.8	4.3
Total	11860	12519	14011	12758	13746	13159	3544	3948	3923	3729	3590	3743	3.3	3.2	3.6	3.4	3.8	3.5
Food crops	6843	7628	8616	7433	8657	8471	1480	1830	1898	1751	1752	2013						

(Food crops = Total - cotton - tobacco)

Source: State Statistical and Forecasting Committee of Uzbekistan.

UZBEKISTAN

Table 6.4: Employment in Agriculture
(in thousands)

	1990	1991
Total	3115.3	3457.4
of which		
Collective Farms	993.4	1090.5
State Farms	950.1	986.2
Temporary Workers and labors in private plot	1153.6	1361.5
Cooperatives	11.1	4.3
Private Farms	4.0	6.7
Other	3.1	5.2

Source: State Statistical and Forecasting Committee of Uzbekistan.

UZBEKISTAN
Table 6.5: Main Aggregates of Animal Husbandry

	1986	1987	1988	1989	1990	1991	1992
Livestock (total)							
(thousands heads)							
Cattle	4099.8	4073.8	4103.1	4130.3	4180.2	4580.8	5112.6
of which cows	1559.4	1555.4	1571.7	1597	1644.7	1856.4	2120
Pigs	728.3	763.1	742.7	728.6	742.9	716	653.6
Sheep & goats	9256.3	8832.1	8539.9	8721.8	8785.6	9229.6	10109.5
of which: astrakhan shee	5245.5	7914.1	4751.2	4880.8	4948.8	5071.9	5218.8
goats	760.8	713.3	699.6	723.6	747.5	823.3	917.5
Horses	88	88.6	90	92.8	97.4	105.2	112.5
Livestock (state & collective farms)							
(thousands heads)							
Cattle	1780.7	1776.4	1777.8	1763.4	1737	1677.5	1633.7
of which cows	458.9	458.1	452.5	442.6	437.9	435.2	434.9
Pigs	714.9	749.7	730.0	715.9	729.4	690.9	620.8
Sheep & goats	5987.2	5703.9	5490.5	5602.9	5525.1	5401.0	5329.1
of which: astrakhan shee	4249	6963.8	3835.6	3982.1	3973.3	3984.2	3925.7
goats	296.1	264.8	249.2	235.6	219.5	203.5	192.7
Horses	69.8	69.2	68.6	69.7	70.0	69.9	68.7
Livestock (individual farmers)							
(thousands heads)							
Cattle	2319.1	2297.4	2325.3	2366.9	2443.2	2903.3	3478.9
of which cows	1100.5	1097.3	1119.2	1154.4	1206.8	1421.2	1685.1
Pigs	13.4	13.4	12.7	12.7	13.5	25.1	32.8
Sheep & goats	3269.1	3128.2	3049.4	3118.9	3260.5	3828.6	4780.4
of which: astrakhan shee	996.5	950.3	915.6	898.7	975.5	1087.7	1293.1
goats	464.7	448.5	450.4	488	528	619.8	724.8
Horses	18.2	19.4	21.4	23.1	27.4	35.3	43.8
Production							
Meat (thousands tons) 1/	330.5	386.0	385.8	404.1	439.6	477.8	484.8
Milk (thousands tons)	2265.5	2438.8	2505.3	2649.5	2836.6	2929.3	3034.2
Eggs (millions of pieces)	1460.6	1947.7	2042.0	2218.4	2333.9	2429.1	2452.9
Wool (thousands of tons)	20.7	23.5	23.5	24.3	25.2	24.4	25.8

Source: State Statistics and Forecasting Committee of Uzbekistan and Ministry of Agriculture
Notes: 1/ include beef, pork, lamb and poultry.

UZBEKISTAN
Table 6.6: Agricultural Production by Type of Farms

	1991 Jan-Dec	1992 Jan.	1992 Jan-Mar	1992 Jan-July	1992 Jan-Aug
Collective farms					
Cattle & poultry raised for slaughter (thousand tons)	61.71	5.50	15.10	32.25	40.25
Milk yields (tons)	531.34	38.20	118.40	254.52	352.79
Eggs (thousands)	68769	3069	12516	30309	38410
State farms					
Cattle & poultry raised for slaughter (thousand tons)	206.85	16.30	47.10	85.12	106.28
Milk yields (tons)	413.14	29.00	82.90	177.98	247.31
Eggs (thousands)	1385665	87336	252399	487949	634671
State farms attached to industries					
Cattle & poultry raised for slaughter (thousand tons)	22.37	2.00	5.20	11.43	13.17
Milk yields (tons)	1.81	0.20	0.40	1.12	1.56
Eggs (thousands)	314	25	68	128	169

Source: State Statitical and Forecasting Committee of Uzbekistan

UZBEKISTAN
Table 7.1. Real Growth Rate in Industrial Production
(percentage increase relative to the previous year)

	1986	1987	1988	1989	1990
All Industry	6.00	2.83	2.75	3.57	1.72
Heavy Industry	7.00	4.67	4.46	2.56	-0.83
Fuel-Energy Industry	9.00	3.67	-0.88	8.04	0.00
Electricity	.9.00	3.67	-6.19	10.38	0.85
Fuel Industry	10.00	1.82	5.36	5.08	0.00
Metallurgy	5.00	2.86	-2.78	6.67	-7.14
Machine-building	7.00	4.67	8.04	0.00	0.00
Petrochemical Industry	15.00	7.83	8.06	-0.75	-4.51
Forestry/Wood Products and Pulp & Paper ind.	5.00	6.67	5.36	6.78	6.35
Construction Materials	-0.30	4.31	2.88	0.93	0.93
Light Industry	5.00	-0.95	1.92	4.72	3.60
Textiles	6.00	-1.89	0.00	3.85	2.78
Clothing	2.00	2.94	7.62	7.08	8.26
Leather and Shoe	0.10	3.90	5.77	6.36	6.84
Agric./food-processing	5.00	4.76	4.55	2.61	5.93
Food processing	4.00	3.85	1.85	0.00	10.00
Meat and dairy products	7.00	8.41	7.76	8.00	-0.74
Fish	12.00	0.00	0.89	5.31	5.04

Source: State Statistical and Forecasting Committtee of Uzbekistan

UZBEKISTAN
Table 7.2. Industrial Production by Sector
(in million rubles, at current prices)

	1985	1986	1987	1988	1989	1990	1991
All Industry	20510.0	21528.0	22041.0	22718.0	23493.0	24733.0	55150.0
Heavy Industry	na	9245.0	9735.0	10034.0	10187.0	10273.0	19947.0
Fuel-Energy Industry	1702.0	1872.0	1916.0	1935.0	2064.0	2090.0	4075.0
Electricity	823.0	911.0	936.0	907.0	984.0	1011.0	1733.0
Fuel Industry	879.0	961.0	981.0	1028.0	1080.0	1079.0	2342.0
Metallurgy	1012.0	1070.0	1099.0	1077.0	1149.0	1166.0	2686.0
Machine-building	2450.0	2609.0	2724.0	3010.0	2986.0	2913.0	5399.0
Pulp and Paper Industry	24.0	25.0	24.0	23.0	30.0	40.0	136.0
Petrochemical Industry	63.0	66.0	69.0	71.0	75.0	70.0	133.0
Forestry/Wood Products	291.0	306.0	337.0	376.0	405.0	418.0	764.0
Construction Materials	1052.0	1036.0	1139.0	1031.0	1007.0	1012.0	2010.0
Light Industry	8417.0	8815.0	8696.0	8894.0	9367.0	9623.0	24863.0
Textiles	6741.0	7122.0	6964.0	7029.0	7333.0	7439.0	20487.0
Clothing	1170.0	1183.0	1205.0	1315.0	1441.0	1558.0	2956.0
Leather and Shoe	495.0	498.0	515.0	536.0	573.0	604.0	1385.0
Agric./food-processing	2666.0	2670.0	2745.0	2850.0	2870.0	3156.0	7674.0
Meat and dairy products	578.0	616.0	649.0	662.0	693.0	675.0	2637.0
Fish	52.0	58.0	58.0	60.0	64.0	69.0	135.0

Source: State Statistical and Forecasting Committee of Uzbekistan

UZBEKISTAN

Table 7.3: Electricity Production and Consumption

(In billion of kwh)

	1980	1985	1986	1987	1988	1989	1990	1991
Production	33930.4	47938.8	52171.4	54754.6	50589.8	55873.7	56324.8	54164.5
Of which:								
Thermal	28999.7	42498.1	47560.3	47991.4	43425.0	50370.4	49676.4	48313.5
Hydro	4930.7	5440.7	4611.1	6763.2	7164.8	5503.3	6648.4	5851.0
Imports (interrepublic)	13256.7	14147.2	13557.1	13797.6	17411.8	16609.4	16471.6	17701.7
Total supply	47187.1	62086.0	65728.5	68552.2	68001.6	72483.1	72796.4	71866.2
Domestic consumption	36313.7	46682.2	48153.8	50049.4	51441.5	53343.4	54167.6	53784.7
Of which:								
Industry	19102.5	24126.2	24589.9	25525.7	26029.0	26996.8	26845.8	25149.5
Construction	788.2	877.4	905.5	940.0	903.7	900.0	902.0	706.0
Households/1.	2655.5	3327.0	3389.4	3431.3	3549.8	3548.4	3542.3	4171.8
Agriculture	8551.3	11435.1	11963.2	12666.5	13368.4	14043.6	14882.8	15576.2
Transport	1206.0	1232.1	1232.1	1251.6	1303.6	1253.2	1240.0	1592.3
Communications & others	955.4	1497.8	1429.9	1441.0	1458.0	1525.4	1467.2	1517.3
Losses	3054.8	4186.6	4643.8	4793.3	4829.0	5076.0	5287.5	5071.6
Exports (interrepublic)	10873.4	15403.8	17574.7	18502.8	16560.1	19139.7	18628.8	18081.5

Notes: 1/ public services & utilities
Source: State Statistical and Forecasting Committee of Uzbekistan

UZBEKISTAN

Table 7.4: 1980 Fuel and Energy Balance

	unit of measurement	total availability	stock Jan 1980	domestic production	other sources	CIS import	domestic consumption	CIS export	stock Jan 1981
coal	1000 mt	8819.6	1022.9	5682.0	-	2114.7	6761.2	1173.4	885.0
firewood	1000 cub.mtr	252.7	36.2	67.0	-	149.5	220.3	0.4	32.0
oil (incl. gas condensate)	1000 mt	8579.8	71.1	1329.4	-	7179.3	8498.8	-	81.0
natural gas	mln. cub.mtr	99311.0	725.4	34840.0	-	63745.6	23397.2	74554.6	1359.2
gas/1.	mln. cub.mtr	299.4	-	-	299.4	-	299.4	-	0.0
hydroelectricity	mln. kwh	4930.6	-	4930.6	-	-	4930.6	-	0.0
metallurgic coke	1000 mt	124.7	14.8	-	-	109.9	111.9	-	12.8
oil coke	1000 mt	220.1	10.1	210.0	-	-	0.2	216.5	3.4
coal bars	1000 mt	142.8	5.8	137.0	-	-	93.1	45.3	4.4
household stove fuel	1000 mt	194.9	8.7	186.2	-	-	58.5	126.4	10.0
diesel fuel	1000 mt	3367.5	151.6	2007.9	-	1208.0	2781.6	434.5	151.4
low speed engine fuel	1000 mt	37.4	10.3	-	-	27.1	25.8	3.6	8.0
gasoline	1000 mt	2871.9	79.9	1285.1	-	1506.9	2426.2	375.6	70.1
aircraft gas	1000 mt	51.3	11.9	-	-	39.4	42.6	-	8.7
kerosin (all types)	1000 mt	1088.5	38.4	736.4	-	313.7	785.5	280.8	22.2
dry gas from oilprocessing	1000 mt	300.1	-	300.1	-	-	300.1	-	0.0
liquidated gas	1000 mt	230.2	7.2	20.1	-	202.9	226.0	0.8	3.4
asphalt	1000 mt	16.2	1.0	-	-	15.2	15.2	-	1.0
black mineral oil (masut)	1000 mt	3639.1	196.4	2332.2	-	1110.5	2966.4	451.3	221.4
electric energy	mln. KWH	47187.1	-	33930.4	-	13256.7	36313.7	10873.4	0.0
thermal energy	1000 gekaltr.	43922.3	-	43922.3	-	-	43922.3	-	0.0

1/produced by underground gasification of coal

Source: State Statistical and Forecasting Committee of Uzbekistan

UZBEKISTAN

Table 7.4a: 1985 Fuel and Energy Balance

	unit of measurement	total availability	stock Jan 1985	domestic production	other sources	CIS import	domestic consumption	CIS export	stock Jan 1986
coal	1000 mt	8656	576	5250	-	2830	7342	843	471
firewood	1000 cub.mtr	90	27	28	-	35	58	-	32
oil (incl. gas condensate)	1000 mt	8175	118	1978	205	5874	8052	-	123
natural gas	mln. cub.mtr	112655	896	34588	534	76637	33723	77369	1563
gas/1.	mln. cub.mtr	157	-	157	-	-	157	-	0
hydroelectricity	mln. kwh	5441	-	5441	-	-	5441	-	0
metallurgic coke	1000 mt	56	2	-	-	54	53	-	3
coke wastes	1000 mt	94	1	13	-	80	77	13	4
oil coke	1000 mt	218	6	212	-	-	18	193	7
coal bars	1000 mt	145	3	142	-	-	134	7	4
household stove fuel	1000 mt	148	6	120	-	22	51	92	5
diesel fuel	1000 mt	3722	144	2006	-	1572	3228	385	109
low speed engine fuel	1000 mt	32	3	-	-	29	23	4	5
gasoline	1000 mt	3129	99	1320	178	1532	2791	258	80
aircraft gas	1000 mt	41	4	-	-	37	37	-	4
kerosin for tech. appl.	1000 mt	130	3	73	5	49	78	50	2
lampkerosin	1000 mt	83	3	79	-	1	35	44	4
aircraftkerosin	1000 mt	632	15	596	-	21	598	17	17
dry gas from oilprocessing	1000 mt	325	-	325	-	-	325	-	0
liquidated gas	1000 mt	258	8	20	-	230	253	2	3
asphalt	1000 mt	16	-	16	-	-	16	-	0
black mineral oil (masut)	1000 mt	3659	161	2281	-	1217	2953	477	229
spent oils	1000 mt	0	-	-	-	-	-	-	0
waste of chem. industry	mln.cub.mtr	62087	-	47939	1	14147	46687	15400	0
electric energy	mln. KWH	52673	-	52673	-	-	52669	4	0
thermal energy	1000 gekaltr.	123	-	123	-	-	123	-	0

1/produced by underground gasification of coal

Source: State Statistical Forecasting Committee of Uzbekistan

UZBEKISTAN
Table 7.4b: 1990 Fuel and Energy Balance

	unit of measurement	total availability	stock Jan 1990	domestic production	other sources	CIS import	domestic consumption	CIS export	stock Jan 1991
coal	1000 mt	11504	1644	6477	3	3380	9403	682	1419
firewood	1000 cub.mtr	103	21	17	-	65	91	1	11
oil (incl. gas condensate)	1000 mt	8340	81	2810	-	5449	8291	-	49
natural gas	mln. cub.mtr	122799	3501	40761	3884	74653	39484	78108	5207
gas/l.	mln. cub.mtr	558	-	558	-	-	558	-	0
hydroelectricity	mln. kwh	6648	-	6648	-	-	6648	-	0
metallurgic coke	1000 mt	57	12	-	-	45	50	-	7
coke wastes	1000 mt	79	17	-	-	62	64	-	15
oil coke	1000 mt	66	11	-	-	55	59	2	5
coal bars	1000 mt	129	-	129	-	-	-	57	72
household stove fuel	1000 mt	114	10	60	44	-	-	2	112
diesel fuel	1000 mt	4089	174	2260	-	1655	3632	353	104
low speed engine fuel	1000 mt	66	11	-	-	55	59	2	5
gasoline	1000 mt	3090	51	1778	32	1229	2746	288	56
aircraft gas	1000 mt	29	9	-	-	20	29	-	0
kerosin for tech. appl.	1000 mt	89	4	74	-	11	69	17	3
lampkerosin	1000 mt	107	10	68	-	29	60	46	1
aircraftkerosin	1000 mt	1069	18	613	1	437	978	78	13
dry gas from oilprocessing	1000 mt	325	-	325	-	-	325	-	0
liquidated gas	1000 mt	385	18	24	-	343	377	4	4
asphalt	1000 mt	219	7	207	-	5	192	22	5
black mineral oil (masut)	1000 mt	4252	398	1657	-	2197	3404	480	368
spent oils	1000 mt	18	-	6	-	12	18	-	0
waste of chem. industry	mln.cub.mtr	106	-	106	-	-	106	-	0
electric energy	mln. KWH	72798	-	56325	-	16473	54169	18629	0
thermal energy	1000 gekaltr.	58714	-	58714	-	-	58709	-	0

1/produced by underground gasification of coal

Source: State Statistical and Forecasting Committee of Uzbekistan

Uzbekistan

Table 7.5: Energy Production for 1991-92
(in thousand tons)

	Coal		Oil and Gas Codensates		Motor Gasoline		Diesel		Mazut		Natural Gas (in million m3)		Electricity (in million kwh)	
	1991	1992	1991	1992	1991	1992	1991	1992	1991	1992	1991	1992	1991	1992
January	510	341	251	278	152	125	178	153	131	105	3949	4128	5443	4870
February	489	501	232	260	166	145	182	174	140	104	3649	3836	5042	4549
March	531	414	252	326	167	154	198	193	156	157	3992	4009	5285	4774
April	546	480	231	279	148	148	178	197	108	163	3430	3470	4463	4580
May	521	416	236	263	165	138	212	173	173	128	3464	3523	4170	4134
June	536	408	218	241	142	111	195	159	150	87	3050	3074	3848	3772
July	534	292	221	242	157	90	196	130	130	89	3041	3086	3891	3970
August	535	413	226	263	142	97	194	152	150	98	3128	3178	4289	3593
September	456	303	224	266							3125	3133	3920	3588
October	528	318	238	290							3411	3573	4430	4364
November	507	392	242	285							3621	3726	4512	4238
December	255	402	260	302							4022	4069	4853	4542
Total	5948	4680	2831	3296	1239	1008	1533	1331	1138	931	41882	42805	54146	50974

Source: Statistical and Forecasting Committee of Uzbekistan

Uzbekistan

Table 8.1 Prices and Inlfations

| | Retail (Goods & Services) | | Wholesale Prices | |
	Index	Inflation rates	Index	Inflation rates
91.12	100.0		100.0	
92.01	242.7	142.7	474.2	374.2
92.02	278.4	14.7	510.9	7.7
92.03	308.8	10.9	562.2	10.0
92.04	428.1	38.7	601.5	7.0
92.05	466.1	8.9	697.2	15.9
92.06	481.3	3.3	756.8	8.6
92.07	506.3	5.2	798.3	5.5
92.08	502.5	-0.8	864.4	8.3
92.09	536.5	6.8	977.4	13.1
92.10	604.6	12.7	1594.3	63.1
92.11	738.7	22.2	2377.5	49.1
92.12	887.1	20.1	2787.9	17.3
93.01	1550.6	74.8	4077.1	46.2
93.02	1753.4	13.1	4546.3	11.5
93.03	2003.6	14.3	5376.5	18.3
93.04	2498.4	24.7	5572.1	3.6
93.05	2907.7	16.4	7457.7	33.8
93.06			9608.4	28.8

Source: Goskomprognostat and Bank Staff Calculations

UZBEKSITAN

Table 8.2: Comparison of Consumer Goods Prices in State & Cooperative Trade Among CIS Cities

(As of end of August 1992, in Rubles per kilogram unless indicated)

	Tashkent	Moscow	Saint Petersber	Minsk	Kiev	Alma-At	Bishpek	Dushanbe
flour	6	13.4 1/	25 1/	16	50	na	na	na
bread	5	13	16	9	9	na	na	na
beef	60	85	90	52	100	99	na	na
boiled sausage	80	150	120	60	na	155	65	98
butter	130	190	190	120	200	219	165	160
vegetable oil	10	46	62	72	22	87	71	50
milk, litre	4	12	11	6	13	13	2.5	5.5
sour cream	50	70	60	34	na	74	52	60
eggs, ten	25	25	31	26	na	22	18	32
sugar	15	65	71	42	70	60	66	72
tea	80	310	230	240	350	172	na	na
vodka, .5 litre	98	121	155	100	na	121	na	97
potatoes	6	20	26	29	22	16	9	10
onions	4.5	20	23	20	23	16	7	na
fresh cabbage	2.5	14	17	19	18	5	5	na
rice	15	43	37	54	na	11	35	25

(As of end of July in 1992, in Rubles per kilogram unless indicated)

	Tashkent	Moscow	Saint Petersber	Minsk	Kiev	Alma-At	Bishpek	Dushanbe
flour	6	12 1/	21 1/	na	36 1/	6.1	na	5
bread	5.33	12.82	10	na	16 1/	3.15	9 1/	3.3
beef	60	77.85	88	50	113.3	92.5	na	60
boiled sausage	na	128.91	114	na	147	172.5	na	87
butter	119	184.95	183	79.5	200	232.5	182	145.5
vegetable oil	10	38.35	65	30	na	80.55	64	8.4
milk, litre	4	9	11	2.8	19	15	2.4	3
sour cream	50	67	61	17	62	78.5	37	32
eggs, ten	25	20.73	24	18	31.25	21.43	18	19
sugar	15	74.21	70	30	na	9	na	65
tea	80	214.34	218	240	na	172	na	148
vodka, .5 litre	98	121.5	163.5	100	122.75	110	250	97
potatoes	3.7	11.39	13	na	19.5	12	94	6.5
onions	3.5	23.08	21	8.53	23	11	6	3.5
fresh cabbage	1.4	13.34	13	16.07	12.25	4.5	na	3
rice	15	35.85	38	na	na	10.7	na	23

Source: State Statistical and Forecastig Committee of Uzbekistan
Note: 1/ High quality

UZBEKISTAN

Table 8.3: Historical Monthly Wages by Sector 1/

(in current rubles)

	1980	1985	1986	1987	1988	1989	1990	1991	1992
AVERAGE	155.5	164.2	165.9	169.7	182.0	193.8	215.4	325.7	2319.0
Material Sectors									
Industry	166.7	178.9	179.7	183.6	198.0	214.1	232.4	386.0	3014.6
Construction	205.4	219.5	218.7	222.7	245.2	260.3	282.1	390.5	2679.2
Agriculture	150.9	154.6	158.2	157.9	176.7	197.3	230.7	325.6	1773.4
Forestry	110.6	132.3	125.2	127.6	130.5	138.8	159.5	208.5	
Transport	185.9	192.8	192.2	194.8	207.6	221.3	247.9	378.2	2647.3
Communications	130.9	142.5	146.4	152.4	167.5	176.8	200.0	320.5	2223.0
Trade (Retail and Wholesale)	129.1	137.6	137.6	134.9	142.1	151.7	180.7	252.6	1456.8
Other Material Production	101.6	109.8	112.3	113.4	117.8	121.9	134.8	230.0	1444.5
Non-Material Sectors									
Municipal Services	117.0	123.4	124.5	126.7	137.1	145.6	163.5	261.0	2035.4
Science, Research & Development	161.8	180.5	184.0	197.1	218.0	247.5	275.5	342.1	2258.7
Education	132.0	149.8	156.2	166.1	171.8	167.7	173.5	290.0	2038.4
Culture	105.6	110.6	105.6	107.7	117.7	116.8	129.7	211.1	1575.1
Arts	116.1	122.1	123.4	122.4	130.4	135.0	143.9	243.5	1575.1
Health Care, Social Security, Sports	120.5	123.4	126.0	135.0	140.7	146.9	159.2	253.1	1824.3
Information services	118.5	127.1	134.8	146.2	159.7	198.6	234.8	363.7	1929.5
Banking, Finance, Credit, Insurance	144.8	153.8	159.4	167.8	173.7	181.5	320.1	549.1	4036.3
Government	144.0	148.2	155.5	164.2	176.5	201.5	286.3	360.4	2526.7

Source: State Statistical and Forecasting Committee of Uzbekistan

1/ For blue and white collar workers.

UZBEKISTAN

Table 8.4: Monthly and Minumum Wages in State Sector for 1992-93

(in Rubles)

		Average Monthly Wages 1/	Minimum Monthly Wages	
1991		325.7 2/	70	
1992				
	January	614	350	As of 1st of January
	Feburary	659		
	March	927		
	April	1158		
	May	1300	550	As of 1st of May
	June	1595		
	July	1908	1000	As of 1st of July
	August	2098		
	September	2660	1350	As of 1st of September
	October	3798	2000	
	November	4316		
	December	5920		
1993				
	January	5541	2500	
	Feburary	6196	3000	
	March	7357		
	April	8386		
	May	9386		
	June	23465		
	July	na	11250	

Sources: Ministry of Labor
Notes:
   1/ Average cross the state sector
   2/ Year average

UZBEKISTAN

Table 8.5: Monthly Wages by Sector for 1993

(in rubles)

	1992 December	1993 Janurary	1993 February	1993 March	1993 April	1993 May	1993 June
1 AVERAGE	5919.9	5541	6196.4	7357.4	8385.7	9386	23465.0
2 Industry	7798.8	7902	9092.8	10229.3	12037.2	13707	31719.5
3 Agriculture	5504.1	3172	3573.9	4654	5411.4	6328.3	13820.7
4 Forestry	3641.9	2697					
5 Transport	6652.9	7269	7811.4	9135.9	10534.9	11317.7	28292.5
6 Communication	6604.1	6330	7806.5	8706.1	9246.2	9882.6	24706.5
7 Construction	7628.1	6331	7172.1	9318.0	10523.2	12539.7	31349.3
8 Trade (Retail and Wholesale)	3438.1	4040	4348.8	4880.2	5344.6	6034.1	15085.3
9 Information and Computing Services	5194.8	5995	7232.5				
10 Municipal & Housing Services	4898.9	6315	6725.0	8591.6	7784.4	8398.8	20992
11 Health Care, Social Security, Sports	3995.8	4233	4413.0	5105.6	5561.8	6158.2	15395.5
12 Education	4403.7	5247	5514.2	6464.0	7316.6	7558.1	18895.3
13 Culture & Arts	3388.4	3727	4557.3	4590.2	6040.1	6979.9	17449.8
14 Science & Research Development	6393.4	5645	6715.4	7491.1	9012.8	10027.5	25068.8
15 Government Administration	6496.6	6840	8249.7	9759.6	10778	11149	27872.5
16 Credits & State Insurance	12764.2	7497	11970.2	18949.3	16676.4	19064.4	47661.0
17 Other Braches	4003.5	4696	5440.4				

Source: State Statistical and Forecasting Committee of Uzbekistan

UZBEKISTAN

Table 9.1: Aggregated Household Monetary Income and Expenditure
(in million rubles, at current prices)

Income	1986	1987	1988	1989	1990	1991	1992.08
A. Total labor income							
1. wages paid by enterprises	10504.4	10965.9	11766.8	12816.4	14427	23530	62412.4
2. other wages & compensations	356	370.5	608.6	1474.4	1622.5	2096.7	3571
3. income paid by collective farms	1718.4	1670.1	1814.7	2117.9	2475.2	3779.6	8578.9
4. income from sale of farm products	1194.4	1279.6	1591.5	1565.7	2047.1	4750.5	5260.3
B. Total transfer receipts							
5. pensions and allowances	2372.3	2501.2	2657.9	2902.7	3415.3	11919.8	
6. scholarships	145.1	147.4	156.1	164.9	192.7	454.7	
7. income from financial system (insurance & interests)	507.6	532.1	643.9	720.2	1566.7	1600.1	17348.7 1/
8. other incomes	396.5	477.9	720.3	812.5	776	990.9	
9. adjustments	13	18.9	41.6	na	na	na	
C. Total income	**17207.7**	**17963.6**	**20001.4**	**22574.7**	**26522.5**	**49122.3**	**97171.3**

Expenditures							
A. Total purchases							
1. retail trade purchases	13548.4	13403.7	14561.1	15710.5	17836.5	30121.7	50844.9
2. purchased services	1384.2	1490.4	1751.9	1899.5	1946.3	2684.7	7726
rent & utilities	428.3	436.8	462.1	479	475.4	541.7	na
communications	75.1	85.3	94.7	108.1	113.5	155.7	na
health & other services	56	67.3	80.7	87.4	105.7	154	na
cooperatives	824.8	901	1114.4	1225	1251.7	1833.3	na
B. Tranfers and savings							
3. taxes, fees, dues & others	1568.8	1639.8	1780.4	1973.5	2341.6	2784	6823.3
4. savings	807.6	851.9	1066.6	1599.2	2159.7	9176.2	3148
5. transfers & money orders	na	na	na	17.8	45.8	121.3	na
C. Total outlays	**17309**	**17385.8**	**19160**	**21200.5**	**24329.9**	**44887.9**	**68542.2**
7. income less expenditure	**-101.3**	**577.8**	**841.4**	**1374.2**	**2192.6**	**4234.4**	**28629.1**

Source: State Statistical and Forecasting Committee of Uzbekistan
Notes: 1/ the sum of iterms 5, 6 and 7.

UZBEKISTAN
Table 10.1: Gross Fixed Investment of State Enterprises

(in million rubles, at current prices)

	1991	1992 est.
Total	9975.2	39692
Industry	2338.7	16790
Agriculture	2701.1	5600
Construction	262.6	700
Transport & Comm.	827.2	2683
Trade & Public Restaraunts	165.7	485
Housing	1406	3776
Communal Services	928.2	5149
Health & Social Security	356.2	1340
Public Education	928.6	2583
Cultural & Atrs	60.9	586

Source: State Statistical and Forecasting Committee

UZBEKISTAN

Table 10.2: Changes in Stocks

(million rubles, at current prices)

	1986	1987	1988	1989	1990	1991
Material sphere	**6068.9**	**1070.6**	**983.4**	**586.6**	**4651.2**	**14740.7**
Industry	45.5	323.2	-942.6	500.0	85.2	11040.1
Construction	604.5	484.4	342.1	170.2	83.6	303.3
Agriculture /1	4877.9	1323.7	1404.5	-1017.2	2270.5	-371.8
Transport	24.6	11.1	111.0	3.2	99.9	3694.1
Communication	48.9	49.4	51.6	48.7	35.8	-167.8
Trade & rel. services	-19.4	-471.8	86.7	229.4	291.7	1606.1
Geology	12.6	-1.8	-1.4	2.6	0.8	1.2
Storage	31.8	-31.5	-28.8	125.0	107.9	-587.9
R&D	5.7	-2.8	63.3	2.1	15.1	555.3
Other branches	436.8	-613.3	-103.0	522.6	1660.7	-1331.9
Nonmaterial sphere of which:	329.5	375.1	-250.9	1204.0	317.3	-2667.7
Housing and communal	315.9	385.4	-238.5	1181.6	281.0	-3174.8
Consumer services	13.6	-10.3	-12.4	22.4	36.3	507.1
Total	6398.4	1445.7	732.5	1790.6	4968.5	12073.0

1/ 1986 figure is biased because stock at end of 1985 did not include collective farms
   Stock of collective farms at end 1986 = 4374.9 mln. roubles
2/ 1991 figure is biased because stock 1991 included also former union enterprises
Source: State Statistical and Forecasting Committee of Uzbekistan

UZBEKISTAN
Table 10.3: Stocks at End of Year

(In million rubles, at current prices)

	1980	1985	1986	1987	1988	1989	1990	1991
Material sphere	16336.2	19933.7	26002.6	27073.2	28056.6	28643.2	33294.4	48035.1
Industry	4738.2	5873.9	5919.4	6242.6	5300.0	5800.0	5885.2	16925.3
Construction	2642.1	2247.8	2852.3	3336.7	3678.8	3849.0	3932.6	4235.9
Agriculture/1	5388.8	7877.8	12755.7	14079.4	15483.9	14466.7	16737.2	16365.4
Transport	291.2	381.0	405.6	416.7	527.7	530.9	630.8	4324.9
Communication	293.3	470.7	519.6	569.0	620.6	669.3	705.1	537.3
Trade & rel. services	1298.7	1875.1	1855.7	1383.9	1470.6	1700.0	1991.7	3597.8
Geology	153.1	241.2	253.8	252.0	250.6	253.2	254.0	255.2
Storage	350.0	495.1	526.9	495.4	466.6	591.6	699.5	111.6
R&D	87.5	94.5	100.2	97.4	160.7	162.8	177.9	733.2
Other branches	1093.3	376.6	813.4	200.1	97.1	619.7	2280.4	948.5
Nonmaterial sphere **of which:**	2500.7	4461.5	4791.0	5166.1	4915.2	6119.2	6436.5	3768.8
Housing and communal	2264.6	4137.2	4453.1	4838.5	4600.0	5781.6	6062.6	2887.8
Consumer services	236.1	324.3	337.9	327.6	315.2	337.6	373.9	881.0
Total	18836.9	24395.2	30793.6	32239.3	32971.8	34762.4	39730.9	51803.9

1/ Agriculture stocks for 1980 and 1985 only include state farms (not collective farms)
2/ 1991 stocks also include former union enterprises
Source: State Statistical and Forecasting Committee of Uzbekistan

UZBEKISTAN

Table 10.4: Gross Fixed Investment at Constant 1984 Prices

(in million rubles)

	1980	1985	1986	1987	1988	1989	1990
Total	**6197**	**6811**	**6980**	**7170**	**7568**	**7529**	**8505**
Material sphere	4442	4649	4645	4592	4702	4573	4960
Industry	1465	1579	1587	1675	1741	1805	1671
Agriculture	2181	2090	2104	2064	2094	1898	2267
Forestry	1	3	3	2	2	4	4
Construction	179	276	252	210	247	246	289
Transport	396	465	464	445	388	382	368
Communication	51	81	81	79	81	84	95
Trade & other material service	155	136	135	115	147	152	249
Storage	14	19	19	2	2	2	17
Non-material sphere	1755	2162	2335	2578	2866	2956	3545
Housing	956	1271	1335	1488	1788	1760	2080
Other non-mat. services*	799	891	1000	1090	1078	1196	1465

* Includes:communal services, health, education, science ,culture and arts

Source: State Statistical and Forecasting Committee of Uzbekistan

UZBEKISTAN

Table 10.5 Capital Investment for Unfinished Construction

(in million rubles, at constant 1984 prices)

	1987	1988	1989	1990	1991*
Total	4869	5222	5441	6095	8438
Material Sphere	3629	3788	3923	4257	5287
Industry	1698	1694	1827	1941	2584
Construction	59	64	103	103	125
Agriculture	1575	1684	1655	1638	1817
forestry	2	2	4	5	8
storage	1	1	3	2	6
Transport	204	233	202	348	451
Communications	44	55	64	80	114
Trade and Catering	43	52	64	131	176
Other material sphere	3	3	1	9	6
Nonmaterial sphere of which:	1240	1434	1518	1838	3151
Housing	364	398	406	451	787
Communal economy	422	517	540	653	1106
Culture and arts	32	42	43	52	86
Public health, social security, physical culture and tourism	147	161	180	241	392
Education	173	187	220	287	606
Other	102	129	129	154	174

* In current prices
Source: State Statistical and Forecasting Committee of Uzbekistan

GLOSSARY

Balance of Payments: A systematic record of the economic transactions between a nation's residents and nonresidents during a given period, usually one calendar or fiscal year. It covers the flows of real resources (including factor services, such as services of labor and capital) across the boundaries of the domestic economy, changes in foreign reserves and liabilities from economic transactions, and transfer payments to and from the rest of the world. Balance of payments accounts comprise two broad categories: the *current account*, which measures merchandise trade, factor and nonfactor services income, and transfer receipts and payments, and the *capital account*, which measures the changes in domestic and foreign capital assets and liabilities.

Capital Flows: Usually refers to the amount of capital moving into or out of a country during a given period. Such international movements of capital may come from either official or private sources. Official sources are (1) governments and government agencies (also called *bilateral* lenders) and (2) international organizations (called *multilateral* lenders). Private sources comprise (1) commercial suppliers and manufacturers, which provide export credits for the purchase of their goods, (2) commercial banks, which provide export credits or cash loans, (3) other private investors, who invest in foreign enterprises in which they seek a lasting interest (*direct investment*) or purchase stocks or bonds issued by foreign companies or governments (*portfolio investment*), and (4) charitable organizations, which provide financial aid, goods, and services as grants.

Consolidated Budget: Refers to a general government budget that presents a structure of all de facto expenditures and revenues that the government incurs and receives. For example, a public enterprise's profits/losses should be considered a revenue/expenditure in the consolidated budget.

Deflator: An implicit price index used to distinguish between changes in the money value of Gross National Product that are due to a change in prices and those that are due to a change in physical output.

Economic Regulations: Regulations to achieve economic goals (that is, the control of monetary policy, lending to priority sectors or individuals, and so forth).

Economies of Scale: Reductions in the average cost of a product in the long run, resulting from an expanded level of output.

Excise Tax: Tax levied on commodities.

Export Credits: Finance provided by lenders in a given country for exports of specific goods or services.

Extra/Off-Budgetary Funds: The funds not explicitly included in the government's budget.

Fiscal Policy: Generally refers to the use of taxation and government expenditure to regulate the aggregate level of economic activity.

Foreign Trade: Trade with countries outside the FSU.

Foreign Direct Investment: Usually refers to any investment in another country which is carried out by private companies or individuals as opposed to government aids.

Grant: A current transfer of capital, goods, or services to a foreign country that creates no or little future obligation to make a similar transfer from the recipient country to the donor.

Gross Domestic Product: The total final output of goods and services produced by an economy and by residents and nonresidents, regardless of the allocation to domestic and foreign claims. It is calculated without deductions for depreciation.

Gross National Product: The total domestic and foreign output claimed by residents. It comprises gross domestic product adjusted by *net factor income* from abroad. Factor income comprises receipts that residents receive from abroad for factor services (labor, investment, and interest) less similar payments made to nonresidents abroad. It is calculated without deductions for depreciation.

Inflation: A sustained rise in the general price level.

Interest Margin [of a bank]: Interest-rate differential between borrowing and lending rates.

Interrepublic Trade: Trade with countries of the FSU.

Investment: The sum of gross domestic fixed investment and the change in stocks (or inventories). Gross domestic investment covers all outlays of the private and public sectors for addition to the fixed assets of the economy, plus the value of changes in stocks (or inventories).

Nominal Wages: Wage earnings that are measured by their money value.

Personal Income Tax: Tax levied on personal income, which is the flow of income that accrues to the individual or household. The income may be from the sale of labor and/or ownership of assets, or it may take the form of a transfer income.

Profits: The difference between the revenue generated from sale of output and the full opportunity costs of the factors used to produce that product.

Prudential Regulations: Regulations that place limits and constraints on banks to ensure the safety and soundness of the banking system.

Rates:

Crude Death
Rate: Number of deaths per 1,000 population.

Birth
Rate: Number of live births per 1,000 population.

Fertility
Rate: Number of children per woman.

Infant Mortality
Rate: Infant deaths per 1,000 live births.

Maternal Mortality
Rate: The rate of mothers who die within one month after giving birth per 100,000 live births.

Savings: *Domestic savings* are defined as the difference between GNP and total consumption. *Gross national savings* are the net factor income from abroad and net current transfers from abroad added to domestic savings.

Seignorage Revenue: Net revenue accrued from money creation.

State Order System: State procurement system that requires that much of state and collective farms and other enterprises be sold to the state at below-market prices determined by the Government.

Stock Market Capitalization: Market price times the total number of outstanding shares in a stock exchange. It is a rough estimate of the size of the market.

Stock Market Turnover: The total value of the shares traded divided by market capitalization. It provides a measure of how active the market is.

Supervision: The means for ensuring compliance with regulations.

Terms of Trade: A measure of the relative level of export prices compared with import prices. Calculated as a ratio of a country's index of export unit value and the import unit value. This indicator shows changes over a base year in the level of export prices as a percentage of import prices.

Value-Added Tax: Tax based on the value-added, which is the value of a firm's output minus the value of the inputs it purchases from other firms. Essentially, it is the sum of the factor income--that is, the wages and profits--of the firm.

REFERENCES

Alexeev, Michael (1991). "The "Storming" of Enterprise Behavior in a Centrally Planned Economy." *Journal of Economic Behavior and Organization*, vol. 15 2:173-85, March.

Alexeev, Michael (1987). "Microeconomic Modeling of Parallel Markets: The Case of Agriculture in the USSR." *Journal of Comparative Economics*, pp. 543-57, December.

Atkinson, A.B. and J. Micklewright. "Economic Transformation in Eastern Europe and the Distribution of Income." *Cambridge University Press*, Cambridge, 1992.

Baeuer, Tomas (1988). "Economic Reforms Within and Beyond the State Sector." *American Economic Review*, vol. 78, pp. 452-56, May.

Bahl, Roy (1992). "Intergovernmental Fiscal Relations in China." *The World Bank Working Papers*, no. 863.

Baranov, A.A., V.Iu. Albitskii, Iu.M. Komarov. "Tendentsii Mladencheskoi Smertnosti v SSSR 70-80 Gody." *Sovetskoe zdravookhranenie 3*, 1990.

Beksiak, Janusz (1987). "Enterprise and Reform: The Polish Experience." *European Economic Review*, 31, nos. 1/2:118-24, February/March.

Belova, N.F. and I.I. Dmitrichev. "Semeinyy Biudzhet Finansy i Statistika." Moscow, 1990.

Bennathan, Esra, Jeffrey Gutman and Louis Thompson (1991). "Reforming and Privatizing Poland's Road Freight Industry." *The World Bank PRE Working Papers*, no.750.

Bennett, John (1991). "Repressed Inflation, Queuing and the Resale of Goods in a Centrally Planned Economy." *European Economic Review*, pp. 49-60, January.

Benston, G.J., R.A. Eisenbeis, P.H. Horvitz, E.J. Kane, and G.J. Kaufman (1986). "Perspectives on Safe and Sound Banking." *MIT Press*, Cambridge.

Blanchard, O., Krugman R. Dornbush, R. P. Layard, and L. Summers (1991). "Reform in Eastern Europe." Cambridge, MA: *MIT Press*.

Boyd, Michael L. (1989). "Policy and the Performance of Bulgarian Agricultural Organizations." *Economic and Industrial Democracy*, vol. 10, pp. 341-59.

Bradburd, R. (1992). "Privatization of Natural Monopoly Public Enterprises: The Regulation Issue." *The World Bank PRE Working Papers*, no. 864.

Brooks, Karen M. (1991). "Decollectivization and the Agricultural Transition in Eastern and Central Europe." *The World Bank PRE Working Papers*, no. 793.

Brown, Stuart S. (1989).   "Export Uncertainty in Centrally Planned Economies and Administrated Protection." *Journal of Comparative Economics*, 13:553-65, December.

Buck, Trevor W. (1988).   "Soft Budget and Administration." *Comparative Economic Studies*, vol. 30, 3:51-70, Fall.

Calvo, Guillermo A. and Fabrizio Corcelli (1990).   "Stabilizing a Previously Centrally Planned Economy: Poland 1990." *Economic Policy : A European Forum*, no. 14, pp. 176-226, April.

_____ and J. Frenkel (1991). "From Centrally-Planned to Market Economies: The Road From CPE to PCPE." *IMF Staff Papers*, vol 38, no. 2, June, pp. 268-99.

Capori, Gerard Jr. (1992). "Reforming Finance in Transitional Socialist Economies: Avoiding the Path From Shell Money to Shell Games." *The World Bank Working Papers*, no. 898.

Casaki, Csaba (1992). "Transformation of Agriculture in Central Eastern Europe and the Former USSR: Major Policy Issues and Perspectives." *The World Bank Working Papers*, no. 888.

Chao, Howard and Xiaoping Yang (1987).   "Reform of the Chinese System of Enterprise Ownership." *Stanford Journal of International Law*, 23:365-97, Summer.

Chen, L., J. Rohde and R. Jolly. "A Looming Crisis: Health in the Central Asian Republics". *The Lancet*, vol 339, June 13, 1992: 1465-1467.

Chen, Tingtong (1987).   "Enterprise Share Flotation in Mainland China." *Issues & Studies: A Journal of Chinese Studies and International Affairs*, pp. 72-91, September.

Corbo, Vittorio (1991).   "Report on Adjustment Lending II: Lessons for Eastern Europe." *The World Bank PRE Working Papers*, no. 693.

Corden, Max W. (1992).   "Trade Policy and Exchange Rate Issues in the Former Soviet Union." *The World Bank Working Papers*, no. 915.

Coricelli, Fabrizio and Ana Revenga (1992).   "Wages and Unemployment in Poland: Recent Developments and Policy Issues." *The World Bank Working Papers*, no. 821.

Debardleben, Joan (1990).   "Economic Reform and Environmental Protection in the USSR." *Soviet Geography*, pp. 237-56, April.

Dhanji, Farid and Branko Milanovic.   "Privatization in Eastern and Central Europe: Objectives, Constraints, and Models of Divestiture." *The World Bank PRE Working Papers*, no. 770.

Dietl, Jerry and Krystyna Iwinska-Knop (1989). "Trade in Poland and the Federal Republic of Germany: A Comparative Approach." *Journal of Business Research*, vol. 19 4:313-24, December.

Dissopoulos, E. and T. Hane (1991). "Market Liberalization Policies in a Reforming Socialist Economy. *IMF mimeo*, August.

Feltenstein, Andrew and Ziba Farhadian (1987). "Fiscal Policy, Monetary Targets, and the Price Level in a Centrally Planned Economy: An Application to the Case of China." *Journal of Money, Credit and Banking*, pp. 137-56, May.

Fischer, S. and Alan Gelb (1990). "Issues in Socialist Economy Reform." *The World Bank PRE Working Paper*, no. pp. 565, December.

Gale, John (1990). "The People's Republic of China: 1978-1990." *International Center for Economic Growth*.

Gelb, A. and Cheryl Gray (1991). "The Transformation of Economies in Central and Eastern Europe." *Policy and Research Series*, no. 17, World Bank.

Gelb, Jefferson and Singh (1993). "Can Communist Economies Transform Incrementally? The Experience of China." *NBER mimeo*.

Gillespie, Stuart. "Safety Nets, Household Food Security and Nutrition in Kazakhstan." *UNICEF/WHO Collaborative Mission to Kazakhstan*, 1 March 1992.

Glaziev, Sergei (1991). "Transformation of the Soviet Economy: Economic Reforms and Structural Crises." *National Institute Economic Review*, pp. 97-108, November.

Granick, David (1990). "Chinese State Enterprises: A Regional Property Rights Analysis." *Chicago and London: University of Chicago press*.

Gray, Chery W. and Peter Innachkov (1992). "Bulgaria's Evolving Legal Framework for Private Sector Development." *The World Bank Working Papers*, no. pp. 906.

Grzegorz, Kolodko (1991). "Transition From Socialism and Stabilization Policies: The Polish Experience." *IMF mimeo*, June.

Hanke, S. and Kurt Schuler (1991). "Currency Boards for Eastern Europe." *Heritage Foundation* (Washington).

Hare, Paul (1987). "Supply Multipliers in a Centrally Planned Economy with a Private Sector." *Economics of Planning*, 21:53-61.

Havrylyshyn, O. and David Tarr (1991). "Trade Liberalization and the Transition to a Market Economy." *The World Bank PRE Working Paper*, no. 700, July.

He, Zhongze (1989). "Brief Introduction to Enterprise Reform in China." *Public Enterprise*, pp. 163-67, June.

Heady, Christopher and Pradeep K. Mitra (1992). "Taxation in Decentralizing Socialist Economies: the Case of China." *The World Bank Working Papers*, no. 820.

Hebel, Jutta and Gunter Schucher (1991). "From Unit to Enterprise? -- The Chinese Tan-Wei in the Process of Reform." *Issues & Studies: A Journal of Chinese Studies and International Affairs*, pp. 24-43, April.

Heesterman, A. (1991). "Inflation and Transition to a Mixed Economy: Can it Work?" *Economics of Planning*, pp. 135-49.

Hewett, E. (1989). "Economic Reform in the USSR, Eastern Europe, and China: The Politics of Economics." *American Economic Review*, vol. pp. 79, 2:16-20, May.

Hinds, Manuel (1990). "Issues in the Introduction of Market Forces in Eastern European Socialist Economies." *The World Bank EMENA Discussion Paper*, no. 0057, April.

Hinds, Manuel and Gerhard Pohl. "Going to Market: Privatization in Central and Eastern Europe." *The World Bank PRE Working Papers*, no. 768.

Holzman, Franklyn D. (1991). "Moving Towards Ruble Convertibility." *Comparative Economic Studies*, vol. 33, 3:3-36, Fall.

Hsu, John C. (1989). "China's Foreign Trade Reforms: Impact on Growth and Stability." *Cambridge; New York and Melbourne; Cambridge University Press*.

Hughes, G. and P. Hare (1991). "Competitiveness and Industrial Restructuring in Czechoslovakia, Hungary and Poland." *European Economy*, Special Issue, June.

Hui, Li Zhi (1992). "China: Important Tax Reform in the Income Tax Laws Concerning Foreign Investment and Enterprise." *Intertax*, pp. 3:163-67, March.

Husain, A. and R. Sahay (1992). "Does Sequencing of Privatization Matter in Reforming Planned Economies?" *IMF mimeo*, January.

Kamath, Shym J. (1990). "Foreign Direct Investment in a Centrally Planned Developing Economy: The Chinese Case." *Economic Development and Culture Change*, pp. 106-30, October.

Kane, E. (1985). "The Gathering Crisis in Federal Deposit Insurance." Cambridge, MA, *MIT Press*.

Klaus, Vaclav (1990). "A Perspective on Economic Transition in Czechoslovakia and Eastern Europe." *World Bank Researcher Observer*, Supplement, pp. 13-18.

Koo, Anthony Y.C. (1990). "The Contract Responsibility System: Transition From a Planned to a Market Economy." *Economic Development & Cultural Change*, vol. 38, pp. 797-820.

Kraft, Evan and Milan Vodopivec (1992). "How Soft is the Budget Constraint for Yugoslav Firms." *The World Bank Working Papers*, no. 937.

Lawson, Colin (1988). "Exchange Rates, Tax-subsidy Schemes, and the Revenue From Foreign Trade in a Centrally Planned Economy." *Economic of Planning*, 22:72-77.

Lebkowski, Maciej and Jan Monkiewicz (1986). "Western Direct Investment in Centrally Planned Economies." *Journal of World Trade Law*, vol. 20, pp. 624-38, Nov./Dec.

Lee, Barbara W. and John Nellis (1991). "Enterprise Reform and Privatization in Socialist Economies." *Public Enterprise*, pp. 101-17, June/September.

Letiche, John M. (1992). "Restructuring Centrally-Planned Economies: The Case of China in the Long Term." *Journal of Asian Economics*, pp. 141-63, Spring.

Lin, Justin Yifu (1992). "Rural Reform an Agriculture Growth in China." *American Economic Review*, March, vol. 82, no. 1, pp. 34-51.

Long, Millard and Silvia Sagari (1991). "Financial Reform in Socialist Economies in Transition." *The World Bank PRE Working Papers*, no. 711.

McKinnon, Ronald (1991). "The Order of Economic Liberalization: Financial Control in the Transition to a Market Economy." *John Hopkins University Press*.

McLure, Charles E. Jr. (1991). "A Consumption-Based Direct Tax for Countries in Transition from Socialism." *The World Bank PRE Working Papers*, No. 751.

Michalopoulos C. and David Tarr (1992). "Trade and Payments Arrangements for States of the Former USSR." *Studies of economies in Transformation*, no. 2, World Bank.

Murphy, K., A. Schleifer and R. Vishimy (1992). "The Transition to a Market Economy: Pitfalls of Partial Reform." *Quarterly Journal of Economics*, pp. 889-906.

Nuti, Domenico Mario (1989). "Opening Up Capital Markets in Eastern Europe: Remonetization and Capital Markets in the Reform of Centrally Planned Economies." *European Economic Review*, vol. 33, pp. 427-38.

Oblath, Gabor and David Tarr (1991). "The Terms-of-Trade Effects From the Elimination of State Trading in Soviet-Hungarian Trade." *The World Bank PRE Working Papers*, no. 690.

O'Brien, John Conway (1991). "The Eternal Path to Communism: From Marx to Lenin and Stalin to Solzhenisyn and Gorbachev." *International Journal of Social Economics*, pp. 10-31.

Osband, K. and Delano Villanuera (1992). "Independent Currency Authorities: An Analytic Primner." *IMF working paper*, WP 92, June.

Owa, J., A. Osinaike, A. Costello. Letter: "Charging for Health Services in Developing Countries." *The Lancet*, vol 340, September 19, 1992: 732.

Pohl, Gerhard (1991). "Economic Consequences of German Reunification: 12 Months After the Big Bang." *The World Bank Working Papers*, no. 816.

Polizatto, Vincent (1990). "Prudential Regulation and Banking Supervision." World Bank, *PPR Working Papers*, WPS 340, January.

Popkin, Barry. "Poverty in the Russian Federation: Demographics and Coverage by Current Support Systems." *University of North Carolina at Chapel Hill*. February 21, 1992.

Portes, Richard (1979). "Internal and External Balance in a Centrally Planned Economy." *Journal of Comparative Economics*, pp. 325-45, December.

Portes, Richard (1989). "Economic Reforms, International Capital Flows and the Development of the Domestic Capital Market in CPEs." *European Economic Review*, vol. 33, pp. 466-71, March.
Portes, Richard (1991). "The Path of Reform in Central and Eastern Europe: An Introduction." *Center for Economic Policy Research Discussion Paper*, no. 559, May.

Radetzki, Marian (1990). "Socialist Transformation: Energy Exports From Centrally Planned Economies." *Energy Policy*, vol. 18, 9:806-88, November.

Rice, E. (1991). "Managing the Transition: Enhancing the Efficiency of Eastern European Governments." *The World Bank PRE Working Papers*, no. 757.

Riveros, Luis A. (1991). "Wage and Employment Policies in Czechoslovakia." *The World Bank PRE Working Papers*, no. 730.

Rondinelli, Dennis R. (1991), "Developing Private Enterprise in the Czech and Slovak Federal Republic: The Challenge of Economic Reform." *Columbia Journal of World Business*, pp. 26-36, Fall.

Sachs, Jeffrey (1991). "Accelerating Privatization in Eastern Europe." Paper prepared for the World Bank's *Annual Conference on Development Economies*, April.

Schrenk, Martin (1991). "The CMEA System of Trade and Payments: The Legacy and the Aftermath of its Termination." *The World Bank PRE Working Papers*, no. 753.

Seleny, Anna (1991). "Hidden Enterprise, Property Rights Reform and Political Transformation in Hungary." *Harvard University, Center for European Studies, Program on Central and Eastern Europe Working Paper Series,* no. 11:1-47.

Sergei, Shatalov (1991). "Privatization in the Soviet Union: The Bargaining of a Transition." *The World Bank Working Papers*, no. 805.

Sundrarajan, V. (1992). "Central Banking Reform in Formerly Planned Economies." *Finance and Development*, vol. 29, 1:10-13, March.

Svejnar, Jan and Katherine Terrell (1991). "Reducing Labor Redundancy in State-Owned Enterprises." *The World Bank PRE Working Papers*, no. 792.

Talley, Samuel and Ignacio Mas (1990). "Deposit Insurance in Developing Countries." World Bank, *PRE Working Papers*, WPS 548, May.

Tanasescu, Dimitru G. (1991).   "Romania Refining Industry Assesses Restructuring."   *Oils & Gas Journal*, vol. 89, pp. 89-93.

van Brabant, Hozef M. (1990).   "Remaking Eastern Europe: On the Political Economy of Transition." *International Studies in Economics and Econometrics*, vol. 23, Norwell, Mass. and London: Kluwer Academic.

van Wijnbergen, Sweder (1991).   "Should Price Reform Proceed Gradually or in a "Big Bang?"   *The World Bank PRE Working Papers*, no. 702.

van Wijnbergen, Sweder (1991).   "Trade Reform, Policy Uncertainty, and the Current Account."   *The World Bank PRE Working Papers*, no. 520.

Vodopivec, Milan, (1991).   "The Labor Market and the Transition of Socialist Economies."   *The World Bank PRE Working Papers*, no. 561.

_____ (1991).   "The Persistence of Job Security in Reforming Socialist Economies."   *The World Bank PRE Working Papers*, no. 560.

Watson, Garry (1989).   "Business Law in the People's Republic of China: 1978-1988."   *American Business Law Journal*, vol. 27, pp. 3:315-74, Fall.

World Bank (1991d).   "Poland: Economic Transformation at a Crossroads."   Draft, November.

World Bank (1991e).   "Microeconomic Response to the Economic Transformation Program: Evidence from the Largest Polish SOEs."   Draft, September.

_____ (1991).   "Measuring Outward Orientation in Developing Countries: Can it Be Done?" *The World Bank PRE Working Papers*, no. pp. 566.

_____ (1992).   "Stagflationary Effects of Stabilization Programs in Reforming Socialist Countries: Enterprise-Side and Household-Side Factors."   *The World Bank Economic Review*, vol 6, no. 1, pp. 71-90, January.

Xu, Lilai (1991).   "China's Financial Reform in the 1990s: A Case Study of Financial Environment in Pudong New Area, Shanghai."   *Journal of Asian Economics*, pp. 353-71, Fall.

_____ (1989).   "The S&L Insurance Mess: How Did It Happen?"   Cambridge, *MA MIT Press*.

Medical Working Group Experts Delegation, *Country Report for Republic of Uzbekistan.* "Pharmaceutical Subgroup."

Medical Working Group Experts Delegation, *Country Report for Republic of Uzbekistan.* "Public Health Subgroup."

Task force on health research for development, c/o UNDP. "A strategy for Action in Health and Human Development." Essential national health research. Geneva, Switzerland, 1991.

UNICEF/WHO Collaborative Mission, Tashkent, 21 February - 2 March. Country Report: "Republic of Uzbekistan, Medical Working Group Experts Delegation to the New Independent States."

United States Agency for International Development. "Uzbekistan, USAID Health Profile (selected data)." April 24, 1992. Center for International Health Information, *USAID Health Information System*, Arlington, Virginia.

World Health Organization. "Highlights on Uzbekistan, WHO Regional Office." Copenhagen, Denmark.

"Emergency Childhood Immunization Support Program: Uzbekistan." *USAID-funded, Reach Project, JSI*, Arlington, Virginia.

"Health Care in the Republic of Uzbekistan." Department of Health Statistics, Statistics Office, Ministry of Health of Uzbekistan, 1992.

"The Looming Crisis and Fresh Opportunity: Health in Kazakhstan, Kyrgyzstan, Tadjikistan, Turkmenistan and Uzbekistan."

"Republican Sanitary and Epidemiology Station." 1991 *EPI coverage for Uzbekistan.*

"Uzbekistan, USAID Health Profile (selected data)." April 24, 1992. Center for International Health Information, *USAID Health Information System United States Agency for International Development*, Arlington, Virginia USA.

"Water Law in Selected European Countries. Union of Soviet Socialist Republics, Food and Agriculture Organization." *FAO: Legislative study, Number 30.* Rome, Italy.

"Narodnoe Khoziaistvo SSSR v 1989 Godu Finansy i Statistika." Moscow, 1990.

"Narodnoe Khoziaistvo Uzbekskoi SSR v 1990 Godu." Uzbekistan, Tashkent, 1991.

"Razvitie Narodonaselenia i Problemy Trudovykh Resursov Respublik Srednei Azii Fan." Tashkent, 1988.

"Sostav Sem'i, Dokhody i Zhilishchnye Uslovia Semei Rabochikh, Sluzhashchikh i Kolkhoznikov." *Goskomstat: informatsionno-izdatel'skii tsentr*, Moscow, 1990.

Distributors of World Bank Publications

ARGENTINA
Carlos Hirsch, SRL
Galeria Guemes
Florida 165, 4th Floor-Ofc. 453/465
1333 Buenos Aires

AUSTRALIA, PAPUA NEW GUINEA,
FIJI, SOLOMON ISLANDS,
VANUATU, AND WESTERN SAMOA
D.A. Information Services
648 Whitehorse Road
Mitcham 3132
Victoria

AUSTRIA
Gerold and Co.
Graben 31
A-1011 Wien

BANGLADESH
Micro Industries Development
  Assistance Society (MIDAS)
House 5, Road 16
Dhanmondi R/Area
Dhaka 1209

  Branch offices:
  Pine View, 1st Floor
  100 Agrabad Commercial Area
  Chittagong 4100

  76, K.D.A. Avenue
  Kulna 9100

BELGIUM
Jean De Lannoy
Av. du Roi 202
1060 Brussels

CANADA
Le Diffuseur
C.P. 85, 1501B rue Ampère
Boucherville, Québec
J4B 5E6

CHILE
Invertec IGT S.A.
Americo Vespucio Norte 1165
Santiago

CHINA
China Financial & Economic
  Publishing House
8, Da Fo Si Dong Jie
Beijing

COLOMBIA
Infoenlace Ltda.
Apartado Aereo 34270
Bogota D.E.

COTE D'IVOIRE
Centre d'Edition et de Diffusion
  Africaines (CEDA)
04 B.P. 541
Abidjan 04 Plateau

CYPRUS
Center of Applied Research
Cyprus College
6, Diogenes Street, Engomi
P.O. Box 2006
Nicosia

DENMARK
SamfundsLitteratur
Rosenoerns Allé 11
DK-1970 Frederiksberg C

DOMINICAN REPUBLIC
Editora Taller, C. por A.
Restauración e Isabel la Católica 309
Apartado de Correos 2190 Z-1
Santo Domingo

EGYPT, ARAB REPUBLIC OF
Al Ahram
Al Galaa Street
Cairo

The Middle East Observer
41, Sherif Street
Cairo

FINLAND
Akateeminen Kirjakauppa
P.O. Box 128
SF-00101 Helsinki 10

FRANCE
World Bank Publications
66, avenue d'Iéna
75116 Paris

GERMANY
UNO-Verlag
Poppelsdorfer Allee 55
D-5300 Bonn 1

HONG KONG, MACAO
Asia 2000 Ltd.
46-48 Wyndham Street
Winning Centre
2nd Floor
Central Hong Kong

INDIA
Allied Publishers Private Ltd.
751 Mount Road
Madras - 600 002

  Branch offices:
  15 J.N. Heredia Marg
  Ballard Estate
  Bombay - 400 038

  13/14 Asaf Ali Road
  New Delhi - 110 002

  17 Chittaranjan Avenue
  Calcutta - 700 072

  Jayadeva Hostel Building
  5th Main Road, Gandhinagar
  Bangalore - 560 009

  3-5-1129 Kachiguda
   Cross Road
  Hyderabad - 500 027

  Prarthana Flats, 2nd Floor
  Near Thakore Baug, Navrangpura
  Ahmedabad - 380 009

  Patiala House
  16-A Ashok Marg
  Lucknow - 226 001

  Central Bazaar Road
  60 Bajaj Nagar
  Nagpur 440 010

INDONESIA
Pt. Indira Limited
Jalan Borobudur 20
P.O. Box 181
Jakarta 10320

IRELAND
Government Supplies Agency
4-5 Harcourt Road
Dublin 2

ISRAEL
Yozmot Literature Ltd.
P.O. Box 56055
Tel Aviv 61560

ITALY
Licosa Commissionaria Sansoni SPA
Via Duca Di Calabria, 1/1
Casella Postale 552
50125 Firenze

JAPAN
Eastern Book Service
Hongo 3-Chome, Bunkyo-ku 113
Tokyo

KENYA
Africa Book Service (E.A.) Ltd.
Quaran House, Mfangano Street
P.O. Box 45245
Nairobi

KOREA, REPUBLIC OF
Pan Korea Book Corporation
P.O. Box 101, Kwangwhamun
Seoul

MALAYSIA
University of Malaya Cooperative
  Bookshop, Limited
P.O. Box 1127, Jalan Pantai Baru
59700 Kuala Lumpur

MEXICO
INFOTEC
Apartado Postal 22-860
14060 Tlalpan, Mexico D.F.

NETHERLANDS
De Lindeboom/InOr-Publikaties
P.O. Box 202
7480 AE Haaksbergen

NEW ZEALAND
EBSCO NZ Ltd.
Private Mail Bag 99914
New Market
Auckland

NIGERIA
University Press Limited
Three Crowns Building Jericho
Private Mail Bag 5095
Ibadan

NORWAY
Narvesen Information Center
Book Department
P.O. Box 6125 Etterstad
N-0602 Oslo 6

PAKISTAN
Mirza Book Agency
65, Shahrah-e-Quaid-e-Azam
P.O. Box No. 729
Lahore 54000

PERU
Editorial Desarrollo SA
Apartado 3824
Lima 1

PHILIPPINES
International Book Center
Suite 1703, Cityland 10
Condominium Tower 1
Ayala Avenue, H.V. dela
  Costa Extension
Makati, Metro Manila

POLAND
International Publishing Service
Ul. Piekna 31/37
00-677 Warzawa

For subscription orders:
IPS Journals
Ul. Okrezna 3
02-916 Warszawa

PORTUGAL
Livraria Portugal
Rua Do Carmo 70-74
1200 Lisbon

SAUDI ARABIA, QATAR
Jarir Book Store
P.O. Box 3196
Riyadh 11471

SINGAPORE, TAIWAN,
MYANMAR,BRUNEI
Information Publications
  Private, Ltd.
Golden Wheel Building
41, Kallang Pudding, #04-03
Singapore 1334

SOUTH AFRICA, BOTSWANA
For single titles:
Oxford University Press
  Southern Africa
P.O. Box 1141
Cape Town 8000

For subscription orders:
International Subscription Service
P.O. Box 41095
Craighall
Johannesburg 2024

SPAIN
Mundi-Prensa Libros, S.A.
Castello 37
28001 Madrid

Librería Internacional AEDOS
Consell de Cent, 391
08009 Barcelona

SRI LANKA AND THE MALDIVES
Lake House Bookshop
P.O. Box 244
100, Sir Chittampalam A.
  Gardiner Mawatha
Colombo 2

SWEDEN
For single titles:
Fritzes Fackboksforetaget
Regeringsgatan 12, Box 16356
S-103 27 Stockholm

For subscription orders:
Wennergren-Williams AB
P. O. Box 1305
S-171 25 Solna

SWITZERLAND
For single titles:
Librairie Payot
Case postale 3212
CH 1002 Lausanne

For subscription orders:
Librairie Payot
Service des Abonnements
Case postale 3312
CH 1002 Lausanne

THAILAND
Central Department Store
306 Silom Road
Bangkok

TRINIDAD & TOBAGO, ANTIGUA
BARBUDA, BARBADOS,
DOMINICA, GRENADA, GUYANA,
JAMAICA, MONTSERRAT, ST.
KITTS & NEVIS, ST. LUCIA,
ST. VINCENT & GRENADINES
Systematics Studies Unit
#9 Watts Street
Curepe
Trinidad, West Indies

TURKEY
Infotel
Narlabahçe Sok. No. 15
Cagaloglu
Istanbul

UNITED KINGDOM
Microinfo Ltd.
P.O. Box 3
Alton, Hampshire GU34 2PG
England

VENEZUELA
Libreria del Este
Aptdo. 60.337
Caracas 1060-A

MAP SECTION